U F O

CONSPIRACY

Schiffer Publishing Ltd®

4880 Lower Valley Road, Atglen, Pennsylvania 19310

CARMEN MCLAREN

Schiffer Books are available at special discounts for bulk purchases for sales promotions or premiums. Special editions, including personalized covers, corporate imprints, and excerpts can be created in large quantities for special needs. For more information contact the publisher:

Published by Schiffer Publishing Ltd.
4880 Lower Valley Road
Atglen, PA 19310
Phone: (610) 593-1777; Fax: (610) 593-2002
E-mail: Info@schifferbooks.com

For the largest selection of fine reference books on this and related subjects,
please visit our website at **www.schifferbooks.com**
We are always looking for people to write books on new and related subjects.
If you have an idea for a book, please contact us at
proposals@schifferbooks.com

This book may be purchased from the publisher.
Include $5.00 for shipping.
Please try your bookstore first.
You may write for a free catalog.

In Europe, Schiffer books are distributed by
Bushwood Books
6 Marksbury Ave.
Kew Gardens
Surrey TW9 4JF England
Phone: 44 (0) 20 8392 8585; Fax: 44 (0) 20 8392 9876
E-mail: info@bushwoodbooks.co.uk
Website: www.bushwoodbooks.co.uk

Designed by Mark David Bowyer
Type set in Pacifica Condensed / NewBaskerville BT

ISBN: 978-0-7643-3893-9
Printed in China

CONTENTS

DEDICATIONS

This book is dedicated to the thousands of men and women who have had the courage to come forward, risking ridicule and more, to report their sightings of Unidentified Flying Objects so that those of us who may have never seen one, knows what is happening and how we have been kept in the dark about it.

And, to my family and friends who have supported my research these past three decades, without whose love and support, this book would not have been possible.

ACKNOWLEDGMENTS

I wish to thank all those people who have helped make this book possible and whose efforts may one day lead to full disclosure, namely the dedicated men and women of APRO, CUFOS, MUFON, NICAP, and all other UFO research organizations that have donated their time, money, and expertise in researching and documenting the UFO phenomenon. Thanks also to all the authors of UFO books who have come before me who have inspired and guided me on this journey, and whose groundbreaking research helped me in completing this book, but especially Ralph and Judy Blum, whose incredible work entitled *Beyond Earth : Man's Contact With UFO* started me on the journey that has led me to this place.

INTRODUCTION

"I feel that the Air Force has not been giving out all the available information on these Unidentified Flying Objects. You cannot disregard so many unimpeachable sources."

~Honorable John McCormack
Speaker of the House
January 1965, *True Magazine*

The sun rose bright and warm on the morning of August 5th, 1608[1] over Nice, France, and it would prove to be a day that would live on in the citizens' memory for a very long time. It was in the early hours that the people of Nice noticed three glowing objects in the skies above the city's Mediterranean Sea port. As the locals watched the three fast spinning objects slowly glide towards their town, the objects stopped near the citadel and remained there for a short time before coming to rest barely feet above the ports' blue waters. The town folks saw the sea begin to roil and heave to and fro beneath these strange craft, and as it did, they noticed a reddish vapor coming up from the boiling sea. Then, much to their shock and terror, two beings exited one of the craft. The witnesses described them as having large heads with shiny eyes, wearing silver and red suits, and each was connected to the craft by some sort of tubing. For the next two hours, the beings performed some unknown tasks as the citizens watched in amazement. The craft remained over the port until 10 PM that night when all three craft flew away quickly to the east.

If this happened today where you live, would you report what you had seen? Chances are, you would not. The factors behind your silence may be many, but probably include fear of being branded as odd, perhaps even delusional or crazy, by the people you might mention it to. Their reaction is due to the fact that for over six decades the government and their lackeys, namely the vocal debunker/pseudo-experts and the media, have created a fiction surrounding the UFO phenomenon. They have intentionally mislead the general public by painting the UFO phenomenon as having grown out of post-World War II fears and anxieties of the growing Communist threat and its effects on a war-weary population. They have withheld the truth by claiming that UFOs are witnessed by untrained, unqualified observers viewing the objects alone at night on lonely highways.

This paved the way for the sightings to be explained away as a misidentification of a known object (usually the planet Venus), a hallucination, or even a fabrication.

They point to those cases where people were looking to garner attention for themselves to stereotype all the reported sightings of UFOs, and in turn, those who witnessed them, even though with a minimal amount of research, these cases are usually easy to identify as hoaxes perpetrated by unstable people. But, by their continual focus on these fraudulent cases and actual cases of misidentifications, the government has been allowed to conceal the fact that most UFO sightings are reported by *normal everyday people* trying to ascertain information about an object that they have seen performing spectacular feats in the skies above the places they live, work, and play.

This is contrary to what the government and their experts would have you believe, thus the fiction they created has been intended to hide these truths. They want you to believe that anyone who reports a UFO has some motive behind making so ludicrous a claim. Usually, they claim the motive is financial gain, as anyone reporting a UFO is somehow trying to make a quick buck by concocting these outlandish stories. The fact that honest, competent people do indeed see and report their sightings of UFOs is often covered up due to the damage it would cause to the huge ongoing charade perpetrated by our government and their hired "experts" since 1947.

CLOUDING WITH FACTS

Why would the skeptics want to cloud the issues with facts! As you will see, the intentional omission of pertinent facts is the cornerstone of the US government's and the debunkers' attempts to pass off the entire UFO phenomenon as one huge flight of fantasy.

The fact is, the government and their hired wordsmiths (the debunkers), are wrong on all counts. Having studied the UFO phenomena for over thirty years, I can say whole-heartedly that UFOs are real and are witnessed by an overwhelming number of competent people. That is not to say that there have not been hoaxes and frauds, as there have and will continue to be. But hear me when I say that there are truths to be had. Being their empowering agents, I feel *we the people* are entitled to no less than knowing these truths, *whatever* they may be.

To ascertain this, the populace must also believe that this phenomenon is legitimate and in need of further study in an open forum by our leading scientists and researchers. That is why I concentrate on sightings by credible people only, with little or no mention of crashed UFOs and abductions to muddy the waters (though the evidence is strong there as well—another book...). To concentrate on either crashed UFOs or the abduction phenomenon is like putting the cart before the horse, as people need to believe that UFOs exist and are actually here before they can believe they have crashed and/or have abducted people! (I do not say this to discredit either field of study, as they both have overwhelming evidence to their legitimacy.) My main goal is to disprove the notions of the UFO phenomena that the government and the debunkers would like you to believe.

I will show you through examples extrapolated from hundreds of books, articles, even television programming concerning UFOs, that what *they* want you to believe is not true. To begin with, UFOs did not appear after World War II; they have been seen from the beginning of recorded history—and will continue to be seen until those beings that control them decide their visitations will cease. I will also show you that UFOs are not seen by only untrained observers; they have been witnessed by scientists, CEO's, Congressmen, Senators, several state governors, two US presidents, thousands upon thousands of trained military personnel/pilots, civilian pilots, and law enforcement personnel throughout the world. You will even find it true that people who witness and report UFOs may serve on juries and find themselves responsible for sentences that put people to death, yet they are not deemed to be reliable witnesses by neither the government nor their vocal nay-saying debunking experts when it comes to the sightings of Unidentified Flying Objects. And worse, often when these same people report their sightings, they are subject to ridicule by the people in government service they entrusted to help them understand what it was they saw or experienced.

THE STORY OF THE CENTURY

You will come to understand why millions of people from around the world, just like you and me, believe that UFOs are real, and hopefully, you will come to believe that the American public needs to be better informed by our leaders as to what they know about this phenomenon.

This is the story of the century. If indeed these flying saucers are from another planetary system(s), would not vigilance be prudent? We as a nation need to place more emphasis on ascertaining the truth behind where UFOs are from and what agenda those that control them seek to follow.

My pursuit of this knowledge that UFO are real, travel wherever they want to go unhindered by any of this world's military, does not make me sleep any better at night, but has brought a better understanding of how the world around me is not always as it appears to be!

But let's ask the questions: If the UFO phenomenon is not real, why has the United States Government spent millions of dollars investigating them through many projects, including the infamous Project Blue Book, and wasted even more money and thousands of gallons of jet fuel chasing these objects that don't exist? Why did McDonnell-Douglas aircraft company, a major Department of Defense contractor, investigate UFOs and their means of conjectured propulsions to try to assimilate any technological advancements into their designs in the 1960s?

A true conundrum: With all these sightings taking place, why would the vast majority of people not believe that UFOs are real? Let's look at an analogy of sorts. Ask yourself this question: Do baby pigeons exist? Though this may sound silly, think with me for one moment. In all your life, have you ever seen one? No? Neither have I, and I have lived in the city my entire life. Does this mean that baby pigeons do not exist? Of course it doesn't! I think it is safe to assume that most well-informed individuals could reason out that mature pigeons had to be baby pigeons at some point. Though baby pigeons are rarely seen, it does not mean that they do not exist. Are you wondering how this relates to the UFO phenomena? Quite simply, many people do not believe that UFOs are real because they have never seen one. Is it normal to have to see to believe? Just ask the apostle Thomas, or any person from Missouri (the Show Me State!): Seeing is believing! Combine this normal human trait with the way the government and the media make light of witnesses and their reported sightings of UFOs, and you will see why the average person disbelieves that other people are seeing strange, unexplainable objects flying through the skies and landing on the roads and fields the world over. Sadly, unlike in the baby pigeon scenario, where if put to the test, I could find a baby pigeon, I cannot go to a certain location and produce a UFO. All I can do is present testimony of those who have witnessed these objects in an attempt to help validate the claim that I and many others around the world hold very dear:

UFOs are real!

My goal is to show you that the skeptics are not truthful in their claims that UFOs are easily identifiable objects or atmospheric phenomena. The government and the very vocal critics in league with them, love to state that the people who witness UFOs can usually be placed into one of the following categories: emotionally unstable publicity seekers trying to make a quick buck, or untrained, unqualified non-technically oriented observers witnessing ordinary things and ascribing extraordinary characteristics and origination. They also like to mention that as far as they know, most sightings involve but a single witness. They claim that multiple-witness sightings are not common place, allowing them to insinuate that when one person has a sighting, it may be easy to explain away because that person was not experiencing an encounter with a UFO; they were most likely having some type of a hallucination or misidentification. Once they have spewed forth these outlandish claims, the average person, not being acquainted with the UFO phenomena, may find it easy to believe these experts of misinformation, which could prompt them to brush aside the possibility that many sane, qualified observers have seen things that defy earthly explanations.

With the government steadfastly behind their claim that UFOs do not exist anywhere but in the minds of those who witness them, compounded by the media's constant focus on just the most controversial sightings and subjects, how do I expect to accomplish my goal and make believers out of the unbelievers? Quite simply, I will tell you the truth. Not my truth, but the plain unadulterated, backed up by facts and figures, truth. I will attempt to convert those who question the existence of UFOs by showing them that what they have been led to believe by the government and their so-called experts is untrue. I will show you that, contrary to what the aforementioned parties have claimed, many honest, competent, highly respected people, as well as members of the military, law enforcement, scientific community and leaders in the government, have all witnessed these things we call UFOs.

I will attempt, also, to dispute the expert's claims that the UFO phenomenon is a recent phenomenon. Many of the critics claim that the UFO phenomenon began after the sighting by Kenneth Arnold on June 24th, 1947. Thusly proving in their own minds their theory that the UFO Phenomena was triggered by the post World War II/ early Cold War paranoid mind set of the masses at large. Their assumptions are incorrect and founded on many untruths. There are researched sightings that pre-date 1947, that exist in mass. The sightings of UFOs date back at least as far as the time man became capable of communicating through words and pictures.

By presenting these startling facts that people have been witnessing this or a similar phenomena since the beginning of recorded history, we will see that from the time that man dwelled in caves right through to this very day, humans have been witnesses to incredible aerial displays by non-terrestrial vehicles. Although this phenomenon only came to the mass media's attention in 1947, it was witnessed and recorded beforehand by many people the world over. A phenomenon so awe inspiring, it, as we will see, intrigued the witnesses so much that they felt the need to record their sightings in art, sculpture, and writings to serve as reminders to future generations of the spectacular sights they had witnessed.

Now this is all fine and well, but many will say, this is only your opinion; the government says they do not exist, so why should we believe you? If they did exist, how could the truth be kept from us for all these years?

The Government Does Not Lie
(Stop Coughing Please)

Now those are hard questions. We all know that the government *does not lie* to us. Nor have they ever conspired to seek information at the expense of the populace. Right? As much as I hate to say it, yes, they have done all of the above. If you don't believe me, just ask the descendents of the men who while imprisoned in the 1940s[2] were injected with Syphilis to see how the disease developed, its symptoms, and the end result of the lack of treatment on a human subject. Or on a larger scale, ask the family members of those people who have developed many forms of cancer in states east of Nevada due to the fallout of radiation from above-ground nuclear testing there in the 1940s and 1950s[3] who were never warned of the danger they were in being downwind from the testing grounds. These stories took decades to break, so I guess it would be possible to keep things from the general public if the government deemed it necessary. Am I making these claims up? No, and if you need further proof, search the Internet from the comfort of your home by referencing the endnotes and bibliography I provide at the end of this book.

By making this claim, am I implying that the government is evil? No. The government has been empowered by us to see to our well being and perseverance. To accomplish this, sometimes secrecy is necessary; the importance of this secrecy will be dealt with later. As 1st Officer Spock of the classic television series *Star Trek* was so fond of saying (and please remember by the way that this saying came from the mind of an American!), "The wants and needs of the many outweigh the wants and needs of the few," and the perennially favorite saying in American culture, "Majority rule, minority dissent" are two slogans from the same body of thought—the body of thought being that sometimes it is necessary that a few may suffer in order to preserve the whole.

The government may honestly believe they are protecting us from ourselves by keeping the truth from us, or by sacrificing a group of people so that the rest of us may benefit from the discoveries made at the expense of those innocent people. The masses at large have come to accept and even ignore things they don't want to know about, especially if these things concern putting others in harm's way to keep them safe. Thus, for most of the mainstream, not questioning authority has become a way of life.

LOGIC MUST PREVAIL

Thus, it is safe to say that things are not always as they are presented to be, and to get to the truth we must weigh all available evidence to make a logical, informed decision on what is truth and what is fiction.

As you read through this book, please keep the following things in mind when analyzing the explanations and conclusions given by the government and it's experts as to what the people are witnessing, and their repeated denials that UFO are not real.

- If UFOs are not real, why has the government spent so much money and allocated so many resources to chasing figments of peoples' imaginations?
- If UFOs are not real, why have intercept aircraft been, and continue to be, dispatched to investigate sightings of UFOs?
- Would the United States Air Force create a policy as to how to deal with UFOs if they were not real? (To add a bit of fuel to the Air Force fire, according to a recent special that aired on the Discovery Channel about aircraft carriers, the average training mission costs the taxpayers of the United States approximately $6,000 per plane. With these prices, which will only continue to rise, why would the government continue to waste our tax dollars on flights of fancy, if they did not truly believe that what they are dealing with are real craft flying through American air space, posing a potential threat to our personal and national security? I can safely say that the military, being the best, most efficient war machine this planet has ever seen, would not issue a policy on how to deal with things that do not exist.

Air Force Regulation 200-2 (AFR 200-2)[4] was issued by order of the Air Force Chief of Staff, covering all aspects of UFO encounters from how to intercept, when to fire, how evidence will be collected and disseminated, and how, when and by who information will be released to the public. This regulation has been altered ten times allowing it to change as the governments' position on UFOs has also changed. The culmination of this policy's evolution was AFR 80-17, enacted in October of 1967, which placed the burden of investigation of UFO reports on the backs of several academic department heads at the University of Colorado, who worked under the name of the Condon Committee, who were placed under contract to the USAF to investigate the matter.

Those of you who have spent time in the military know that regulations might as well be written in stone by the Almighty.

Regulations are created due to real events that would or could impact the performance of military personnel as they carry out their duties in protecting the people and Constitution of the United States of America to maintain discipline.

WHAT'S GOING ON?

So what is the big deal? If they are hiding this from us, what else has or is happening that we should know about? If nothing else, by proving to you that what the government would like you to believe about the UFO phenomena is false, that in fact it is all too real and deserving of more positive attention than it receives, I hope to show you that there are discrepancies aplenty. So, yes, question authority, make sure the facts you are receiving are true. If you see that the facts presented to you by the government and their experts are not the truth, as is the case of UFO material for the last six decades, you may begin to question other things you hold to be true. This may lead to a better understanding of the world around you.

So please read on, as you will learn that:

1. UFOs have been around for thousands of years.
2. They have been witnessed by large groups of people over large population centers.
3. Qualified, well-respected people have seen and reported similar objects and experiences from the four corners of the world.
4. UFOs are picked up on radar which verifies that some tangible objects have been seen in the sky above, not a mass hallucination as often has been claimed by the government and their debunkers.

For the most part, only those sightings where the names of those people who experienced the sightings, the time and date of the sighting, and where it occurred have been included. As you will notice, in the earlier sightings, due to the passage of time, the names of those involved sometimes have been lost or forgotten. From 1947 on, only sightings where the previously listed particulars have been met are used. Some persons have requested to remain anonymous when making the report, but their sightings have been included due to the standing and/or qualifications of the witness and the impact their sightings has had on the UFO community worldwide. By doing this, I have afforded anyone with some free time to hurry down to his or her local libraries to see if the sightings were reported in their local newspapers. More importantly, by providing the names and places of residence of those people who experienced the sightings that are included herein, it can be determined by checking the local directories during the year quoted to see that these people actually existed. This eliminates the possibility that others, or I, created the people and then fabricated a story of an encounter with a UFO to help prove a theory that UFOs are real, and witnessed by sane, competent people.

If you wanted, you could prove that these people did indeed live in the towns listed, but this would not prove that they weren't lying about what they saw. Nothing I write could prove that every person listed in this book did not fabricate the stories they recounted about encounters with unknown aerial devices.

The question then becomes: Why would they lie about such a thing? Would it be worthwhile to lose their place in their local business, religious, or professional communities, to report something that the government claims does not and never did exist? Would you make up such a story at the risk of losing so much? Probably not, and neither did they. In order for people of the caliber included herein to make such a report, they must have had an encounter with an unknown object that affected them deeply enough to risk ridicule and ruin to report it to the proper authorities.

Search as you may, you will never find a person who has reported their sightings and earned a million dollars for doing so. These people have reported their sightings in an effort to find out what it was they saw. Because try as they might, their minds could not rationalize what it was they saw, as these crafts are not indigenous technology. They out-perform even the fastest, most agile jet fighters this country has to offer with ease.

I feel safe in saying that when you are finished reading this book, you will be among those of us who want answers to what these things are, where they come from, who the overlords are that operate these UFOs—and most important: why they are here!

—Carmen McLaren

The radiation levels for Silo B were consistent with those found in the ███████████████████████ and all records pertaining to the ████████████████ of the aforementioned ████████████████ remain highly classified. The southwest sides, shown in Figure 2B, completed in ████ created an impact site of approximately 75 acres with a surface area measuring the length of ███████████████████████████ All official documentation relating to the ████████████ ████████████████████████████████████ ████████████████████████████████████ ████████████████████████████████████ ████████████████████████████████████ has been destroyed.

Chapter 1

Introduction to UFOlogy

"Unidentified Flying Objects—sometimes treated lightly by the press and referred to as "Flying Saucers"—must be rapidly and accurately identified as serious Air Force Business in the Interior Zone."

~Operations and Training Order from the Inspector General of the USAF to Base Commanders, December 24th, 1959

Possible Reasons for the Government's Need For Secrecy

The government's refusals to acknowledge the factuality of objects flying into American airspace at will, taking surveys of the people, places, animals, and other indigenous life forms is not fiction. As we have seen, the USAF has rules of engagement for encountering UFOs, thus the government believes these objects are real enough to create regulations concerning them. So the question is why would the government keep such information secret? Why would keeping secret their knowledge that UFOs exist, have and continue to visit our world, and may have even crashed at several sites throughout the world be such an important part of government policy?

There are many reasons why they may need to maintain secrecy, but we shall examine just these: mass hysteria, the need to protect national security, and undermining governmental authority. Before continuing, it is very important to mention that not all foreign governments treat the subject the same way that our governing body does. The governments of France, Russia, Belgium, and Brazil all openly discuss the UFO phenomena with its citizenry, and the United Kingdom has just released volumes of previously classified documents concerning their military's encounters with and the investigation of UFOs. In these countries, the reports are investigated by organizations within the government and some, but perhaps not all, of the findings are reported to the people. The witnesses who step forward can be assured that they will not be the objects of ridicule. Instead, they are part of the process of finding out information and answers. So why aren't we?

MASS HYSTERIA

To paraphrase from Tommy Lee Jones' character, "K," in the hit movie *Men in Black,* a person is smart; but people are stupid. When most people are confronted with a problem they will try to reason out the who, what, where, when and how of the problem with the tools they have available. No matter what the problem at hand may be, we all try to rationalize why and how things happen, allowing us to come to terms with it. When we internalize a problem we tend to concentrate on just the problem, keeping outside stimuli out of the reasoning process. However, when several people get together and are confronted by a problem or a situation, a mob mentality often takes over. Then instead of concentrating on a solution, many will begin to focus on their emotional response to the stimuli. Emotions being what they are, and people being emotional beings that tend to share their emotions and usually do not concentrate on logic, they focus on fear, hatred, or some other strong emotion. And, as we have seen, once a group becomes caught up in this emotional response, bad things can and often do happen.

THE MARTIANS ARE COMING!

This exact thing happened in the United States before the modern era of UFO sightings put UFOs and aliens into the conscience mind of many Americans. Though it is a well-known story, it serves as an excellent example of what may happen if the populace believes that: "The Martians are coming!"

On October 30, 1938, Orson Wells and his Mercury Theater broadcast a rendition of the H.G. Wells story, *The War of the Worlds,* over the CBS Radio Network. To add a touch of realism, the story was set-up as a series of bulletins breaking into a musical broadcast, much as the *Breaking News* cuts into our present-day television broadcasts as events transpire. When the broadcast began, Wells let it be known that this was a rendition of the H.G. Wells classic story, then proceeded to state this three more times throughout the broadcast. The newspapers that printed the radio shows in a guide, much like our television guides, spelled it out in black and white that the Mercury Theater would be presenting Wells' classic story that evening.

So why than did mass panic occur? Why were the switchboards of police stations, radio stations, and newspapers flooded with callers wanting to know how long they had before the Martians razed their neighborhoods? Why were there thousands of urbanites racing from their homes to guard against the Martian gas by holding handkerchiefs to their faces and making a mad dash to get out of the city? Some were so distraught at the radio broadcast and subsequent clogging of phone lines and traffic jams that hospitals in different areas of the country actually treated people for shock in their emergency rooms. All of this was in response to a drama broadcast over the radio!

Although people had fair warning as to what was going on, they went off the deep end, making snap decisions without waiting long enough to hear one of the several announcements that this was indeed a radio dramatization. Caught up in the fear of the unknown, they rushed around like lunatics, when in reality nothing but a radio show was happing that night in the not too distant past.

Could something like this happen again? Would we lash out due to fear or hatred and let mob mentality rule? There is no way of knowing what would transpire if we were told that UFOs are here, have been here, and we can do nothing to prevent them from carrying out their agendas—and I am sure this weighs in on the government's need for secrecy. I do, though, like to believe that we as a nation have matured a great deal since the 1930s, and we would not lose our collective minds if we were informed that UFOs are real.

Let's explore why hysteria could result from the masses finding out that, yes, we are being visited by beings whose agenda will be carried out without much resistance from this planet's governments. If we look to our own history, we will find that anytime a technologically superior civilization comes in contact with a technologically inferior civilization, the inferior civilizations' culture ceases to exist or is all but forgotten about by the majority of their people. There exist many, many examples we could cite, from the Romans conquering their entire known world and forcing their culture on the conquered, to the plight of the American Indians. It has continued right into the twentieth century. When tribes of Indians isolated in South America, but especially Brazil, as recent as the late 1980s, finally came into contact with Western civilization, their culture of sharing, love, and providing for the common good went out the window. They began to acquire goods, as simple as things like shirts and hats; and soon, those who did not have them began to steal these items from those who did. The Indians did not even have a word for stealing in their vocabulary until they needed to invent one after becoming "civilized." These were people who thought jetliners flying overhead were gods of flight; now they wait for the Brazilian government to take care of them, when they used to take care of themselves, having let their hunter-gather culture totally fall by the wayside. If this could happen to them, could it happen to us?

If we were to come into contact with a race of beings so advanced as to be able to travel across the universe or through time, would our societies suffer the same fate? Should we be so arrogant as to believe our culture, our belief systems and our lives would not radically change? Would we willingly or by force begin to worship new gods? Could the fabric of our families, our nations, or our species withstand so radical an event? I do not know; nor does anybody else.

Protecting the National Security of the United States of America

Let me first point out that we will not be discussing how UFOs could be a threat to national security; instead, we will be discussing how the knowledge of the truth behind the UFO phenomena could compromise US national security.

How could knowledge be dangerous? you ask. First, if the government admitted that it had in its possession crashed alien crafts that they were studying and extrapolating technology from, it could potentially cause many problems. Acknowledging that they had gained technology they could use offensively or defensively against other governments sometime in the future could result in some type of preemptive action to prevent our gaining a strategic advantage.

Is it not coincidental that historically we are usually the first nation to make scientific leaps and bounds? We were the first to crack the atom allowing us to make weapons and power, and first to create stealth bombers and fighters that are virtually cloaked from radar's detection. Yet, had it not been for Soviet and Chinese espionage, they may still be our exclusive secrets.

If we are reverse engineering UFOs, how many more of these great leaps forward await us? Such leaps would certainly make other nations step up their spying efforts, which could lead to their discovery of these and other things we don't want them to know about. How long before that creates increased tensions? All are scenarios that could lead to confrontations of one sort or another, none of which has a good outcome for any of us.

Likewise, some sightings may indeed be misidentification of US aircraft, including those under development by the black operation divisions within the government. If there was a concentration of UFO sightings in an area and the government came right out and announced that it was not alien craft, but instead, a test flight of an experimental aircraft, any espionage unit worth their salt would be concentrating on that area and its environs. Thus, secrecy is a necessary endeavor, but for the government to operate such a machine of misinformation is not wise. The aforementioned nations that keep the UFO investigations in an open forum have their own research and development programs/facilities, and a need to maintain secrecy. They don't operate under the same game plan as our government; they don't concentrate on the outright deceit of the people who empower them. They endeavor to find the truth or a facsimile thereof. And though these efforts may be halfhearted or a muse, they are open in sharing information and admitting that UFOs are phenomena worth researching.

When all is said and done, the research indicates that there is no good reason to deny that the UFO phenomena is real, nor is there a reason to ridicule those who see them, as it is possible to maintain national security without perpetrating such actions. This is why so many people believe in some type of conspiracy or another being conducted by the government. They ask: Why not admit that they do not know what these objects are, but they are striving to gain a better understanding of them?

A case in point: When the Center for Disease Control announces a new disease, like the H1N1 virus and back in the 1980s the HIV virus, did they not admit the diseases were out there and they were working to find a cure? Of course, they did so to educate the people, who could then try to take preventive action so they did not contract these new scourges. Had they hid the information the way information about UFOs is hidden, many more people could have been infected and died. But wisely, they shared the facts for the benefit of all.

Why not, then, treat the UFO phenomenon in an open manner? Whenever trickery and deceit is used, someone is usually trying to hide something. Is that *something* they are hiding the truth about an answer regarding why the aliens are indeed here and how it will impact us? Only time will tell.

Undermining our Government's Authority

Again, let's make it clear; we are speaking in reference to how the *knowledge*, not how the actual UFO, could undermine our Government's Authority. If the teachings of one man can be most associated with influencing how our forefathers came up with our system of government, that man would be John Locke. He theorized that man came to form governments so that they could safely devote time to their pursuit of life, liberty, and property. A civilized group of people created a government by banding together to insure their safety. To create this government, they had to first be willing to part with some of their possessions (taxes). If attacked, these individuals who banned together must be willing to give up not only their wealth, but some must be called to make the ultimate sacrifice and perhaps give up their lives to see to the protection of the group as a whole (like our military men and women do). They had to be willing to part with a certain amount of their freedom, as the government had to have authority to make laws, rules, regulations, and assign consequences to those who broke them. These same individuals also had to be willing to give up a portion of their property through taxation to pay for the government that protected them. Now, if that government failed to protect them, or stopped looking out for the populaces' well being, the people retained the right to change the government through election of new leaders, or if necessary, by revolt.

These ideas have been the basis for many governments' creation and overthrow. Our system of government is based on these ideas, and every time we lose confidence in our elected officials, we replace them through the power of the ballot. Many countries, like England, France, Russia, Spain, and even the good old U.S.A. have had civil wars to change or try to change the system of government controlling their respective nations. What has all this to do with why the government denies the existence of UFOs? Well, let's review. According to Locke's Doctrine, if a government cannot protect its citizenry, it runs the risk of ceasing to exist. If the United States federal government admitted that it could not protect the citizens of our great republic from being harassed, or even abducted by those in control of the UFOs, then it may run the risk of ceasing to exist. Far-fetched? Perhaps. Possible? Definitely.

How the nation would react to the government admitting it could not protect its people from an outside invader is not known. Would the people want to do away with the government we now have? Who knows? But why admit to the people that the government could not defend the citizens from an outside attack, when right now those beings in the UFOs whom the government cannot defend us against are not attacking; they are merely reconnoitering. Would it not be easier to deny that these beings and their crafts are here, then admit that the American Federal government is powerless to defend the people from this possible threat? Absolutely.

It is a very likely scenario that the United States federal government fears having to acknowledge to the world that it cannot keep its skies free of trespassing craft, nor certain members of its population free from forced interaction with the UFO occupants. If a foreign government tried to send some craft into our airspace and then abducted people from their vehicles or homes, there would be a swift, effective response to keep a similar incident from ever happening again. But since these objects are technologically superior to ours, our response at the present time is consistent but ineffective. To admit defeat or the possibility of defeat is not the American way. Besides, once you admit to a weakness, certain countries may try to exploit that weakness creating a larger problem for the people then the government's refusal to admit that UFOs exist.

Some say that so big a secret could not be kept from the people, but as we have shown, such secrets can and have been kept from us. Medical and radiation tests conducted on the unsuspecting populace have probably continued to occur. Even during the height of World War II, the Manhattan Project was kept secret from the public until the use of the Atomic Bomb on Japan. Notice that whenever research that needs to be kept secret is identified, it is carried out in an isolated area. The desert near White Sands, New Mexico, holds as many secrets as does the desert near Groom Lake, Nevada. Thus, I think it is safe to say that there are many reasons why the government needs to maintain a certain level of secrecy where UFOs are concerned.

What needs to be questioned is why the government keeps us in the dark through a ministry of misinformation. The only way to end this farce, is to make believers of you, the general public. I am not trying to make you believe information about where the UFOs come from or why they are here; I will leave those things for you to reach your own conclusions about. What I wish to accomplish is to raise a curiosity in you so that you will also like to find out the truth behind the UFO phenomena and the government's repression of information. By using reports from people who are entrusted with securing the streets, borders, and skies of this nation as well as reports by those entrusted with providing for the economic, political, and scientific well being of us all, I hope to be able to prove to you that the whole UFO phenomena needs a closer look by everyone.

The end result may impact every person on this planet.

Basic UFOlogy

Before you immerse yourself in the multitude of eyewitness accounts that follow, I think it would be prudent to review some of the basic elements associated with the study of Unidentified Flying Objects. Remember though, this is just an overview, as our concentration will be the UFO phenomena, not the history of the study of it.

First off, what is a UFO? Quite simply, a UFO is an Unidentified Flying Object, or more to the point, any object observed that you couldn't identify as a plane, helicopter, balloon, atmospheric phenomena, cloud, moon, star, planet, or other conventional object.

Origins of the UFOs

Where do they come from? Though there are many schools of thought associated with this question, no one can give a definite answer as to the origin of the objects witnessed during these sightings. Some believe that the beings and their machines of interstellar travel originate from outside of our solar system. Some believe they originate from here on earth from beneath the seas or from the subterranean regions below the seven continents. There are those who imply that these travelers may transcend time, not space, meaning the UFOs and their crews originated on Earth sometime in the future and have made their way back through time. Which is correct? I can't say with any absolute certainty, nor can anyone else, save the beings that pilot these fascinating objects.

If they are interstellar voyagers, their approach to gathering information on the flora, fauna, and indigenous species that inhabit our world are parallel to the way humans gather information about the other forms of life on our own world. Many researchers have theorized that, quite possibly, some of the overlords of the UFOs may indeed be future humans coming back in time, to conduct research or perform experiments. The abductees have always claimed that the beings they encounter are bi-pedal humanoids, with two arms, legs, hands, feet, and eyes, as well as some sort of nose and mouth. No matter what language the abductees speak, the beings doing the abducting have no problem communicating with these humans in their native tongues. There are even instances of English-speaking abductees witnessing these beings communicating in Spanish or another earth-based language while onboard the strange craft flying unchecked through the skies over our cities and towns. And most importantly, many of the occupants seem quite capable of breathing the same air we breathe, leading many to suspect they either come from our planet or one incredibly similar. Of course there are those people, namely the debunkers, who believe that the entire phenomena has no basis in reality, thus there is nothing being seen and nobody of any consequences observing these UFOs. However, that is just their paid opinion, not a conclusion reached by a thorough analysis of the facts.

As those who have seen them know, and those of you who are interested in learning more about this phenomena will see, the distance the viewer is from the object is of the utmost importance. A sighting of an object hovering twenty-five feet above the highway asphalt seen by a retired Air Force pilot makes for better proof that the phenomena is a legitimate mystery, than a report by farsighted, average Joe's sighting of a mysterious light in the night sky. A sighting of an object at close range would help to alleviate misidentifications, as the viewer should be able to distinguish the familiar (plane's wings, helicopter noise) from the unfamiliar (silent, wingless object with no means of propulsion). Thus, sightings have been classified into many categories to allow those reading about the sighting to get a better idea of the circumstances under which the object was seen. These categories, as postulated by J. Allen Hynek, include nocturnal lights, daylight discs, radar-visual, and Close Encounters of the I, II, III and IV kinds.

TYPES OF SIGHTINGS

NOCTURNAL LIGHTS

These are sightings of lights high up in the night sky made between the hours after sundown and dawn's first light. A light in the night sky is not an uncommon event, as the sky is full of lights; after all, it is home to millions of stars, comets, meteors, seven other planets, several planetoids, and one large moon. What makes some of these sightings of interest is the fact that varied well-trained individuals have seen lights fly across the sky at tremendous speed, stop, zigzag, reaccelerate to blistering speed and make ninety degree turns as effortlessly as a figure skating gliding across the ice.

Daylight Discs

During the day, it is easier for the human eye to discern the identity of an object. Most well-trained observers can tell when an airplane or helicopter is passing overhead. But, when we see familiar things under unfamiliar circumstances, we may mistake them for UFOs, when in fact they are normal identifiable objects (IFOs). Once I saw a large cigar-shaped object flying over my hometown of Troy, New York. The object was passing before my eyes at a very slow pace, and it appeared to be very large, thus I felt sure it was no known aircraft. But as I continued to watch the object make its way west across the Hudson River Valley, my excitement waned, as I saw the wings and four huge propellers of a C-150 Transport Plane lumbering toward the Stratton Air National Guard Base in not too distant Scotia, New York. But, because it was daytime, I waited to ponder all possible scenarios contributed to my identifying this object, even though the angle I was viewing it from surely made it appear alien to me. My point here is this: In my investigation of UFOs, both in the field and in books and magazines, I have concentrated on sightings where the object viewed could not be anything except a UFO. When deciding which sightings to include here, I have strove to include only those sightings that there could be no other explanation, except that the witness was viewing an unknown craft. You will not find sightings by John Q. Public, who witnessed a strange light in the sky after a night of partying, as no expert would consider their testimony as reliable. What you will see included are sightings by reliable individuals from all walks of life either alone, in small groups, and even a select number of sightings of the same object by many people in nearby or distant locations. When these observers, who are better trained than I am, see disc or cigar-shaped objects intruding into American airspace, report these sightings to the proper authorities, risking ridicule in their search for a logical explanation, you can rest assured that what they have seen was not a normal object we would come to expect to see in the sky above.

As with the nocturnal lights, daylight disc reports should only be interpreted as UFO sightings when the object displays characteristics not associated with identifiable aircraft. Some of these characteristics would be silent operation of large stationary objects, unheard of speed and maneuvers, and the ability to appear and disappear. These discs have been sighted in every nation on earth, and recently, their images are frequently being captured by persons using some type of hand-held video recorder.

This has allowed sightings to be captured and shared for analysis with experts, helping to alleviate some of the debunkers' claims that people lie about what they have seen, as the images are right there on film.

The best types of sightings in these two categories are those objects that are witnessed by multiple observers. It is easy to misidentify a familiar object when viewed from only one angle, as it may be an angle you have never witnessed the object at before. Therefore, if the object is viewed by different people from different angles, chances are, if it is a familiar object, one of the witnesses will recognize it. For instance, let's take my encounter with the C-130 mentioned before. Although I did not recognize its side profile, when it turned, the profile I am more accustomed to allowed me to see that it was a plane and not a UFO. In this case, I did not move, the plane moved. But, when the objects that are being sighted move in one direction only, any single observer gets only one view of this object. That is why triangulation, or viewing the same object from several vantage points, is very important when researching and recording any sighting. If the C-130 remained on a constant heading, I may have ended up reporting a UFO, while a person viewing it from the front could easily tell that it was clearly a plane.

To illustrate this, take an object familiar to you, one preferably that you often see from a single vantage and turn it so you get a view you are not familiar with. Without turning it, or moving so that you get another view, could you readily identify this object?

Radar-Visual

These are the best reported sightings of UFOs made by any observer. They occur when a UFO that has been sighted by some observer(s) also appears on the radar screens at the local commercial and/or military airport or on an air craft's onboard radar. To me, these reports are the best proof that refutes the claims by the government and their experts that UFOs are not real, but are hallucinations, swamp gas, or the planet Venus. The proof is in the fact that the object being viewed by witnesses must be made of some type of material that reflects radar signals to appear on a radar scope, thus they are tangible, not imaginary. At last check, we do not have radar that picks up mental images, stars, or the planet Venus, thus these objects must exist in the sense that they are physical objects capable of reflecting radar.

Returning a radar blip proves the objects are real. The only mystery remaining is what they are, from where they originate, and why they are here.

Close Encounters of the First Kind

This category consists of sightings made of an object in close proximity to the viewer, where there is no contact made between the object and the surrounding environment.

Most typically, these are sightings that would match my previous example of the retired Air Force officer who witnesses an object hovering over the highway, in close enough proximity that he/she could rule out the possibility that the object was a plane, helicopter, Venus, or swamp gas. Unfortunately, besides the witness' testimony, there is no record or proof that they witnessed this object. Leading me to include only sightings where reliable, and when possible technically trained, witnesses are involved, in an attempt to circumvent claims by detractors of the witnesses' ability and veracity, when including accounts in the text that follows.

Close Encounters of the Second Kind

These encounters are similar to CEI's (close encounters of the first kind) in every aspect, except that in these incidents the object leaves a record of its visit behind. Drawing on our Air Force retiree again, if he was to have a CEII (close encounter of the second kind), the UFO sighted hovering over the highway would have left a scorched spot on the pavement where it hovered. Or, the tops of the neighboring tree line would be bent, snapped, or burned as the object left the scene of the encounter. These sightings tend to help prove that the persons involved did see something, as hallucinations don't leave a trail or burn marks. Thus a CEII is an encounter where the UFO leaves a physical trace of its visit.

Close Encounters of the Third Kind

These sightings are similar to CEI and II's in that an object is sighted in close proximity to the observer, it leaves physical traces of its visit, but in this scenario, the observer witnesses the crew of the vessel. The "Crew" refers to the occupants, beings, aliens, UFOnauts, or whatever names you would like to assign to those creatures responsible for piloting these craft. In some sightings, one or more people witness the crews of these craft as they go about repairing, adjusting, or somehow interacting with their craft, or as in many cases, the crews are witnessed as they busy themselves collecting soil, plant, or animal specimens and returning to the interior of their craft and taking off as mysteriously as they had arrived.

Close Encounters of the Fourth Kind

When the crew decides they would like a look at the human witnesses within the confines of their ships, the witness is said to have had a Close Encounter of the Fourth Kind. These sightings are the basis behind the Abduction Phenomenon, which we will touch on later. Although I have said it before, please keep in mind that any of the sightings included in the following text are made by reliable people who have a vested interest in not making up a lavish story due to their position in society, business, government or their respective churches. Most of the sightings of CE IV's included, with the exception of the Hill's abduction, are from people in the military or law enforcement, to my reckoning, the best people to make detailed observations of encounters they have had with Unidentified Flying Objects and the crews that operate them.

When witnesses have reported these close encounters with unknown craft, certain similar side effects on the people, animals, and inanimate objects exposed to the craft have been recorded throughout the world. These side effects are not permanent like scorched roadways or damaged trees and vegetation, but they are also proof of some interaction between people and UFOs. Hallucinations, planets, and atmospheric anomalies do not usually have side effects on the people, animals, and inanimate objects that come in contact with them. The most common side effects that a close encounter has on people are nausea, vomiting, and skin/eye irritation. Animals and birds react with intense fear, creating quite a ruckus when the objects are near. Sometimes the crickets and toads that usually fill the night with their musical rhythms go silent when the craft draws close. Many times, watches and clocks have been known to cease functioning at the exact time the craft is overhead. It has also been frequently reported that a UFO has interrupted television and radio reception, as well as the flow of electrical current through high-tension wires. Thousands of instances of cars and trucks stalling when an object is near, and returning to normal operation when the object leaves, have been reported throughout the world. Only vehicles that are powered by diesel engines are immune to the electromagnetic side effects associated with being in close proximity to a UFO. Thus, these objects can leave many non-permanent traces that act as proof of their visit to the small blue planet we call home.

THE ROLE OF THE SKEPTICS

Now that we have briefly examined the theories as to the origins of UFOs and how they are classified, I think it would be worthwhile to examine another facet to the UFO phenomena: the debunkers. I refer to the people who have taken it upon themselves to ridicule witnesses into silence. As debunkers, not opponents to the UFO phenomena, they are not open-minded investigators searching for answers; thus it is not a give and take relationship. They have already determined that UFOs don't exist, and then they set out to warp the facts of reported sightings to conform to the guidelines of their beliefs. They are so successful because most carry a title, like Ph.D., which impresses those caught in the gray area between belief and disbelief in the UFO phenomena.

This can best be illustrated in a recent NBC special in which several police officers are interviewed concerning their sightings of objects flying over the back roads of Ohio, (covered later). So close were some incidents, that one police officer and his cruiser's encounter ended with a stalled vehicle and a very bewildered patrolman. The debunker in this case, carrying that *magical* title, Ph.D., concluded that the officers involved obviously witnessed Venus, which happened to be uncommonly brilliant that night. How Venus shrunk down to the size reported, traveled over highways in rural Ohio, stopping over a cruiser long enough to stall the engine and then continue on its way was not covered by this debunker. The disturbing part of this debunker testimony was the ease in which he sullied the reputation of a trained police official, well versed not only in his patrolled landscape but with the very reputable responsibility of daily protection of the general public. To imply that this officer could not differentiate between a planet and a flying "craft" along the back roads of Ohio is unconscionable.

This begs the question: Why would the debunker want to cloud the issue with the facts of the case? All that could do is prove his thesis incorrect.

This is but another way debunkers try to explain away any and all UFO sightings and the whole UFO phenomenon in general. Venus is a popular visitor to the airspace over the United States. How it is mistaken for a metallic object with an array of lights hovering near the tree line is even a greater mystery than the UFO phenomena itself! There are however, many types of these nonsensical answers given by the skeptics.

Venus is not alone in its misidentification by competent observers. Ask any skeptic and you will be told that these *untrained witnesses* are not seeing UFOs; they are seeing IFOs (*Identified* Flying Objects). The skeptics claim that the lights/discs in the sky and craft hovering over the highway that measure from 25 feet to 500 feet across, are easily identified, but what they are is never mentioned.

As you read through the sightings included in the text ahead, notice that before 1947, anytime a UFO was reported in the press of the day, it was reported without skeptics and/or critics chiming in with their ridicule and nonsensical answers. Once the government reversed its first claim that the wreckage found in the New Mexico desert near Roswell was not a flying saucer as had been reported by Major Jesse Marcel, labeling it instead a downed weather balloon, all bets were off in giving the public a thorough unbiased account of sightings by the media in all its incarnations. Once this story hit, it seemed to signal that from that point on, all sightings had to be explained away in conventional terms. As you will see, the sightings made are always explained away as misidentifications of stars, planets, meteors, aircraft, or debris from our space program, or meteorological devices/anomalies. And in their tireless effort to get the most sensational story, the media naturally concentrate on the most controversial aspects of the UFO phenomenon—instead of focusing on the sightings by competent, well trained witnesses.

In the 1950s, the media found it profitable to concentrate their efforts on reporting the stories concerning "Contactees." The Contactees were groups of individuals who claimed that they were in regular contact with our "Space Brothers" on our neighboring planets, who through these specially selected humans, wanted to help us solve all our problems. Thus, everyone who saw a UFO was classified as being similar to these misguided folks: that is, crazy! All other reputable sightings were overlooked, dismissed, and ridiculed in the media.

Some of the "experts" will take the scientific highroad and explain that UFOs cannot be real as it is impossible for beings from other solar systems to travel to our little corner of the galaxy. They presuppose they are experts in an area where no earthling has any experience: interstellar travel. They espouse their belief that covering the distances between galaxies that UFOs must to reach Earth, as being contrary to the laws of physics that we accept as universal constants. Thus, interstellar travel is not possible.

Debunkers do not, however, always report all or know all the facts. Noted, researcher Stanton Friedman pointed out in a lecture conducted in New York City, that there are things we don't yet know or understand, and one day soon a discovery may be made that will prove that man can cover great distances in shorter periods of time than is now theorized by leading experts. To drive this point home, he gave the following example: In 1941, a Dr. Campbell theorized that it would take a rocket weighing 1 trillion tons to reach the moon. He arrived at this using the, then accepted, formula that for every 1 pound of payload, it would take 10 pounds of propellant to get a rocket into orbit. However, when it was actually accomplished in 1969, 38 years of research and development in conjunction with many new discoveries, allowed NASA to reach the moon in a rocket weighing in at a measly 3,000 tons. Thus, what was deemed impossible was ascertained in less than four decades thanks to breakthroughs in technology and engineering. If this could happen in less than four decades, is it not possible we will be traveling to other galaxies within a century? Likewise, couldn't a civilization that is most likely older than ours already have made the necessary discoveries to make interstellar travel a reality for them? My belief is that no matter how long it may take us, sooner or later we will get there.

So I suggest that you please keep the following in mind when reading the skeptics' claims in regards to the motives behind why people report seeing UFOs. Although neither researching the facts nor interviewing the witnesses is conducted by these pseudo-experts, they seem to make it into the spotlight more often then the so-called publicity seekers who actually have had the sightings. I often wonder why no journalist has asked the debunkers if they in fact are not trying to make a quick buck off of maligning the character and intelligence of those individuals who have had an encounter with the unexplained... After all, they are doing exactly what they claim the person who reported the UFO is trying to do: gain fame and fortune from the sighting of UFOs. By ridiculing those who have had sightings, through interviews and writing books, these debunkers make a comfortable living, while most witnesses are rewarded with scorn and hardship for trying to ascertain what it was they saw or experienced by reporting what they had seen to the proper authorities or the media. The irony is truly sad.

Chapter 2

From Primitive Man to the Victorian Era

"I believe extraterrestrial intelligences are watching the earth and have been visiting us for millennia in their flying saucers."

~Dr. Herman Oberth
Co-inventor of the V-2 rocket

Primitive Man and the UFO Phenomenon

In the immediate post World War II years, the world was a very different place than it is today. Having just helped to defeat the two greatest menaces to freedom this planet has ever known, Americans wanted nothing more than to sit back and begin to enjoy the American Way and the fruits of their prosperity. A way of life that would have been lost if the Axis armies where allowed to triumph. The peace was short-lived, as the Soviet Union went from ally to antagonist in the span of several months. Now, having seen what the harnessing of the atom could do, Americans waited on edge to find out if the Red Menace could and would develop nuclear weapons or other secret weapons to be used in their quest for world domination.

To keep this threat at bay, Americans gladly handed over their taxes to help develop new weapons that could help safeguard our country against any threat. However, people began to see objects in the skies. Objects that not only looked radically different, but also performed never-before-seen maneuvers while flying at unheard of speeds. At first, it was thought that these objects were secret weapons being developed by the United States or the Soviet Union. Their nerves being frayed by three years of intense warfare and so short a respite from conflict, the people wanted answers pronto, preferably one that would allow them to sleep easier at night. So the government came up with one. UFOs don't exist; thus they are no threat and should not concern the people of the United States. Oddly enough, most people believed this line, after all the government would never lie to the people, would they?

In hindsight, when taking all this into consideration, it is easy to see why the government was able to dupe Americans into believing that these sightings of craft that could out perform all aircraft known to our military were not real nor were they any threat to national security. When the sightings began, they came in slowly. This allowed the government the opportunity to come up with monologue replies that UFOs were not really unidentified objects from a foreign government, on or off this planet. Instead they were ordinary aircraft viewed in extraordinary circumstances. Or conversely, they were extraordinary (new) aircraft viewed under ordinary circumstances. But, when the reports started to pile up, and hundreds of reports were made each day, to be sure the administration's line was towed, the government had to set up a ministry to provide misinformation. It was these same people who came up with the Venus, swamp gas, weather balloon, and similar ludicrous explanations as to what people were seeing in the skies over the United States.

One explanation the government came up with was very convincing to most people. It seems so logical to those unfamiliar with the UFO phenomenon, that it is still used by many today. The government and their experts reasoned out the following: If the flying saucers are real and originate from elsewhere, why were they not reported before the populace was suffering from a nationwide nervous disorder caused by tensions from the Cold War? The experts deduced that if these objects where not a recent phenomenon caused by the stress every American was under from the constant threat of having their way of life destroyed by the Communist menace, why had they not been sighted before Kenneth Arnold made his report in 1947? If they were not products of overactive imaginations, should not there be a litany of sightings occurring on an ongoing basis throughout recorded history?

This was excellent deductive reasoning; the only problem with it is that unbeknownst to most people, what the government told them was not true! The truth is that mankind has been witness to these or similar craft on an ongoing basis since the beginning of recorded history. Banking on the fact that 99 percent of the people would not know of these old sightings, they went ahead with this debunking theory, and use it still today as but one way to discredit those people who claim to have seen these craft that the government claims do not exist.

The UFO phenomenon has always been very much a part of the human experience. Since discovering ways to communicate, man has tried to convey what goes on in his environment. Stone-age man painted pictures on rocks and cave walls depicting important things they experienced during their everyday life. Likewise, as man evolved, they continued to paint, sculpt, or draw things, as well as pass down stories through both the written and spoken word, depicting people, places, or things that profoundly affected them. With the exception of tabloid media reports, the tradition of recording only important events continues to this very day.

Thus, I have attempted to include only those paintings, sculptures or stories from our ancient ancestors that to me depict similar beings, objects, and events that have been recorded by people in the last several decades that have come into contact with Unidentified Flying Objects. The reason these reports from our predecessors are important is quite simple: These ancient men and women had never been exposed to oral stories or painted pictures of aliens, rocket ships, or invasions from space. They had no preconceived notions created by stories from prolific writers of science fiction. When creating histories on cave walls in paint or through the written word, the similarities to events today are not coincidental. The similarities come from the fact that they witnessed the same objects and beings in the sky and on the ground that thousands of people are seeing today. If they were going to embellish on their paintings, sculptures, or written histories, the flights of fancy they could come up with would be relative to the technology they witnessed around them. Children create imaginary friends, not imaginary beings coming out of metallic discs. Likewise, the Greeks and Romans, when creating their folklore and the imagery associated with their gods, they did not arrive in silver discs and impart great knowledge. They were human in form; rode chariots pulled by winged horses and were endowed with supernatural powers. They used things from everyday life when describing their stories of wonders, as that is the technology they were familiar with. It is when the paintings, stories, and traditions use imagery that would not be normally associated with their surroundings that we should sit up and take notice.

When not busy providing the basic necessity for their survival, our Cro-Magnon ancestors developed a highly stylized method of depicting the world around them through the painting of figures and objects on the walls and ceilings of the caves they called home. Their artistic renderings of the landscape around them, the animals that represented food, comfort, and danger, all can be found throughout Europe, with a high concentration existing in the caves near Les Trois Freres, in the Pyrenean Mountains of France and in the mountains of Spain.

One such gallery of Cro-Magnon art can be found in the province of Santonder, Spain. Within this 600-foot cave, there are many paintings made by our not-too-distant ancestors. Picture if you will, standing inside a cave, stone walls surround you as you make your way within. On either side of you are hundreds of depictions of the animals that were the lifeblood of these cave-dwellers' existence. Artistic renderings of bison, reindeer, and bears grazing for food in lush grasslands, or charging through timber to escape their capture by these ancient hunters. Now gaze upwards to the ceiling of the cave. Painted here are discs of many sizes and shapes. If there, you would be witnessing what appears to be a categorized listing[1] of the UFOs that have been encountered within the last sixty years; and as the pictures show, these objects were seen in the Paleolithic age.[2] The sun is in its rightful place high in the sky, centered on the cave's ceiling. Looking closer at these objects, you can deduct right away that this is not a mediocre rendition of birds. If the artist could paint such lifelike scenes on the walls of plants, animals, and humans, could he not paint birds in the sky that looked similar to real birds? But upon closer inspection, you begin to see discs that look like two saucers placed on top of one another, while others resemble hubcaps with antenna protruding from their oval shells. All these objects are in the sky hovering near the sun. None are depicted in trees or on the ground, where birds they hunted could be captured. If you could see them first hand, you would not think for one second that they are a likeness of birds. You would know what they represent upon first sight, a Cro-Magnon's man encounter with Unidentified Flying Objects. They could not be in possession of overactive imaginations, as they had no idea that man could build machines to fly in the sky. If these objects were to represent that, would they not have painted men with birdlike wings? Wings were the only mode of flight the caveman usually witnessed, so chances are they would associate flight with wings. There is even a painting on the wall of a cave near Pech Merle that has an object on the ground, and next to it there is a depiction of the large headed bug-eyed being that looks eerily similar to the central figure in the abduction phenomenon of our time, known as a "Gray."

Paintings are not the only way that visitation by UFOs and their crews to earth have been documented. As noted in great detail in Ralph and Judy Blum's excellent work, *Beyond Earth*, sometimes their visitations were recorded through the acquisition of knowledge. Many tribal societies from around the world share similar beliefs and rituals, though isolated by thousands of miles. The indigenous people of the present-day Americas, especially those in the Southwestern United States, Mexico, Peru, and Argentina all share stories of the great elders who came from the skies. These great elders had great "Medicine" as they imparted great knowledge to the tribes. Western scientists, until quite recently, didn't make some of these same discoveries that the original inhabitants of the Americas already knew. This would include calculating pi and the exact time in a lunar and solar year.

These tribes honored the benevolent elders through story and song, as well as dances and rituals where the braves of the tribe, dressed in helmets that exhibit a striking resemblance to the helmets worn by our own astronauts. There also exists incredible artifacts ranging in size from a handheld idol to the extraordinary Nazca Lines, lines forming figures visible only from thousands of feet up in the atmosphere, created to celebrate the great wisdoms imparted by these great Medicine Men from the heavens.

African tribes also have stories, customs, and artifacts similar to those presented above. There is one impressive example of the gift of great knowledge to an ancient people. They possessed this knowledge for hundreds of years, yet western science could only verify it in the last few decades. About 300 miles south of Timbuktu, in Mali, Africa, situated on the Bandiagara plateau, is the ancestral land of the tribe known as the Dogon. Like most people, they hold their religious beliefs quite dear. The central belief of this religion has knowledge about the creation of the universe, as well as all customs, and in fact their entire culture, being given to their elders by an amphibious extraterrestrial race known as the Nommo. According to legend, these benevolent beings arrived on earth in "Arks" several thousand years ago from their home. Their home is a planet in the Sirius system, some 8.7 light years from our solar system. The Nommo told the Dogon people facts they could not have guessed or made up. Central to these is that Sirius, the Dog Star, has an invisible highly dense companion star, which travels around it in an elliptical orbit once every 50-earth years. This information has been verified by western science as follows: In 1862, western astronomers witnessed the companion star, dubbed Sirius B, a giant White Dwarf as professed by the Dogon, and in 1926, our astronomers determined that it was a highly dense star, exactly as the Dogon have claimed for tens of centuries. These stories, though not a report of an encounter per se, reveal that ancient people did have close encounters of the first, second, third, and fourth kinds, and preserved them in their culture through painting, sculpture, written and oral traditions, and their customs. The information these primitive peoples had could not have been guessed at, leading many researchers to the conclusion that the tribes did indeed receive information from some highly evolved, technologically superior source. The only question is, who were these givers of these far seeing beliefs?

ENCOUNTERS WITH UFOS BY EARLY CIVILIZED MAN

Ancient texts are full of stories that could be interpreted as encounters by ancient man with UFOs and their occupants. However, since I have tried to incorporate only those stories or works of art by our ancestors with many similarities to the current UFO phenomenon, many had to be left out of the following section. Those included will illustrate my claim that UFOs have been here since the beginning of recorded history, and those things seen and or experienced were very similar to what goes on around us today.

Without a doubt, the Egyptians were one of the most advanced civilizations of their era. Less well known then their incredible architecture and complex culture is the fact that these advanced people had many encounters with strange craft hovering in their skies. Though they were taken as bad omens, or as messages that the gods were angry, the details are remarkably similar to sightings today. The following account was recorded circa 1504-1450 B.C. by scribes of the House of Life during the reign of Thutmose III. This well-documented case so troubled the chief scribes that they had to consult the Pharaoh, their living god, ruler of all Egypt, to gain his wisdom and words of comfort on what they had witnessed. According to the account that appears in the annals of Thutmose III, the event took place in the 22nd year of the Pharaohs reign, in the third month of winter, at the sixth hour of the day. The encounter began when the towns' residents in the Pharaoh's Royal City pointed out a "Circle of Fire" that hovered above the city to the sage scribes, whom, they were sure, could tell them what it was they were witnessing. The scribes noted that the object was as long as it was wide (a square or circle perhaps), and emitted a foul order (ionized air?) as it hung silently in the daytime sky. Sound familiar? It returned daily. After several days of this, it returned with several more objects just like it. The objects were so numerous and bright that they outshone the midday sun. The scribes, so troubled by this, traveled to see the Pharaoh. He was also concerned, so much so that he rallied his army to march on the Royal City, hoping that seeing the most powerful fighting force of the time would scare the objects away. It did not work. Much to his and the scribes' relief, several days later, the objects left as mysteriously as they had arrived.[3]

Could they have seen Venus, swamp gas, or a strange cloud formation? If the Egyptian military was anything like ours, not wanting to admit inadequacy, they probably invented stories to explain these objects away. As you will see later, the victim of the Gulf Breeze, Florida, sightings and abductions, Ed Waters, reported an object with a ring of lights (fire?) around its base that emitted an odor like ammonia as it passed overhead. The Egyptian encounter, much like the cave paintings in Spain and France, depict mans' encounters with machines we have come to call UFOs. Then, like now, these objects cause both fear and wonder in the people who witness them. The reaction of our ancestors is identical to ours, and unfortunately, we know the same amount of information about the objects now as they did then.

The Old Testament of the Holy Bible, as well as other writing by scholars of the Judeo-Christian schools of thought, are rich with accounts of mans' encounter with strange phenomenon. Some of these are feats that could be performed not only by a supreme being, but also by creatures of an advanced race. Some of these, like the parting of the Red Sea, talking clouds, pillars of light appearing out of nowhere, or the moving star that guided the wise men to the stable were Jesus was born, share some similarities to events associated with the current UFO phenomena. To myself, the accounts that follow are descriptions of close encounters that the people who are among the cornerstones of our religious beliefs had with extraterrestrial visitors to Earth.

EZEKIEL

Ezekiel was the first prophet to be called by God outside of the Holy Land. His calling came to him in Babylon, where he lived after his deportation from the Holy Land by Nebuchadnezzar in 597 B.C. The following is the best, most vivid account in any ancient text of an encounter between ancient man and a UFO. This account is taken directly out of the Book of Ezekiel, Chapter 1, verses 1-28. The prophet describes his encounter as follows:

> I looked and beheld a whirlwind coming from the north, a great cloud of fire… with a great brightness about it….Out of its mist there came the likeness of four living creatures…They had the likeness of a man…hands, feet, faces…Their appearance was like burning coals of fire…and out of the first being went lightning…as I beheld the living creatures, I behold one wheel upon the Earth by the living creatures…

The prophet goes on to describe how the creatures floated around the wheel as they went about "working" on their craft. The only noise he notes is a sound that reminded him of great rushing water. Ezekiel, believing he was seeing a manifestation of God, bowed down in homage to the Almighty.

Does this not sound identical to countless reports made in the recent past? An object lands; its occupants get out, give the ship and the surrounding area the once over, and go as mysteriously as they had arrived. It goes without saying that his peers held Ezekiel in high regard. If Ezekiel were trying to get across to other Israelites the greatness of God, wouldn't it be easier and more effective to create a story that would have had more of an impact on the people of his time. Recounting a tale of God's greatness using fire and brimstone to punish evil doers would have been more relevant to his peers than describing in such perfect detail the landing of a UFO and the description of the features and movements of the crew.

ENOCH

From the first *Book of Enoch* comes an account so similar to the reports of abductees, it is startling. This account was translated from the *Coptic* by R.H. Charles in 1912 and was published by Clarendon Press in Oxford, England.

And lo! The Watchers called me, Enoch the scribe. And the vision was shown to me thus: Behold, in the vision clouds invited me and a mist summoned me, and the course of the stars and the lightning's sped and hastened me, and the winds in the vision caused me to fly and lifted me upward, and bore me into heaven. And I went in till I drew nigh to a wall that was made of crystals and surrounded by tongues of fire, and it began to affright me. And I went into the tongues of fire and drew nigh to a large house which was built of crystal. Its ceiling was like the path of the stars and the lightning's, and between them the fiery cherubim, and their heaven was clear as water. A flaming fire surrounded the walls, and its portals blazed with fire. And I entered the house, and it was hot as fire and cold as ice: there were no delights of life therein: fear covered me, and trembling got hold of me. And I looked and saw therein a lofty throne: its appearance was as crystal, and the wheels thereof as the shining sun.

This account parallels recent accounts in the appearance of the craft, the abductees being taken aboard and shown great, yet strange things. Could Enoch just be a great storyteller? Of course, but if he had not had an experience so similar to those that are presently associated with the abduction phenomenon, would he have been able to describe it in such vivid detail? I doubt it highly.

JACOB

Jacob, the son of Abraham and Rebekah, and twin of Esau, also had a close encounter with an unidentified flying object. In the Book of Genesis, Chapter 28, verses 1-19, we find Jacob en route on foot from Beer-Sheba to Haran. When night encroached in around him, he decided to bed down for the night at a site near a temple in Luz. He lay down and was soon fast asleep. He awoke suddenly, being bathed in a brilliant light. Though he could not see anyone, he heard a voice explaining who he was. Coming down from some place on high was what Jacob referred to as a stairway, brilliantly illuminated, as if by the sun itself, turning the surrounding night into day. The "stairway" had angels drifting up and down as they went about carrying out their assigned duties. When he awoke in the morning, Jacob was convinced that he was in the presence of God the night before; so he took the rock from under his head, poured oil on it and set it up as a memorial stone, and renamed the place Bethel.

Correct me if I am wrong, but don't these accounts sound identical to the reports made by abductees today? The reports are exactly the same in every way; from their being bathed in bright light and levitated onboard a craft, to the description of the interior of the craft and the abject fear felt by Ezekiel, Enoch, Jacob, and recent abductees to their respective experiences.

One or two things can explain the similarities between accounts of long ago and today. Either people who have encounters with UFOs are experiencing the same or similar encounters as our ancestors did, or those who report them today are researchers and theologians, who make sure that their accounts matched those made by figures from the past in every detail. As many of the people in Asia, Africa, and Oceania have never read these accounts, yet have the same experiences, it leads me to believe that the answer is obvious. The events and accounts are similar then and now, because the same things that happened in the past are happening today. Who says history never repeats!

UFOs in the Medieval World

Although we have jumped several centuries, please do not infer that UFOs were not seen between the time of Enoch and the Middle Ages. There were mass sighting during the heydays of the Roman Empire. But, since these sightings do not meet the guidelines I have adhered to while writing this book; they will not be included. So we will start this section off with an account of a witnessed abduction that comes to us from France in the years when King Charlemagne set upon his throne, circa 800 A.D.

Lyons, France

Within plain sight of the townspeople of Lyons, France, three men and a woman were seen too consort with the men who flew a flying machine.[4] These four villagers were whisked up into this machine and taken up into the heavens and shown miraculous wonders. When their fantastic voyage was over, they were slowly lowered to the ground from on high (perhaps by a tractor beam?) while the flying machine hung silently overhead. Once returned to their village, they were met by a frightened mob. The townsfolk knew man could not fly, thus the men who operated this abomination must be in league with the devil himself, using sorcery to fly through the air and raising people off the ground only to lower them once again. Their four neighbors must also be sorcerers, guilty by association, as they were seen to fly up to and down from the ship. Ordinary people could not do that. The fact that these four people had no control over what transpired around them was not known to those same neighbors who would have burned them at the stake as heretics, witches, and warlocks, had it not been for the Bishop of Lyons' intervention.

The Bishop, whose logic was the basis for all the logic used by our government in similar circumstances, reasoned to the townspeople that since people could not fly, they obviously could not have seen these four people floating to and from a machine that could not have possibly existed! (This man could have worked for Project Blue Book!) Likewise, in a testament to the basic nature of the masses at large, the people of Lyons unconditionally believed this authority figure, much like people today have believed the misinformation bring put out by our government for over six decades.

JAPAN

Similar things happened in Japan on September 12, 1235.[5] One General Yoritsume was bivouacking with his troops in the lovely Japanese countryside. When night had permeated their camp, the general and his men became the unsuspecting witnesses of an amazing aerial display. The night sky was alight with strange bright objects that flew overhead. They came from the southwest horizon, and passed overhead, looping, swinging, and swaying through the night sky, as they made their way to the northeast horizon. Much to the dismay of the frightened men, this displayed continued for several hours. Even though the lights ceased to pass overhead long before dawn arrived, calm did not return to the troops until the morning sun had vanquished the fearful night.

The general ordered his scientific advisors to explain what he and the men had witnessed by sundown. The scientific advisors knew they had not witnessed comets, meteors, or shooting stars, as these natural phenomena do not change course, nor do they do loop-to-loops, as the lights had done the previous night. The advisors debated throughout the day, but could not find an answer to the general's question. As night drew near, the advisors knew that soon they had to have an answer for the general. In the event the lights returned, the general wanted an explanation he could give to his men to prevent another widespread panic. When the general came to find out what his great thinkers had come up with, he was informed that what they all had witnessed was a new type of natural phenomena: The wind was causing the stars to sway! Luckily for the general and his science advisors, the lights did not reappear that night, and this highly irrational explanation did not have to be used to explain the unexplainable to a group of highly disciplined, yet very scared men.

THE MONKS

In the Middle Ages, the religious people throughout the world were often charged with keeping and passing down knowledge from one generation to the next. Many times, Monks were the prototypical jacks of all trades: they dedicated their lives to God, translated works into languages the masses could understand and were teachers to these masses throughout the known world. Therefore, when they had sightings of unknown phenomena, you can rest assured that what they recorded was what they encountered. The following are several examples of Monks sighting objects never before seen by themselves, or those people who depended on their wisdom, strength, and knowledge.

To quote Estelle Getty's *Golden Girls* character, Sophia: Picture this, Midnight, New Years Day, 1254, St. Albans, Hertfordshire, England. While involved in a late night prayer ritual on that crisp, cold winter's night, the residents of this Abbey bore witness to the sudden appearance of a bright UFO in the clear night sky. The monks watched in awe as a flying ship of impressive, yet elegant, design,[6] bathed in the most splendid colors, passed over their Abbey in dead silence, sending the monk into pray in an effort to rid themselves of this unwanted intruder to their communal home.

Thirty-six years later, the monks of the Byland Abbey in Yorkshire, England, had their own encounter with a UFO. That evening, the routine chores of several of the monks were interrupted when a fellow monk who was in a highly agitated state summoned them outside. Once outdoors, the monks saw what it was that so alarmed their excited colleague. Floating effortlessly over their abbey was a large, silvery disc-shaped object.[7] This object so frightened the monks, that until it went on its merry way several hours later, the monks were in feverish pray to the Savior to keep them safe from this unholy visitor to the night sky above their normally peaceful abbey.

Both of these incidences were recorded by the monks in their Abbey's records for safe keeping, and to enlighten the generations that came after them in how to deal with visitors from the unknown: Pray and hope they go away!

Arras, France

All Saints Day November 1st, 1461 began like any other autumn day for the people in Arras, France.[8] The shopkeepers plied their trade and the local farmers prepared their fields for winter. The familiarity of the day was cast aside, when a ship with fire coming from its aft quarters silently passed over the petrified residents of this small rural community. In his *Memoirs of a Freeman in Arras*, Jacques Duclerc, a distinguished counselor and chronicler to the court of King Philip the Good, put into words a detailed account of this sighting. He describes what he saw thusly,

> A fiery thing like an iron rod, as large as half the moon, was seen in the sky [over Arras] for a little less than a quarter of an hour.

We cannot say what these folks saw, but we can be sure that it was not a fireball or meteor. Although both could appear cylindrical like a ship, and be followed by flaming trail, neither of these could move so slowly through the sky that it would take almost fifteen minutes to pass over the town.

Erfurt, France

Another fiery object was witnessed in the village of Erfurt in 1520. The villagers witnessed an aerial performance by a disc-shaped object. The disc was not only brilliantly illuminated, it also projected beams of lights outward, as two smaller fiery orbs circled the main object. The trajectory of all the crafts took them over this small, bewildered village, in plain view of all the religious persons, social and business leaders, as well as the average citizen, as they went about their business of the day.

We can be sure this was no misidentification of aircraft, nor a natural phenomenon, as they do not emit beams of lights. There is only one thing these craft could be: Unidentified Flying Objects. The only question we cannot and never will be able to answer is where did these craft come from?

The New World and More New Sightings

The Old World did not have a monopoly on sightings of strange craft in the sky. As settlers from the Old World made their way across the Atlantic Ocean, the sightings of strange objects in the skies followed them. These explorers were without a doubt among the bravest adventurers that this world has known. They left the world they knew and set off on adventures into something that most humans avoid at all cost: the great unknown. These sojourners would not have had a chance to start news lives in the New World had it not been for the great explores of the sea. These were men of steel, who sailed wooden ships throughout the cold, rough seas of the world in search of routes to the Orient.

At Sea Near Bimini

On one such adventure, these men of steel became like frightened children. After several weeks at sea, the sailors on an expedition began to wonder if they truly would reach land. On the night of October 11, 1492, as unbeknownst to them, they were closing in on the New World, (estimates put their position as off the coast of present day Bimini) the men on watch began to see bright objects as they flew across the sky, on a level trajectory, from horizon to horizon.

The crew became so frightened that they awoke their captain. Once on deck, he also witnessed these strange glowing objects as they made their way across the night sky. He, like his crew, became quite bewildered at what they saw, but being the captain he was, he managed to calm his crew down by reminding them that God worked in many mysterious ways. A short time later, land was sighted and these strange objects that had caused great fear were looked back upon as good omens, pointing the way to safety of the harbors of the New World.

Now, who are the people who say that only weird, delusional people see UFOs? If this is true, then our nation has a national holiday that pays tribute to a kook! The captain mentioned here is none other than Christopher Columbus, who at the time of the sighting was on his first expedition to the New World. He recorded this account in his log, a log that would be scrutinized upon his return to Spain. Seafarers were and are accustomed to seeing natural phenomena in the crisp, clear sky over the oceans of the world. These objects were obviously something that neither he nor his crew had ever seen before.

Around Boston Harbor

The New World's Massachusetts Bay Colony was home to many famous people and events. Some less known events within the colony, all but ignored by historical studies, occurred in and around Boston Harbor. The most amazing occurrence happened on the night of January 18th, 1644, and was reported by John Winthrop's *Journal.*[9]

On that night, James Everell and two fellow colonists had their hands full as they navigated a barge down the Muddy River, on their way to Boston Harbor. While going about the business of sailing the barge down the river, the three-man crew noticed an oddly bright light in the night sky. Odd as this light was, their attentions remained focused on getting the barge safely to its destination. Without warning, night became day when the light swooped down out of the sky, and hung over and just upstream from the barge as it sailed downstream towards the harbor. So bright was the object that it illuminated not only the men and their barge, but also the banks of the river and the tree line beyond it.

The crews' utter amazement soon turned into abject terror as the UFO began to drag the men and their barge upstream against the current, back in the same direction from which they had just sailed. After what seemed like forever to these terrified men, the object released its hold on the barge and flew off at high speed.

The men rowed for all they were worth for the shore. Once they had reached the safety of the riverbank they found that their encounter had witnesses. Several locals had seen a bright light coming from the river and decided to see what was the cause of the illumination. They told the crewmen that, much to their surprise, once they had arrived on the riverbank, they did not see a fire. Instead, they saw the crew struggling to maintain control of their barge as this brightly illuminated object attempted to pull them upstream for a full twenty minutes. As it attempted, in their words, to hijack the barge, the object threw off sparks and was followed by a trail of flame. Had residents of the area not witnessed their encounter it certainly would not have been reported in a printed journal. Instead, Mr. Everell and his crew would've been the butt of jokes in pubs throughout New England.

SIGHTINGS BY 18TH AND 19TH CENTURY ASTRONOMERS

Sailors were not the only people of this time period that bore witness to the strange phenomenon that we call UFOs. There was a similar group of people, who would have had plenty of opportunity to view the strange craft that, like now, traveled throughout the night skies. This next series of reports comes from astronomers of the day.[10] They, more than anybody, would have had ample opportunity to witness these objects, as their work required them to study the skies. Thus, it is safe to assume that they would not have mistaken natural phenomena for the objects they saw, and since planes did not yet exist, there can be but one answer to what they witnessed: UFOs.

ASTRONOMER SIR EDMUND HALLEY

The evening of March 6th, 1716 was one that Sir Edmund Halley would not soon forget. As on any other clear night, the famed astronomer was using his telescope to pursue his true love, astronomy. It was on this night, however, that he came face to face with the unknown. As he busied himself in exploring the heavens, Halley noticed a light strong enough to illuminate the room, coming in the window from the nighttime sky. Feeling this was odd, as the sun had just set and the light was far brighter than moonlight, Halley proceeded to venture outside to see what could possibly be creating this intensely bright light.

What he found shocked him so much that he made special note of this peculiar encounter. Much to his surprise he saw a large glowing object hovering relatively close by his observatory in the night sky. He noted the time, 7 PM, and for the next two hours he sat bathed in the light of this truly alien object.

Halley noted that the object emitted enough light so as to allow a book to be read outside at nighttime. The light did not encompass the entire sky, just an area that included his home, observatory, and a portion of the immediate property. At 9 PM, the light intensified so much, Sir Halley noted that it seemed as though "more fuel was added to the fire."

Although he later found a comet made famous in the intervening years, I would be willing to bet that this incident impressed him much more than the discovery of the comet that bears his name. He could explain what a comet was and why it did what it did. The object he saw that night he could not explain any better than the leading scientists of today.

ASTRONOMER CHARLES MESSIER (FRANCE)

Likewise, the French astronomer Charles Messier had a similar encounter outside his home in France. As he stepped out of his house into the midday sunshine, the astronomer's attention was drawn to several rather large disc-shaped objects as they slowly made their way across the beautiful afternoon sky. From his description we can tell that what he saw was similar to the discs that had been reported by many people across the world as well as across the plane of time.

Reverend W. Read (London, England)

The next century saw more of the same.[11] During the Great Exhibit in Hyde Park, a well-known London astronomer witnessed through his telescope, a procession of large discs making their way quite leisurely through the London skies. On September 4th, 1851 the Reverend W. Read was scanning the morning skies above London from the confines of his home, when an object caught his eye. Reverend Read went to his telescope to train this instrument on the peculiar object making its way through the heavens. What he saw were many brightly illuminated disc-shaped objects flying through the daytime skies, high above the largest city in the world at that time. His sighting continued for six hours as squads of these discs made their way to their unknown destination.

Oxford, England

Several years and a short distance away, another astronomer sighted objects that he too could not explain. From the Radcliff Observatory in Oxford, England, astronomers sighted a large glowing object in the clear skies on the night of June 8th, 1868. For in excess of four minutes, he witnessed a large glowing object as it drifted across the night sky. He became certain that the object he was viewing, whatever it may have been, was surely controlled by some form of intelligence. What convinced him of this was the way the object changed course. From its original heading, it changed course and headed westward for awhile, then changed course again as it proceeded to head in a southerly direction, only to turn 180 degrees and streak off to the north, vanishing in short order as it flew over the northern horizon.

French Academy Member M. Trecul

The following is an account of the sighting made by one M. Trecul, a member of the French Academy of Science, on August 20th, 1880. As he scanned the skies, his attention was drawn to a large cigar-shaped object, pointed at both-ends and emitting a whitish-gold illumination. As the object slowly made its way over the French countryside, the astronomer witnessed something even more unexpected and amazing than this truly foreign craft. As the object floated by, it seemed to open up, and from within it, came a smaller brightly lit object, which left a flame-like trail as it sped quickly out of sight along the same or similar trajectory that its parent craft was on. Imagine that, a scientist sighting a "Mothership" releasing a smaller scout ship, and all of this occurring sixty-seven years before the modern UFO era began.

ASTRONOMER JOSE BONILLA

August 12th and 13th, 1883 were days that Mexican Astronomer Jose Bonilla of the Zacatecas Observatory did not soon, if ever, forget. Perched by his telescope, approximately 11,000 feet above sea level, Bonilla was observing the sun's solar flare-ups. According to record , Bonilla observed and photographed a series of ovoid-shaped objects as they passed somewhere in the 92 million miles between the Earth and the sun. Most of these objects appeared to be dark, yet others seamed to give off a glow.

Within two hours, he had counted 283 objects as they crossed the length of the sun's disc-shaped outline. Due to the field of view being so large, Bonilla was able to see the objects before and after they passed across the face of the sun, which enables him to note that, every so often, one of the discs would shoot off beams of intense light in all directions.

The next day, he recorded seeing 116 bodies cross through his telescopes' field of view as he attempted to study several phenomena singular to the sun; not watch disc-shaped objects as they flew through space!

NOTABLE 19TH CENTURY SIGHTINGS FROM AROUND THE WORLD

The following sightings will consist of sightings by scientist, military personnel or multiple witnesses, which have allowed me to rule out hallucination by an individual as the cause of those sightings not made by trained observers. As you will see, many of these sightings were witnessed by several or more people, and in some instances, for in excess of two days! Besides, not often do several people have the same hallucination when located in various points of observation.

PINEROLO TURIN, PIEDMONT, ITALY

October 12th, 1808 was your atypical autumn day for the people in the village of Pinerolo, Piedmont.[11] After a hard day of harvesting the last of that year's crops in the nearby fields, the villagers, while on their way to their homes, had an encounter with the unknown. While walking home, the villagers sensed something was amiss. The usually quiet farm animals were having a full-blown fit, almost as if a wolf or some other predator had found its way into their pens. Concern began to mount as they drew closer to the animals as predators usually waited for the cover of darkness to ply their trade. To see a wolf lurking about in the daylight would truly be out of the ordinary. What they saw was many times odder than that! The cause of the commotion was a brilliantly lit disc-shaped object that by its course had drifted over the pens of the animals as it made its way across the skies above their small village, leaving frightened animals and awestruck townspeople in its path.

EMBRUM, FRANCE

In the French publication *Annales de chimie et de physique*, dating from September 15th, 1820,[12] Francois Arago reported on an encounter with an unknown object in Embrun, France. Multiple witnesses were present for the sighting of two aerial phenomena: one quite ordinary, the other quite extraordinary. The first phenomenon was an eclipse of the moon, a common yet infrequent phenomenon. It is what the crowd that had gathered to witness the eclipse saw during the eclipse that left the longest lasting impression. As the moon's surface was being covered by the shadow of the Earth, the gathered spectators saw a line of several round objects that moved along very military-like in a straight line. When the lead object felt a change of course was necessary, each object that followed would turn at the same exact spot that the lead object turned, much like the movement known as the column right or left practiced by troops on review. Much to the chagrin of the modern debunkers, I think we can presuppose that the witnesses were not watching meteors, as they, like planets and stars, cannot turn with the precision of a military marching band.

EAST OF THE MISSISSIPPI RIVER, OHIO, NEW YORK

Refocusing our sites back on the good old USA, you will find that our next sighting is very similar to the last. Over a two-day period from November 12-13, 1833, those people living in the states east of the Mississippi River were treated to a spectacular meteor shower.[13] The residents of Poland, Ohio, and Niagara Falls, New York, were more fortunate than most, as they also were treated to the aerial performance by large Unidentified Flying Object.

Just south of Youngstown, in the small town of Poland, Ohio, at 9 PM on the evening of November 12th, the Honorable Calvin Pease was sitting on his front porch with a small assembly of friends and relatives awaiting the beginning of the meteor shower. The aerial display they saw was more than anyone had anticipated, surely it was odder than any other sight witnessed by anyone in the group at any time in the past. Mr. Pease claims that he and his crowd witnessed an object, shaped like a pruning hook, flying through the night sky, on a heading that took it through the area of the sky where the constellation of Ursa Major could be seen. Though no height was recorded, the assembly estimated the object looked to be twenty feet long and eighteen inches wide as viewed from arms' length! To give you an idea of how enormous this craft must have actually been, a Boeing 747 flying at altitude will be completely blocked out by a quarter held at arms' length. Since it can be assumed that the object was flying in Earth's atmosphere, whatever the object was, it was of incredible size!

In Niagara Falls, New York, the meteors were first seen at or around 2 AM in the early morning hours of November 13th, 1833. Not long thereafter, those people watching the skies above Niagara Falls also sighted a large, luminous, oval-shaped object that many were heard to say reminded them of a dining room table. The object was much larger and brighter than the meteors seen falling from the heavens. The object, as it made its way from west to east, was seen to shine bright beams of lights from many different angles and points of origins on its surface.

Now I do not claim to be an astronomer, nor any type of scientist for that matter, but I would bet that no meteor, shooting star, fire ball, or asteroid would emit beams of light from any or all sides as it streaked through the night sky. Also keep in mind that anything "falling" out of the sky like a meteor would have a trajectory that would intersect with the ground, not take it from one horizon to the next.

The Brig, Victoria

We have spoken previously about the bravery of the men of steel who sailed the oceans in their wooden ships. That is not to say that sailors plying the sea today are not as brave; they are still among the hardest souls alive. Their jobs, however, have become a little easier thanks to the technological progress of the last few centuries. And even though during the Industrial Revolution they made large, sturdy vessels, lessening the worries by their crews, sometimes these crews were often the unsolicited witnesses to strange phenomena.

One such occurrence that may forever remain unexplained happened to the men aboard the brig *Victoria*. While sailing to Newcastle, England, from the Isle of Malta, approximately 100 miles out of port, the *Victoria*[9] and her crew encountered a sudden vicious storm, followed by their sighting of several UFOs. On June 18th, 1845 at 9:30 PM, while sailing in calm weather, the ship and its crew were suddenly beset with a freak and intense squall. Suddenly, the mast went over the side as if carried away by a large storm surge. For two long hours, a strong wind from the east battered the ship. Then, as suddenly as it came upon them, the wind ceased. Once more the ship was calm. Then, the crew noticed that the air had become almost unbearably hot and a strong stench of sulfur permeated the atmosphere. In the midst of a boiling sea, approximately one half mile from the ship, emerged three bright, shiny objects. They rose from the ocean and hovered for ten minutes before speeding off into the dark night sky.

Some doubters would take this report, subtract the UFO sighting out of the picture and tell you that the ship's crew had an encounter with a meteor. The rushing of air, sulfur smell, and churning sea certainly would be associated with such an encounter. However, most meteors go *into* the ocean, not come *out* of it!

Another possible explanation would have a submerged volcano erupting in the area, throwing molten rock into the atmosphere. This also sounds like a plausible explanation until you consider the facts. Molten rock could be shot out of the water, but it would not hover for ten minutes and then speed off into the night sky!

This encounter represents the type that I find most believable. Here we have a sighting by the crew, both enlisted men and officers, manning a ship in the largest navy of their era. All well-trained observers, hopefully not inclined to tell tall tales, as the consequences of those stories could impact the entire British Empire, who encountered three unknown objects as they came from beneath the brine and flew off into history. These men made a detailed description of their encounter, including the effect the UFOs had on the air and water around them. Could they be lying? Sure, but would they? Probably not, as what possible benefit could reporting such an incident to the English Maritime Board bring, except ridicule and possible dismissal from the service had the Admiralty not accepted the word of their well-trained sailors.

Wilmington, Delaware

Another good multiple-witness sighting took place not on the sea, but in the historic seafaring town of Wilmington, Delaware. The sighting received widespread coverage in newspapers from Philadelphia to New York City. The spectacle was witnessed by many residents of the city as they sat out in the cool night air of July 13, 1860.

As was the practice of the day, many city dwellers retired to the outdoors, as the night air was cooler than their brick and stone houses, which resonated with heat from the afternoon sun well into the evening. On this particular night, many evening constitutionals and conversations were interrupted when a pale blue light originating from overhead, illuminating different areas of the city. The best vantage point must have been the intersection of 5th and Market Streets, as the most detailed sightings reported came from the people who were stopped dead in their tracks by this uninvited interloper. The sight these startled residents saw was unbelievable: Moving slowly over the area at about the speed of a trotting horse, approximately 100 feet above the rooftops, was a 200-foot-long object, glowing the pale blue light that had mysteriously surrounded them. In front of this amazing machine was an intensely black cloud-like object guiding the object on its course. Behind it flew three deep red spheres, glowing as if filled with blood. The aerial procession crossed Market Street and continued on a southeasterly heading that made it pass over the Delaware River near the mouth of the Christina River, where it turned and headed towards Newcastle,[14] eventually disappearing from sight—but not the minds of the people who had just witnessed this remarkable object.

If the government had a pre-Civil War misinformation ministry, they would be hard pressed to so easily explain this sighting away. Hundreds of people from throughout the city and the surrounding area witnessed these large, unknown objects from many different locations. Heck, I don't think even the ever-creative folks from Project Blue Book could have convincingly explained this one away!

BONHAM, TEXAS AND FORT RILEY, KANSAS

The next account is taken from one of the many books of the late Frank Edwards, a man I like to refer to as "The Paul Harvey of the Occult." In his book, *Stranger Than Science*, he reports on an interesting case that comes to us out of the town of Bonham, in the great state of Texas.

In 1873, the town's residents, but especially the field hands harvesting cotton, were terrorized by silvery disc-shaped objects that repeatedly swooped down at them from out of the daytime sky. This so spooked a nearby team of horses that they bolted from the field, throwing the driver off the wagon they were attached to, down to the ground, where he died from injuries inflicted by the wheels as they passed over his body.

About an hour later, the same or similar objects buzzed the parade grounds of Fort Riley, Kansas, tormenting the horses the Cavalrymen road to such an extent, that the commanding officer had to end the Pass and Review exercise, as they were embroiled in utter turmoil.[15]

DENISON, TEXAS

An interesting report concerning a farmer's encounter with a UFO can be read from the microfilm files of the *Denison Daily News* of Denison, Texas. Its January 25th, 1878 edition contains the following report:

> Mr. John Martin, a farmer who lives some six miles north of Dallas, while out hunting, had his attention directed to a dark object high up in the northern sky. The peculiar shape, and the velocity with which the object seemed to approach, kept his attention... When first noticed it appeared to be about the size of an orange, which continued to grow in size....After gazing at it for sometime...the object was nearly overhead, the object had grown in size ..and appeared to be going..at a wonderful speed...when directly over him it was about the size of a large saucer and was evidently at a great height.[16]

NEW YORK HARBOR

On April 12th, 1879, two astronomers independently witnessed a UFO hovering high above New York Harbor. Harry Harrison of Jersey City, New Jersey, and Spencer Devoe of Manhattenville, New York, both witnessed the same object at the same time while watching the heavens through their respective telescopes.

Mr. Harrison, having watched the object for three hours, noted that the brightly glowing object was circular and remained stationary in the sky as the stars moved past it due to the earth's rotation. Mr. Devoe described the object as "wonderfully brilliant" and from his calculations from observation, the object was a half mile wide and at an altitude of roughly eighty miles. Both men noticed the next night that the strange object was gone. Mr. Harrison decided to contact the Naval Observatory in Washington D.C. to report this strange anomaly, but they, as today, showed no interest in his sighting. So, instead his story was submitted to and published by both the *New York Tribune* and *Scientific American*.[17]

KATTENAU, GERMANY

The early risers in Kattenau, Germany, were startled by events they saw unfold in the early morning hours of March 22nd, 1880.[18] As the sun began to brighten the morning sky and villagers began heading off to their day's toil, those unfortunate souls who were out and about came face to face with objects they never dreamed existed. As the townsfolk trudged their way towards their respective places of employment, they began to notice that the clouds in the sky were not alone. Much to their amazement they saw luminous discs heading for their town. When they had reached Kattenau, the animals became so frightened and raised such a ruckus that most people who were asleep were soon outside trying to ascertain the cause of all the commotion, only to find these strange discs in the skies above their homes!

These are excellent examples of daylight discs as seen by simple folk more than 120 years ago.

AUTHOR'S NOTE:

Interestingly, the report from the *Denison Daily News*, like many of the others, matches word for word, description for description, with the reports submitted by people today. As I have said before, these are the same or similar craft being seen then as today. Notice the farmer's description of the object as being "like a large saucer," almost seventy years before Kenneth Arnold described the craft he'd seen likewise.

H.M.S. VULTURE

Here is another encounter that points to the possibility of the re-visitation of earth by the same groups of beings. On May 15th, 1879, the H.M.S. *Vulture* found itself sailing the waters of the Persian Gulf on that warm spring night when the ship was confronted by two UFOs. At the helm that night was an old salt by the name of Commodore Pringle, and it was by his hand that the account was recorded into the ship's logbook.

The encounter with the UFOs was quite sudden; one minutes they are sailing the calm seas, the next minute two objects were coming down out of the sky aimed at his vessel. One hovered off the port side and the other off the starboard side. He describes them as appearing very similar to two large wheels with spokes. Each rotated, one clockwise, the other counter-clockwise. When they had finished looking the vessel over, they departed rapidly.

Is it coincidence that these two objects were wheel shaped and witnessed in the same geographic area that Ezekiel had his sighting of similar objects thousands of years before? Or could it be that these visitors had returned to record the progress made in the area where they had been assigned to collect data for whomever and whatever purpose so many years before?

Adrianople, Turkey

From out of the land of the Ottoman Turks comes our next report of encounters between man and Unidentified Flying Objects. The residents of Adrianople, Turkey, were treated to quite an aerial display on the cool autumn night of November 1st, 1885.[19] On that night, not very high above the city, the locals bore witness to the slow overhead passage of a large oval-shaped, brightly illuminated disc of unknown origin. Amazed onlookers first noticed the object at 9:30 PM. The huge object, said to be four to five times the diameter of a full moon, seemed to be content to hover over the city, making it clearly visible to the entire city and its environs. Whatever it was gave off a brilliant glow. Witnesses reported the glow was equal to having ten electric lights illuminating a given area, thus turning night into day for the duration of the encounter. The following morning, around the break of day on November 2nd, in a nearby port, a bright blue "flame" of light was reported, as it circled the town and the boats lashed to the pier. The light reportedly hovered just 15 feet off the ground, providing enough light to illuminate the interior of the houses and boats it hovered near and their frightened inhabitants.

None of the sightings in this section could be blamed on hallucinations, as these mental events are highly localized and are witnessed by just the person having it. So what were the objects all these people saw?

Chapter 3

1889-1946

Forgotten Observations and Happenings

"Gods and Sky People were forgotten as the Industrial Age thundered over the western world."

~John A. Keel

South Bend, Indiana

Our next encounter will require us to go back to Christmas Eve, 1889. According to the local newspaper reports, on that snowy night in South Bend, Indiana, young Oliver Larch volunteered to brave the snowy cold and go out to fetch some water from the well for his mother, who was busy preparing the Christmas Eve meal. As the family reveled in the joy of that magical night, little did they know they would never see Oliver again! Not more than ten seconds had passed after Oliver left the house, than he was heard screaming. His father and several party guests grabbed lanterns and ran outside. As they made their way across the porch, they could see the boy's footprints were alone in the snow, and had come to a sudden end. They could hear his screaming dissipating as if he was being carried up into the night sky. Oliver was never seen again.

Virginia and the Carolinas

Though some people living south of the Mason-Dixon Line were still seeing red in 1893 from the War Between the States, thousands were witnessing a luminous object as it made its way quite leisurely through the skies above Virginia and the Carolinas.

The residents of Virginia first sighted the object on December 20, 1893. They noticed an object that was flying parallel to the ground as it flew over the mountainous terrain. What was even odder was that it was not reflecting the sun's rays; it was illuminating itself, using what was termed by some as by an "electrical device" (out of respect to the recent invention that was at the time sweeping across America). The object would seemingly glide along until enough people were watching it, then disappear into the distance. Interestingly enough, each time it was reported, the object remained in sight for fifteen minutes and then disappeared at high speed off over the horizon.

So what was it they all saw? Curiously, they attributed the objects' illumination to be caused by some electrical means, a testament to the fact I mentioned earlier: People will associate things they cannot understand with the technology they have witnessed around them.

THE AIRSHIP WAVES OF 1896 AND 1897

The first wave of UFO sightings to occur in the United States began in the fall of 1896. People from all walks of life from far and wide were seeing "airships" as they made their ways across America's skies. The objects sighted were called airships, but make no mistake about it, the people did not see Zeppelins or dirigibles. The name comes to us from the fact that the people of this time had known that inventors in Europe and America were trying to perfect lighter-than-air ships that could transport people from one area to another.

I can say with some certainty that the objects viewed were not lighter-than-air dirigibles due to several facts. The first airships did not operate at night as they did not have lights, nor were the new pilots experienced enough to navigate anywhere through the darkness. The man with the best design, one Hungarian-borne David Schwarz, did not get his craft off the ground until November 13th, 1897. Once airborne in Berlin, Germany, he could only stay aloft for a few miles, which makes it impossible for him to have been responsible for the sightings in America, especially a year earlier. Another pertinent fact is that the Wright Brothers were still several years from testing their heavier-than-air flying machine. Thus those who witnessed these objects were not misidentifying aircraft—that we can be sure of! The people called these objects airships, because they saw ships flying in the air.

One thing is for sure: These people did not have to worry about ridicule, as the government had not yet made their claims that UFOs did not exist. They felt comfortable reporting what they saw, because the reporters made their stories front-page news in papers from San Francisco to Boston, and all points in between. It would be worthwhile to look at the microfilm copies of your hometown newspaper from that time, as you will see these reports were taken seriously by all involved; nowhere will you find ridicule of the observers, only truthful uncertainty. They were trying to find out what was going on in the skies above them.

SACRAMENTO, CALIFORNIA AND BEYOND

Sacramento, California, was the first place these mysterious airships (read UFOs) were seen. On the night of November 17th, 1896, the first of many reports of strange lights were reported to have been hovering over the state capitol. *A Wandering Apparition* and *A Queer Phenomenon* are just a few of the headlines that were run by local newspapers in the days that followed, showing the bewilderment the witnesses felt to having seen a sight so foreign to their senses. Though many reported having seen just a light in the sky, many reported that the light was attached to a large cigar-shaped chassis of odd construction that drifted against the wind through the cloudy night sky.

The good townspeople of Sacramento would not have to wait very long for the return of this odd machine. On November 21st, the object was once again sighted as it made its way over the city, except, many more people saw it on this occasion. Shortly after it vanished from the sight of the residents of Sacramento, it was seen flying over the nearby town of Folsom. Later that same night, it was seen over San Francisco and its environs, with many articles printed the next day in the local papers.

By November 23rd, 1896, these mysterious lights were reported over nineteen other California cities including, Los Angeles, Fresno, Santa Rosa, San Jose, and Bakersfield. From these sightings came a report by two Methodist ministers from Knights Ferry, who reported that they not only saw the light in the sky, but also as it rested on the ground, and took off once more to continue their aerial survey of the Golden State. A tugboat captain also had an encounter with an illuminated cigar-shaped object as it sped across the night sky.

Every State Between the Rocky Mountains and Atlantic Ocean

Up in Tacoma, Washington, a resident observed a strange object as it hovered near Mt. Rainier. For the better part of an hour, he observed the object as it darted from place to place, all the while it was emanating colorful beams of light in every direction. Much like today, the leading thinkers of the time could not come up with a plausible answer to what it was all these people had seen. Though there was sporadic sighting across the country, by December 1896 the sightings had all but ceased.

Having taken a break over the winter, the sighting of these unknown craft returned full force in March of 1897. On the 29th of that month, scores of people in Omaha, Nebraska, watched in utter amazement as a huge bright light flew over their city, stopped, hovered awhile, then flew off to the northwest and out of their sight forever. Now, heading south, thousands in Kansas City, watched this same object or one very similar, as it put on nearly the same aerial display as the people of Omaha had seen. In Everest, Kansas, witnesses described the object as looking like a giant canoe with searchlights of various colors passing overhead.

On April 19th strange objects were seen by tens of thousands of people across the Midwest, all who described seeing a large metallic object as it glided effortlessly across the skies, in the days and nights for most of that week. When witnesses viewed the object through a telescope in the daylight, they reported the object appeared metallic and was shaped like a cigar with short stubby appendages. When the object was sighted at night, it gave off a slight glow, while green, white, and red lights blinked around its perimeter. It was seen over several days in a swath of land stretching from Denver, Colorado, to St. Louis, Missouri. Like most other unexplained sightings, the object vanished from the skies as mysteriously as it had arrived. These airships/UFOs were seen in every state between the Rocky Mountains and the Atlantic Ocean. Twice they were even observed as they floated over the Capitol in Washington D.C.

1900-1919

Bournbrook, England

The sighting of unusual craft did not end with the end of the nineteenth century. The first sighting we will review is slightly different than most I have offered up to now, and will continue to do so throughout the text. It is a the story of a sighting by a young man from England in 1901. Though he witnessed this alone, and he is not what would be called a trained observer, his account echoes those of many other witnesses who would have CE III and IV kinds a half a century later.

This young man's name was kept under wraps because of his families standing in Edwardian England. While walking home from an errand one afternoon, he came across what he described as a large cylinder with a turret on top coming down to rest in the fields near his home in Bournbrook, England. As he stared at the strange sight, much to his dismay, a door opened up in the side of the cylinder. Out came two small men who were a little more than a meter tall, dressed in what he called strange uniforms, including helmets with wires or tubes connected to the uniform itself. He crouched down so as not to be seen, allowing him to view their actions. When he was noticed, the little men, through the use of body language and hand signals, made it clear to him that he was not wanted near their craft. He didn't have to be asked to leave twice, and made a fast break toward his house. Much to his surprise, the object left as suddenly as he had.

Now some may say that this young man may have made up this story. This is quite possible. Would it not have been easier to make up a story of fanciful highwaymen or mythical creatures than to describe in intimate detail an encounter with occupants of an unidentified flying object, that is accurate enough to parallel the encounters people would have decades later?

Darby Family Sighting

In June of 1904, Tony Darby was on his way to the well on his family's farm one night at approximately 10 PM when he sensed that something was not quite right.[1] As he surveyed the area, he noticed that near the barn, about 500 feet in front of him, two orange disc-shaped objects hovered about 6 feet above the ground. He described them as being orange wagon wheels that were glowing brightly, but did not light up the surrounding area. Upon seeing these objects, he made a mad dash for the house and summoned his mother and brother outside to see these fantastic objects. Once outside, Tony, his mother, and his brother, Joseph, began to walk slowly towards these objects. When they had covered about half the distance, the glowing orange discs, in unison, began to retreat very slowly away from them, keeping their formation every inch of the way. When they stopped, the objects ceased their retreat. When the family moved toward the objects, the objects slowly retreated.

All members of the family agreed that the objects had to be under intelligent control to perform movements like these. The next time the family halted, the objects continued their retreat. The family pursued the objects until they found themselves on a small ridge. From this vantage point, they watched as the objects glided 6 feet off the ground throughout the entire valley, until they had disappeared into the dark surrounding countryside.

Having told their neighbors about their experience, the Darbys went to the local authorities and were directed to a member of a local government agency. When the man from the agency arrived (probably dressed in black), he promptly assessed the situation and informed the Darbys that they had seen swamp lights, or as it would be called some 50 years later, swamp gas. Having seen swamp lights before, the Darbys knew what they had seen that night wasn't swamp gas or lights as it had never before moved in accordance with pursuing humans. Amazingly, even all these years later, when other law abiding, taxpaying citizens consult the government, they still see fit to reply with the same nonsense!

Ann Arbor, Michigan

The year 1904 was quite busy for ordinary people who encountered extraordinary objects. Near Ann Arbor, Michigan, two men came face to face with a UFO while on their way to shop for groceries.

Walking through Dixboro, a suburb of Ann Arbor, W.M. Covest and Arthur B. Eldert, noticed a light in the purplish evening sky. As the light got closer, they realized that it was not a shooting star or meteor, but a craft flying under its own control. Mr. Covest noted that it reminded him of the ironclad ship *Merrimack*, with a strange orange light flooding out of its "portholes." After leveling off, the craft began to bank upward at a sixty-degree incline and then it shot off out of sight. Although ridiculed by their friends and neighbors for telling of their sighting, the men remained steadfast in the belief that what they encountered truly was not of this Earth!

Encounter in the Atlantic

The following encounter at sea is taken from the March 1904 issue of *Weather Review*. The report comes from the sighting the crew of the USS *Supply* had while navigating the Atlantic:

> The lights appeared beneath the clouds, their color a rather bright red. As they approached the ship, they appeared to soar, passing above the broken clouds. After passing above the clouds, they appeared to be moving directly away from the earth. It was egg-shaped, the larger end forward. The second was about twice the size of the sun, the third about the size of the sun. Their near approach to the surface appeared to be most remarkable. That they did come below the clouds and soar instead of continuing their southeasterly course is also certain. The lights were in sight for over two minutes and were carefully observed by three people whose accounts agree as to the details.

We can discount that what they saw was neither an astrological phenomena nor an aircraft. No planes or dirigibles of the time could fly at the speeds that are mentioned here or for that matter out over the Atlantic Ocean. Venus doesn't make it into Earth's atmosphere any more frequently than meteors make course adjustments. So the question remains, what did they see?

Vermont

The next sighting is one of several included that was made by persons that few people would have doubted their integrity or their ability to truthfully recount the details of their encounter with a UFO.

July 2nd, 1907 was passing by like most summer days in upstate Vermont. The majority of the townspeople were basking in the infrequent warm weather, making their plans for celebrating America's 131st birthday two days later or perhaps sipping iced tea from a shaded front porch. Standing in the middle of downtown Burlington that afternoon, at approximately 2 PM, were two of the towns leading citizens: the most Reverend Bishop John S. Michaud and then ex-Governor Woodbury. They were conversing with a third man while enjoying the warm breeze blowing off the Green Mountains when they, as well as the rest of Burlington, were taken aback by a very loud, nearby explosion. Looking around to try to determine what caused the thundering roar, the Bishop saw a torpedo- (cigar) shaped object floating about 50 feet above the treetops, and some 300 feet from where they were standing.

Bishop Michaud described the object he saw as being about six-foot long and approximately eight inches in diameter. As it was floating very slowly over the treetops, he noticed that though the object was very dark in appearance, the object was surrounded by a halo-like yellowish glow extending twenty feet out from the object itself.

From a vantage point a short distance away, Mr. Alvaro Adsit corroborated the claims made by the reverend. He, like the Bishop, had seen the torpedo-shaped object, agreed with the size, shape, and color, and was equally mystified by its coming and goings in the clear blue afternoon skies above their normally sleepy northern Vermont hometown.

LOWESTOFT, ENGLAND

Much like the fleet, we are headed back to sea for another encounter between a ship's crew and an unidentified flying object. According to a log entry from October of 1908, while sailing about thirty-five miles out of Lowestoft, England, J.H. Stockman, the captain of the HMS *Superb*, noticed an unusually large and bright star in the clear cool autumn night. As he continued watching this star, much to his amazement, the star began to move down out of the heavens toward his ship.

As the light approached, the captain, wanting to see what it was that was approaching his ship, had one of the ship's mates set off a flare into the dark night sky. The two men stared in disbelief as this object sent a small red light out to greet the flare they just sent up. The resulting light from the flare and the red light allowed the men to see that the light was attached to a large cylindrical object made out of a dark metallic material. Again they sent up a flare, and again the object responded with a light of its own, only this time the light was blue not red. Not wanting to send the wrong signals, nor provoke this object in the sky the captain, now joined by most of his crew, continued to watch this baffling object as it appeared to study their ship.

A short while later, the object began to move and picked up speed until it was once again lost among the millions of lights in the star-filled night sky.

PETERSBOROUGH, ENGLAND LAW ENFORCEMENT SIGHTING

Here is the first sighting recorded here by law enforcement officers. I place a high value on these sightings, as the police throughout the world are trained as observers. They are trained to observe people, the times, and places of the things they do, all in order to get a thorough understanding of what is normal for the people and places they protect and serve. This makes it easier for the officers to tell when something out of the ordinary is happening so as to prevent harm to the citizens they are sworn to protect. Part of their job is grounded in the faith that the people of the community have in their ability to protect and serve. Thus, when a law enforcement officer reports having had an encounter with the unknown, chances are, you can bank on the truth and accuracy of their accounts. To make up such a story would put their ability to instill faith and gain the trust of the people they serve in great peril, severely hampering their ability to do their jobs.

Our next sighting comes to us from jolly old England. In the early morning hours of March 23rd, 1909, a Petersborough policeman, or "Bobbie" as they are called across the pond, was walking his beat when much to his surprise he saw lights flashing on buildings a short way down the street. With his club in hand and whistle at the ready, the officer raced down the street to stop what he assumed was a burglar plying his trade armed with one of those new Torchlights employed to brighten the darken residences of unsuspecting victims.

When he turned the corner, the whistle must have feel to the ground as his mouth gapped open in awe of the sight in front of him. The light was not from a burglar holding a flashlight; it was a searchlight of some kind roaming the streets as if in search of someone or something. Stranger still, the light was shining down from the heavens from a large object that was moving across the sky at a fairly rapid speed. The officer reported the object moved silently against the wind that was blowing through the streets of pre-dawn Petersborough, eliminating any chance that what he witnessed was a plane and dirigible of that day and age. Natural phenomena can be ruled out as it is not likely a meteor or swamp gas would have spotlights. The object sighted, as all the others we have reviewed thus far, remains unidentified.

LA PORTE, INDIANA

Indiana was a "hotspot" of sightings in the first decade of the twentieth century. Let us return there for another amazing encounter. In October of 1909, the Reverend Ruth Smith and members of a group from her church were riding in a horse-drawn wagon through the dark countryside surrounding La Porte, Indiana. Her excellent account is taken from a National Investigative Committee on Aerial Phenomenon (hereafter referred to as NICAP) report[2] and is as valid a report as any included herein.

At around 10:30 PM that night, the horses drawing the wagon reared repeatedly as a "blinding light" flashed across the countryside. As she looked up, she saw that a large object at about a forty-five degrees of elevation was responsible for the blinding flashes of light. She describes the object as looking like "two inverted bowls, separated in the center by a row of lights."

As she recounted in her report made years after the sighting, the lights scanning the countryside were being emitted from this object in long streams that reached all the way to the ground, and were brighter than the brightest floodlight. The Reverend also reported that this object had a halo-like ring of light surrounding it. Several minutes after the object popped into view, it began to slowly move toward the wagon and its occupants. At approximately 10:45 PM, the object "blinked out as if one were turning off a light" bulb.

What makes this sighting very credible to me is the description of the object's arrival and departure. As you will see often times, the witnesses, especially those who have witnessed the objects around Gulf Breeze, Florida, report that the objects blink on and off. They are not insinuating that the objects flew in and left at tremendous speed. What they are describing is an object that materializes and dematerializes at will, a feat that our technology cannot or will not be able to attain in the foreseeable future. This is but another link in the chain of events reminding us that these objects have been here since the beginning of recorded history and will be here long after our demise. We are merely spectators of an amazing phenomenon that has incredible craft performing incredible feats as they ply the byways of the mysteries of both time and space.

BOSTON AND WORCESTER, MASSACHUSETTS

On December 20th, 1909, the citizens of Boston, Massachusetts, witnessed a large luminous object as it made its way over their city. Three days later, the same or a similar craft was spotted over Worcester, Massachusetts. The good people of Worcester out and about doing last minute Christmas shopping on the cold winter evening of December 23rd were taken by surprise when a large luminous object, fitting the description of the one reported in Boston three days earlier, drifted over their city. The object was reported to be searching the heavens with a strong "headlight." After a brief visit, the object disappeared, only to return again several hours later. Once again, the object became the center of attention, as it flew in over the city and remained stationary above the middle of town for around a quarter hour. The object began to slowly move to the south, then headed east, a course it remained on until it disappeared out of sight on its way back to wherever it had come to Worcester from that winter's eve.

BLYTH, NORTHUMBERLAND, ENGLAND

As I am sure you have noticed, there have been many reports by sailors aboard ships at sea. One possible reason for this is that the ships are usually isolated in the vast expanses of the world's oceans. This would allow the UFOs to observe the craft and the humans on-board with little or no interference.

The *St. Olaf* was a prime candidate for the visitors to get a chance to study humans in their natural environment. The *St. Olaf* was a Norwegian freighter plying the shipping lanes a few miles off the coast off Blyth, Northumberland, England, in the frigid waters of the North Sea. The crew noticed a bright, glowing object as it made its way through the dark sky, fairly close to the swells of the rough sea. Once overhead, the strange light slowed down and proceeded to match the course heading and speed of the freighter. For several long minutes it hung over the ship in absolute silence. Then without warning, this aerial device shone five bright spotlights into the ship's bridge. Once their observation was completed, the craft sped away from the *St. Olaf* at high speed.

The captain and crew watched, still awestruck by their close encounter, as the object stopped over another steamer about a mile distant. Again, the object trained its spotlights on the ship and after several minutes, it once again left at high speed. This time, however, the object flew out of sight over the far horizon.

If these visitors wanted to observe how humans would react to a stressful situation, they picked the perfect laboratory. These men at sea knew they were alone. Likewise, they had neither a quick exit nor anywhere to run. Thus they were stuck right there and had to deal with the events unfolding around them. This captain and crew passed the test with flying colors. Though they were doubtlessly frightened, they were merely passive observers in what could have become a confrontational situation.

Madison Square Park, New York

According to an article appearing in the *New York Tribune*[3] on August 30th, 1910, hundreds of New Yorkers relaxing in Madison Square Park were treated to an aerial display straight out of the *Twilight Zone*. Around 9 PM two nights previous, a black metallic object was witnessed as it flew in silence over the crowded park. The next night, a crowd of eager persons, including reporters alerted during their work shifts, gathered in the park in hopes of a repeat performance. Their eagerness did not go unrewarded. Later on that evening, those present in the park witnessed the overhead passage of a cigar-shaped "fuselage" with red and green lights as it once again flew silently over the crowded park. Some speculated that a brave pilot had over flown the park, but as Ralph and Judy Blum point out in their phenomenal work *Beyond Earth : Man's Contact with UFOs*, there were only thirty-six registered pilots in the United States in 1910, and none where anywhere near the southern tip of Manhattan Island. The closest pilot was on the ground in his home on Long Island. Secondly, the object did not have wings, and was said to appear as though it was made out of metal. Planes of the day were shabby wood and canvas contraptions that had several visible sets of wings. (Remember that these were the days of the planes with two and three wings.) Nor were these early planes rigged out with any type of lights. Additionally, they could not operate in the updrafts of the early skyscrapers surrounding the park, including the 300-foot tall Flatiron Building and the then newly-completed tower of the Metropolitan Life Insurance Building, which rose to the then-remarkable height of 700 feet, just east across Madison Avenue.

But it is the silent operation that makes it truly impossible for these objects to have been planes. If you have ever heard them at an air show, you would agree that the piston engines of the day were very, very loud, thus they would have been very easy to hear over the din of the city as they echoed through the concrete canyons below.

Youngstown, Ohio

On a cool October evening in 1917, John Boback who had missed the last streetcar out of Youngstown, Ohio, was walking along the railroad tracks on his way to his home in Mt. Braddock, Pennsylvania. Mr. Boback describes his encounter as having taken place around 12:30 AM.[4] Off to the side of the tracks he was following, in a small field, he came across a landed craft shaped like a saucer with a dome on top. The saucer was ringed by a couple of rows of lights and a platform resting on the ground. He estimated the object was about as big as an automobile. Quite startled by his observation, he froze to observe this mysterious illuminated craft for several minutes. As he studied it, he saw portholes through which he was sure he could see diminutive figures inside the landed craft going about some business which looked to be related to operating the craft, like sailors on a ship.

Suddenly, he was jolted by a shrill sound and the object lifted off the ground and began a gradual climb out of the field and into the star-filled night very slowly. At first he thought that maybe this was one of those airplanes he had heard about, but had never seen. This, however, he immediately dismissed when he finally saw a plane, as they were nothing like the object he saw in the field that autumn night.

The Roaring Twenties

The 1920s were a strange time in the United States. Having proved that we were a world power by helping France and the United Kingdom make the world safe for democracy, the American people returned to the normal business at hand: making money! There was an unparalleled economic boom, no alcohol, and a Renaissance in the arts and sciences. If there was ever a time when people did not need to have their attentions attracted by unknown objects to make up for some missing component of their psyche, it was the 1920s. However, there are many accounts of encounters that people both far and wide continued to have with these unidentified objects, despite the absence of bars and legal alcohol to fuel their imagination. The following sightings draw heavily from a series of articles entitled *Unsolved Mysteries from the UFO Archives*, by Jerome Clark and Lucius Farish appearing throughout the 1975 volumes of *UFO Report*. (This was an excellent magazine from the 1970s which did exactly what its title implies: report on sightings of UFOs.)

Mt. Pleasant, Iowa

First off is a sighting from Mt. Pleasant, Iowa. On June 3rd, 1920, at approximately 10 AM, Clark Linch was involved in one of his favorite activities: fishing. While enjoying his respite, Mr. Linch noticed a strange bluish egg-shaped object coming down from the bright blue morning sky. The object settled down about fifteen feet from where he was standing. Not daring to move, Mr. Linch observed the craft for a quarter hour from the spot where he had first seen it. The object silently lifted off the ground and slowly ascended into the blue sky where it soon disappeared, as its color matched that of the surrounding sky. (This is a fact to make note of, as it will factor into a CE IV sighting from England that we will review later). Once the object had left, he examined the site where the UFO had come to rest and found that the grass was not harmed in any way it was only matted down under the weight of the vehicle.

Wathena, Kansas, and Rushville, Missouri

Five days later more objects were seen throughout the area between Wathena, Kansas, and Rushville, Missouri. Over 200 residents of these rural areas reported seeing a large cylinder-shaped object as it floated through the air between these two mid-western towns. Witnesses described the object as being a very large cylindrically shaped object; dark in color that traveled just 75 feet above the ground. When it finally reached Rushville, it made a ninety-degree turn and proceeded towards a large bank of clouds about two miles away. After it had slowly ascended into the distant cloud bank, the object was not seen again. The object had caused such a stir, that the *Gazette*, a newspaper in nearby St. Joseph, Missouri printed an Extra, in which the people who had witnessed it recounted details of this incredible encounter.

North of Freeport, Texas

Later that same year, another fisherman had an encounter with an unidentified flying object. While fishing in the early hours of one autumn morning about fifty miles north of Freeport, Texas, on the Gulf of Mexico, C.B. Alves, having just landed a fish worthy of mounting back at his home, came upon something even more spectacular than his new trophy.

Looking up, Mr. Alves spotted a fast-moving disc -shaped object moving directly towards his position. After unsuccessfully trying to wake his fishing partner, all Mr. Alves could do was stand and stare at the approaching object. Before the disc reached his position, at about 100 yards out, it turned and headed south. Much to his surprise, there were three other discs following in a single-file formation. He described the discs as looking like two silver plates placed on top of one another. They were about twenty-five feet in diameter and ten foot at their apex. The first and last appeared to have had a pink hue enveloping them: The middle two were surrounded by a greenish hue. He watched them as they flew off into the morning sky on a heading that put them on a course towards Freeport.

DETROIT, MICHIGAN

Something odd occurred in Detroit, Michigan, on a warm summer night in 1922. As we have seen, many odd occurrences have taken place throughout history, but this one comes straight out of science fiction. As a young couple sat "parking," as it was then called, in their automobile, something odd enough to capture two embraced lovers' attention passed overhead. Once freed from their tangled embrace, the couple saw a large object drifting slowly and in complete silence through the evening sky. As it drew closer, they noticed the object had large portholes or windows. The closer it came, the more frightened they became, as they began to see the shapes in its windows. These shapes soon took on a form. The couple reported seeing at least twenty "bald dwarfs" intently staring at them. What better a scene could explorers ask for than to come across two indigenous creatures so obviously performing a mating ritual in their primitive mode of transportation!

INDIANA

In 1923, two men, who in later life would become esteemed members of the faculty of De Pauw University, came face to face with an Unidentified Flying Object.[5] While driving west on US 40, approximately where it intersects with Indiana State Route 100, Dr. A.W. Crandell who would go on to chair the history department and Dr. H.E. Greenleaf, who would go on to chair the math department at De Pauw University, witnessed a slow-moving, sizable object. This object was slowly traveling towards their car, moving parallel to the highway at a height of 500 feet. As it came closer they saw that the area below this huge aerial ship was bathed in an intense red light. The saucer-shaped object was rotating slowly on its axis in a bone-chilling silence as it made its way through the Indiana night. The object crossed the highway diagonally across the path of their car and disappeared so fast that they could not tell if it sped away at great speed or vanished right before their eyes.

PACES, VIRGINIA

If you had to rate those people in a given profession who would be very accurate at identifying aircraft in the early years of aviation, who would be at the top of the list? Given the fact that you are obviously above average intelligence (after all you are reading this book), I would venture to say that you put people who work in the many fields of aviation right at the top of that list. That's what I would have said, and having said that, our next report comes from a man heavily involved in helping expand the reaches of the airplane in the earlier years of American aviation.

R.A. Marshall, Jr. of Mannboro, Virginia was an employee of the W.L. Price Company, a concern that helped establish the Atlantic-New York Airmail Beacon Route. In the days when planes used markers on the beacon towers to navigate Mr. Marshall's job was quite important. He was charged with the upkeep of these towers throughout eastern Virginia. It is safe to say he was familiar with the airplanes of the day, as he'd seen them throughout each and every workday.

It was on an atypical workday in the fall of 1926 that Mr. Marshall witnessed a flying machine unlike any he had ever seen. Towards the end of the day, around 4 PM, while seventy-five feet up a beacon tower replacing needed parts, an object sighted in his peripheral vision caught his attention. As soon as he trained his eyes on the object, he knew something was amiss. In the still air he could hear no engine noises coming from this object that, from his position, approached from the southern horizon. Any thought as to the object being a dirigible was quickly squashed by the speed the object traveled. Most startling to him, and the most troubling part of the sighting, was the observation he made as the craft passed overhead: It had no wings!

Now, though he was not intimately aware of all the facts concerning lift and drag, he knew a plane, being heavier than air, needed wings to supply lift, and a propulsion device to supply thrust. Neither was present on the unidentified flying object he witnessed over Paces, Virginia.

Author's Note:

Very infrequently have I included in this work an encounter where a single untrained observer observed an unidentified flying object. The following three accounts were reported by men who, while alone, were visited by one of these mysterious craft we know as UFOs and its pilots. It was not vogue at the time to report having an encounter with strange flying ships or the crews that fly them. It is due to this element in conjunction with the description provided by the following witnesses, which parallels those reports from forty, and fifty years later, that has lead me to include these within this chapter.

Bakersfield, California

As Richard Sweed drove through the outskirts of Bakersfield, California in his car, the last sight he had planned to see was an odd aerial craft, but that is exactly what he encountered. The sighting took place on October 18th, 1927. As Mr. Sweed meandered down the deserted highway, he came upon a large vehicle that straddled the road in front of him. As he slowed to a stop a short distance from the object, he was at a loss, for he had never seen anything like it in his life.

Resting on the highway in front of him was a bluish-gray metallic disc that he estimated to be sixty feet in diameter. Around its edge was a row of windows, each covered by what looked like a lens of some sort. He observed this marvelous machine for several minutes, before the craft lifted off the ground. As it sped away at tremendous speed, on an incline of about forty-five degrees, Mr. Sweed reported he could hear a slight whining hum. Once the ship had departed, he got out of his automobile and went to the spot where the craft had rested on the highway. Though there were no marks on the road; all the sand on the pavement had fused into many small glass crystals that now lay strewn over the width of the asphalt roadway.

The chance remains that Mr. Sweed made up this story, but I find it curious with which his details match those given countless times throughout the world over the last sixty-plus years. From the size and shape of the craft to the noise it made and the traces it left. This case could have been reported yesterday and the testimony would be exactly the same. Mr. Sweed witnessed a visit by a craft whose operators have systematically visited every corner of our planet for as long as we have kept records.

Yakima, Washington

On a sunny spring afternoon in 1928, at about 4 PM local time, just outside of Yakima, Washington, 17-year-old Floyd Dillon was driving down a dirt road in a rickety old Model T Ford. His mind awash with images of youth in spring, the last thing he expected was to have a close encounter with the unknown. While driving along quite distracted by the beauty of the season, Floyd soon came upon a sight unlike any other he had ever come across. Flying gingerly above the terrain at an altitude he estimated to be seventy-five feet, was the damnedest flying machine he had ever seen before or since. He described the object he saw as a flying hexagon made from a shiny metal substance.[6] The object was dark olive in color, and had a dome on the upper portion. He estimated that the object was twenty-two feet wide and seven feet thick at the center.

As if this was not startling enough, as the machine came closer, our intrepid observer noticed that there was a window running vertically up the dome. Upon closer examination of the window, Floyd saw a figure piloting the craft that was coming into position just in front of the car, as if this out-of-worldly explorer wanted to get a look at the car and its passenger. The window was positioned in such a way that though Floyd could see the figure had a head, arms, and a torso that was covered by a blue uniform of sorts, he could not distinguish any features of the pilot onboard this extraordinary craft. After a short time, the vehicle rotated on its axis so that the window faced away from the car in which Floyd was in, and sped off at a tremendous speed.

India, Tibet and Mongolia — the Kukumor District

While on an expedition in 1929 that took him through India, Tibet, and Mongolia, Nicholas Roerich kept a journal logging the events that unfolded around him.[7] On August 5th, while in their camp in the Kukumor District, half-past nine in the morning, he and his group saw a huge oval reflecting the morning sunlight as it traveled from north to south. Many used field glasses to view the object as it passed over their camp and headed away on a southwestern trajectory. Barring hallucinations inspired by oxygen deprivation, the people on this expedition truly had a sighting of an unidentified flying object while traveling near the top of the world.

The Franklin Roosevelt Years

Maybe it was from the great strain felt around the globe caused by the worldwide economic upheaval that sightings were sparsely reported during the early 1930s. Of those reported, only the following one from the late 1930s measures up to the standards established earlier. This is not to say that sightings were not happening, because chances are, they were; they just weren't being reported as people everywhere were more interested in surviving than reporting odd things they may have seen. As we will see, sightings of a higher caliber, quite coincidentally, resumed in the months just prior to the start of the largest, most destructive, deadliest war the human race has ever waged.

Pittsburgh, Pennsylvania

While sitting on their front porch in Pittsburgh, Pennsylvania one warm summer night in July of 1939, Mr. and Mrs. J.M. Williams spotted a strange object as it floated over the steel capital of the world. Trained in the methods of observation from his fifteen years of service to his country in the United States Navy, Mr. Williams recalls that it was about 9:30 PM when his wife spotted the object as it made its way over the center of the city through the overcast Pennsylvanian skies.

The object appeared to be similar in shape to a giant sword hanging in the night sky. If you held a ruler at arm's length, that would give you an idea of the size of the object, claimed Mr. Williams. Without a doubt it was quite large. Though he did not notice any sound coming from the object, Mr. Williams did notice that a haze about the same color a car's head lamp would emit surrounded it. He was quite impressed that throughout the sighting, which lasted a full fifteen minutes, the object remained perfectly still and completely silent. As he and his wife watched the object in the sky, it disappeared behind a passing cloud, not to reappear over the city that night.

Utica, New York

As the Great Depression was becoming an unpleasant memory, world events began to deteriorate, so much so that within months of the Williams sighting, most of the world would be at war. After Germany invaded Poland, the British and French came to their aid and soon the Second World War was raging uncontrolled across Europe. It would be almost two and a quarter years before the United States would enter, as we were dragged into the contest on December 7th, 1941, when the Japanese Empire tried to take the US Navy out of the war in one quick blow: They bombed Pearl Harbor.

Some two weeks later, a veteran of the First World War, who saw action in France, had an encounter with an object that by the end of the decade would be known in most homes throughout the country as a flying saucer. On December 22nd, 1941, George Bogner was making his way through the streets of his hometown of Utica, New York, at about 2:15 PM.[8] As he was about to cross through the intersection of Agnes Avenue and Pleasant Street, a glimmering object in the afternoon sky caught his gaze. Looking up, he saw a silvery disc-shaped object hovering somewhere between 300 and 400 feet above the homes in the neighborhood. The object, which he estimated to be 100 feet in diameter, looked to him to be made out of a material similar to the color of chrome. It stood in stark contrast to the gray overcast skies. Bogner, an electrical technician by trade, was amazed that he heard no sound coming from the machine as it passed overhead at what he estimated was 300 miles per hour.

The length of his encounter was no more than ten seconds, but he was profoundly affected from the sighting of so amazing a machine. When he reached his home, still somewhat dumbfounded from his encounter, Mr. Bogner fumbled for words to describe to his wife what he had just witnessed. Before he could get out all the details, his wife informed him that at the same time she had seen what she called a "shiny object" as it streaked across the skies above the city of Utica. Though they reported their sighting to the local media, they did not opt to discuss the matter openly for fear of ridicule by their peers, even though they were sure they had witnessed something not of this world.

The Battle of Los Angeles

The next account is a little-known classic. It is a microcosm of the whole UFO phenomenon. Thousands of people see a UFO, including military personnel who engaged the intruder. Yet when questioned about it, the government claims to have no record of the incident, until several decades later when they are forced to release the information thanks to the Freedom of Information Act.

The evening of February 12th, 1942, started off as calmly as possible for a city in a nation at war. Later that night and into the following early morning hours of the 25th, this serenity would be shattered by a most baffling incident. At 2:25 AM, at least one million Southern Californians[9] were startled out of their beds by the blaring of air raid sirens across the city of Los Angeles and its surrounding area. The city was blacked out as the Civilian Air Warning System manned their stations to report sightings of any aircraft. The members of the 4th Interceptor Command Squadron had been warming up their planes in anticipation of receiving orders to prevent any enemy planes from reaching inland targets.

Although that order was never given to these pilots, at 3:16 AM, the anti-aircraft guns of the 37th Coast Artillery Brigade began to rapidly fire 12.8 pound anti-aircraft shells at unknown intruders, that the search beams were scanning for in the night sky above Los Angeles. The gunners finally had a target to aim for when the searchlights converged on a large object with lights ringing its exterior, hovered stationary and in silence over the metropolitan area. Shells were fired continually until 4:14 AM; then sporadically throughout the early morning hours, until 7:21 AM (almost five hours later), when the All Clear was sounded, signaling to the residents of Los Angeles that the danger had passed.

For almost five straight hours, the residents of Southern California were terrorized by an intrusion of some foreign craft that could not be made to leave by the nearby United States military forces. The threat was taken very seriously that morning. The artillery fired live rounds into the night sky to drive off the invading foreign craft. Not only wasn't the intruder driven back it was not even damaged. This large round object that easily moved from a standstill to over 200 MPH while ascending and descending from 9-18,000 feet was not from Japan or Germany. It was not even from this planet! The air defense forces fired over 1,430 rounds at the object, and though witnesses claimed to have seen the explosions caused by the impact of the shell with the ship (force field?), no damage was done to this intruder.[10]

What was the object over Los Angeles that night? It wasn't enemy planes as no bombs or any other type of weapons were used, and after intensive interrogations of captured pilots and naval officers, the military ruled that no enemy planes or ships were near California on the day in question. The sheriff of Los Angeles County and the Secretary of War vocalized their concern that Mexico was allowing Japan to secretly launch planes: a nonsensical claim that was shortly proven incorrect. The Secretary of the Navy informed the local authorities that no US ships or planes were in the area that night.

So what was it that made the military fire over nine tons of shells into the air that night? Shells that when they ceased their upward momentum would fall back to earth on unsuspecting people, places, and things! Pray tell, what was the official explanation as to what was behind the night of terror suffered by these California residents? Even with all the reports of the large object in the sky by the residents and members of the Civilian Air Warning System and the 37th Coast Artillery Brigade, the government's official explanation was that "jittery war nerves" caused trained men to toss almost 20,000 pounds of artillery shells into the air.

Speaking only for myself, I would not feel safe with military personnel in possession of such firepower that fired at a mass hallucination. The people of southern California did not feel this way toward their coastal defenders, as they had witnessed the same craft that the men who manned the artillery fired so many shells at, in a valiant but futile effort to protect those people they were sworn to keep safe.

What do you think was done to follow up on this incredible encounter? As incredible as this sighting was, the facts of the case were shuffled around until it was purposely lost within the government's huge bureaucracy. Truth was finally exposed and made known to the general public thirty-two years later, thanks to the Freedom of Information Act. (A great big "Thank you" should go out to the authors of the Freedom of Information Act, without which we would not know what we now do about many of the mysterious incidents that have happened throughout the last six decades.)

Foo Fighters

The people of Los Angeles were not alone in their interaction with strange objects in the sky. Throughout the Second World War, pilots from every nation that had planes in the sky had encounters with what came to be known as "Foo Fighters." The somewhat small balls of strangely hazy lights would seemingly follow the planes as if observing what was going on, without ever directly interfering. Each side thought these strange objects were secret weapons belonging to the enemy. These secret weapons did not attack, so the pilots came to believe that they were "psychological warfare" weapons aimed at their own psyche, not at their flying fortresses. When they did not cease to follow the aircraft, their appearance was attributed to mirages or mental apparitions brought on by the military version of "Jittery war nerves" termed battle fatigue.

Now how many of you reading this would put a person who would begin to have hallucinations under stress in the seat of a very expensive fighter or bomber? I would say none of you would do something this ludicrous, and neither did the government. Because they could not give a concise explanation to these strange objects plaguing our pilots, they simply decided they did not exist! Laying the groundwork for their wonderful explanation as to what the people of this and other countries have seen for last several millennia.

Solomon Islands

The following accounts are but a few of the thousands of encounters that occurred during America's involvement in World War II. Keep in mind that those not reported do not lack credibility, I selectively chose just a few so you could see that this was and is an ongoing global phenomenon.

Just west of Guadalcanal in the Solomon Islands is the small island of Tulagi. On August 12th, 1942, Stephen Brickner, a member of the 1st Marine Division,[11] was sitting on the edge of his foxhole during a lull in fighting with the Japanese Imperial Army. As he was cleaning his trusty M-1 rifle and trying his best to relax, he was instantly jarred back into fighting mode by a blaring air raid siren. The signal sounded at 10 AM local time, and until something happened, all the marines could do was watch and wait for whatever it was the enemy was about to throw their way.

As tension mounted for Brickner and the other Marines, finally it happened: The silence after the siren sounded was broken by the thunderous sound of propellers and piston engines. So loud was it that Stephen Brickner felt there must be hundreds of planes flying very low as they advanced on their position. Once that thought had crossed his mind, he pondered the strange fact that for the first time ever, he heard the engines of the planes before he saw them. (Much like a car coming down the road—you can see it, and as it gets closer, you begin to hear the drone of the tires on the road and the engines exhaust, the same holds true with planes.) The marines began to look around for the planes they could hear but not see. Finally a formation came into view, and as he suspected it was quite large. But what were they? Sure he could hear engines, but as the objects flew overhead, it soon became obvious that these were no ordinary planes.

Brickner describes the formation as having 150 "aircraft" flying in several straight lines of 10-12 craft per row. These "aircraft" were shaped like discs, without wings or tails, or any visible signs of propulsion. The craft were flying faster than any planes he had ever witnessed. As they crossed above the tropical island, they reflected sunlight off their silvery-metallic surface each time the craft seemed to wobble. Once past, the engine-like noise did not die off gradually, but ceased like a radio had been shut off. No threat was made by or towards these strange objects.

Indeed this was a strange encounter for these battle-hardened Marines. Many like Stephen Brickner would remember the strangeness of this encounter better than most of their experiences during their visit to these beautiful, but treacherous South Sea Islands.

CHRISTCHURCH, NEW ZEALAND

Soldiers and air crews were not the only military personnel to spot UFOs during the war. A military nurse had a sighting while waiting at a train station in Christchurch, New Zealand, late one summer night in August of 1944. Looking up the tracks to see if the train was nearing the station, the nurse was surprised to see a large object just to the side off the tracks a short distance up the line from where she waited. Overcome by curiosity, she slowly made her way along the tracks in the direction where the object rested. The features became clearer the closer she got.

The nurse described the object as appearing to be an "upturned saucer," with windows or portholes on its exterior beaming light through them from the craft's interior into the surrounding night. As she came within feet of the object, she peered through a rectangular window. Inside the machine she could see the strange machinery and apparatus that must have controlled the craft, and much to her surprise, the beings that piloted it. There were two humanoid beings staring at a third who had just stepped out of the craft through a hatchway from what she felt was the front of the ship. As she peered around to see him, the being floating outside the craft caught sight of her and hastily floated back into the safety of his ship. Having seen the beings frightened the nurse greatly. As she turned to make a hasty getaway, the ship shot straight up into the heavens and out of sight.

Though a military nurse may not be familiar with all types of aircraft, having stood within arm's length of the craft, I tend to believe that what she saw was no conventional craft of 1944. Besides, humans just can't float through the air, but whatever she saw, could.

PALEMBANG, SUMATRA

During a bombing run, approximately 100 miles north of Palembang, Sumatra, an Army Air Corps bomber was paced by a strange yellow light as they flew through the night sky on their way back to base. Having delivered their payload to an enemy stronghold, Captain Alvah M Reida,[12] who was based out of 468th Bomber Group in Kharagapur, India, was piloting his bomber through the dark night skies.

About one half hour later, the right gunner and the copilot both noticed a yellow object pacing the aircraft about 1,500 feet out, at about the 5 o'clock position off the starboard wing. At that distance, it appeared to the two men to be a disc-shaped object about five- to six-feet in diameter and encircled by a halo of light. Assuming this to be some radio-controlled tracking device, Captain Reida proceeded to initiate evasive maneuvers.

Despite all of his gallant efforts, the crew could not shake this device. Every time they moved the plane, the glowing disc kept pace by moving just enough so as to remain in virtually the same position relative to the bomber. Unnerved by this, the crew soon realized that all it could do was watch and wait, hoping this object was not armed nor gunning for them. After what must have seemed like forever, without any warning, the luminous disc made a sudden ninety-degree turn and accelerated into the surrounding clouds, out of sight of the shaken crew.

Florida

How many people would have the audacity to accuse the man who was the Assistant Chief of Flying Safety at the Tactical Air Command of being an untrained, unqualified observer? Would anyone claim he was making up a story to gain fortune and fame? The answer is no in either case.

On August 1st, 1946,[12] almost a full year after the war was over, Captain Jack E. Puckett, who was on his way to becoming the Assistant Chief of Flying Safety at the Tactical Air Command, was flying a sleek C-47 through the clear blue Florida skies. He had taken off from Langley Field and was flying his aircraft on his way to McDill Air Force Base, when about thirty miles outside of Tampa he crossed over into *The Twilight Zone*.

As he busied himself flying his plane, Captain Puckett's attention was turned from his instruments to a strange cylindrical object hurtling through the sky ahead of him. At first he thought the object was a meteor, but as it approached his plane, his first assumption was proven incorrect. About 1,000 yards out, the object made a forty-five-degree left turn, crossing in front of the plane and continued on its course, disappearing at high speed. His new view of the ship convinced him that not only wasn't it a meteor, it also was not any aircraft known to him.

He described the object as being shaped like a cigar and about twice the size of a B-29 bomber. The object appeared to be metallic and had luminous portholes on the exterior. The object was in view until it crossed over the horizon. The captain estimated the object was in view for 2.5 to 3 minutes and traveled about 75 miles to 100 miles. When this is calculated out, the object had to be traveling at least 1,500 MPH and up to 2,000 MPH, depending of exactly how long the object was in view and how far it traveled. Although most interceptors can reach these speeds today, they are 4 to 5 times the maximum speed of the fastest aircraft in any country's inventory in 1946.

It wasn't one of *ours*, nor was it one of *their* planes. Then what was it? Could it have been a meteor or fireball as the captain had suspected? No, meteors do not change directions. Could it have been lightning or some other natural phenomena? Not likely, as natural phenomena do not have windows. Could it have been a weather balloon or other aircraft? No, nothing except a UFO could accurately describe what he saw that day.

CHAPTER 4

1947-1949

THE EMERGENCE OF THE MODERN UFO ERA

"RAAF Captures Flying Saucer on Ranch in Roswell Region – more details of Flying Disc are revealed"...

~*Roswell Daily Record*
Headlines from an early July edition

RICHMOND, VIRGINIA

We will begin this chapter with a sighting that predates the "Big One" made by Kenneth Arnold by a mere two months. While studying a cloud formation over his hometown of Richmond, Virginia in April of 1947, a weatherman was fascinated to see an unknown aerial object. Due to his initial request to remain anonymous, we must refrain from using his name, and will simply refer to him as *him* or *the weatherman.*

The weatherman was observing the atmospheric conditions the old fashioned way: by looking up into the sky. Before satellites and Doppler radar, weathermen had to observe the wind at high altitude by measuring the speeds of high-altitude clouds visually. Thus, instead of being in a studio behind a computer, they were outdoors very often, checking the barometer, temperature, wind speed, dew point, and the like, in order to make their best guess at a forecast. Our weatherman was observing clouds through a thedeolite—a small mounted telescope, very similar to a surveyor's transit. As he scanned a distant cloud bank, he noticed a strange object in his field of view. (Remember, as a weatherman, he would be familiar with natural phenomena, planes, and weather balloons, as he would see these things on a regular basis because his job required a lot of sky-watching.) What he saw was none of these.

What he saw he described as a disc-shaped object with a flat bottom and a domed top. The weatherman tracked this object as it effortlessly made its way across the sky in the opposite direction of the wind. The object hurriedly disappeared over the far horizon, leaving him very perplexed, as he tried to figure out what it was he'd just witnessed. He reasoned that the object was not any natural phenomena, as most atmospheric phenomena doesn't glint in the sunlight as if made from a reflective metal. Nor was it a weather balloon as it traveled against the wind. It was not any type of aircraft that he had ever observed, as he saw neither wings nor propellers/jets. What was it this weatherman saw? If it were just two months later, he would have called the object by the now familiar name coined by the media: a flying saucer.

BAKERSFIELD, CALIFORNIA

Less than two weeks before Kenneth Arnold had his sighting, a pilot over California came face to face with an unknown aerial craft.[1] June 14th, 1947 started out very much like any numerous working days for pilot Richard Rankin. While on the last leg of his familiar run plying the airways between Chicago and Los Angeles, Mr. Rankin witnessed a "squadron" of ten objects as they raced through the heavens in tight formation. It was around 2 PM PST, just outside of Bakersfield, California, that Rankin came into contact with what he described as a most incredible sight. Racing in tight triangle-shaped quasi-military formation were no fewer than ten thirty to thirty-five-foot wide disc-shaped objects, reflecting the sun's light off their metallic hulls. The pilot estimated the objects were traveling at close to 600 MPH, which was faster than any plane aloft in 1947.

Quite understandably, the pilot was baffled by what he saw, but even more so at his inability to get any satisfactory answers from those in the Civilian Aviation Administration. What makes this report even more astounding is the fact that this report mirrors the next in every way, and the next is the best-known sighting of all.

THE CASCADE MOUNTAIN CHAIN

Ten days later, the same or a similar formation of craft were seen by another pilot while he was flying through the scenic Cascade Mountain chain. On June 24th, 1947, 32-year-old Kenneth Arnold took off from Chehalis, Washington in his own single-engine airplane on a clear, beautiful early summer day. His destination that day was Pendelton, Oregon. While in the air, he decided to join in the search for a missing Marine C-46 transport plane because the government was offering a $5,000 reward for information leading to its recovery.

Having flown for about an hour without locating the plane, Mr. Arnold was enjoying the beautiful scenery when his attention was attracted by sunlight being reflected off of something below. Looking in the direction from where the reflection had come, Mr. Arnold, sure he was going to see the crashed C-46, probably began formulating ways to best spend the $5,000 he was going to receive for discovering the whereabouts of the lost plane. Much to his surprise, the sunlight was being reflected off the silver skin of a squadron of nine saucer-shaped objects flying through the atmosphere, much like saucers skipping across water, in what he termed an echelon formation. The objects were close to the terrain, as they zigzagged through and around the higher peaks.

Arnold timed the craft as they made their way from Mt. Rainier to Mt. Adams. It took the squadron only 102 seconds to cover the forty-two mile distance, putting their speed at approximately 1,657 MPH. He had the objects in sight for almost three minutes.

Once he arrived at the airfield in Pendelton, he gave his account to waiting newsmen, and from there, the rest is history. The story made headlines around the world, and is responsible for the Air Force becoming involved in the investigation of reports concerning Unidentified Flying Objects. An interesting aside is the fact that this case, even with the worldwide attention it received, and the pressure it put on the Air Force, was never satisfactorily explained. It is this sighting that many researchers attribute too having set off the modern era of UFO reports. It was also this report that debunkers like to point to as being the first time a UFO was reported. As we have seen in the opening chapters, contrary to the debunkers' claims, these objects have been sighted since the dawn of recorded history and continue to this very moment, with no foreseeable end in sight.

Bisbee, Arizona

The last week of June in 1947 would prove to be ripe with sightings of UFOs by qualified observers. Three days after Kenneth Arnolds' sighting, a retired Army Major had an interesting sighting while going about his everyday activities. At 10:30 AM the morning of June 27th, 1947, retired Major George B. Wilcox watched approximately nine objects as they flew through the sky approximately 1,000 feet above the mountains near Bisbee, Arizona.[2]

Upon closer examination, the retired Army officer noticed that these objects had no wings or tails, nor did they emit any noise. Studying them as they flew by, Major Wilcox described the objects as being disc shaped and of light color. He also noticed that, moving through the skies, the discs seemed to rock back and forth as they made headway through the atmosphere. The objects were traveling very fast out of the major's line of sight, vanishing to his eye, but not to his memory.

Just about the same time, and only a short distance away on the other side of town, Mr. John Petsche, an electrician at the Phelps-Dodge Cooper Mines of Bisbee, and several other employees saw the same or similar craft as they "wobbled" through the sky above them.

This type of sighting, where several people see the same object(s) from different locations are avoided like the plague by the debunkers as they are incredibly hard to disprove, as the similarity of descriptions from witnesses who had no contact and thus could not compare notes to create similar stories, in the very least proves that the objects were there. And by the description given by a trained Army Major, this craft certainly was not of this earth!

Lake Meade, Nevada, and Montgomery, Alabama

The next day, June 28th, 1947, would be a busy day for Air Force personnel on both sides of the American continent.[3] At 3:15 PM, an Air Force pilot was flying his F-51 fighter when he had a sighting just several hundred miles north of the Arizona town our two previous sightings happened. As he piloted his craft near Lake Meade, Nevada, the pilot was startled by the sudden appearance of six objects as they flew past his right wing and out of sight at tremendous speed.

About six hours later, and several thousand miles to the east, four more Air Force personnel had an encounter near Montgomery, Alabama. Two pilots and two intelligence officers from Maxwell Air Force Base were witnesses to the over-flight of a large glowing object as it zigzagged across the star-filled skies of central Alabama. The object was first seen by the four officers near the western horizon. It utilized sudden intense bursts of speed to propel it in its odd flight path through the star-filled sky. After one such burst of speed, the object made a sudden ninety-degree turn and accelerated at high speed out of sight towards the southern horizon, a maneuver still not attainable even with sixty-plus years of technological innovations. Here is a trend you would not expect to be developing if you believe the spiel that the debunkers put forth. Much to their chagrin, many of the first sightings of the modern UFO era were made by highly trained officers in the United States military!

Roswell, New Mexico

Sandwiched in between these excellent sightings was an event, which I hesitate to mention due to the lack of tangible, consistent documentation to back up any claims that have been asserted. I am not insinuating that the event did not occur, as it did, and probably played out as the main witnesses have reported. I will briefly mention what is alleged to have happened in the desert near Roswell, New Mexico during the summer of 1947 that still has the world community debating it to this day and then we will move on.

Since the true date has been in dispute by the leading experts for quite some time, we will leave the time frame as late June or early July. Many local residents have claimed that a flying disc was seen to falter in flight after being hit by lightning. The wreckage was strewn over a large area near a local's ranch. When this rancher noticed the "wreckage," he called the authorities. The Air Force eventually showed up, and the officer sent, one Major Jesse Marcel, proclaimed that the material found was from a crashed flying saucer, giving us the quote we used to introduce this chapter.

Of course, the powers that be in the Air Force hierarchy denounced this press release and determined that the wreckage found was that of one of those pesky weather balloons. Thus a controversy was born! I do not mean to detract from the importance of this event; instead, I was brief in the synopsis because I have tried to stay away from such highly controversial occurrences in an effort to maintain focus on my reason for writing this book, which is to prove that the UFO phenomenon is significant enough to have a more detailed analysis carried out by all the governments of the world, so that we the people can be better informed about what is happening in and around the skies above us.

Emmett, Idaho

July bought a great surprise to the Air Force, as these sightings of flying saucers did not stop as projected. Instead, they continued to pour in at an increasing pace. The Fourth of July weekend brought two very intriguing accounts. Over the holiday weekend, United Airlines flight 105 had a strange encounter with several Unidentified Flying Objects.[4]

Westbound from Boise, Idaho, on its way to Pendelton, Oregon, Flight 105 was airborne for less than ten minutes when they encountered several UFOs over Emmett, Idaho. At approximately 9:16 PM MST, Captain E.J. Smith and copilot Ralph Stevens, the crew and passengers of Flight 105 came in contact with the UFOs just after ascending to the 8,000-foot level. At first, the pilots thought they were witnessing a cluster of small planes, but upon further examination they soon realized that what they were seeing were unlike any planes they had ever seen before.

Captain Smith described the objects as being circular and flat, like a disc that was illuminated. They flew by in a tight formation and passed just to the left of the airplane. The plane was passing over the Blue Mountains as things began to return to normal in the cockpit and cabin. Copilot Stevens spotted another group of discs closing in on the plane at a slightly higher altitude. These objects also flew by the plane at great speed, on their way to God knows where.

Twin Falls, Idaho

The second sighting of note that happened on that holiday weekend in 1947 also occurred in the skies over Idaho. A group of picnickers celebrating America's birthday with food and fun at a popular resort area near Twin Falls, Idaho, had their attention diverted from merry-making by a daytime exhibition by aerial craft of unknown origin.[5] Several families enjoying the afternoon sun were amazed to see a display that would rival any fireworks display put on anywhere in the country that night. No fewer than thirty-five UFOs leisurely drifted across the blue cloud-free sky.

The objects were described as metallic discs that reflected the bright afternoon sun. The objects moved slowly, yet purposefully. Some folks were convinced that whoever was in control of these objects must have been interested in the festivities on the ground, as they seemed to drift and stop as if reconnoitering the area below. Having so many witnesses can exclude the possibility of hallucinations, as widespread daydreams are not likely, and in fact, what they saw truly were solid, real unknown aerial objects.

Muroc Air Force Base, California

Several days later on July 8th, 1947, Muroc Air Force Base in California, was the site of yet another encounter by humans with unknown craft that once again appeared to be interested in the activities on the ground.[6] Early in the day, as two military engineers made their way across the compound, they were very surprised to see what they described to their superiors as two metallic discs slowly making their way across the sky above the base. The objects were moving so slowly that the engineers claim it took several minutes to fly overhead. Later that day, at 9:20 PM to be exact, a group of base personnel witnessed a large circular object, as it made its way overhead. In contrast to the previous report, these observers reported that there was only one craft, and it was moving a bit faster at approximately 300 MPH and flying much higher at what the witnesses estimated as close to 7,500 feet and against the prevailing wind.

Boise, Idaho

The very next day, July 9th, 1947, the editor of *Statesman's Aviation* had an encounter with a UFO as he flew over Boise, Idaho, the hometown of the now famous Kenneth Arnold. While flying his National Guard AT-6 on a routine mission, at approximately 13,000 feet, the editor known to us as Mr. Johnson, encountered a large, round, black object as it darted in and around the clouds around him. Thinking that what he was viewing was a reflection on his canopy, he proceeded to pull the canopy back to its fully open position. Much to this pilot's surprise, the object was right there in front of him, thus informing him that what he had seen was no reflection, but a real craft flying rings around his plane. So as any good pilot would do, he attempted to try to close in on the unknown object. What happened next left Johnson in awe and amazed. As he tried to close on the object with his AT-6, the object, as if sensing what he was trying to do, suddenly and instantly, shot straight up, rolled over 180 degrees and disappeared from his sight. This object, as Johnson I'm sure would concur, truly was not of this world!

New Mexico

Although there were many, many reports of UFO sightings from across the country after Kenneth Arnold's sighting made headlines, we will include only one more account from that fateful year. On July 10th, 1947, there was a sighting by a gentleman who would not fit into any of the debunkers' presupposed dispositions. This witness *was* rather technically oriented, having achieved a Ph.D. in astronomy. He certainly *was not* seeking publicity, as he was and is still internationally well known in scientific circles. And although he had seen countless wonders through his telescope, the object he saw that warm July day would remain etched in his memory until he passed on some years later.

Dr. Clyde Tombaugh, who discovered Pluto in the 1930s, had an encounter with a UFO while driving down a New Mexico highway. At about 4:50 PM on the afternoon of July 10th, 1947, the good doctor noticed an elliptically shaped object reflecting the bright desert sunlight as it "wobbled" across the sky above him. As he watched the object, it flew into a cloud bank and remained hidden for a short time. After a brief period, the object emerged from the cloud bank, hovered for a moment, and then shot straight up and out of sight at what Dr. Tombaugh estimated to be close to 900 miles per hour. It was the object's ability to generate such fast acceleration that convinced Dr. Tombaugh that this was indeed a "Novel Aerial Device,"[7] or as we would call it: an unidentified flying object.

Southeast Ohio and Northwestern Kentucky

January 7th, 1948 started out like most other mid-winter days for the residents of Southeast Ohio and Northwestern Kentucky. No one had any indication that the events of that day would be infamous sixty-odd years later. Maysville, Kentucky is a small town some 100 miles east of Louisville. On January 7th, 1948, the state police barracks near Maysville began to receive calls from residents of the surrounding area. All reported the same thing: a strange object flying through the skies over their homes. The state police, having no expertise or experience in investigating these reports, contacted the local military installation, Godman Air Force Base. They asked the information officer if they had any planes on maneuvers, or had any odd craft in the area that could have accounted for the reports the local people were making. Godman informed the police that they had nothing in the air.

Feeling as though they had fulfilled their obligation to follow up on the reports, the officers attributing the reports to the misidentification of some atmospheric phenomena, and continued with their daily routine. However, any chance of shutting the books on these sightings came to a screeching halt minutes after the police had spoken to Godman Airbase. Not long thereafter, the phones began to ring off the hook as people from the surrounding communities began to flood the state police with sightings of the same or similar objects as reported earlier. All the people calling in were reporting an "ice cream cone-shaped" object flying at a good clip over the homes of many frightened residents. Soon the good folks at Godman, as well as the Army Air Force base near Wilmington, Ohio, were seeing the same object that the local townsfolk had witnessed. For over forty-five minutes, Godman Airbase Commander Colonel Guy Hix and his executive officer Lieutenant Colonel Garrison Wood, tried to identify the object and plot a course of action to stop this object from freely over-flying these military installations. The solution to their problem manifested itself once a decorated World War II flyer flew into Godman airspace: They would have this experienced flyer investigate this strange object for them.

As 25-year-old Captain Thomas Mantell lead a squadron of four National Guard F-51 fighters on a routine flight that as happenstance would have, took them near Godman Air Force Base, he received a request to investigate an unknown bogey hovering in the sky near this vital airbase. He answered the request in the affirmative, and although one of the planes was a little low on fuel, they proceeded north to investigate this bogey. When Captain Mantell gained a visual fix on the object, he pushed the F-51 to the limits trying to close the gap between his plane and this unknown bogey. Leaving the squadron behind, all of whom were headed for a nearby airfield for refueling, Captain Mantell began to give chase to this object that was pulling away from one of the fastest planes of the day. The faster Captain Mantell went, the further the object climbed into the atmosphere. As he gave chase, Captain Mantell reported to Godman that he was chasing the object, which appeared to be a metallic object. (It is worth mentioning here that he did not report a bright light or a glowing object.) He was informed by ground control that he had passed the 15,000-foot limit, meaning he was headed into oxygen-starved air with no onboard oxygen supply to supplement his breathing.

His wingman, who had been refueling at nearby Standidford Field, was soon in the air once again. Unbeknownst to them, their chase would soon turn into a rescue mission from which they would bring back only bad news. Captain Mantell radioed the field to inform them that, "I have the object in site; it's huge and climbing!" and after a short pause, "I'm going after it!" That was the last thing the tower or anyone else heard from the decorated war veteran.

Captain Mantell lost his life that day, becoming the first-known fatality of the UFO phenomenon. Witnesses on the ground reported seeing the fighter pursue the red cone shaped object until, inexplicably, the fighter began to fly in circles and then dove nose first, falling almost 20,000 feet until it broke apart shortly before it impacted the ground in rural Kentucky. By the time his wingmen returned to help him, Captain Mantell was already dead.

The media circus that followed was something never before seen in this section of the country. As the cry for an accounting by the government explaining what had happened to Captain Mantell surged, the official explanation offered by the government was classically logically unsound.

The government claims that the highly decorated flying veteran, Captain Mantell, who so gallantly served his country in World War II, had died from losing control of his aircraft, due to oxygen deprivation, while chasing the planet Venus! One would think that the government could come up with a better cover story. This one fell apart quite easily when logical thinkers examined it! His cause of death is indisputable. Climbing into air with little oxygen can readily cause a blackout. The circling motion and sudden dive are evidence that this is probably what happened. The object, however, could not have been Venus as the government had claimed, as a quick check of the astronomic tables of the day, show that Venus was not in that part of the sky at the time Captain Mantell was pursuing the UFO. Nor would Venus look like an ice cream cone made from a metallic material capable of flight within the earth's atmosphere. Nor can Venus be picked up on radar meant to track aircraft. I think you would agree that a planet would not appear as a metallic cone by a fighter pilot who was giving chase. It may however appear as a bright light or a glowing-object flying at high altitude. Neither of these descriptions fit what Captain Mantell reported seeing that day. When this theory began to fall apart under scientific dissection, the government then claimed that it was a weather balloon that he had chased until he passed out and subsequently crashed. This explanation is no better than the first, as it is quite safe to say that a balloon could not climb through the atmosphere faster than a high-powered aircraft! The best reason as to why these explanations were false is the fact that no highly trained, battle hardened fighter pilot, would put their life at risk chasing what should have been readily apparent as a star or a balloon. Captain Mantell gave his life chasing an unknown object, becoming the first recorded death of a human who had come into contact with a UFO. A close friend of Captain Mantell said it best, when delivering the following as part of a eulogy:

> Captain Mantell was pursuing something he considered important enough to risk life and limb, and take a tremendous toll on his family. Captain Mantell died trying to identify an invader in United States airspace.[8]

Alabama, Georgia, North Carolina, Virginia

July 24th, 1948 found Captain Charles Chiles piloting his big Eastern Airlines DC-3 on a flight plan that originated in Houston, Texas, and terminated in Atlanta, Georgia. Little did either he or his passengers and crew know that they would be making a detour through, forgive me Mr. Sterling, *The Twilight Zone!* The plane taxied down the runway at Houston and was in flight by 8:30 PM CST. Once airborne, the crew soon realized that the beautiful July evening was perfect for flying. The sky that night was dotted with clouds and full of stars. The first couple hours were spent uneventfully attending to the business of flying the plane and seeing to the passengers comfort, all the while observing the spectacular night sky. As beautiful as the night sky was, sleep soon conquered most of the passengers.

Around 2:45 AM EST[9] as Captain Chiles piloted his plane over the outlying area of Montgomery, Alabama, he noticed a strange light off in the distance. Having stared at the light for a couple minutes, not wanting to foolishly cause any unnecessary alarm amongst the flight crew, Captain Chiles pointed out the light to his copilot, John Whitted. They both watched as a light approached from the 12 o'clock position, at a much higher speed than any jet plane they had ever seen. As the light rapidly closed in, Captain Chiles, fearing a collision, made a sharp turn to starboard in hopes of avoiding a sure catastrophe. The sleeping passengers were jarred awake in wild bewilderment wondering what was going on. Those who were not sleeping saw the same strange object as the flight crew had, as it rocketed by the plane causing severe turbulence in its wake. The pilots had the best view of the object as it passed approximately 700 feet off their port wing. They, as several of the passengers, claimed that a cigar-shaped object, not unlike the fuselage of a B-29 minus wings and tail, with two rows of windows emitting a bright light, passed by their aircraft at an astonishing speed, then made a rapid climb into the night sky and was lost from their field of view inside the steeply turning aircraft's cockpit. In its wake was a tremendous amount of turbulence, as well as a pronounced red-orange flame/exhaust that spewed from the rear of the craft as it passed by. The witnesses also noticed an intensely deep blue light being emitted from the bottom of the craft.

Unbeknownst to Captain Chiles, his crew and the passengers who witnessed this unknown craft, were not alone in their sighting. Shortly after that sighting, an aircraft crew chief stationed at Robbins Air Force Base in Macon, Georgia, watched as a "strange" glowing object streaked across the night sky. And shortly their after, a pilot aloft near the North Carolina-Virginia border spotted in the southern horizon a incredibly bright "shooting star" that, much to his surprise, flew parallel to the ground as it made its way on its northeasterly course.

These multiple sighting of what in reality was the same craft viewed as it made its way east by northeast from Montgomery, Alabama, passed Macon, Georgia and on through to a site near the North Carolina-Virginia border, did not make the captain's, nor copilot's, reporting their sighting any easier. Once they had landed, they were ordered to a debriefing. They explained exactly what happen, what they saw, and had several passengers back up their accounts verbatim.

The authorities squashed their report, giving the usual meteor explanation and wanted nothing more to do with this fantastic encounter. As is always the case, the authorities could not explain how a meteor could fly parallel to the ground, and then ascend at terrific speed. Nor did they dare to venture a guess as to how windows got into the solid rock or metal interior of a meteor. They knew then, as today's authorities now know: These objects are not meteors or swamp gas or misidentified airplanes; they are exactly as their name implies—Unidentified Flying Objects.

North Dakota

Our next case is also a report made by a pilot, though this time a military pilot, of his encounter with an unknown object over the skies of North Dakota. At 8:30 PM on the night of October 1st, 1948,[10] while piloting his P-51 back to base from a rather lengthy training mission, North Dakota Air National Guard Captain George F. Gorman, on final approach to the base, radioed to the Fargo Airfield flight control tower for landing instructions. Fargo tower informed him that he was next in line to land; the only other traffic was a piper cub, whose outline was plainly visible to him against the background of the city lights, below and ahead of his plane.

Not a minute after receiving this transmission from the tower, Captain Gorman was startled by the close passage of some craft off the right wing of his P-51. Upset by the high speed and close passage, but before initiating any action, this well-trained officer once again contacted the tower to inquire what the hell just buzzed his fighter. The tower assured him that he was the only traffic on their radarscope as the piper cub had landed a few seconds previous.

Since the tower had no information on this craft, the captain decided to take matters into his own hands. As he increased the manifold pressure, his airspeed increased dramatically—as I have mentioned previously, the P-51 was one of the fastest planes of its time. As he closed to within 1,000 feet of the light, he soon realized that the ball of bright white light was quite small, only about eight inches in diameter. The light increased its speed and quickly pulled away from the fighter on a heading back towards the Fargo tower. Then, in one quick movement, the light made a sharp left turn and began to climb into the atmosphere at terrific speed.

As Captain Gorman brought his plane around once again and tried to close the gap between the light and his plane, the light, without stopping, instantaneously reversed direction, and was now on a collision course with the fighter. Captain Gorman, sensing the danger, put his fighter into a steep dive, and was relieved to see the ball of light pass over his canopy and head up into the star-filled night.

Having survived this harrowing "dogfight," Captain Gorman once again made his final approach to the base in Fargo. Here he faced an even bigger challenge: telling his superiors that he encountered and gave chase to an object that was unlike any flying craft he had seen before, putting himself and an expensive piece of Uncle Sam's hardware into harm's way.

What was it that Captain Gorman chased? We can rest assured that it was no star or planet, as they usually aren't less than a foot in diameter. Nor could the powers that be allege that it was a meteor, as the sudden turns and the increasing/decreasing of speeds would rule this out. Even ball lightning could not account for this sighting as lightning, though it may fly by or near an aircraft, does not change directions to give chase. What was it that Captain Gorman saw? Could it have been a small remote-controlled vehicle from a larger vehicle at a higher altitude, reconnoitering the skies above Fargo? As is too often the case, the truth has not as of yet surfaced.

Author Note:

I hope you are not distressed by the fact that I have included so many sightings by pilots in the post Kenneth Arnold period thus far. I wish to assure you that people from all walks of life from around the globe were having encounters with unknown aerial devices. I have chosen to fill this section with reports from pilots, both military and civilian, due to several facts. Firstly, the time was rapidly approaching when the military brass and aviation authorities would bring pressure on pilots not to publicly divulge their encounters with UFOs, nor even file a report with the control towers they were dealing with. Ridicule and loss of jobs were used as methods to intimidate pilots who did not bend to the will of those above them. Secondly, pilots, by their very nature, make the best witnesses when dealing with UFO encounters. They are familiar with all atmospheric phenomena, meteors, lightning, and other airplanes. To pilot a plane, you must also be a good judge of speed, direction, and inclination, and be an above-average observer. Pilots are well compensated and are the recipients of much prestige. Thus, there would be no reason for them to make up stories that would draw attention to them, nor would they need to make extra money by making up reports of encounters with UFOs. The fear of the loss of their jobs would also be a major motivator in influencing how they conduct themselves. Therefore, when a pilot comes forth to report their encounters with Unidentified Flying Objects, I tend to believe that what they are reporting is the whole truth, and nothing but the truth. I believe you would agree that pilots could make more money flying planes then authoring short fictitious stories.

Fukuoka, Japan

Flying in a propeller-driven aircraft that required two officers, one pilot, and one radioman to fly successfully, sat 1st Lieutenant Oliver Hemphill and 2nd Lieutenant Barton Halter when they had their chance encounter with the unknown while out on routine patrol to keep the skies over Fukuoka, Japan safe.

On that night of October 15th, 1948,[11] at approximately 11 PM local time, the radioman, 1st Lieutenant Halter, noticed that the radar waves his plane was emitting were bouncing off an unknown object somewhere in the dark night sky ahead of their aircraft. To be sure his radar set was not malfunctioning, he asked the pilot if there was a bogey out in front of the plane. Sure enough, once the pilot's sight was trained on the sector of sky the radioman had alerted him to, he saw the object that was painting a return on Lieutenant Halter's screen. They called the tower at flight control to see if there was any other traffic in their vector, to which they received a negative reply. They were then in agreement: the object needed to be investigated.

So Lieutenant Hemphill brought the plane around to intercept with the bogey. As they gave chase and started to close in on the unknown to make an ID, the object, still about 12,000 feet from the fighter, suddenly shot off into the distance at an incredible speed. Radar contact was re-established in short order and again the plane tried to close in on the object, with similar results. This scenario was played out five more times, as if the UFO was playing mouse to the fighter's cat. On their last attempt, the object disappeared out of sight.

Lt. Hemphill described the object as a circular light, about the size of a fighter with no visible wings, tail, or means of propulsion. He also concluded from this game of cat and mouse that the object was consciously aware of the fighter and its intentions. Each time the plane closed in on the object, it would "bounce" out of radar contact by shooting up or down and even made 180-degree turns to scoot away from the hounding beams emitted by the fighter's radar.

With no explanation from their superiors once they returned to base, these aviators were left without any answers to what they had encountered that autumn night in the skies over occupied Japan.

Washington, D.C.

Dateline November 18th, 1948,[12] at 9:45 PM EST, an Air Force pilot in flight over the nation's capital reported to ground control that he was observing a light moving north to south over the airspace of Washington, D.C.'s Andrews Air Force Base.

The object was described by the pilot as a large, brightly glowing white light. Curious as to what was making its way unhindered over the skies of the nation's capital, the Air Force pilot throttled up the plane to try to close in on the object, thus allowing him to make a positive ID. The pilot managed to close within a half-mile of the object, at which time he proceeded to flash his landing lights to alert the craft to his presence. The object responded by accelerating at a tremendous rate over the top of the pilot's T-6. He then turned his plane into a climb in an attempt to intercept the unknown object. The pilot wanted to corral the object in such a way so as to put it between his T-6 and the moon, the light from which he believed would allow for a positive ID. This never came to be, as the object could not be caught by the T-6. The pilot described the object from his close passes as a dark gray oval-shaped object surrounded by the glowing white haze, that although was smaller than his plane, was definitely under intelligent control.

By itself, this was an amazing encounter between a well-trained Air Force pilot and an unidentified flying object that out maneuvered this USAF jet as it flew across the restricted airspace above Washington, D.C. What makes this such an exceptional sighting is that at the same time this "Sky jockey" was chasing the UFO in the skies above the capital, three of his fellow servicemen witnessed the entire encounter from their vantage point at Andrews AFB.

On the ground two officers and a Master Sergeant watched as the plane closed in on the object, its rapid acceleration and the plane's fruitless chase. They all agreed that whatever it was the pilot in the sky was chasing, it certainly did not originate from any US air base! The quasi-experts at Project Grudge, a government think tank assembled to explain away UFO encounters, without any investigative efforts, declared that the pilot had an encounter with a high-altitude weather balloon. Given the fact that a balloon could not out-fly a trained fighter pilot in a jet aircraft, and that the air weather service proclaimed that it had no balloons aloft that night, did nothing to sway the experts' opinions: They remained adamant that the object was a balloon. (Heck, I bet that under the proper circumstances, they would have revealed that the moon is made from blue cheese! I guess the old saying is true, anything is possible.)

Author's Note:

As 1948 was drawing to a close, the United States Air Force, as well as the air forces of the rest world, suddenly were faced with the prospect of dealing with a new facet to these encounters with unknown objects. There began to emerge a trend of sightings from around the world where pilots, military personnel, law enforcement officers, and many "men on the street" reported having come in contact with large green fire balls that made their way through the skies above cities and towns worldwide. When the reports started coming in from the average person, the great minds at the Pentagon and throughout the government theorized that these witnesses, who were not technically trained, were seeing military flares as they drifted across the sky. Why there were so many flares being set off over populated area was never explained. The plausibility of this cover story soon was blown to shreds when both military and civilian pilots began to see these fireballs, and if pilots could not discern a flare from a flying craft, then I don't know whom I would trust to.

New Mexico

On December 5th, 1948 two aircraft, one military and the other civilian, both had close encounters with green fireballs as they flew through the dark New Mexico skies. The military plane, a C-47,[13] was flying over the sand-strewn landscape near Kirkland Air Force Base, when the crew noticed a green ball of light approaching the plane from below. The light came to the same elevation as the plane, remained there a short time, then climbed up into the upper atmosphere and out of sight.

One of the crew vocalized what they were all thinking: "What was that?"

The first suggestion, that they had witnessed a meteor, was quickly shot down, when one of the crew mentioned that meteors come down, they don't go up! After more discussion, the crew decided that they should report what they had seen, so at around 9:30 PM local time, they reported their encounter to a less-than-amused radioman at the Kirkland flight control tower. Before the operator could form any opinion about the mental well being of the flight crew on the C-47, he received another report from a passing commercial airliner.

At roughly 9:35 PM, a Pioneer Airline's DC-3, aloft that night bound for Albuquerque, came into contact with the same or a similar "fireball" as the crew onboard the C-47. Flying just east of Las Vegas, New Mexico, about 100 miles from their destination, the copilot onboard the Pioneer DC-3 saw a bright reddish-orange glow off in the horizon. He studied it for a moment, making note of trajectory and speed and determined that it was much too low and slow to be a meteor, especially since it was flying on a parallel trajectory to the ground. The copilot pointed this object out to the pilot, and not long thereafter, the object made a sudden course correction and began speeding toward the DC-3. The object changed color from red-orange to a bright green as it accelerated towards the airplane. (Could the object have been ionizing the air around it as a bi-product of its propulsion, as it sped towards the plane?)

Concerned that the object may collide with his DC-3, the captain put the plane into a sharp right turn. So tight a turn in fact, that if not for the experience and skill of the flight crew, the plane could easily have dived into a spiral and ended up as a flaming heap of charred metal on the desert floor below. Once the crew regained control of the plane and the passengers, they too radioed the tower at Kirkland Air Force Base at approximately 9:35 PM; just five minutes after the report had come in from the C-47.

When the Pioneer Flight landed and the passengers and crew had deplaned in Albuquerque, they were met by anxious intelligence officers for an extensive debriefing. Unfortunately, like all other encounters with government officials, these UFO witnesses took more information into the meeting than they would take away. They had told the authorities what they had seen, but the authorities either couldn't or wouldn't divulge what it was that these two aircraft had encountered that night in the skies above New Mexico.

Author's Note:

There are only two sightings I have deemed worthy of including from 1949. One is a second encounter by a rather distinguished gentleman we have met once before. The other is a rare encounter between a UFO and a military officer who works with weather balloons and their tracking devices on a regular basis.

Southwestern United States

Our first encounter once again takes place in the desert of the southwestern United States. While relaxing on the porch of his home with his wife and her mother on the evening of August 10th, 1949,[14] the discoverer of Pluto, Dr. Clyde Tombaugh was involved in his favorite past time: sky watching. While relaxing in the cool night desert breeze, Dr. Tombaugh and his companions spotted an object outlined against the night sky. The object was cigar shaped and appeared to be made from a dark metallic substance. There were two rows of rectangular lights from which a soft yellow light emanated. (Please note the similarity of this craft to the one witness by Chiles and Whitte!) He believed that the object he saw, due to its size and shape, the rectangular windows, was truly an unidentified flying object.

Dr. Tombaugh, having seen two UFOs, supports my claim that people who are technically trained and are familiar with atmospheric phenomenon have and continue to see Unidentified Flying Objects. This lends credence to my claim that UFOs are real.

New Mexico

Our second encounter from 1949 occurred in the morning hours of April 24th. Commander R.B. McLaughlin, a graduate of the United States Naval Academy at Annapolis, was working with his crew of technicians, engineers, and scientists. All were hard at work on the grounds of the White Sands Proving Grounds making preparations for their launch of a Skyhook Balloon.[15] As a precursor to releasing the 100-foot-diameter balloon, the team had sent a small weather balloon aloft that bright April morning in order to get an idea of wind speed in the upper atmosphere. Commander McLaughlin's Team was using a thedeolite (a small instrument not unlike a surveyor's transit, that is built around a 25x telescope) to track the balloon as it made its way up two miles. Another of his staff measured the angle and time of the balloon's ascent, while a third documented the findings with pen and paper.

In the midst of this scene, a fellow member of their team began to shout excitedly as he pointed to a region in the sky just to the left of the weather balloon. They soon saw that what he was pointing to was a silvery-white metallic-appearing object as it gently moved across the morning sky. When they all had realized the gravity of the situation, one team member trained his thedeolite on the object, while another noted the time, 10:30 AM, and then reset his stopwatch to time the event. The transcriptionist recorded what was happening in his journal. The sighting lasted one minute, and in that time period, the object dropped from 45 degrees to 25 degrees above the horizon; then it suddenly accelerated straight up and out of sight.

After the sighting was over, the team sat down to analyze what they had seen. What the scientific computation pointed to was incredible, to say the least. What they found was that they had witnessed the passing of some rather large unknown craft, performing feats unheard of then or now. In other words, they had witnessed a UFO. The object calculated out to be roughly 40 feet wide and 100 feet long, was cruising along at 420 miles per *minute* at 296,000 feet of elevation. The team as well as their commanding officer came to a startling conclusion: They had proof that the "Flying Saucers" were real.

Here we had a whole team of trained, technically oriented people, who know what weather balloons looked like under all circumstances, who had tracked an object and recorded their observations for analysis. What they saw was real. It was not a comet, meteor, or lightning. It was not swamp gas, birds, or insects. It was no aircraft, and certainly wasn't what would have been to them an easily recognized weather balloon of any type. And since a whole team of people saw the same thing, one through a 25x telescope, the object was not a hallucination, dream, or illusion. It was a vehicle of unknown origin.

Unfortunately, the team faced the daunting fact that their superiors were not interested in a report that substantiated the existence of flying saucers.

Chapter 5

The Early 1950s
The Korean War Years

"I can assure you that Flying Saucers, given that they exist, are not constructed by any power on earth."

~President Harry Truman
Press Conference, April 4th, 1950

From what I have seen and read, the fifties were a kind of American Renaissance. I cannot verify this as I was not yet born, but from the events that occurred politically, socially, and economically, I would say this would be close to the truth. America had finally come into its own. Having helped defeat the Axis Powers, fighting a two-front war since the day we were involved, America truly showed its military and industrial might, as well as its long-term ability to lead the world into a peaceful, prosperous era. Although we fought another war, err, Police Action in Korea, the United States went through many years of economic growth, which helped people ascertain so good a lifestyle across so many socioeconomic planes as to be truly a remarkable accomplishment. The Cold War was raging, but for the most part peace reigned throughout country.

One thing that did not change, however, was the continual sightings of these unknown aerial "craft." In fact, the number of sightings increased remarkably. Though the number of reported sightings by unqualified observers increased rapidly, sightings by those people who I would consider competent observers (pilots, military/law enforcement personnel) also continued on a steady upswing. (Please continue to keep in mind that the sightings you are about to read *are not* the only reports made in the fifth decade of the century, as there were thousands of sightings reported and tens of thousands more sightings that went unreported. What you will read are a select number of sightings made by those individuals who meet the qualifications defined in the beginning of this book.)

The powers that were in both the Air Force and the United States federal government, began to bring pressure on the pilots and military personnel to keep them from coming forth in the public domain with the intimate details of their encounters with UFOs. By silencing these highly trained individuals, the government hoped to make this rapidly growing phenomenon go by the way side. Fortunately, reports continued to come in from pilots and military personnel who bucked their superiors in an effort to bring the truth to the forefront. Likewise, all across our country and from around the world, other well respected individuals, like doctors, lawyers, politicians, clergymen, and law enforcement officers began to come forward with their reports of encounters with Unidentified Flying Objects. The phenomenon would not and has not gone away and the truth about their existence can be kept quiet only so long! People, being curious creatures do and will continue to search for the truth; we can only hope the government one-day will make a good faith effort to tell us exactly what the truth is.

TENNESSEE AND ARKANSAS

The decade was still young when the first of our very numerous reports from the 1950s was made. Our first report comes from the flight crew of a long-forgotten airline called the Chicago and Southern Airways. (I guess naming airlines like railroads just wasn't cricket!) The plane and its flight crew were flying from Memphis to Little Rock on the night of March 31st, 1950[1] when they had a close encounter with a flying saucer.

For the most part, the flight that night was quite routine. The DC-3 that Captain Jack Adams and Copilot G. W. Anderson were flying was a very user-friendly plane to fly—leaps and bounds ahead of what was being flown five to ten years previously. As they piloted their big craft through the unusually crisp and clear late winter's night sky, the unexpected happened. At precisely 9:29 PM CST, the copilot noticed the captain leaning forward in his seat, and as he was staring intently out the windshield, he could be heard to say, "What is that?"

As copilot Anderson focused his eyes in the general direction that Captain Adams was looking, he too saw a large craft as it effortlessly made its way through the night sky. They later described the object they had seen as being disc shaped and ringed with portholes emitting a bright bluish-white light. On the apex of the disc was a white light. This at first led them to believe they were witnessing another aircraft that had veered off course, putting it on an intersecting flight path with the Chicago and Southern Airways DC-3. The pilots were soon convinced that the object they were witnessing was not a plane, as it flew in front of the DC-3 and they could see no wings or tail, nor any landing lights. When asked if they were sure it was not another plane, Captain Adams quipped that he and his copilot *knew* it was no plane. The object passed so close, that if it had been another plane, they could have read the call numbers on the tail!

Another obvious case of an encounter by qualified, technically trained observers whose encounter with a UFO was shrugged off by the powers that be, in their ongoing attempt to bury the truth as to the true nature of the flying saucer phenomenon.

Author's Note:

The next two reports come from April of 1950 and are more examples of sightings made by people on-board an airplane in flight. What makes these two special, is that these two sightings were made by qualified, technically trained people; the pilots and flight crew, as well as multiple witnesses; they being the passengers on the planes. These reports have to be placed among those that are most believable, having so many factors present that successfully detract away from the possibilities of misidentifications or hallucinations.

South Bend, Indiana

The first of our two encounters happened on the night of April 27th, 1950.[2] An aircraft on route to Chicago was flying a level course at 2,000 feet just outside of South Bend, Indiana, when the plane and its crew came into contact with a bright red, disc-shaped UFO.

According to flight crew and passengers, the object was rotating on its axis as it flew past the plane, so much so that it appeared like a wheel on edge, rolling through the sky. The pilot, whose name has been lost due to the passage of time, wanted to get a better look at this object, so he turned his craft to bring it closer to the red disc. As soon as the plane drew slightly closer, the disc sped off at what the pilot estimated as close to 500 MPH. The disc slowed down once and descended to the altitude of roughly 1,500 feet. Then, almost instantaneously, the disc either sped off at the speed of light, or disappeared into thin air. (Either way, the speed of its exit is enough to prove to any thinking person, that the object sighted was no plane, meteor, or other atmospheric anomaly.)

Northern Indiana

Four days after the plane had landed in Chicago, in the same general vicinity of Northern Indiana, the crew and passengers of a DC-3 were visited aloft by a UFO that all of those who witnessed it agreed looked like a large mass of molten metal[3] flying past their unsuspecting eyes.

Flagstaff, Arizona

On May 22nd, 1950, Dr. Seymour Hess, who at the time was the head of the Meteorology Department at the Florida State University and an associate of the Lowell Observatory in Flagstaff, Arizona, had an encounter with a cigar-shaped object, which he recorded in a signed letter that he mailed off to the NICAP[4] (National Investigations Committee On Aerial Phenomena). In his letter, he states the he saw the object between

12:15 and 12:20 PM, May 20, 1950, from the grounds of the Lowell Observatory. It was quite visible to the naked eye. He then grabbed a pair of four power binoculars, and from his time viewing it, he calculated what he was seeing was a disc-shaped object, three to five feet in diameter, flying at a height of 6,000 to 12,000 feet. He also noted that the object had to be under its own propulsion as it moved against the wind.

It is safe to say that Doctor Hess is of the highest caliber of observers. His experience in meteorology and at the Lowell Observatory would have allowed him to identify some sort of plane, helicopter, or atmospheric anomaly. So the question remains, exactly what was it that Dr. Hess saw that day?

Mt. Vernon, Virginia

The night of Memorial Day, May 30th, 1950, found Willis Sperry piloting his big four-engine American Airlines DC-6 out of Washington, D.C.'s National Airport. The plane swiftly climbed into the sky and away from the D.C. area as it made its way towards its destination in Tulsa, Oklahoma.

While flying near Mt. Vernon, Virginia,[5] at approximately 9:20 PM EDT,[6] the copilot brought the captains attention to a strange sight in the sky, directly ahead of the aircraft. As they drew closer, they could tell that the object blocking their flight path was a large, dark object. At first, the captain thought he was witnessing some hotdog fighter pilot flying without his lights on, breaking most of the rules laid down by the Civilian Aviation Authority. This thought soon passed when the captain could not reconcile the fact that this object was not moving; it was hovering motionless in the night sky in front of the DC-6!

Captain Sperry, struggling to set aside his inquisitiveness, quickly turned his thoughts to that which he had always trained to do: make the safety of his passengers his paramount concern. Concerned that his speed would soon cause a mid-air collision with this unknown, hovering object, he attempted to avoid a sure collision by taking evasive action. Knowing the plane would respond to gravity faster than the engines could accelerate upward, Sperry pushed the wheel down, putting the big plane into a nose-first dive. As the plane dropped like a rock, the disc, now reflecting the moon's light, sped off, passing the plane and again hovered some several hundred yards off the DC-6's left wing. Immediately, as training dictated, Captain Sperry reported the encounter to the control tower back at the National Airport in Washington, D.C. The radar operator at National Airport reported that he had the DC-6 and an unknown object painting a return on the screen of his radar set, but the object could not be a plane as none had filed a flight plan that would have come so dangerously close to the DC-6.

As the captain was concluding his conversation with the tower, the object moved further away from the plane, pausing in front of a bank of clouds, where it was illuminated by that night's recently risen moon. The captain and copilot, both well-trained observers, described the object as resembling the conning tower of a submarine. The object began to circle the plane around the tail section and came directly into the copilots line of sight on the right side of the plane.

At that very moment, an anxious radar operator at Washington's National Airport chimed in over the airways, "Still no other traffic in the area!"

This aerial ballet played itself out when the UFO disappeared into the cloud bank it had hovered in front of shortly before the game of tag between it and the DC-6 had ensued.

Unfortunately for Captain Sperry, his reporting of a UFO that looked like the conning tower of a small submarine lead to nothing but misery for the experienced flier. He was constantly ridiculed by his peers, and soon became the butt of many jokes, proving that even qualified, well-respected observers are not immune to the ridicule of small-minded people. Thus, it is understandable why many more people do not come forward with reports of their sightings of Unidentified Flying Objects.

The good captain was somewhat vindicated in June of that year when Mrs. Paul Trent, a farmer's wife, had a picture she had taken of the same or a very similar object that was seen by Captain Perry and his copilot, published in *Life Magazine*. But, the humiliation and loss of professional standing that Captain Sperry suffered for reporting his encounter with a UFO was never to be undone.

Alamogordo, New Mexico

Our next encounter comes by way of an electronic engineer working out of Holloman Air Force Base. The base itself is located nine miles west of Alamogordo, New Mexico, and is a mere thirty miles north of the infamous White Sands Proving Grounds. This engineer, having seen several other objects in the recent past in the skies of the New Mexico desert, was convinced that there was merit to these reports of Unidentified Flying Objects,[7] even if the scientific community in general scoffed.

On a hot summer day in early July of 1950, the engineer had just finished his lunch with several co-workers, when the phone rang. On the other end of the line was an agitated field technician who was phoning to inform them that a UFO had been spotted. After getting the lowdown, the engineer and his companions went to another range sighting station, where they could track the object with a thedeolite. Having rushed the whole three miles to the next station, and thanks to the azimuth and elevation readings supplied by the technician, in no time at all they had the object in sight. Through the 25x telescope on the thedeolite, the engineer could see the side profile of a large cigar-shaped object, reflecting the sun off of its highly polished metallic surface through a yellowish-orange hue that surrounded the object.

The object had several dark-gray ports running along its fuselage. Shortly after the thedeolite had been focused on the object, it began to move about the sky in such a way as to give the viewers a good look at all four sides. The object then began to drop in fast, but controlled dives. Wanting to get a triangulation of the object, one of the engineer's coworkers with him at that moment, called a third field station to have them get a fix on the object. Before that could happen, the object disappeared.

SAWBILL BAY, ONTARIO, CANADA

For an executive and his wife, both who will remain anonymous at their request,[8] the afternoon of July 2nd, 1950, radically evolved from the familiar into the fantastic. The catalyst, as you may have guessed, was their unexpected encounter with an unidentified flying object.

Out for a relaxing day of sailing, the corporate executive and his wife, as they will be referred to as from this point onward, managed to navigate their boat into a small cove of Sawbill Bay, in Ontario, Canada. The cove was hidden from the mainland, and had many overhanging branches, just perfect for a couple looking from some quality time alone! Having pulled their boat onto the shore for a secure mooring, the couple proceeded to spread out their blanket, and settle down to a romantic picnic lunch, alone in the secluded cove. Relaxing and trying to forget about the hustle and bustle of the corporate world, the couple had eaten their full and were toasting the beauty of the day with tea brought in an extra-large thermos when the damnedest thing happened: The air around them began to vibrate! The executive described the vibration as being similar to a shock wave from an explosion. He realized that this could not be the cause of the vibration. Had it been a shock wave from an explosion, he would have heard an explosion soon after the vibrations began. With the vibrating showing no signs of stopping, the corporate executive proceeded to climb up an out-cropping of rock to have a look around and ascertain what it was causing the vibrations. Upon reaching the summit, he soon saw what it was creating the vibrations.

Not far down the coastline from the mouth of the cove where he and his wife had taken refuge in from the work-a-day world was a large silver disc hovering just above the waterline. He dashed down to tell the Mrs. what he had just seen. Once he had filled her in, they were both on their way to the top of the rock to have a long look at this alien machine. What they described seeing, was a silver disc that looked like two pie plates placed on top of each other. Around the center, placed at four-inch intervals, were small black protrusions. They estimated the disc to be about fifteen feet thick at the center, twelve feet thick at the edges, with a circumference of somewhere near forty-eight feet.

Moving about as if performing some important tasks were several small, odd-looking creatures. The couple described them as human-like automatons, because to them, they looked as if they moved like the robots that they had seen in any number of serials while at the movies. Both of them heard a humming noise coming from the craft as the little men manipulated what looked like hoses—some of which seemed to be drawing water into their ship, while others seemed to be discharging something into the water. To avoid detection by these visitors, the couple decided to take cover in the nearby bushes. One last look revealed that the men and hoses were back inside the ship and all hatches had been sealed up tighter than a drum.

The object began to slowly float away from where it had hovered. As it did, the couple noticed that the water near where the object had hovered was reddish-blue with a tinting of gold here and there. B.J. Eyeton, chief chemist for the Steep Rock Mining Company where the executive who had the encounter was employed, reports that there had been many sightings of this or a similar craft up and down the coast near the cove where they had had their lunch and subsequent sighting.

As astonishing as this report seems, it is very similar of many sightings to come throughout the world in the years to follow. We can either dismiss this report as a product of two over active imaginations. Or we can believe that a high ranking executive with a large mining company would not risk his self esteem and high paying job, by creating stories about flying discs with little robotic men. I believe it is safe to assume that these two well-to-do people had an honest to goodness close encounter with a flying disc and those beings that operated this particular vessel. And lucky, they were willing to share their experience with the rest of us. I will let you make up your own mind on this one, but citing the facts at hand, your conclusion should be reached quite easily.

KOREA

In the early morning hours of one fine September day in 1950,[9] six well-trained navy pilots took to the air from the deck of their aircraft carrier on a mission to strafe a truck convoy believed to be carrying vital supplies that Communist North Korea planned to use against the Democratic South and their allied United Nations Troops, lead by the USA. These planes required two officers: one pilot and one radar-gunner. The flight's take-off and early stages of the mission were all routine, almost boring to the action-seeking fighter crews anxious to hone their skills in the art of aerial warfare.

It was at approximately 7 AM local time when the flight was approaching the valley where the convoy was thought to be passing through. While flying in formation at 10,000 feet, all eyes were scanning the ground for the convoy and the skies for enemy aircraft. What follows is an eyewitness account by one of the pilots on this mission who wished to remain anonymous.

As he was scanning the ground for the convoy, he noticed two large circular shadows moving rapidly across the terrain below, approaching the squadron from the north at high speed. Not wanting to have the squadron caught in an ambush, the crewman diverted his eyes from the valley floor to the skies in front of the plane. Hoping to zero in on the enemy planes and take them out before any harm could come to a single plane in his formation, the officer scanned the skies until he found what it was that was causing these shadows. Much to his surprise, the objects he found were not MIG fighters. What lay in front of his eyes astounded the young officer. Using his radar and a built-in guide on the canopy of his plane, the radar-gunner estimated that the objects casting the shadows were 1½ miles ahead of his plane and 650 feet in diameter! The objects must have spotted his squadron, as they came to a dead stop and began hovering at about a mile's distance from the planes.

As the ships remained stationary, the radar-gunner began to stare at the objects to ingrain their image into his mind's eye. The objects he saw that day were of the classical disc shape, only much, much larger. They appeared to be made out a gleaming silvery metallic substance. Both craft were enveloped in a reddish hue. From ports along the mid-section of each craft came bright pastel-colored light.

It soon became evident to him that the whole squadron had seen these craft, as each crewman was pointing at the object to draw the others attention to it while maintaining radio silence. Much to the dismay of the crews, these objects became fascinated with the aircraft! As the planes approached and passed the objects, the objects soon were keeping pace with the fighter-bombers, while maintaining an equal distance from the planes as they all flew over the Korean countryside. Soon thereafter, the operators of these huge crafts' inquisitiveness must have got the better of them, as both discs began to circle the squadron as it continued on course laid out in their mission's orders.

As the strange craft literally flew rings around the squadron of fighter-bombers, this radar-gunner decided to break radio silence and radioed the carrier. Much to his dismay, he could not raise her. Soon thereafter, his radar set conked out, sending him to the verge of panic. What where these things, and what did they want? So as not to panic, the radar-gunner began to recall his training, and once more began making mental notes of these alien ships, as he was sure they were observing his craft and their actions. He noticed on their next fly by that the discs' undersides were jet black and made from some sort on non-reflective material, not at all like the sides and top of the craft. Suddenly, as if done with their inspection of these US Navy fighter-bombers, the two discs once again resumed their original course and accelerated out of sight.

Once they had returned to the aircraft carrier, each of the crewmen was interrogated individually and then together as a group. Then, they and their aircraft were tested for residual radiation. Although they never found out the Geiger Counters readings, they were later informed that the dials of their instruments were luminous and the film in each of the planes' gun cameras had been completely ruined. Although their superiors tried to convince these six young men that they had a close encounter with a natural phenomenon, what they saw can only be described as Unidentified Flying Objects.

What is upsetting to many is the fact that the people who are entrusted to protect our country are lied to and threatened to keep quiet by their superiors, whenever they have an encounter with these odd aerial devices. So I'll ask you the question that eats away at my soul, where does the lying end, or doesn't it? How can we tell who in the government to believe, when those high ranking officials are readily willing to lie to the men and women who put their lives on the line to protect our freedom whenever they see fit?

Albuquerque, New Mexico

From August of 1951 comes our next case, where a couple in their own backyard came into contact with an oddly shaped UFO that would become very familiar to UFO researchers almost four decades later. In the yard of their home on the outskirts of Albuquerque, New Mexico, an employee of the Sandra Corporation, a highly restricted subsidiary of the Atomic Energy Committee,[10] and his wife were enjoying the cool evening air in the early evening hours of August 25th, 1951, when they spotted a highly unusual object in the sky above their home. Being in such close proximity to Kirkland Air Force Base, the couple had grown accustomed to witnessing overhead flights of military planes, but never before had they seen anything like this!

They both seemed to spot the object at the same time and agreed that the object was passing overhead at approximately 1,000 feet. They described the object as being shaped like a V, or as we now refer to it as boomerang shaped. They estimated the size as 1½ times the size of a B-36 Bomber, a craft they frequently saw flying over their house. The large object frightened them by the way it moved so quickly without making any noise as it passed overhead. They noticed no portholes, landing lights, or any visible means of propulsion. They did report the object was dark in color with a single light-colored strip running along the edges. They had never seen an object like that before, and probably were never fortunate enough to witness another one again, well not one they would talk about anyway.

Some may attribute this couple's sighting to an over-flight of one of the experimental flying wings. As an experimental aircraft, it would not have been seen frequently by the general public, accounting for its strangeness to the couple. But the single and most convincing argument that this craft was not the famed Flying Wing is the fact that this wing was built with propellers first and jets on a later model. Neither could cruise at 1,000 feet in total silence, and these wings were by no means 1½ times the size of a B-36. What this couple saw is the same type, or a very similar type of craft, that was seen throughout the Hudson Valley in the 1980s and in the desert around Phoenix, Arizona in the late 1990s.

SPOKANE, WASHINGTON

January 20th, 1952 was a night that bought dismay to the intelligence officers stationed at Fairchild Air Force Base near Spokane, Washington. Early in the evening, around 7:20 PM PST,[11] two Master Sergeants, who by the way were intelligence/surveillance experts, noticed a strange oddly bright light in the sky as they walked down a street within the base's compound. As the light continued towards them, they stopped at a point where they had a clear view of the sky. The two men were shocked that this light was not a plane. Instead, what they saw was a large bluish-white sphere of light approaching their position from the east.

As they continued to watch this unidentified flying object fly towards them, the irony of the situation struck them full force. Since they were involved in military intelligence at the base, they had interviewed several pilots who had claimed to have seen an object very much like the one they were now observing. They did not take the reports seriously until that very moment—as often is the case, it takes seeing an object to make believers out of many people.

The object flew smoothly and silently, and left a bluish trail, as it made its way across the Washington countryside. Their military training soon kicked in as they began to make mental notes of how and when the object passed landmarks and geographic formations in an effort to estimate speed, elevation, and trajectory.

On the 21st, they requested and received reports on weather conditions and local air traffic flight plans. Soon thereafter, having rechecked all the available information, the sergeants came to what was for them, some astounding conclusions. Since there was no air traffic in the sky over the base at that time of the evening when they'd had their sighting, they rationalized that what they saw was no plane. The weather report told them that there was a slight breeze blowing from the west, with a cloud ceiling being at 4,700 feet. From their calculations, whatever they saw was traveling at 1,400 MPH, or more than three times faster than most planes aloft in 1952. What unnerved them the most was the fact that this object flew silently with no means of propulsions, and even though it crossed the sky at close to Mach 2, there was no sonic boom! The two men could only come to one conclusion: They had seen an unidentified flying object. And from this day on, they would not so easily dismiss the reports they received from pilots at their base.

WONSON, KOREA

Just over a week later, there was another encounter with unknown aerial phenomenon by active military personnel of the United States Air Force. On January 29th, 1952,[12] while flying their B29 at 20,000ft over the town of Wonson, Korea, the pilots were surprised to see what they at first took to be a meteorite flying towards them on a level trajectory. The closer the orange fireball approached, the quicker the crew lost faith in their original hypothesis. Meteors, due to the pull of the earth's gravity and their lack of any means of propulsion beyond inertia, cannot fly through the atmosphere perfectly level. They usually have a downward trajectory that intersects with the earth's surface. The next event totally unnerved the crew and lay to rest any theory that what they were observing was a meteor or any other type of natural phenomenon.

As the object came closer, the crew noticed that the object was actually slowing down! The object not only slowed down, but when the plane was at its closest in proximity to the object, it actually appeared to stop and hover in place! As the object hung motionless, the hue around it changed from orange to a green. As the plane passed this odd object, the crew began to feel relief, hoping that once past it, the object would continue on its original heading, which was in the opposite direction of the plane! Much to their dismay, once the color change was complete, the object, reversing its original course, began to pace the B-29. The crew watched anxiously as the object paced the plane for around five minutes, then, as if answering the crewmen's prayers, the object accelerated away, until it was lost over the horizon.

ARIZONA

Once again, had the prior case been an isolated incident, it could have been easily explained away. However, the same or a similar object was spotted later that day all across the continental United States, including encounters with a separate B-29 crew and a sighting by over 165 people in Arizona.

KIRKSVILLE, MISSOURI

In March of 1952,[13] a TWA pilot flying a C-54 cargo plane from Chicago to Kansas City made an unusual discovery while going about the business of flying his big plane. Flying above a solid overcast, at about 2:30 PM CST, the pilot, while speaking to a control tower in Kirksville, Missouri, happened to glance out the cockpit window at the number two engine, which had been losing oil pressure. Much to his surprise, off in the distance was a silver, metallic disc. The object remained in place, flying in tandem with the aircraft, though some several thousand feet away, for over five minutes.

The captain decided to take a closer look, and turned his plane in such a manner so as to close in on this unknown object. The copilot mentioned to the pilot that this could be a weather balloon. Not wanting to appear foolish chasing something so ordinary, they returned to their original heading and continued on course to Kansas City. The captain began to believe that the object might just be a balloon that was appearing to follow the plane as the copilot suggested, when he discovered that the object was still following the plane, making the captain once again wonder what it truly was.

To put the question to rest once and for all, the pilot decided to make a 360-degree turn. Knowing that if the object truly was a balloon, it would stay put, making it disappear for part of the turn, and appear over the right wing when the turn was half-complete and back over the left wing when the turn was completed. The pilot began a tight turn to the right, and although at first the object dropped off the left wing, whatever it was it accelerated just enough to remain visible off the left wing for the entire turn. This was no balloon, as any object that could stay off the wing of a C-54 at several thousand feet distance had to be a mighty quick object.

The pilot was now determined to get a better look at the object, so he took the plane into a sharp turning climb, and dove down directly at the object. Using gravity to assist the four engines that he had increased to full power, the plane closed in on the object, and the disc dipped down into the overcast and out of sight. As the plane was about to enter the clouds, the pilots saw the disc shoot straight up and out of sight.

When the plane leveled off, the pilots discussed what they had seen, until once again the light came on for the number two engine. They then knew that they had to get to Kansas City as soon as possible.

What they had seen was never reported to the CAA. In fact, a United Airlines pilot who had talked with the pilot of the C-54 shortly after their encounter gave the report to Edward Ruppelt, the ex-chief of the Air Force Project investigating flying saucers. Exactly what these pilots saw will never be known thanks to the government's policy of silencing witnesses, especially military personnel and airline pilots.

So we shall call it what it truly was, a UFO.

JAPAN

While flying his propeller-driven reconnaissance plane at 6,000 feet over occupied Japan on a regular patrol that 29th of March 1952, Lieutenant David Brigham was surprised to see an F-4 Thunderjet fly along side his plane. Suddenly, a small silvery-metallic object about eight inches in diameter pulled up alongside the F-4. According to Lieutenant Brigham in the report he filed, the small object began to pace the jet about twenty feet above the jet's fuselage. The object then jumped over to the right wing of the jet, appearing to flip over once as it passed through the slipstream created by the oval-shaped fuel tank on the end of the wing.[14] After the jet passed by, the object streaked off.

Lt. Brigham estimated that the object was in view for approximately ten seconds. Once back at base, Lieutenant Brigham was debriefed and gave a fully detailed account to his superiors. This account was released to the wire services and made its way around the world in short order. Soon, the world had heard of this pilot and his sighting, yet the government made no formal effort to investigate what he had seen. Nor did they try to explain to the people of the United States and the world exactly what was flying rings around military aircraft anywhere and anytime they wanted.

UTAH

At approximately 11 AM on July 2, 1952,[15] Warrant Officer Delbert C. Newhouse, his wife and two children, while driving to their vacation destination, spotted a strange object in the summer sky. They were enjoying the ride that morning through the Utah countryside until they were about six miles outside Tremonton. That is when Mrs. Newhouse spotted something strange in the sky. The object appeared so out of place with what she was used to seeing in the sky, that she asked her husband to pull over to the side of the road. Once the car had stopped, Mrs. Newhouse got out of the car for a better look. Joining his wife, Warrant Officer Newhouse was surprised to see ten to twelve objects flying in a "rough" formation. What amazed him the most, being an aerial photographer who graduated from Naval Photographic School and having logged more than 3,000 hours of flight time, was that he did not recognize the objects streaking across the Utah countryside.

Remembering he had brought his camera on vacation with him, he proceeded to pull his Bell and Howe Auto-master 16mm motion picture camera he used at work out of his luggage and load into it Kodak Kodachrome Daylight film. He immediately exposed thirty feet of film, following the objects as they flew by. As he filmed the objects, he wished that they would fly by or behind a known geographic landmark so he could estimate size, speed, and possibly elevation. Unfortunately, the objects remained on a straight heading, flying through the bright blue sky without changing elevation or heading. Suddenly, one of the objects reversed course and began to fly back in the direction from where it came. W.O. Newhouse decided to film this object, but it accelerated out of view over the horizon. When he searched the sky to draw a bead on the main squadron, he found they too had flown off into UFO history.

Upon examination of the film at Wright Patterson Air Force Base, the images on the film could not be identified. The government could not just explain this sighting away as not only had a trained observer saw something unusual, he also shot film of it! After intense scrutiny, the experts at Wright Patterson could only give a definite answer as to what was not on the film. They safely concluded that the objects were not natural phenomenon, birds, planes, nor weather balloons. And since the film was taken in broad daylight, no one could claim that this warrant officer chased Venus with his movie camera. What is on that film remains a mystery to this day, as no explanation has ever been given. File this one away in the annuals of history as an unknown!

AUTHOR NOTE:

As you have probably discovered, there are many variations on theme where UFO phenomenon is concerned. Sometimes the craft are tremendously fast, while others are incredible slow. Some objects are huge, while others are tiny. The same holds true for how the objects are viewed. One or a few people see some UFOs, while whole communities see others. Some objects are seen up close and personal, while others are spotted flying many miles above.

INDIANAPOLIS, INDIANA

The following report is one where literally thousands of unsuspecting people became observers and believers in the UFO phenomenon. On July 13th, 1952,[16] local radar in Indiana picked up an unidentified flying object on their scopes as it flew over the countryside on a level trajectory at about 5,000 feet, at an unusually high speed, and from the information, it appeared that the object was on a heading that would take it directly over downtown Indianapolis.

Shortly thereafter, remaining on a steady course and speed, the object made its way over the state's largest city. Moments after radar had shown the object to have passed the city, police, sheriff, newspaper, radio, and airport switchboards began lighting up with people trying to find out what the hell they just saw fly overhead. The radar showed that the object was flying too fast to be a plane. There weren't any flight plans filed by civilian or commercial flights on that heading at that time that day. The local officials had no answers for the thousands of people who called their offices, all wanting to know one thing: What flew over Indianapolis that summer day? They did not know then, and we probably will never have the answer to that mystery.

NORFOLK, VIRGINIA

This flap reached its pinnacle the next day, July 14th, 1952.[17] That night found 1st Officer William Nash and 2nd Officer W.H. Fortenberry scheduled to take their fully loaded Pan American Airlines DC-4 on a flight from New York City to San Juan, Puerto Rico. It was a very long, but routine flight for the pilots who had logged thousands of hours in the air in their combined twenty years experience. The plane was airborne and soon reached cruising altitude.

As their big DC-4 neared Langley Air Force Base near Norfolk, Virginia, at around 9:15 PM EST, both pilots attention was simultaneously drawn to a large glowing object, crimson in color, as it made its way on through the night skies over Virginia. The object was dead ahead, but about 1,000 feet below the DC-4 by the pilot's estimate. The closer they got, the more it became obvious that what they were witnessing was six large disc-shaped objects flying in tight formation. Each appeared to be about 100 feet in diameter and 15 feet thick. The pilots calculated by the way the objects were closing, that the UFOs were flying at close to 12,000 MPH.

As the discs sped toward the DC-4, the lead object, having as the pilots termed, "noticed" the airliner, slowed down to take a look. Likewise, all the craft slowed down considerably, perhaps to get a better view of the pilots, their crew, and the passengers onboard the airliner. Satisfied with their examination of the DC-4, the objects "flipped up onto their edges, and in a V-formation accelerated up to their original high speed and continued on their original heading. Then, the pilots noticed two more discs flying below their plane. They linked up with the six original discs, and joining their formation, sped out of sight over the horizon.

At their next scheduled stop, Miami, Florida, the two pilots made a report of what they had seen and were forced to wait out an interview with officers from the Air Forces Office of Special Investigation. Once they had informed the Air Force of what they had seen, the USAF officers began a futile attempt to explain away the sightings that night while flying to their rendezvous with destiny.

SIERRA NEVADA MOUNTAINS

The July flap did not end with the Nash-Fortenberry sighting. Our next sighting occurred almost a fortnight after their sighting. July 24th, 1952, was a perfect day for flying: The sky was clear as a bell and the atmosphere was quite tranquil. Truly the type of day pilots and everyone wish all could be like. On this perfect day, two United States Air Force Colonels were enjoying their flight from Hamilton Air Force Base near San Francisco, California, as they were heading east towards Colorado Springs, Colorado. As they crossed the Sierra Nevada Mountains somewhere between Sacramento, California and Reno, Nevada, these two experienced Air Force Officers could have had no inkling as to what was about to happen.

They were flying eastward on what was known as "Green 3,"[18] an aerial highway linking California and Salt Lake City, Utah. At around 3:40 PM PST, one of the colonels spotted what he first thought was a squadron of planes flying towards them at the 10 o'clock position. At first these two colonels (whose names were withheld at their request in the original report) thought that because of the size and speed of the craft, they were observing a three-plane squadron of F-86s flying in V-formation. This belief was shattered when these three objects accelerated and rapidly closed the distance between them and the colonels' plane. The objects were now close enough to be identified for what they really were: Unidentified Flying Objects.

The colonels instantly knew these three objects were not F-86s. They were triangular-shaped craft, silver in color, with no tails or visible cockpit windows. They noticed no means of propulsion, yet they traveled at what the colonels estimated at six times the top speed of the F-86. The objects were gone as fast as they had arrived, and the colonels honestly believed that they had witnessed craft built by an intelligence alien to ours.

Upon touchdown in Colorado Springs, the two colonels, wanted to report the objects they had seen intruding over American airspace to the proper authorities. So they contacted Air Defense Command Headquarters. As it turns out, this was not the best thing they could have done! As soon as the colonels described the objects as being triangular and excessively speedy, the desk jockeys back at headquarters informed these two full-bird colonels that they had seen three F-86s! The officers rebutted that they could easily have identified any aircraft in the United States arsenal. What they saw were not F-86s.

Those at headquarters, however, decided they did not want to deal with this sighting, so they referred the sightings and the colonels over to the Air Forces' special investigating body that concentrated on investigating UFOs, Project Blue Book. Once the information was transferred to them, Blue Book personnel began to check with Flight Services, a series of airports linked together to track flights, to see if any F-86s had flown anyplace near the flight path of the colonels. Flight Services confirmed that the closest silver F-86s were thousands of miles away. Next they checked with all local airports and meteorological stations to see if anyone had launched weather balloons near the time of the colonels sighting. They were informed that no balloons were aloft at that time. When they had exhausted their avenues of investigation and ended with naught, they filed this encounter under "Unidentified." Notice if you will, that the people at the Colonels HQ and those at Blue Book tried to prove that the objects were everyday objects seen under odd circumstances, which is a legitimate way to investigate. What they did not do is investigate what the objects were once they could not assign any rational explanation to them.

Why investigate when you have no plans to solve a mystery? You will see, this is a common practice by the government when they cannot prove that what they believed to be, actually was something entirely different.

EASTERN ATLANTIC OCEAN, NORTH OF BORNHOLM ISLAND

In September of 1952, the North Atlantic Treaty Organization was holding a training exercise in the Eastern Atlantic Ocean, off the coast of Denmark and Norway. The operation was code-named "Operation Mainbrace."[19] Six member nations and New Zealand participated in the operation that began on September 13th and concluded twelve days later on the 25th. Eighty thousand men, 1,000 planes and 200 ships carried out maneuvers in a show of force, solidarity, and cooperation to drill home the point to the Soviet Union that the Free World would remain free. A demonstration of force such as this is expected to get the attention of many spectators. Unfortunately, some of the spectators who witnessed this event remain unknown to this day.

The night of September 13th, 1952, found the Danish destroyer *Willemoes* sailing north of Bornholm Island, just where she was scheduled to be for that evenings exercises. During that night, Lieutenant Commander Schmidt Jensen and several other crewman saw a triangular-shaped object, emitting a strange bluish glow as it flew across the sky at a high rate of speed. Counting the time it took to go from being directly over their heads to disappearing behind the southeast horizon, Lieutenant Commander Jensen was able to calculate the speed of the object as being close to 900 MPH or more! Not knowing if this was part of the maneuvers or not, as you never know what those ingenious Yanks might have come up with, Jensen did not sound the alarm and did not report anything unusual until after the exercise had concluded.

YORKSHIRE, ENGLAND

At 11:00 AM GMT on the morning of September 19th, 1952, a British Meteor fighter jet, having finished its role in that day's exercise, was on final approach to land at Topcliffe Airfield in Yorkshire, England. On the ground watching the jets approach were Lieutenant John W. Kilburn and several others English airmen. When the jet began to bear down on the airport, those watching its approach noticed what appeared to be a silvery disc-shaped object that seemed to be following the plane as it attempted to land. When the jet began to fly its holding pattern, which was a giant circle around the airfield, the object was seen to hover quietly over the field, spinning on its axis as it hung very still in the sky. Those on the ground, wanting a better view of the object, began to make their way toward the area where the disc hovered. As they made their way closer, Lieutenant Kilburn and the others watched in disbelief as the disc went from a standstill to what was estimated at over 1,000 MPH in an instant. The object made a quick in-flight course correction and disappeared over the distant horizon.

USS Franklin D Roosevelt

The following day, September 20th, 1952, the personnel onboard the USS *Franklin D Roosevelt*, an American aircraft carrier participating in the military exercises, witnessed a silvery disc as it flew over the big ship. As luck would have it, this day a person armed with a camera was present when the object was sighted. A reporter by the name of Wallace Litwin snapped a photo depicting a silver disc, that had been seen by many of the men onboard the American warship. The photo was developed and studied by the experts on hand, and when they could not decide what the object was, the photo and story was sent on to the quasi-experts at Project Blue Book. Like those who studied the photo before them, the folks at Project Blue Book had no idea what the picture depicted, so off the story and photo went into Project Blue Book's file of unidentified cases, never to be fully investigated nor have any conclusions.

North Sea

The very next day, six British pilots were flying in tight formation above the North Sea, as they made their way back to the main fleet. The pilots witnessed the passage of a shiny sphere of unknown origin as it rocketed past their squadron. They turned to give chase, but the UFO easily out-distanced them and was lost over the horizon. The planes abandoned the chase, and returned to their previous heading to take them back to their base of operations. As they closed in on their destination, one of the pilots caught sight of the UFO as it tailed the squadron at a safe distance. Without warning, the pilot broke formation, and pushing the plane well beyond the safe limit, once again gave chase to the unknown object. As was the result the first time around, the British jet was left far behind this obviously superior craft.

This was not the last time the object would make an appearance. Several days after the exercises concluded, sightings of this or a similar craft spread across Europe like a wildfire. The most reported sightings came from an area encompassing southern Denmark, western sections of the old West Germany and Southern Sweden. The outbreak of so intense a number of sightings brought experts from the United States Air Force's Project Blue Book, US Naval and Air Force Intelligence, the British Air Ministry and many experts from other member NATO countries together to try to make sense out of what was going on, by trying to identify what was being seen throughout North Central Europe. Needless to say, every report mentioned above from September of 1952 remains unsolved, and the crafts that were witnessed remain unidentified.

Gulf of Mexico

As 1952 began to wind down, the number of UFO reports remained consistently high. Our last sighting from that year reportedly took place on December 6th, 1952.[20]

Lieutenant Coleman was a radar officer onboard a B-29 that was flying three miles above the Gulf of Mexico at 5:25 AM CST that cold winter's morning. There was a full moon illuminating the still-dark, early-morning sky, as the big bomber roared back to base.

When the plane was about 100 miles off the Louisiana coast, Lieutenant Coleman noticed a blip appear on his radarscope. When the radar had made its next sweep the blip had moved a great distance through the air, and on his set. Feeling the scope was giving false readings, he made a quick check of the instrument, and it appeared to be functioning properly. Again the blip had moved a great distance in just the space of time it took for the radar to make one full sweep. Given the distance covered in the time since it first appeared, Lieutenant Coleman was staggered when a quick computation showed that the object was moving in excess of 5,000 MPH, or almost seven times the speed of sound! Then, Lieutenant Coleman spotted four more objects on his screen. This time he was not alone, as the other two radar sets in operation on the plane were now watching the same super-fast objects as they hurtled through the dank gulf air. The objects passed the plane so fast that the only thing the crewmen knew for certain was that they were of a strange bluish color. They could not say what shape the objects were or any other details.

Soon after the first UFOs had sped by, another squadron of blips appeared on the radar sets. They also roared by at fantastic speed. Before they had time to wonder what was to happen next, a third wave of unknown craft appeared on their radarscopes, except this time, the UFOs were on a collision course with the bomber! The plane was lumbering along, in comparison to the speed of the UFOs, thus it did not stand a chance of getting out of the unknown crafts' way. Suddenly, the five UFOs slowed to the bombers pace and followed behind it for a short time. The objects then split up, and once around the B-29, regrouped and continued on their original course.

As if they had not had a strange enough quarter hour, the radar-men all witnessed the appearance of one incredibly large half-inch wide blip on their radar screens. The five much smaller blips merged with the huge blip, and then they all departed the area at what was calculated to be 9,000 MPH or Mach 12!

The crew had a routine conclusion to the rest of their flight. Air Technical Intelligence Center was very interested in the crew's story, as they were unaccustomed to having flight crews report witnessing aircraft carrier size objects moving at 9,000 MPH! Needless to say, A.T.I.C.'s conclusion came back as: Origin – Unknown.

DETROIT, MICHIGAN

Our next account comes by the way of an interview conducted by a well-known author and paranormal researcher Brad Steiger. The man involved, one Lieutenant Colonel Howard Strand,[21] recounted the events that unfolded on a bright morning in March of

1953. Lieutenant Colonel Strand was piloting his F-94B on a routine practice session high in the sky above the outskirts of Detroit, Michigan. To test Air Force readiness and response time, somewhere on this particular patrol, he was supposed to encounter some Navy aircraft, whose goal was to successfully penetrate Detroit airspace.

Strand recalls that about thirty minutes into the flight, the local control tower began tracking an unknown blip on their radar. They relayed the information and coordinates to the Colonel who, figuring that these were the Navy's planes, set an intercept course and accelerated to attack speed. Shortly thereafter, Lieutenant Colonel Strand spotted a formation at his eight o'clock position, flying directly over downtown Detroit. Instantly, he made his move. Dropping the nose of his plane down, to benefit from the pull of gravity, he began a power dive down toward the formation below. As he increased speed and decreased the distance to the bogeys, something struck the colonel as being not quite right. Speaking to the radar man seated under the canopy behind him, Strand asked for a radar fix. And although the tower had the objects on their screens, the planes radar set picked up nothing. Colonel Strand became increasingly uneasy; the nearer he drew, he still could not identify the craft in front of him. Suddenly, it hit him: these objects had no wings! As he looked closer, they had no tails and no engines either! Just then his radar-man informed him that objects were painting a strong target, which incidentally would allow the weapons to be locked on target.

Taking his eyes off the objects for just a moment, Strand looked over his shoulder to ask if the objects were locked on by targeting-radar. Negative, was the response. When he turned back around just a second later, the objects were gone. Surprise soon turned to downright bewilderment. How could objects just disappear? Strand contacted the ground radar to inquire if they still had the blips on their screens. They had them in front of the plane and increasing their speed. The colonel searched the skies in front of him and saw nothing. Acting on a hunch, Strand began to search the skies at higher altitudes, just in case the vanishing act pulled by these craft was in fact a sudden change of altitude. He saw nothing. The objects remained on the radar screen but invisible to this well-trained pilot's experienced eyes. Although what he saw that day has never been identified, Lieutenant Colonel Strand knows one thing for absolute certainty: The objects he saw that day, though unidentified, were real!

His conclusion is sound as only solid objects return strong blips on radar, which eliminates hallucinations, hysteria, and swamp gas. Likewise, the objects seen could not have been any types of meteor or conventional craft. A meteor would only disappear had it crashed into the ground, leaving quite an impression and causing a lot of noise and destruction, especially one that impacted near Detroit, Michigan. Conventional craft would not become invisible while remaining on a radar screen, and even today, solid objects not in a magician's handbag, cannot just disappear!

BLACK HAWK AND RAPID CITY, SOUTH DAKOTA

The next account I have labeled as one of the best reports of an unidentified flying object ever recorded. I labeled it as such due to the fact that multiple witnesses at different locations, two different types of radar, and two experienced pilots in different locations, all within a short period of time, saw the same object. The sighting began soon after nightfall on August 13th, 1953.[22] Since all involved sought anonymity, their names were not included in the original account. Nonetheless, a spotter for the Ground Observer Corps called in to her local reporting center, to inform them that while on watch, she had just observed a large bluish light hugging the local terrain, flying low in the sky near the Northeast horizon. The reporting center immediately contacted the tower at Ellsworth Air Force base in Rapid City, to inform them of what one of their observers had seen just ten miles to the west near Black Hawk, South Dakota.

The base's radar was repositioned to allow it to scan the area where the Ground Corps Observer claimed to have seen an unknown object. Much to their surprise, the radar operator found the object painting a strong return right where the observer told them it would be. Having studied the return for several minutes, to be sure it was not some anomaly or atmospheric phenomenon, the Warrant Officer on duty that evening decided to see if the object could be located by the height-finding radar. It could and it was determined that the object was now at 16,000 feet.

The Warrant Officer phoned the Reporting Center to be put through to the observer in Black Hawk to see if what they saw coincided with what she was seeing. She confirmed that it was. Satisfied that the object was real and solid, the Warrant Officer decided the object deserved looking into. Before he could take any action, the observer screamed into the phone that the object was moving in a southwestern direction, towards Rapid City, South Dakota. The Warrant Officer ordered two of his men outside to watch the skies.

Shortly thereafter, one shouted into the tower that a bluish white light had just come into view overhead, on a course that would indeed take it into Rapid City. That was enough for the Warrant Officer. As fate would have it, Ellsworth had a plane in the air on a routine patrol mission. The plane was currently flying a holding pattern, and quickly, the Warrant Officer, with vector and locations in hand, radioed the flyer and requested he go and intercept this unknown interloper. The jet was vectored south, which would take it over the base and on an intercept course with the unknown light.

Once the pilot had the object in sight he gave chase. Pushing the F-84's jets to the limits, the pilot began closing on the object. When the plane had closed to within three miles, the object performed a sudden and impressive burst of speed witnessed by the pilot, the radar, air force men at Ellsworth, and the ground observer in Black Hawk.

There could be no question about it; they all were witnessing the same unidentified flying object.

The F-84 gave chase, and when it had once again closed within three miles, the UFO accelerated off again. Thus began the game of cat and mouse. These actions began to worry the pilot, as nothing could run away from an F-84 with such tremendous speed. What would happen if it began to chase the plane! He knew he could neither out run nor out maneuver this object, and was quite relieved when his jet began running low on fuel. Thus, so as not to crash, he had to return to base. The plane disappeared from radar briefly, and when it returned, the Warrant Officer noticed that about ten to fifteen miles behind the plane, the UFO was following it as it made its way back to base. The pilot claimed afterward that when he found out that he was being followed by the large, speedy, and very maneuverable object over the desolate Black Hills, it was more than enough to unsettle his nerves.

As the F-84 neared the base, an intercept jet was waiting on the tarmac to initiate a new mission. Once the second pilot got the okay from the tower, it was in the air in pursuit of the unknown craft. Once again, the craft would not allow the jet to close within three miles. The second pilot, like the first, could not believe how easily the object could out-distance the interceptor. Unfamiliar with all the confirming the Warrant Officer had done, pilot #2 thought the object might be a reflection on the canopy from one of the multitude of lights on and in his aircraft. He switched off all lights inside and out, and the object remained right where it had been. Not convinced yet, the pilot, wanting to prove that the object was not solid, decided to switch on his targeting radar. Expecting a blank screen, the pilot was quite disconcerted when the object showed up on his targeting radar, meaning whatever it was, it was solid!

For the first time in a long while this experienced pilot was scared. He had fought the best planes the Third Reich could produce over Europe and the best MIGs the Russian could supply to the North Koreans, but never had he come across anything like he was seeing that night. The targeting radar struggled to get a lock on the speedy, agile object. Once it locked on the object, the bluish light accelerated even faster than before, and disappeared over the horizon as mysteriously as it had appeared in the skies over South Dakota that night almost six decades ago. Here, for the first time, a UFO was spotted and confirmed through triangulation by highly trained and experience observers, preventing anyone from the Air Force or Project Bluebook form explaining this away as a sighting of a common object seen under unusual circumstances. As you might suspect, this sighting has never been explained.

SAN RAFAEL VALLEY, CALIFORNIA

Another sighting made by a member of the Ground Observation Corps happened just over two weeks after our last report. On the humid summer night of August 28th, 1953,[23] a member of the Ground Observation Corp was scanning the skies above the San Rafael Valley in California for any enemy aircraft that might have slipped through the radar scans of surrounding air bases. The observer, a member of the Corps since World War II, was having quite an uneventful night, as clouds where the only intruders blocking out the stars that evening. The bliss and serenity of that August night was shattered when the observer noticed a squadron of fourteen objects breaking through a bank of clouds. As any good spotter would, he raised his field glasses to get a better look, and as he did, thinking to himself, how strange it was that he did not *hear* the approaching planes. He followed the fourteen objects as they made their way across the sky on a western trajectory. As he watched them, he soon realized that these objects were unlike any planes he had ever seen!

The objects were cigar shaped, without wings, tails or any visible means of propulsion. The lead object soon made a sharp turn, and almost instantly, the other thirteen-followed in unison. Their new course lead them back into a cloud bank, and out of the observer's sight, never to be seen by him again. As a trained observer, familiar with aircraft from around the world, who was quite use to looking up into the night sky, I rest assured that what this man saw on that fateful night in August of 1953 were truly objects not manufactured or flown by any nation on earth!

NEAR PHILADELPHIA, PENNSYLVANIA

October 19th, 1953 found its way into the annals of UFO history due to the excellent encounter by an American Airlines DC-6's crew and passengers and some craft from another place or time.

At approximately ten past midnight in the wee morning hours of October 19th, 1953,[24] Captain J.L. Kidd was piloting his DC-6 at 8,000 feet, just fifteen minutes out of Philadelphia bound for National Airport in Washington DC. It was a beautiful night. The bright moonlight illuminated the scattered overcast. So clear was it, off to their right, the crew and passengers could see the glow of the lights of Baltimore some thirty miles distant as they flew over the Conowingo Dam, which was busy holding in check the Susquehanna River.

Glancing over at his copilot, Captain Kidd noticed he was staring at something ahead of the aircraft. What he saw baffled him. Out in front of the plane, flew a disc-shaped object. It was reflecting the bright moonlight as it made its way across the night sky, passing in and out of the scattered clouds. The captain wanted to get a better look at the object that was now hovering, so he decreased airspeed. When the object did not move he yelled to the copilot to flash the intensely bright landing lights at the object in case it did not see the approaching aircraft. As soon as the bright light had hit the hovering disc, the unexplainable happened! The disc returned "fire" by shining an even more intense light into the cockpit of the DC-6!

Bewilderment soon changed to terror as the captain was snapped back to reality because the disc had changed its position and was heading towards the DC-6 and closing fast. Captain Kidd knew he had to get the passengers and crew out of harms' way, so, as we have seen many times before, he put the plane into a gravity-assisted nosedive. Those not buckled into their seat, as was the case with many of the passengers, were sent flying. They dropped 3,000 feet before the pilots could get the big plane back under control. The disc was seen to pass too close for comfort over the top of the DC-6 soon after the dive began.

When the situation was well under control, Captain Kidd radioed air traffic control to explain what had just transpired and see if there was any other known traffic in the air that could have been responsible for almost causing a mid-air crash. The tower answered in the negative. Luckily for the passengers and crew, the rest of the flight was uneventful.

Upon arrival at Washington DC, the crew first saw to the passengers injured in the flight by making sure first-aid workers were on scene or on their way. Immediately thereafter, the crew reported their near miss with the CAA. The debunkers steered clear of this case. So as not to put it in the public spotlight, the CAA promised to investigate the cause of this incident and fill the pilots in with what they found. They also managed to keep the sighting out of the headlines, as it would be counter-productive to their ministry of misinformation to debunk so dangerous an encounter. They would find it hard to laugh off the account of the highly skilled pilots, and even harder to explain to the public how so many people were injured in a flight, and no one knew what had caused all the injuries.

This was truly a chilling encounter between the DC-6 and a UFO. Had the two collided, or the pilots not been able to regain control of the DC-6, many people would have been killed, and the list started by Captain Thomas Mantel, of humans who have died after coming into contact with a UFO, would have increased in size exponentially. Needless to say, the pilots were never informed as to what they had seen, nor has the government ever come up with an answer as to what it was these two pilots almost flew their DC-6 into that night in 1953.

Soo Locks, Michigan

Slightly more than a month later, on November 23rd, 1953,[25] the Air Defense Command radar at Kinross Air Force Base locked on to an object out over Lake Superior, just to the west of the base's location near Soo Locks, Michigan. The base commander ordered an F-89C jet interceptor into the air for a closer look.

As soon as the radar station had the jet on its scope, they gave the pilot a heading that would bring him into direct contact with the unidentified blip. The light remained on the radarscope, and as the jet closed in, no one could have guessed what was to come. As the jet drew nearer, the two blips on the radar screen merged and then disappeared as if the jet had crashed into the unknown object and nothing but wreckage had plummeted into the frigid waters of Lake Superior. The radar operators thought that their sets were malfunctioning. But after re-calibrating the sets, they still had no images being painted on their screens. Several long minutes passed after the base lost radio contact with the fighter. It was never regained. The pilot never returned. When the story of what had transpired began to circulate around the surrounding community, the official answer given was that the unknown blip was a Canadian C-47 that had strayed off course, and had returned to base safely.

This is yet another made-up answer, as the Canadian Air Ministry had no record of any of its C-47 flying anywhere near there on the night in question. As for the pilot of the interceptor, no mention was made. Only the United States Air Force and the operators of the mysterious blip know what actually happened to that brave flyer 160 miles out and 8,000 feet above the largest of the Great Lakes, that autumn night.

Northern Japan

To close out this chapter and the calendar year of 1953, we have a sighting made by military pilots in the air over occupied Japan. In December of 1953, Colonel D.M. Blakeslee was flying an F-84 Thunderjet over northern Japan. Ahead of his position he spied a cluster of glowing objects[26] as they appeared to travel in a spiral motion along the far horizon. Colonel Blakeslee gave chase, but soon realized that there was no way he could catch these high-speed discs. So he returned to base, where he reported to his superiors his encounter with a disc-shaped craft that was surrounded by smaller discs revolving around it as the whole cluster flew at a high rate of speed away from his fighter.

The brass at his base had tried to laugh off this encounter as hallucination brought on by fatigue. But the fact of the matter is, Lieutenant Brigham had an encounter with the same, or a similar, object the previous year over Japan. It is highly unlikely that two different pilots had the same hallucination nearly a year apart! So the conclusion can be made that either both had seen an unknown object as it made its way across the skies of Japan, or this particular area is plagued by free floating, apparitions capable of speeding away from a powerful jet interceptor.

Chapter 6

The Rest of the 1950s
Baseball, Hotdogs, Apple Pie, and UFOs

"Reliable reports indicate there are objects coming into our atmosphere at very high speeds and controlled by thinking intelligences."

~Rear Admiral Delmar Fahrney
Former US Navy Missile Chief

The Police Action in Korea had come to an end, but the UFO sightings continued to pour in, so let's get right to them!

Near Long Beach, California

We will begin the sightings from 1954 with yet another encounter between a UFO and an airliner in flight. While piloting United Airlines Flight #193, Captain J.M. Schidel had no idea that April 14th, 1954[1] would remain one of the most memorable days of his life.

At approximately ten minutes to midnight, the DC-6 that Captain Schidel was piloting was hugging the California Coast near Long Beach. Suddenly, from out of nowhere, a large, dark object with an intense red light was hurtling towards his plane at break-neck speed. His description was vague due to the speed of the approaching craft and the immediate action the captain had to take. The object was on what appeared to be on a collision course. So Captain Schidel put the plane into a sudden, steep turning climb. The object passed by unharmed just below the plane's fuselage.

Those onboard did not fair that well. The turn was so sharp and sudden that many people received bumps and bruising from colliding with the seats and arm rests. One stewardess was sent crashing into the galley, shattering her ankle in the process, and one passenger, C. Barber of North Hollywood, California, was thrown down the aisle, breaking a leg in the process.[2] The official report as filed with the Civil Aeronautics Board states the plane had a near mid-air collision with an unknown craft. As usual, the powers that be did not investigate this case to find out what was streaking through the air nearly killing a planeload of the same American citizens they were suppose to protect.

Washington, D. C.

Shortly before noon on May 13th, 1954,[3] two electronics experts who wished to remain anonymous, were testing a radar set. No sooner had they finished their tests, when they noticed that the set was tracking an unusually high and fast object as it passed uncomfortably close to our nation's capitol. If the scope was right, this object was not only high and fast, but also tremendous in size! Both agreed that there must be a kink in this set that they had not worked out. So they switched on another set. Much to their surprise the object now registered on two sets simultaneously! This convinced them that something was actually flying overhead. Now what should they do next?

Through some quick computations, they discovered the object, which they estimated to be 250 feet wide, was about 15 miles above Washington, D.C. As they watched the returns it painted, they saw that it was flying a huge rectangle over the city. They decided that others needed to see this, so they alerted other radar installations to the crafts elevation and position, and sure enough, they spotted it also. With several radar stations tracking the object, there could be no doubt that it was actually up there. The only question was, what was it?

After almost three hours of flying, this strange pattern in the skies above D.C., the object began to move away from the city on a westerly heading, then with a burst of speed, accelerated off the screens of all the radar stations tracking it. Little did the radar operators know that while they watched this odd aerial geometric ballet unfold, other people were watching it with them. At the same time they were tracking this object on their radar sets, a military transport flight crew witnessed a glowing orb high in the sky over downtown Washington, D.C. Likewise, two police officers on duty at Washington's National Airport also witnessed a glowing orb as it flew its odd course over the capitol from 12:45 PM till sometime past 2 PM.

No explanation was offered to those who saw it, as the government felt no need to investigate the sighting of an unknown craft as it hovered over our center of government for close to three hours. This sighting is one of the few where radar tracked an object that was also seen by independent observers in the air and on the ground. These factors place this unknown sighting in a class all by itself.

Dallas-Fort Worth, Texas

Four days later, the lead story in the *Dallas Times-Herald*[4] for May 17th, 1954, was centered around four jet pilots who played a game of aerial tags with several UFOs. Marine Corps Reserve pilot Major Charles Scarborough was in command of a group of SF-97 jets. While going about their routine flight, the small squadron of jets was suddenly surrounded by sixteen silvery, disc-shaped objects. The terrified pilots try to stay calm and on course as these unknown and unwanted visitors began to play ring around the jets, flying through the skies at several hundred miles per hour. The UFOs flew in a circle around the jets while maintaining forward momentum—which is quite an impressive performance to say the least. After several minutes of this terror-go-round, all at once, the sixteen craft, seemingly unimpressed with the best aerial machines earth could put forth, disappeared as quickly as they had arrived.

The relieved pilots returned to base and reported what they had seen. Once more the critics kept silent, hoping that American's short attention span would drive this incident from the collective conscience. No debunker could successfully argue that four United States Marines pilots, flying very expensive planes, over highly populated areas, would all become temporarily insane. Had they tried, it would have been the skeptics who would have been ridiculed into silence.

Seven Island, Quebec, Canada

Having been airborne for only thirty minutes in the first leg of a trip that would take flight #510-196, a big Boeing Strato-Cruiser belonging to the British Overseas Airways Corporation,[5] from New York City to London, England, Captain James Howard was ordered into a holding pattern above Rhode Island by Boston flight control. After twelve minutes of circling, Captain Howard asked for permission to proceed on his way. He was given the okay to go ahead, providing he avoided flying near Boston, by detouring over Cape Cod. Once they were well past Boston, he returned to his original course, which would take the plane up the coast of Nova Scotia towards Greenland and then out over the Atlantic Ocean.

Sometime later, the plane was flying over the St. Lawrence River near Seven Island, Quebec, Canada at close to 19,000 feet. The captain was noticing some broken clouds below the plane, when an odd sight caught his eye. Below the broken clouds, at about the 8,000-foot level, Captain Howard saw several objects flying a parallel course and speed. The objects became more readily visible as both they and the plane crossed into Labrador, as the concealing clouds had scattered. The objects had climbed to almost the same altitude as the plane was flying, keeping the same speed as the plane as they ascended.

The flight crew and those passengers who were not asleep were all witness to these odd objects pacing their plane. Captain Howard describes what he saw as one large dark gray object that appeared to be pulsating or changing shape. Six smaller globe-shaped objects ringed that larger one and all flew in a tight formation through the skies over Canada.

Captain Howard radioed Labrador Radar Control to inquire if they had any idea what it was flying in tandem with his plane. They did not know, but requested more information and for a description of what he was seeing. Captain Howard described the objects to Labrador Control Tower. They proceeded to radio an F-94 airborne just a short distance away to check out what Captain Howard and his passengers and crews were witnessing. As the fighter pilot closed in, Captain Howard began communicating with the other pilot directly so as to vector the jet interceptor into position. As the fighter drew nearer, the seven objects vacated the vicinity. Once on the ground for refueling, the flight crew was questioned at length by the Air Force's Intelligence officers, who were not surprised by the sighting. They even went to lengths to inform the crew that there had been several other sightings in the area that month alone, however, the Intelligence Officers could not explain what it was that flew with Captain Howard's plane that night over Canada.

Vernon, France

Lest we forget that the UFO phenomenon is global, I think that it is high time to include a sighting from elsewhere. So the next report we will study comes to us from France. In the evening hours of August 24th, 1954, Bernard Miserey, a businessman in Vernon, France,[6] had just arrived home, parked his auto and came out of the garage, when he noticed a pale light illuminating his hometown.

His eyes became transfixed on a cigar-shaped object he estimated to be 300 feet long, that hung perfectly still and silent as it hovered over and illuminated a portion of Vernon. Several minutes of observation had past when, much to his surprise, the cigar-shaped craft's lower portion opened up and from inside dropped out a smaller disc-shaped object. The smaller object at first appeared to be in free-fall, then as if gaining its bearings, shot towards the spot where Mr. Miserey stood. Much to his pleasure, the disc continued to fly right over his position and continued on out of sight. This was to be repeated three more times in succession. The discs that dropped from the cigar-shaped object had a red glow to them that intensified as they accelerated through the atmosphere. After a brief interval, a fifth disc dropped from the belly of the cigar-shaped UFO, but this one did not fly off into the distance. This one took up position above a nearby bridge. It remained there for several minutes, and then it too shot off out of sight. After the last disc had made its way over the horizon, the large cigar-shaped craft slowly disappeared into the upper atmosphere.

Mr. Miserey's sighting lasted a full forty-five minutes, and unbeknownst to him an army engineer on the southwest side of town and a local constable making his rounds also witnessed this spectacular event. Had this object been viewed by only Mr. Miserey, a hallucination would have had to be considered as an explanation. The two other witnesses prove that this was not so, however, this provided little comfort to the three men who wondered what it was they saw that night, as no explanation has ever been brought forth.

Italy

November of 1954 found Italy awash with reports of sightings of what Italians call Dischi Volanti or as we know them flying saucers. On October 30th, a large crowd was standing outside near the church of Sante Marie of Maggiore. One member of that crowd was Italian diplomat Dr. Alberto Perego.[7] The gathered crowd was watching as two white orbs silently moved around the sky at about 6,000 feet of elevation.

This was followed a week later by an even more impressive sighting by Dr. Perego and others. He recalls that on November 6th, he witnessed not two, but dozens of orbs, as they darted silently through the skies above Italy's Tuscolano District. The sighting lasted from 11 AM to 1 PM. The objects appeared to be flying at between 720 MPH and 840 MPH at a height he estimated as ranging from about 21–24,000 feet. Sometimes the orbs would leave a short, white trail as the moved around the sky creating formations and then abandoning them, and then would repeat the process all over again.

Around noontime, Dr. Perego witnessed two squadrons of twenty craft, each flying in V-formations. One squadron came from out of the east, the other from out of the west, and met in the sky, directly above the Vatican. He counted slightly over 100 of these orbs in the sky, a veritable fleet of UFOs! Thin filaments of fiber-like substances began to fall out of the sky, bringing forth the first reported instance of what has come to be called the Angel Hair phenomenon.

The following day, Rome's daily newspapers did not have one word printed concerning the objects in the sky the day before. But they would have another chance to cash in on the story as the orbs appeared once again in the afternoon of November 7th. The orbs made their last appearance in the skies over Rome that month on the morning of the 12th. No explanation was given to Dr. Perego by the Air Defense Headquarters, nor by the Chief of the Air Defense Ministry when inquired regarding what it was that he had seen. Though it would take several years before Dr. Perego could come to terms with what he saw, as having witnessed alien machines did not set right with him, he went on to become the most vocal supporter of the UFO phenomenon that his country has ever seen.

Soviet Union – Trans-Caucasus Region

Although there were many, many reports of flying saucers in 1955, I have chosen to include only two. These are the only two occurrences I could locate that pass the qualifying exam for inclusion in the book. Both of these encounters where reported by technically trained, competent observers, who had too much to lose to go off creating stories to grab the media's attention. The first encounter we shall review was classified as Top Secret for over two decades. The Freedom of Information Act was the vehicle used to bring this report to the rest of the world, after it was hushed up due to its ultra sensitive nature.

The following is an account that describes the encounter several American officials had while traveling through the rolling steppes of the old Soviet Union. The officials involved included:[8] Lieutenant Colonel E. U. Hathaway, a US Army staff officer, assigned to the powerful Senate Armed Forces Committee, Ruben Efron, a consultant to the Armed Forces Committee, and Senator Richard Russell R-Georgia. On a train trip somewhere between Atjaty and Adzhijabul in the Trans-Caucasus Region, at approximately 7:10 PM local time, the US contingent witnessed the vertical takeoff of two disc-shaped craft. The objects rose to about 6,000 feet and then proceeded to accelerate out of sight into the darkening northern sky. The objects were described as disc shaped, with a stationary light on the top of each disc. They appeared to be rotating to the right as they flew overhead. No wings, tails, mean of propulsion, nor sound were detected by any of the witnesses.

The sighting's details were wired to the United States Air Force by the US Air Attaché at the US embassy in Prague on October 13th, 1955. This report was classified for obvious reasons. It would have been easy for the average Joe to mistakenly assume that since there was a sighting of the classically disc-shaped UFO in the old Soviet Union, they must originate there. Thus with the number of reports of UFO in the 1950s, it is easy to see how this type of information could have caused wide-spread panic. It could have been assumed that not only was the Red Menace coming, they were coming via UFOs that the US military could do nothing to stop! So, for once, I agree that it was better to keep this particular sighting out of the public domain.

MOJAVE DESERT IN THE AMERICAN SOUTHWEST

Our next encounter occurred in November of 1955. While crossing the Mojave Desert on the Union Pacific's *Challenger* passenger train, Mr. Frank Halstead, Curator of the Darling Observatory at Duluth, Minnesota and his wife witnesses an object as it made its way across the American Southwest. While enjoying the views of the spectacular mountain ranges outside of Las Vegas, Nevada, the Halsteads saw an object low in the sky that appeared to be a blimp flying in the same direction the train was traveling. As he watched the object, he soon felt that this was no blimp, as it appeared to be four times as long as the largest blimps he had ever seen.

The object had paced the train for five minutes, when the Halsteads noticed a second object, as it seemed to appear from thin air just to the rear of the first object. They described the first object as being around 800 feet long and cigar shaped. The second object was smaller yet still a respectable 100 feet in diameter, and disc shaped. Mr. Halstead based his calculations on the relative size of the objects as compared to the size of surrounding trees, which the objects flew past as it paced the train. Both objects remained in view for several more minutes before they both ascended very slowly, until these two huge machines had disappeared in the upper atmosphere.

Here is just another example that shows that the claims made by the government and their hired skeptics that competent, well-trained observers, who would be familiar with anything flying through the skies, do not have encounters with UFOs is false.

Cape Jesup, Greenland

We begin 1956 with very interesting reports from friends and foes overseas. Our first report comes to us from the old Soviet Union. The report came to the west via Valentin Akkuratov, a well-known Soviet pilot, who was chief navigator for the USSR on their flights above or through the North Pole. He reports that while on a routine survey of the ice flows near Cape Jesup, Greenland, he and the crew of a Tupolev 4 airplane observed an unidentified flying object. The pilot brought the plane down out of the clouds to fly in calmer, clearer weather. When they came out of the clouds, they spotted a strange object a short distance off their port wing as it flew a course parallel to the plane's. Believing this to be a new addition to the American arsenal, the pilots deemed it wise to prevent contact with this incredible vehicle, by climbing back into the clouds. Forty minutes later, the plane ran out of clouds to fly through near Bear Island, and awaiting their probing eyes was the strange craft, flying the same course and distance from the plane as it had before the pilots went back into the safety of the clouds.

He described the object as a large Pearl colored lens, with wavy, pulsating edges, without any visible wings, tail, windows, engines, or vapor trail.[10] Now that they could no longer avoid the craft, they decided that while it was there, they should gather as much intelligence on it as possible, so the authorities back home could try to devise a counter to this new American threat. Having alerted the authorities at their home base in Amderma, the plane made an abrupt course change and turned sharply to port to get closer to the object. As they changed course, the UFO followed likewise; changing its course just enough to remain the same distance and position off the plane's port side. After almost twenty minutes of playing follow-the-leader, the UFO accelerated ahead of the plane and then began to ascend into the bright blue sky at a speed that all the crew agreed was faster than any plane, American or Soviet, that they had ever encountered before.

Paris, France

Our next sighting comes to us from France. It occurred on the night of February 19th, 1956,[11] and was witnessed by not only professionally trained air traffic controllers on radar, but also with the naked eye by passengers and crew of an Air France jetliner as they flew over the French countryside.

At approximately 10:40 PM local time, the air traffic controllers at Orly Airport in Paris, France, were astonished to see a large blip come into view on their radarscopes. The controllers estimated the size of the object as twice as large as a big jetliner. They watched in disbelief as the object hovered for a while, then sprinted at high speed over the countryside to another town. The controllers, noticing this pattern of flight, managed to track and time the craft on one of its quick trips. The object at one moment was hovering over the town of Gometz-le-Chatel, and half a minute later it had flown eighteen miles to hover over another part of the French countryside, having reached a speed in excess of 2,100 MPH, a speed no conventional craft of any size could achieve in 1956!

Not long after this feat, a smaller blip appeared on the radarscope, which would turn out to be a quite conventional: an Air France DC-3 Dakota flying over the French military installation at Les Mureaux. The two craft, though 800 feet apart in elevation were on a converging course. Then a radioman at Orly contacted the plane to inform the crew that they had unknown traffic in their vicinity. With coordinates in hand, Radio Officer Beaupertuis soon caught sight of the UFO through one of the cockpit windows. In a report that Captain Desavoi and the crew made to the French Ministry of Civilian Aviation, the captain of the Air France plane reported that the object was of incredible size, with a random pattern of lights attached to a superstructure of indeterminable dimensions. All stressed that whatever it was in the sky that night, it was no civilian or military aircraft known to any of his crew. The radar operators, who witnessed the blip on their screens for over four hours, concurred that the object on their radar screens was certainly very different from the planes they normally tracked on their journeys through the skies of France.

Schenectady, New York

Our next encounter brings us back to the United States, and quite close to my hometown. In the evening hours of April 8th, 1956,[12] American Airlines flight 775 took off from the Albany (New York) County Airport headed towards Syracuse. At the helm were Captain Raymond E. Ryan and First Officer William Neff. It was a beautiful night for flying with light wind and a sparse scattering of clouds. At 10:20 PM, the plane had climbed to 6,000 feet and was above Schenectady, New York, about ten miles west of

Albany, when the flight crew noticed a very brilliant white light approaching their aircraft. Thinking the light to be the landing lights of an oncoming plane, the crew banked the twin-engine Corsair, in an attempt to put distance between themselves and the unknown craft that was quickly approaching them. The object made a sudden right-angle turn and accelerated away from the plane. As the object slowed from its incredible acceleration, the intense light began to fade. The object was still out in front of the American Airlines Corvair when its light faded away to blackness.

Captain Ryan, fearing a possible collision, hit his intense landing lights. No sooner had the plane's lights began illuminating the overcast ahead, then the now-bright orange object suddenly reappeared, some eight to ten miles ahead. Immediately, Captain Ryan radioed Griffis Air Force base in nearby Rome, New York. They concurred that they could also see the object, and though their radar was not up and running, they were scrambling two jet interceptors. Griffis informed the pilots that they should be on the lookout for them very shortly.

Another witness on the plane, a stewardess named Phyllis Reynolds, was in the cockpit when the controller at Griffis, without any authority to do so, ordered the pilots to change course and try to close the gap between the plane and the unknown object. The lack of fighters arriving on the scene and the anxious twang in the controllers' voices, inspired Captain Ryan to change course and pursue the unknown object. This however proved futile, as the object accelerated almost out of sight and headed out towards Lake Ontario and north towards Canada.

Both pilots concurred, that whatever the object was, it was no conventional craft. Knowing that there was no way to catch the object, the two experienced pilots, gave up the pursuit of the UFO and turned the plane back towards Syracuse. Both pilots and the shift supervisor on duty in the tower at Griffis, who watched the object through binoculars, all agreed on their description of the UFO. The object was round, much larger than any star in the sky, and changed color from white to orange to red during its high-speed voyage over New York's Mohawk River Valley.

Though the object was viewed by two well-trained and highly experienced pilots, a stewardess, and Air Force personnel at Griffis Air Force Base, who all concluded the object had no conventional explanation, upon the conclusion of his investigation into this case, Donald Menzel, debunker emeritus, concluded the object was the planet Venus.

Bloomington, Indiana

Later on in the spring of 1956, four boys had an encounter with a low flying UFO as they fished a water-filled quarry near Bloomington, Indiana. At about 3 AM in the morning, the boys, who had fallen asleep, were suddenly awakened by a loud humming noise accompanied by an intense white light. The boys watched as the lights moved slowly overhead, crossed the quarry and disappeared behind some trees in the direction of a local stone mill, that had been closed for several months.[13]

The boys ran around the edge of the quarry and through the woods, purposely keeping the mill between themselves and the light. When they found the courage to venture out onto the train tracks that ran along side of the mill, the boys came face to face with a large glowing orb as it hovered some 15 feet above the ground and 100 feet distant. The humming the boys heard as it flew over the quarry was now absent, but they all reported getting a warm sensation on their skin from the intense light produced by the hovering object. After several minutes, the objected emitted an even higher pitched hum, and rose up into the night sky until it disappeared from their sight entirely.

Frightened by what they had seen, the boys ran the entire two miles to the nearest police station to report it. This incident could have been disregarded by the police as a boyhood prank, but the officer who took the report felt that something had truly frightened the boys, so he passed the report along to the proper authorities.

When researcher Frank Edwards arrived on the scene the following day, he, the police, and the boys all went out to the mill to have a look around. Once on the scene, the boys pointed out the place where the UFO had hovered and sure enough, the leaves on all the surrounding trees, right near the spot where the UFO had hovered, were burnt, withered, and dying. When the night watchman was interviewed, he admitted that he had seen both the object and the four boys, but had not reported the incident due to fear of being ridiculed.

Two days after the incident, the Bloomington Police had the four boys interviewed by a psychiatrist from nearby Indiana University, who concluded that although he could not identify or even speculate as to what the boys had seen, one thing was absolute: He thoroughly believed that the boys were telling the truth about their experience with the UFO they had encountered two nights previous.

ENGLAND

The night of August 13th and into the earlier hours of August the 14th brought shear havoc to the air bases of the United States and the United Kingdom in and around coast of England.[14] The sightings took place over two air bases, both manned by US and UK forces. The first air base, Royal Air Force base Brentwaters is located on the English coast, some thirteen miles from Ipswich, England. The other base involved is Lakenheath Airbase, located some forty-four miles further inland than Brentwaters.

At approximately 9:30 PM local time, USAF personnel at Brentwaters Royal Air Force Base, tracked an unknown return on their Ground-Controlled Approach radar as it flew in a straight line over the base from a position twenty-five miles east-southeast of the base to a position twenty five miles west-northwest of the base, at a speed calculated to be in excess of 4,000 MPH! Another unknown blip was painting a return on their radar sets at 10:55 PM. This blip also flew a straight-line course from a position thirty-five miles east of the base to a position thirty-five miles west of the base, at the same or even greater speed.

The tower personnel at Brentwaters decided to contact their counterparts at Lakenheath to inquire if they had witnessed any unusual returns on their radar. They had a sighting by the pilot of a C-47 cargo plane, who reported spotting an intensely brilliant white object as it passed below his plane at incredibly high speed. At 11:10 PM, two radar sets at Lakenheath and three ground observers all witnessed the passing of two, round, white, glowing objects as they flew a rectangular flight plan above the plains of Southwest England.

From the observers' reports and the returns on the radar, these objects could fly at high speed (between 600 and 800 MPH) and make the ninety-degree turns necessary to complete the rectangular shape without slowing down! Just after 11:30 PM, the Radar Air Traffic Control Center team supervisor at Lakenheath conversed with Chief Fighter Controller at nearby Neatishead Royal Air Force Base, and they decided it was high time to scramble a fighter to get a better look at what was happening high in the skies above these military installations.

A Venom night-fighter was scrambled from Battle Flight, located at RAF Station Waterbeach, just outside of Cambridge, England. The flight control teams on the ground vectored the fighter to the area where the two UFOs, which had suddenly merged into one return, was flying its rectangular course. Once the fighter had the object in sight, it began to close. The UFO, in just a matter of seconds, discontinued its rectangular pattern, and in one quick, blisteringly fast movement, took up position behind the approaching fighter. The pilot asked for a vector, as he and his radar-man had lost sight of the object. Ground control informed him that the UFO was now in back of his fighter and evasive action should be taken immediately.

The pilot tried desperately to shake the UFO off his tail. As you may have guessed, the UFO could not be out maneuvered, and remained right where it had started, about 1,200 feet behind the plane. To assist the pilots' efforts to shake the bogey from his tail, another Venom fight was dispatched and vectored to that area. But, before the second fighter arrived on the scene, the UFO proceeded to accelerate out of sight and off all radarscopes.

The object that frayed many nerves that night was not seen again, and little did these men know that some quarter century later, their two military bases would be in the forefront of one of the most controversial sightings/encounters ever recorded!

New Mexico

A little before 8 AM local time, one morning in September of 1956, the people of New Mexico who traveled Interstate I-70 where amazed or terrified (depending on whose point of view you are quoting), when a large disc-shaped object with a dome on the upper-half landed in full view of the commuters on this busy New Mexico highway.

The ship touched down about 150 feet from the highway at a spot less than twelve miles from Holloman Air Force Base and the White Sands Proving Grounds.[15] The craft caused the cars closest to it to stall and many others drivers' radios also died. The stalled cars backed up traffic for miles, which gave those stopped closet to the craft, including two full-bird Air Force colonels, two sergeants, dozens of base employees, and a whole assortment of civilians, almost a full ten minutes to observe the craft before it took off emitting a loud whirling noise.

Holloman Air Base went nuts! Immediately, the base commander notified the Pentagon as to what had happened. They responded by flying out a team of Air Force Intelligence officers and CIA experts to Holloman to debrief the entire personnel of the base. All personnel were assembled in a large hangar and questioned, and then sworn to absolute secrecy as to what they had witnessed on their way to work that morning.

The report made via wire back to the Pentagon from the debriefing team stated exactly what the brass did not want to hear: Whatever it was these people saw, it was not made by any country on this planet! This leaves a very clear conclusion: The object seen was obviously swamp gas illuminated by the light from a late setting Venus, whose magnitude was obviously enhanced by refraction through an inversion layer of super heated air, right? Just ask the debunkers or those folks who worked at Project Blue Book... I am sure they would agree with this utterly ridiculous hypothesis!

East of Jacksonville, Florida

Early in the next calendar year, 1957, another DC-6 had a near collision with an unidentified flying object. This time, it was a Pan-American Airways' DC-6 piloted by Captain Matt Van Winkle.[16] Captain Van Winkle had left New York City and was bound for San Juan, Puerto Rico.

At approximately 3:30 AM, flight #257 was on schedule over the Atlantic Ocean, though flying slightly farther west than normal due to a course change administered to avoid rough weather. The flight was about 150 miles east of Jacksonville, Florida, when the pilot was startled by an intense light coming from below and slightly to the right of his plane. Once his eyes began to adapt to the bright light, Captain Van Winkle saw that the source of the bright light was a large disc-shaped object streaking upwards through the night sky towards his aircraft. To avoid a mid-air crash, he, like Captain Schidel before him, pulled back hard on the wheel. And just like before, the steep climb the plane was put into by the pilot helped the flight to avoid the unknown object, and sent passengers hurtling throughout the cabin. Many of these passengers had to be treated for minor injuries upon arrival at San Juan. No debunker tried to explain this sighting away, as once again, one of those objects that do not exist almost killed scores of people, and the less the general public knew about this near mid-air collision the better.

Boainai, New Guinea

Our next encounter is truly incredible! I would like to preface this account with several statements of fact. First of all, no matter how bright or how close the planet Venus is to our planet, it does not, and could not hover close to the ground. Likewise, if a group of people were having a mass hallucination, if one member tried to communicate with this hallucination, each member would not have the same mental response, as each persons' mind processes information differently; only the one communicating should receive an answer to their inquiry. With that said, lets delve into one of the best encounters ever.

Having finished his dinner and retired to the porch of his residence at a missionary school in Boainai, New Guinea, to relax and participate in a little sky watching, the Reverend William Booth Gill, an ordained Anglican minister, and graduate of Brisbane University, had no clue as to the events that would soon unfold.

Once outdoors, looking up from the porch, the Reverend Gill spotted Venus shining brightly in the night sky. Another light, that appeared even brighter than Venus, caught his eye in an instant. The light appeared to be getting bigger which meant only one thing: It was getting closer! Not wanting to witness this phenomenon alone, Reverend Gill called to one of the teachers to come outside. Sensing the excitement, several students also made their way out to the porch.

The light began to slow as it closed the distance between itself and the ground. Finally, all assembled could see what was causing this spectacle: A large disc-shaped craft, some thirty- to forty-feet wide, was now hovering close to the ground, about 400 feet from the small group of stunned witnesses. Although it settled down closer to the ground, it never actually landed. According to a signed statement made by all those present, the object had four legs projecting out of the bottom, and a dome estimated to be twenty feet wide and ten feet high, covering the top. On top of the dome, a small deck ringed the object. On this deck, not long after the craft came to rest, four small, man-like creatures appeared. These small men busied themselves as if repairing the craft, and as they did so, at an interval of thirty seconds, a narrow shaft of bright blue light was emitted skyward for about five seconds, looking very much to those assembled like a beacon or signal.

In the signed statement, Reverend Gill states that he felt compelled to attempt to establish contact with these small beings. Thus, the next time one of the small beings seemed to be looking down at the assembled audience, the reverend waved one hand over his head. Even in the diminishing light, the small being must have seen the reverend, as it returned the signal by waving his appendage over what appeared to be his head! The teacher that Reverend Gill had called to the porch waved both arms over his head, to which two of the beings responded likewise. Next the reverend and the teacher waved their arms and hands over their heads and all the beings responded in kind. The young students assembled were very excited, and began shouting to the small beings, but no sound was returned from the beings on the ship.

One of the boys went inside and returned with a flashlight. By the time he had returned, the figures had apparently gone below decks. In light of this he shined the light at the craft, without any response. Much to the groups' disappointment the object was soon airborne and once more under way. Over the next few days and nights the same or a similar object came back and hovered over or near the school, but never came as close as it did during the first night they had observed it.

All persons involved in the sightings helped compile and signed an eleven-page report that the Reverend submitted to the government of New Guinea. Since the sighting was not made in the United States or near any of our military installations, our government, nor their debunkers, offered up any explanation explaining exactly what it was the reverend and other members of the mission school saw those nights in June of 1957.

EASTERN LOUISIANA AND TEXAS

In the early morning hours of July 17th, 1957, an Air Force RB-47H, on a routine training mission, came in contact with an object of unknown origin for more than an hour. The RB-47H was a plane that was equipped with electronic intelligence gear used to gather intelligence information and deploy countermeasures against enemy radar. Six highly trained Air Force officers staffed it. The plane took off on its mission from the runways of Forbes Air Force Base in Topeka, Kansas. That night's plan was to fly south to the Gulf of Mexico, practice navigation and gunnery exercises, then fly home through Mississippi, Louisiana, and Texas, where they would practice some intelligence gathering and countermeasures.

The weather was quite clear that summer night, no storms or showers were expected anywhere along their flight plan, putting the crew in a good mood as they could expect a pretty easy mission. When they had finished with their navigation and gunnery exercises, the pilot turned the plane northward, and at 34,500 feet, the plane was heading for the coastline on the last leg of its training mission. Traveling at 500 MPH as they crossed the coastline near Gulfport, Mississippi, a ground station picked up a return on their scopes that seemed to be circling the Air Force plane. When the plane did not call in for any request for local traffic, the ground operator took the reading to be an error. When the aircraft reached Meridian, Mississippi, they turned westward. Shortly thereafter, at about 4:10 AM local time, while flying over eastern Louisiana, the pilot and copilot saw a bluish-white light that appeared to them to be on a collision course with their plane.

The object, as if reading the pilots' minds, suddenly changed course and passed in front of the plane and disappeared into the distance. The above mentioned ground station, having heard the discussion of this near miss, tuned his equipment towards the new position, and once again picked up the plane and the same blip he had observed circling the plane a short time earlier. Twenty-nine minutes later, the pilot of the RB-47H sighted what he described as a huge light that he suspected was attached to something even larger that he could not see, flying slightly to the right and 5,000 feet below the plane. A minute later, the pilot and copilot saw two red objects.

This new sighting led the pilot to request and receives permission from the Air Defense Command at Duncanville, Texas, to pursue the objects. The pilot also requested all available help that this ADC air station could supply. The pilots continued at 34,500 feet and 500 MPH as it chased these intruders who were 5,000 feet below their aircraft. The plane closed the gap in distance between itself and the UFOs at approximately 4:50 AM, when the UFO stopped dead in the air, and the plane, 5,000 feet above, overflew their intended prey. The object was lost from radar for a minute, but contact was made once again at 4:52 AM. At 4:55 AM, the plane now close to Mineral Springs, Texas, notified the ADC base in Duncanville, that they were running low on fuel and needed to return to base. Having turned for home, the pilots once again gained a visual fix on the UFO at 4:58 AM, and they last saw it about twenty nautical miles northwest of Fort Worth.

So here we have a series of Unidentified Flying Objects that were sighted visually by pilots, on radar and on intelligence gathering electronic equipment, which should have warranted some type of investigation by any number of government agencies. Project Blue Book did investigate this case, and came to the conclusion that all of the trained military personnel in the air and on the ground did not know that they were tracking and chasing American Airlines flight #655. (If the USAF could not distinguish between a UFO and a jetliner, as Project Blue Book implies with their explanation, how could they so successfully achieve air superiority in every conflict we have fought since?) Nice try Blue Book...

SANTA CATARINA, BRAZIL

On August 14th, 1957, a Varig C-47 cargo plane departed from Porto Alegre Airport in Rio Grande do Sul, Brazil, on its way to Rio de Janerio. The pilots that night were Commander Jorge Araujo piloting the craft, and Edgar Soares acting as copilot, both highly experienced pilots.[19] Cruising at 6,300 feet over the Brazilian state of Santa Catarina, at approximately 8:55 PM local time, copilot Soares, having lifted his eyes from the cloud cover below, spotted a glowing object off the left wing of their big plane. In one quick movement, the object closed the distance between itself and the plane, crossed in front of the plane, and coming to a dead stop to the right of the C-47. When it took up its position here, the planes' engines started to misfire and the lights in the cabin and cockpit began to dim almost to the point of shutting off altogether.

The crew became very apprehensive, as loss of the electrical system could spell big trouble for the C-47. Then suddenly, the UFO dived straight down and out of sight below the thick layer of clouds at 5,700 feet. Once the UFO had left, the plane's engines and electrical system returned to normal. Both pilots, as well as the radioman, Rubens Tortilho, and two stewards, Jose Machado and Alfonso Schenini, all saw the object. All agreed that the object had a saucer shaped bottom that glowed with a weak yellowish hue, and a dome on top that shone brightly from a strange green luminosity.

Araujo radioed their airline's headquarters to report what they had just encountered. Several days later, the report leaked out and made the headlines in papers across Brazil and South America. The Brazilian military made no attempt to cover up or debunk this report. (Note that Brazil did not collapse from within, nor did its social, economic, and political structure's implode for providing full disclosure. ...Lessons to be learned—if our government wanted to.)

PORTUGAL

A squadron of F-84 Thunder-Jets belonging to the Portuguese Air Force, were airborne for a routine navigational practice mission on the night of September 4th, 1957, when they had a forty-minute encounter with an Unidentified Flying Object. The night was clear and the moon almost full, which equaled excellent visibility for the fliers. The mission consisted of four pilots: Captain Jose' Ferreira, the flight commander, and Sergeants Alberto Covas, Manuel Marcelino, and Salvador Oliveira. Once they had reached Granada, at just past 8 PM local time, the plane's mission called for them to change course and head for Portalegra. It is at this point that Captain Ferraira noticed an unusual light sources emanating from just above the horizon to the left of his jet plane.

The pilot to Ferraira's right notified the captain that he was seeing the same object, and soon the other two pilots spotted the odd light. To all of the pilots, the unknown object looked like a huge star, except the nucleus was changing color from green to blue to yellow and to many different shades of red, while the entire light seemed to scintillate. Suddenly, the object swelled to five or six times its original size, confirming the pilots' suspicion that this was no star, lightning, plane, nor balloon. Then it shrunk down to a small yellowish light at just a fraction of the size it had been originally. The object continued to swell and shrink, and none could determine if the size fluctuations were due to growing and shrinking, or moving closer than fading back to its original location.

At 8:38 PM, the squadron abandoned its original mission and began to pursue the unknown object. The planes adjusted their course several times, yet the object always remained ninety degrees off their left flank. Satisfied that the object was not stationary, the squadron soon closed the gap between itself and the UFO. When they were above it, the pilots noticed it was shaped like a curved bean held at arm's length,[20] red in color and emitting a yellow beam of light. Three other yellow circles of light, approximately one-tenth the size of the main craft, could be seen just to the right of it. As the planes and the objects closed in on the town of Coruche, the large object made a sudden turn, as did the small circles shortly thereafter, and began streaking towards the jets. The lights passed below and behind the jets and were soon lost in the darkness of the night sky.

The rest of the flight was uneventful, as it would be hard to match or top the excitement these pilots had for a good portion of their mission that night. They landed without any further incidents, and there was no attempt by Portuguese authorities to ridicule members of their Air Force due their encounter and near collision with several Unidentified Flying Objects.

New Mexico

On routine patrol at the White Sands Missile Range on November 3rd, 1957, Military Police Corporal Glenn Toy and Private James Wilbanks, were not at all alarmed when they saw a rather bright star in the night sky. But there was something odd about how bright it was, and both men felt the size of this "star" seemed rather large. So the two soldiers kept a cautious eye on this object. As they went about their business, their suspicions were justified.

The bright light began to grow larger as it began its descent over the most restricted area of the base. They watched in shock as the object came to rest just fifty feet above the area of the base where atomic bombs were once stored. The object, which they described as being shaped like an egg, about 225 to 300 feet in diameter, and glowed intensely with a strange white luminosity. Suddenly the light went off, the soldiers claimed it was much like a flame being extinguished, only to flare up long enough for the craft to come to rest on the ground about three miles from the soldiers' position. Upon touchdown, the light once again went off.

The officers reported the incident to their superiors, who all but ignored it until the same thing was seen by another patrol in the same general area just hours later. At 8 PM,[21] Specialist Forest Oakes and Specialist 3rd Class Barlow also saw a bright object hovering over the bunker where the atomic bombs were once stored. The object suddenly shot up at a forty-five-degree angle, hovered high in the sky blinking for several minutes, and then disappeared altogether.

Something tells me that inferior military police officers would not guard so sensitive a base, and those stationed there would be of superior observational/cognitive ability. Thus a question remains: Exactly what did these four military police officers see that night in November of 1957 in the skies above and on the soil within one of the most secure areas on this planet? An answer has never been forth coming from the military or the federal government.

Merom, Indiana and Brazil

November 4th, 1957 was the second day in what would become a memorable week for UFOlogists throughout the world. On this night, the Gilham family of Merom, Indiana, would have an encounter with a UFO that none would soon forget.

Rene Gilham, an iron worker in Terra Haute, his wife's, and his children's dinners were all interrupted when a neighbor's child rushed into their home to tell the family of the oddest looking star that was in the sky above their small community. Wondering if this could be one of those UFOs he had heard so much about, Rene led his family out into the street in front of their home to take a look at this peculiar star.

Once out in the street, the Gilhams found themselves staring with their neighbors, who had came out a short time earlier, at the sky above their homes. There they watched a circular object hang completely motionless. The object was silent, awash in a white glow, and appeared to be about 300 feet above the ground and about 30 to 40 feet in diameter. Suddenly, the object began to project bright blue beams of light down onto the street.

With this development, the Gilham's neighbors hastily retreated to the safety of their home. The lights passed over Mr. Gilham as they made their way up and down the street. Unnerved, Mrs. Gilham took the kids into the house and beckoned for Rene to follow. He stayed outside watching the object and its lights for a full ten minutes, being illuminated by the bright blue lights several times before the object made a swift and permanent exit from the skies above his home.

Mr. Gilham was hospitalized a short time later for severe burns to the parts of his body that were directly exposed to the light coming down from the UFO. His burns were treated and recorded by Dr. Joseph Dukes of Dugger, Indiana.

A short time later, at the Itaipu Brazilian military installation, guards on duty saw the same or a similar object as it hovered over their base. The guards reported that as they watched the glowing orb hover over the base, they began to feel concern over the strangeness of the object they were watching. This unease was magnified when the object flew overhead, stopped, and began to descend closer to the men. As the orb moved closer to them, they were overcome with fear and sounded the general alarm. Much to their dismay, as they did, the base was plunged into total darkness as it lost all electrical power.

The orb was so close overhead that the ground around them began to look as if the sun was out. By the time order was restored,[22] the UFO was gone, and the guards were found on the ground severely burned by the light given off from the orb as it descended over their guard shack.

Now, it is safe to say that these objects had to be ships of some design that were able to enter the airspace above the heartland of the United States and a Brazilian military base and severely injure three people. The usual explanations, Venus, swamp gas, weather balloons, ball lightning, etc, could not be applied to either of these cases as none of the above could have caused similar burns to three people on two different continents. So what was it that all these people saw that so drastically changed their ideas and concepts about their and our place in the universe. The answer is easy, they saw a UFO. What UFOs *are*, is where the real mystery lies.

Orogrande, New Mexico

Earlier in the day of November 4th, James Stokes, an employee of the Holloman Air Force Base, was driving near Orogrande, New Mexico, when the radio in the car died. Not long thereafter, his car began to sputter and finally stalled out altogether. As he guided his stalled vehicle to the side of the road,[23] Stokes saw a group of people, a short distance ahead, standing by the road and pointing skyward. Looking in the general direction the people were pointing, he saw a large oval-shaped object flying towards where they all stood staring in awe. The object flew over the cars, turned around, and made a second pass before flying off for good.

As the object passed overhead, Stokes swore that he felt some type of heat on his face. He saw no portholes, wings, nor engines as the object flew overhead at what he estimated as 3,000 feet of altitude and at approximately 760 MPH. Several hours after the sighting, Stokes noticed that the areas of his hands and face where he had felt heat as the UFO passed overhead, were itchy and red as if sun burned. Stokes made an official report to his superiors at Holloman, and although he would not soon forget the sighting, he, unlike Mr. Gilham and the guards prior, would suffer nothing more than some red, itching skin as a by-product of being exposed to an Unidentified Flying Object.

New Mexico

As the great J. Allen Hynek states in his book, *The UFO Experience*,[24] the following report shows the way that Project Blue Book disregarded quality sightings so they would not be forced to change their position on the existence of Unidentified Flying Objects and their capacity to fly in and out of our air space at will.

Later the same day as the prior sighting, November 4th, 1957, at 10:45 PM local time, two controllers were working their shifts in the 100ft control tower at Kirkland Air Force Base in New Mexico. One of the controllers looked up into the night sky to gather some information on the existing cloud cover. Along with the clouds he saw a bright white object flying below the clouds at approximately 1,500 feet altitude at nearly 200 MPH. He then contacted the radar installation to try to identify the light that was flying over the base. The radar men watched as the object turned and made a quick descent in the vicinity of Runway 26.

One of the controllers, thinking the light was a plane with a confused pilot, tried to radio the aircraft, but could raise no one. As it slowly flew overhead, the controllers got a look at it through binoculars. They described an oval object about fifteen to eighteen feet long with one powerful bright light on its underside. The object then slowed to less than fifty MPH and was seen to descend into a restricted area of the base. The object reappeared and began to head on an easterly course about 300 feet above the ground. It then made a sharp turn, veering off into a southeasterly direction and began a speedy ascent, climbing high and fast, until it was gone from sight.

A short time later an Air Force C-46 took off from Kirkland, and no sooner was it airborne, its radar picked up the same or a similar unknown object hovering over the southern outer-marker of the north-south runway. The object sprung to life, coming around and behind the C-46 and proceeded to follow the cargo-plane for fourteen miles. It then ceased trailing the plane, and returned to hovering over the outer marker for a few more minutes before fading off of the radar screen permanently.

The object was visually in sight for six minutes by the controllers, and for twenty minutes by the radar operators at the base and onboard the C-46. Thus we had a sighting of the same UFO by many trained observers, using both the human eye and radar, at three different locations (Control tower, radar installation, and the C-46) and all Project Blue Book could do was to claim that the object was indeed a misguided aircraft.

How you may ask, could two control tower operators, one a twenty-three year veteran, and the pilots of a C-46 not recognize a plane when they all saw it with their own eyes? Good question. How could a plane appear as this object did through the binoculars, and accelerate like it did are questions Blue Book could not and would not answer. Likewise, why the officials did not press to find out who the pilot was who buzzed aircraft and landing strips at Kirkland Air Force Base is another riddle that no one attempted to solve.

US Coast Guard

Our last reported sighting from 1957 comes from a branch of the United States Armed Forces that we have not heard from in a while: the Coast Guard. During the morning of November 5th, 1957,[25] the Coast Guard Cutter *Sebago* was on routine patrol under the watchful eyes of Commander Waring. At 5:10 AM, the ship's radar picked up an object that appeared to be circling the ship. The unknown blip then stopped, hovered, and shot ahead at great speed, a pattern it would repeat over and over. Some eleven minutes after the object was first tracked on radar, four of the ship's crew who had gone deck-side, could make out the object with their naked eyes as it performed high in the sky above their ship.

Lt. Donald Schaefer, Quartermaster Kenneth Smith, Radioman Thomas Kirk and Ensign Wayne Schottey all reported the object as being disc shaped and very shiny as it circled and stopped and sped ahead in the skies overhead. The object soon departed from the eyes of the topside crew and the screens of the radar below, but would not soon be erased from the mind's eye of each and every man that bore witness to this aerial display.

This sighting ends a very active week of UFO reports and the calendar year of 1957 as far as this work is concerned. As you will see, as the 1950s wound down, the number of sighting may have declined, but the quality of the sightings remained high. People continued to see Unidentified Flying Objects as the 1960s approached and would continue to do so right up to the moment which your eyes read these words.

New Mexico

On a warm summers evening in 1958,[26] a mechanic (whose name is withheld at his request in the initial interview) on duty at Holloman Air Force Base witnessed a UFO as he worked on a plane attached to one of the many squadrons in the multitude to the air wings of that base. As he was repairing the landing gear on a Lockheed Martin F-104 interceptor, the mechanic, just by chance, glanced out at the landing strip, and much to his surprise, he saw a disc-shaped object hovering silently just several hundred feet away. As he watched the craft, it began to withdraw what he assumed was its landing gear. At this point, he alerted another mechanic, and while both gawked at the object in complete awe, it took off at great speed and disappeared out of sight.

A few days later, Air Force officials at the base interviewed the mechanics. The interrogation included having them look through a book with three hundred pages of UFO pictures, and after they had picked out the craft they had seen, they were sworn to secrecy and made to sign affidavits attesting to this.

INDIANA

Our next sighting took place onboard a train traveling from Monon, Indiana to Indianapolis, Indiana, on the evening of October 3rd, 1957.[27] That ninety-mile trip usually went off without a single hitch, but the crew aboard this freight train had no idea what they would encounter that fateful evening.

There was a five-man crew assigned to the train that night. It consisted of Engineer Harry Eckman, Firemen Cecil Bridge (who had accumulated 450 heavy bomber hours in the Air Force), Head Brakeman Morris Ott, Conductor Ed Robinson, and Flagman Paul Sosby. Bridge, Eckman, and Ott were in the cab of the diesel locomotive and Sosby and Robinson were fifty-six cars, or roughly one half mile, behind the locomotive, in the caboose. If they needed to communicate with each other, they did so by FM radio. They all were in constant contact with dispatch located in Lafayette, Indiana.

According to Bridge, it was just about 3:20 AM when the train passed the junction at Wasco, when the three men in the locomotive noticed four lights in the sky ahead of the train. At first, the lights were dismissed as stars, but upon closer observation, the three men noticed that the lights were moving towards the train, thus eliminating any chance that they were any type of star or planet. The objects were flying in an echelon formation.

The objects were described by Bridge as four big, soft-white lights, which crossed over the tracks at an estimated speed of sixty MPH, about one-half mile ahead of the train. Since the objects were so low, the guys in the caboose could not see them. Bridge contacted them via radio and filled them in as to what they were observing about one mile ahead of the caboose's position. Once past the train tracks, the object came to a dead stop, then doubled back over the tracks in the direction of the caboose.

Robinson and Sosby watched from the caboose's cupola as the four lights flew over the entire train at what they estimated to be a couple hundred feet. Once the objects had flown overhead, the crew had a better look, and subsequently, all accounts agreed as to the description of the objects. They described the objects that flew over the train as being disc shaped, about forty feet in diameter, with a white fluorescent glow that made them appear kind of "fuzzy" around the edges. None heard any noise coming from the object, yet all agreed that they may have made a noise, only it wasn't as loud as the racket made by a freight train in motion.

The objects then, single file, made a turn towards the east and began to move away from the tracks. As they did, the crew in the locomotive could see them again. All bore witness that as the crafts sped up, they glowed brighter, and each object, starting with the lead object and ending with the last one, would shine brightly, then go out, and repeat the pattern as they flew off into the distance. The objects were lost from sight for two or so minutes. The four objects reappeared down the tracks behind the train and proceeded to once again head towards the train. The objects closed to within 200 feet of the caboose. They traveled down the tracks, two on edge, two at a forty-five degree angle from the others.[27]

As they closed in, Ed Robinson got a powerful flashlight and shone the beam on the objects that had descended to treetop height. The objects scrambled and regrouped. Another dose of the light made them keep their distance as they followed the train down the tracks. The objects followed in back and along side of the train until it reached Kirkland, Indiana, where they disappeared into the night sky as mysteriously as they had arrived.

Bradford, Pennsylvania

American Airlines flight #713 was non-stop service from Newark, New Jersey to Detroit, Michigan. At the helm of the American Airlines DC-6 was the very experienced Captain Peter Killian. He was a fourteen-year veteran, who incidentally, had racked up a staggering four million miles of flight time while employed by American Airlines.[28]

The flight, for the most part, was very normal. The flight left Newark on February 24th, 1959, was on time and remained so as the crew kept to their schedule and routine, right up to 8:20 PM. Five minutes earlier, the last of the dinner trays had been cleared from the cabin by flight attendants, Edna LaGate and Beverly Pingree.

As the flight passed over Bradford, Pennsylvania, first officer John Dee noted the planes position and recorded that the DC-6 was flying over scattered clouds, at 3,500 feet, and cruising along at an airspeed of 350 MPH. While he was busy recording these statistics, Captain Killian's attention had been diverted to three bright white lights in the sky. The objects were flying a single-file formation, and were higher than the plane and slightly off towards the south. Thinking that these were stars, Captain Killian found the constellation of Orion and compared the lights to it, and these three objects were much larger than the largest stars in the sky. They also glowed with a yellowish-white light, and upon closer examination, these lights were moving faster than the plane!

Suddenly, one of the objects broke formation and sped towards the plane. Before any evasive action needed to be taken, the object slowed down and began to pace the plane at a safe distance, as if it only meant to get a closer look at what surely was a novel flying device to whom or whatever was controlling the unknown craft. From its precise flying, Captain Killian became quickly convinced that this object, which appeared to be three times the size of his DC-6, was definitely under intelligent control. With the precision of its first movement, the object returned to the formation of other lights. The captain alerted his first officer to the presence of the three visitors.

After a brief discussion, they decided it would be in the best interest of everyone aboard to alert the passengers of the objects presence as well. This, they felt, would avert a sudden panic in the event one of the objects became overly curious and ventured very close to the plane. Once the announcement was made informing the passengers of the presence of the three objects and the pilots' intent to remain on course, Killian and Dee returned their attention to the objects.

Once again, one of the objects broke formation and sped towards the plane. Though this one ventured closer than the first had, it still maintained what the pilots felt was a safe distance. It also returned to its formation in short order. The captain then wisely put out a call over the radio to any airliners in the area to inquire if they were seeing the objects near his plane.

Within seconds he had his answer. Two American Airlines flights, one just north of Eire, Pennsylvania and the other over Toledo, Ohio had been witnessing the phenomena for ten minutes. And unbeknownst to Captain Killian, there was other witnesses to this aerial ballet. According to United Airlines Captain A.D. Yates, he and his crew, as well as the crews of United Airlines flights 937 and 321 all saw these objects and were in agreement that they certainly were not any known aircraft. Shortly after Captain Killian received confirmation from his fellow American Airlines pilots that they also saw the objects, the three UFOs returned to their original course and speed and were quickly out of sight.

Before he had landed, Captain Killian issued a full report to the American Airlines authorities in Detroit, hoping that this would be the end of the story. It was not. Onboard the airliner was the manager of a Curtis-Wright airplane factory, one N.D. Puncas. He tipped off the local papers by reporting to them that in a clear, unobstructed sky, he had seen three glowing objects flying under intelligent control in and out of formation—a sight he claims to have never seen anything even closely resembling in his entire life. The story hit the wires, and soon, the authorities at American Airlines were forced to release Killian's account of what happen in the skies over Pennsylvania that cold winter night.

As the story spread across the country and raised many eyes coast to coast, the Air Force was soon required to explain exactly what it was that was witnessed by Killian and others. They (in their infinite wisdom) proclaimed that twelve pilots, six planes full of passengers, and one aviation expert, with all their combined experience and specialties had all misidentified three stars they were all viewing through broken clouds. And as far as the Air Force was concerned, that was the end of the story.

First off, stars would have been recognizable to twelve pilots. Secondly, as First Officer Dee noted the broken clouds were below the plane, and as Killian reported, the lights were above the plane. And last but not least, stars do not suddenly fly closer to an object and return to formation repeatedly.

CHAPTER 7

1960-65

THE KENNEDY-JOHNSON YEARS

"Flying Saucers, Unidentified Flying Objects, or whatever you call them, are real!"

~Senator Barry Goldwater

Brigadier General, USAF Reserve

1964 US Presidential candidate

The early 1960s were an interesting time in American history. Although we were officially enjoying the post-war peace, man, woman, and child alike were constantly on edge, worrying about the "bomb." America was spending a large portion of its Gross National Product on military goods to eliminate any strategic advantage being ascertained by the Soviet Union. Music and movies were changing, and a little movement headed by Dr. King began a full court press to acquire equal rights for all Americans.

A new decade meant new sightings, so let us get right to the them.

RED BLUFF, CALIFORNIA

While driving down a back road just outside of Red Bluff, California at about 11 PM the night of August 13th, 1960, two California Highway Patrol officers sighted what they thought was an airliner crashing a short distance ahead of them. Officers C.A. Carson and S. Scott brought their patrol car to a halt, and then got out to investigate and provide whatever help they could.

As they watched the object, what had appeared to be the fuselage of an airplane, suddenly reversed its rapid descent and then climbed several hundred feet and remained there motionless. They soon had their pistols at the ready as this strange craft began to descend and come closer to them. The object came within pistol range, according to the officer's report, and while it was that close, it was impossible for the officers to radio back to base. The object came to within 200 feet of the car and then returned to its original position overhead.

The close encounter allowed the officers to discern that the object appeared to be metallic and cigar-shaped with two large lights, one on each end that swept the entire area. When the object began to move off towards the east, the officers found their radio was once again in working order. They called into report what they had seen, and requested some back up and a radar confirmation from nearby Red Bluff Air Force Radar Station. After a quick call by the dispatcher, the personnel at Red Bluff confirmed that they were tracking an unknown in the vicinity of the officers.

The object was in view that night by police and civilians throughout Tehama County. In fact, other law enforcement officers saw it as well. About an hour before the two CHP officers had their sighting, a Tehama County deputy sheriff on duty at the county jail saw the same object. Deputy Clarence Fry reported that he had seen a pale-yellowish oval object that had lights on either end, as it hovered in the sky some distance from his location at the jail. Not knowing about the two CHP officers having their own sighting, Fry, wanting witnesses to his sighting of a UFO, marched several prisoners outside to watch the UFO. They reported that at approximately 1:45 AM the following morning, the original object was joined by another object[1] and both disappeared as they headed out over the eastern horizon.

The next day, when Carson and Scott went to the base to request some verification that the radar at Red Bluff had tracked the object, the officers in charge informed them that no such object was tracked. When they requested to speak with the radar operator on duty the night before, the officer in charge, one Major Malden, denied their request. A few days later, after a meeting by the "Brain Trust" at Project Blue Book, their official explanation was that two CHP officers, a deputy sheriff, and many other witnesses, who had sighted an object that was also tracked by radar for over two hours that night, had bore witness to the atmosphere's refraction of the planet Mars and two stars, Aldebaran and Betelgeux![2] Quite an incredible tale from the folks at Blue Book! Had they done their homework, like the officials at NICAP did, they also would have known that none of these celestial bodies were in the sky that night. Nor could they have been picked up by ground-based radar. The police officers, for the record, stated that what they had witnessed that night was not stars, nor could anyone, no matter *where* they worked, convince them of that.

CRESSY, TASMANIA

Before the evening of October 4th, 1960, the Reverend Browning, an Anglican minister and Tasmanian Secretary to the World Council of Churches, did not believe in UFOs. But, at 6:10 PM that evening, all that would change! While standing outside of his home in Cressy, Tasmania,[3] the Reverend accompanied by his wife, saw a large, dull-gray, cigar-shaped craft, which they estimated to be nearly 300 feet long. According to Mrs. Browning, the object moved very slow, and as it approached, it came to a complete standstill in the sky above their home. After what they estimated as a period of about half a minute, the cigar-shaped object was joined by five smaller discs, which had rapidly descended from a cloud bank and join the larger object as it hovered motionless.

The Reverend described the smaller craft as being disc-shaped with a dome on top and flat on the bottom. He estimated their individual size to be approximately thirty feet in diameter. Soon, all the objects had departed leaving the Reverend and his wife with memories that would last a lifetime. The Brownings were not going to report what they had seen until other neighbors told them that they had seen the same thing. One neighbor, Mrs. Doris Bransden, described it as having been a fantastic sight where a lot of smaller ships flocked around a bigger one.

Local aviation authorities reported that no known air traffic had been aloft that evening. The Reverend's sighting was not taken lightly. So convinced were the local authorities that they forwarded it to Canberra, where it was brought before the Australian Senate for discussion on October 18, 1960. What they had seen, or what should be done to investigate this sighting, were conclusions not reached by the authorities in Australia, thus what the Reverend and his wife saw that night remains a mystery.

Soviet Union

Because of the indirect route it took to come out in the western press, the next account is not as concise as most, but intriguing nonetheless. The old Soviet Embassy in London is the source of this account, which originated with the Soviet Aviation Institute. According to British researcher Derek Mansell,[4] sometime in early 1961, a Soviet-made An-2P mail plane took off from an airfield near Sverdlovsk bound for the small city of Kurgan on a routine mail delivery flight. There were seven crew members on board, plus a moderate load of mail and packages. When the aircraft was approximately 100 miles from Sverdlovsk, the pilot was radioing in his altitude, air speed, and position/ heading, when, according to the Soviet account, an Unidentified Flying Object was tracked on radar, and almost instantly, the plane disappeared off the ground control's radarscope.

There was no emergency declared by the pilot, and no SOS issued. The plane was just gone, and likewise so was the unknown object. Understandably, the UFO was not the major concern of the air traffic control tower, as a whole plane and its crew had just vanished. Thinking that the plane was befallen by some sudden and cataclysmic collision, a search was organized and underway very soon after the plane had vanished from sight. The searchers knew where to look as the pilot had radioed his position just seconds before his plane disappeared.

So the search, consisting of several helicopters and many troops headed out towards the area of the plane's last known position expecting to be recovering the plane, its contents, and crew—one piece at a time. When the searchers finally found the plane, they were very, very shocked. Expecting to find a trail of debris leading up to an impact site, what they found was just the opposite. They were all shocked when they came upon the plane intact, sitting in a rather small field of tall grass, surrounded by dense, pristine forest. The aircraft looked as if it had been placed there, like a child putting down his toy plane in the backyard. There was no landing path and the field was not long enough for a normal landing to have taken place in any case. Nor was there any crater or gully. Most of the grass around it was thoroughly undisturbed.

About 100 meters from the plane, the searchers found a perfectly circular patch of grass that had been depressed and burnt by an object that had to have settled down from overhead. When they gained entrance to the plane, they found no one! No one in the cockpit, no one in the cargo bay, and no one in the galley! The mail was untouched, and when they were turned over, the engines started on the first try. Upon closer inspection around the outside of the plane, the searchers could find no path or footprints the crew would have left, had they exited the plane. When the troops reached the nearest settlement, the crew was nowhere to be found. The crew was gone, and would never be seen again by their comrades, families, or friends.

It was suggested that the crew staged this as a ploy to escape oppression and defect to the west. If this was true, they could have flown the plane towards the west and taken their chances with being caught and shot down. The location of the plane on the ground showed that the plane was traveling further into the heart of Soviet territory, not out of it. Thus, although I feel safe in the assumption that the crew was not trying to defect, I cannot answer the more important question of what happened to them? Why have they never been heard from since? Unfortunately for them and their families, these are questions to which we still have no answers to.

The Barney and Betty Hill Experience

This next account is a very controversial case due to the claims made by those involved. Both were professional people living a quiet life in Portsmouth, New Hampshire, until the night of September 19th, 1961. It was this night that Betty and Barney Hill had an encounter with a UFO and its occupants on a lonely stretch of New Hampshire highway that made history. Betty Hill was employed as a social worker. Barney Hill worked as the Assistant Dispatcher at a post office in Boston, Massachusetts. She was white, he was black, and in 1961 interracial couples tried desperately not to draw attention to themselves, as integrating the races was not a widely accepted idea. If they wanted to draw attention to themselves, it surely would not have been with a story of seeing a UFO and of a subsequent abduction by those beings within. Just being who they were was enough to cause a stir just about everywhere they went, so why draw more attention to themselves by creating a story of alien abduction? The fact is, this story is true, and because of the bravery of the Hills' in coming forward with their claims convinced me of this, and persuaded me to include their amazing tale. The following account is derived from the story they recounted to John Fuller in his book, *The Interrupted Journey*, a book well worth reading if you find this story interesting, as the entire book is devoted only to their story, nothing else.

A Trip To Remember

The Hills had gone on an extended weekend driving trip that would take them from their home in Portsmouth to Niagara Falls for a short stay, and then a return trip where they would detour through Montreal. Well, on the last leg of their trip, they had just entered back into New Hampshire, having crossed the US/Canada border in Vermont, no more than thirty minutes previous, when they stopped at a diner to grab a quick bite. They left the diner at 10:05 PM and expected to be home by 2:30 AM or 3 AM the latest. They resumed their trip down US Route 3, when near Groveton, New Hampshire, about 100 miles northwest of their home in Portsmouth, they noticed an exceptionally bright star-like object as it moved through the southwest sky.

At first, they thought they were seeing a falling star, but when it continued on in its upward trajectory, they thought maybe it was a plane or a satellite. The Hills continued their drive, watching this object, pulling to the side of the deserted road several times so Betty could get a better look at the object through the couples 7 x 50 binoculars. Barney tried to convince her that the object was probably a jetliner on its way to Montreal. Then on one stop, near Canon Mountain, they let their dog, Delsey, out for a bathroom break, and watched as the object made a sudden course change and circled around as if it had spotted them and they were coming to investigate.

Barney was perplexed as to why an airliner would make a sudden course change like that, and grabbing the binoculars from Betty, he two saw what appeared to be an elongated disc-shaped craft, which he wanted very much to believe was a plane's fuselage as viewed from the side. Betty reminded him that if it was a plane, it should not be following them and they should hear its engines. Barney became irritated and felt it would be wise for them to continue on their way. They were alone on a highway in an isolated region that was less than sparely populated, and if it was indeed a plane, maybe it was in trouble and they had no access to a phone or other people where they were, thus no way to call for. He put their 1957 Chevy Bel Air into gear and resumed their trip down Route 3, paced by this odd light.

He told Betty that he felt the object had seen them and was playing games with them, more in an attempt to comfort himself than Betty. They drove on, Betty watching the object as it passed behind the trees off to the right of the car, and Barney trying hard not to notice the light, commented on how he was worried about a car coming at them on the wrong side of the road from one of the many blind curves on the twisty turning US Route 3. Once over Canon Mountain, they past a motel, Betty remembered thinking that they could end this whole ordeal by bedding down there for the night, but neither suggested it. Instead they focused on the object in the sky, Betty wondering what it was, Barney trying to convince Betty and himself that it was a plane of some kind.

The object veered closer to the car, and as it did Betty peered at it through the binoculars. She could now see that whatever it was, it was very large and had two rows of windows from which light poured forth. Betty asked Barney why he didn't pull over to get a look at this fantastic machine. He said that it would surely disappear before he could do that, but stop he did, right in the middle of the highway. He took the binoculars and got out of the car, motor running, headlights on, and as he looked at the craft, it swung across the highway from the passenger side of the car to the driver's side, about 100 feet in front of him. It continued to float across the landscape until it settled down in a field off to his left.

Strange Beings and Sounds

For reasons unknown to him, Barney began to walk towards the object that was scaring the hell out of him. A short distance later, he stopped on a little knoll overlooking the object in the field below. Betty, had not noticed Barney walking away from the car at first, but when she did, she began to yell to him to return. Barney was transfixed on the sight he was seeing through his binoculars. He could see figures inside the craft through the rows of windows, and they appeared to be looking back at him! He had never seen creatures like this before. Their eyes terrified him.

All at once, all but one, stepped away from the window in unison and Barney became frightened. He suddenly felt that they may be coming outside, and with that he pulled himself out of the daze he was in and ran screaming back to Betty and once in the car he tore out of there like a bat out of hell! Screaming that he was sure they were going to be captured by the craft, he ordered Betty to watch in back of them for the ship. She complied with his request, but all she could see was darkness. Suddenly, the entire car was filled with a deep, penetrating beeping noise that made the windows tremble and their chests vibrate. They had escalated to a state of hysteria, when suddenly they became very at ease and relaxed. Soon they felt drowsy, and then the beeps stopped, and they didn't remember anything until a second series of beeps started and then faded.

They found themselves driving along US 93, about seventeen miles from Concord, New Hampshire, or fifty miles from where they last recalled being. They arrived home a little past 5 AM, unable to account for the extra two hours it had taken them to reach their destination. For the next several weeks each was plagued with nightmarish dreams of little men in matching uniforms stopping the car and taking them aboard a strange craft. Under hypnosis, both recalled that they indeed had been taken from their cars and into the object (craft) where they were subjected to a battery of tests.

Tests

This is all well and fine, and makes for a gripping encounter with a UFO by two level-headed, down to earth, professional people that many quasi-experts have shrugged off as a flight of fancy, and may have been forgotten altogether had it not been for two starling facts that came out of the hypnosis sessions.

Betty had claimed that one of the test these beings performed was a pregnancy test, where they inserted a needle into her navel to see if she was pregnant. Several years later, with some improvements in our own medical techniques, women began undergoing a similar test by earthly doctors, and it is known in medical terms as Amniocentesis.

Secondly, Betty claimed she had asked the leader of the beings where they had come from, and he showed her a "star map" that included the stars where his home and Betty's homes were. She was able to reconstruct this map that contained Sol and Zeti Reticuli 1+2 in one of the sessions she had under hypnosis. After years of study, Marjorie Fish, was able to prove that Betty's map showed how the stars of Zeta Reticuli 1+2 and Sol would look if viewed from Zeti Reticuli's point of view.

If this case was a hoax, their stories, and these two *coincidences* are truly remarkable. What actually happened on that dark highway fifty years ago is something we can never be absolutely sure of. But until someone can prove the account provided by Betty and Barney Hill as false, my gut feeling is that they were telling the truth about their experiences that night in September of 1961.

Salt Lake City, Utah

Waldo J. Harris, a pilot from Salt Lake City, was looking forward to his flight on October 2nd, 1961. He was going to be flying his private plane only a short distance, and the weather was clear, with no haze and not a cloud in the sky. While sitting on the tarmac awaiting clearance to take off from Salt Lake City's Utah Central Airport, Harris spotted a large, gray object off in the distance. Thinking it nothing more than another plane on approach to land, he proceeded to takeoff, and was quite surprised that the object was still in the same place, even after he was airborne.

Harris studied the object closer and decided that he was wrong, the object was no plane, and it was unlike anything he had ever seen. He radioed the tower to inform them that he had just seen a UFO and was going to change course to try to get a better look at the object. He told the tower that the object, which appeared to be a gray disc hovering with a slight rocking motion, was off to the south at about five miles distance at an elevation of about 6,750 feet, and that, as it so happened, was his intended heading. When he had closed to within two miles or so of the object, the disc departed, by rising vertically and headed south.

When it was over the Lake Omni Station, the object halted, and then disappeared over the western horizon in a matter of seconds. Harris, and six others on the ground, including a mechanic, a pair of pilots and the owners of the airport observed the object, with the owners having watched it through binoculars. All gave the following description of the object, agreeing that it was saucer or disc shaped, like two plates put together, and the material from which it was made reminded them of sand-blasted aluminum.[5] It was 50 feet in diameter and about 10 feet thick at the center. None of the observers saw any wings, tails, engines or windows.

Harris was in constant communication with the tower at Utah Central, as well as the Federal Aviation Authorities contingent at Salt Lake Municipal Airport. Thus, as he described what he saw, the information was funneled through the channels, and Blue Book was soon on the scene, telling Harris and the other six observers that they had seen a weather balloon.

The likeliness of all of these people mistaking a weather balloon for a flying saucer is slim to none to say the least. But, since Blue Book made a determination as to the cause of this UFO sighting, the matter was closed and no further follow-up was ever done.

Author's Note:

The year 1962 brought to us the following accounts, which I want to preface by saying that although the details are somewhat lacking than most accounts, these are accounts that were made by either competent civilian observers or members of the armed forces/airline flight crews, all whose word I would take over any members of the government or their officers of misinformation.

East Coast USA and Utah

What would you say if I told you that a UFO was tracked on radar for the better part of an evening, as it flew over highly populated areas, was chased by jet interceptors, and seen to explode in mid-air by multiple witnesses? Would you say that this little whimsical tale was science fiction? Well, it was not.

It happened on April 18th, 1962.[6] A UFO was first spotted over New York State by a wide array of radar operators' on the East Coast. The object, seen by many observers on the ground, was described as a "bright red" glowing mass as it headed west over the most populated states in the United States at that time. It was tracked by radar as it made its way to Utah. It was in no hurry, as it took enough time out to land next to a power station, which was rendered useless for sometime after the object left the vicinity.

Shortly after it took off, the object was intercepted by jet fighters, which pursued and, according to local papers, destroyed the object in the skies over Utah, as witnesses on the ground observed it explode while still aloft. Whether it self-destructed or was destroyed by air-to-air missiles, is not as important as the fact that chances are, you've never heard of this incident before reading it here today—the perfect tribute to the government's ability to silence news it did not want to leak out when they are motivated to do so.

Bristol, England and Argentina

Internationally, reports were high during the last week of May 1962. On May 24th, an Irish International Airlines Viscount jet airliner had a near miss when they came into contact with a UFO. The plane was on course from Cork, Ireland, to Brussels, Belgium. Behind the controls was veteran pilot Captain Gordon Pendleton.[7] He was piloting the airliner at 17,000 feet, flying near Bristol, England, when the crew and passengers spotted a brown disc-shaped object with ten antennae-like projections around its rim, approaching the plane about 3,000 feet below and to the side.

As the object closed the distance between itself and the airliner, the captain radioed in to Bristol what he was seeing and asked for radar confirmation. No sooner had the object blinked on the radar operators' screens, with what the captain described as an amazing burst of speed, the UFO darted up and out of sight.

Later that night, a "well to do" woman in Argentina was picked up by local authorities in a state of utter fright and panic having come face to face with a similar object as the one Captain Pendleton had seen over England, when she walked out into her yard on her somewhat isolated ranch. Upon further examination, authorities found a burned patch of lawn about eighteen feet in diameter, in the exact spot outside of her home that she had claimed the UFO was resting when she saw it.

Two days later, eighteen enlisted men and three officers of the Argentine Army reported having watched a silvery disc land in a clearing and take off a short time after. When they left the bridge they were building to investigate what they had seen, they also found traces on the ground of the landed craft. These burnt spots, or physical traces, as they are commonly referred to in UFOlogy, proved that the people were not imagining the objects they saw, as hallucinations cannot burn the grass. What they saw, was quite simply, just another UFO!

A short time thereafter, Captain Joe Walker was flying the experimental X-15 rocket plane at several thousand miles per hour,[8] when he looked up and noticed a squadron of UFOs following high above him on the outer edges of the atmosphere. When the story broke that a test pilot had seen and recorded with his wing camera a flight of UFOs following one of our top-secret air craft, the military informed the world that the objects following the X-15 were indeed "Giant Ice Flakes," though they did refuse all requests to view the tapes by anyone who requested to do so. So much for ice, and it's been said that the only flakes involved in this were the people in the government and Project Blue Book.

Buenos Aires, Argentina

When you go to work each day, do you ever say, *Boy I hope to see a UFO today!?* No? Well neither did the entire staff employed at the Auto Union DKW Car Plant in Sauce Viejo, in the northwest sector of Buenos Aires, Argentina, when they went to work on July 19, 1962. All 150 employees agreed that the object was cigar shaped[9] and was headed in a northeast direction when it passed overhead at what they estimated to be about 300 feet. They could see no wings or engines, and reported that before the object climbed rapidly out of sight, it was emitting blinding flashes of light. Many of the witnesses said that this was the same object that they or people they knew had seen overhead several times in the recent past.

Cowboys and Aliens

The following month, a calm day of fishing in August for actor Clint Walker took a turn for the weird. Clint Walker was a regular on the television series *Cheyenne,* but surely must have felt that what he would see that day was taken from the script of another show, *The Twilight Zone!* He reported that while fishing with a buddy on a local river,[10] he happened to look up from the smoke break he was taking to see a disc-shaped object as it came down the river, about six or so feet above the water's surface. The disc-shaped object traveled very slow, and in complete silence. Mr. Walker noticed that a small circle of the water rippled and waved, or as he called it "danced," directly below the UFO as it made its way down river. Once the object had passed, he and his buddy decided that they had had enough of fishing for that day, and beat a quick path to their vehicles and the safety of their homes.

Author's Note:

The years 1963 and 1964 were the calm before the storm for the UFO phenomenon and all the people connected with it. Though there are few reports included herein from these two years, they are no less important in terms of the ongoing phenomenon. Let us remember for one moment that just because there were not a lot of reported sightings, does not mean good, quality sightings did not occur. I am quite sure they did, but they, like many crimes, for reasons unknown, just were not reported. So let us begin with a reported sighting that ranks as one of the most detailed accounts made by a law enforcement officer ever. It truly is one of the classic examples of competent, highly trained observers that claimed to have come into contact with things that most people can't or don't want to understand.

Socorro and La Madera, New Mexico

It was 5:50 PM local time[11] during the afternoon of April 24th, 1964, and Officer Lonnie Zamora was in his police cruiser chasing a speeder who was heading south on Park Street in Socorro, New Mexico. As he passed a local church, his eyes and ears were drawn to a loud roar and blue flame just off to the right of the road his cruiser was speeding down. Thinking that he may have just witnessed a plane crash, Officer Zamora decided to break off the chase with the speeding car and go to investigate exactly what it was that had caused the explosion and flame.

As he rounded the bend, one possible explanation popped into his mind and soon he was afraid that some local teens were fooling around with explosives left in the abandoned dynamite shack that was close in proximity to where the flame seemed to be coming from. The main road soon turned into a dirt trail that led up and over a mesa, on the other side of which sat the dynamite shack. As he came down the slight incline, Officer Zamora saw what looked to him to be an overturned car approximately 450 feet ahead. Next to the "car" he saw two small children "puttering about." Alarmed that these kids could be in danger, Officer Zamora was about to increase the speed of his car to get to the scene faster, but suddenly he stopped the car altogether.

As he started to drive again and drew closer to the object which was resting in a small gully off to the side of the dirt road, it looked less like an overturned car, and more like a large white egg, with no doors or windows visible, resting on the ground on three pod-like landing gear. On the side of the object was a red "insignia" that stood out in stark contrast to the smooth white surface of the object. The kids began to take the form of small adults dressed in white coveralls, much like a mechanic might wear. As his police cruiser moved closer, one of these beings turned and looked at the car, with what Officer Zamora claims was intense surprise.

He radioed into headquarters and requested a backup cruiser be sent out, recalling that the whole situation began to bother him greatly due to the oddness of everything he was seeing. Once out of the car, he took several steps to try to get a better look at the object and its occupants. Having taken just a couple steps away from the cruiser, his head began to ache as an ear-splitting noise permeated the entire area. Looking over towards the craft, he immediately saw that the little people were gone, and a large cloud of dust was being blown out from underneath the "egg."

Scared, Zamora, got face down on the ground, and then looked up in time to watch as the craft began to lift up off of the desert floor and slowly gain altitude. He then saw the bright blue flame it was emitting from its under-belly as it distanced itself from the officer. He recalled that it took off diagonally, thus allowing it to gain altitude and distance at the same time.

Officer Zamora's fright began to subside when the roaring noise ceased as quickly as it had begun. He watched the object as it slowly floated about fifteen feet above the desert, just clearing the roof of the dynamite shack. A short time later, the object disappeared behind the rugged desert landscape as it traveled off on a southwestern heading. Seconds after the craft disappeared, the backup cruiser containing Sergeant Chavez pulled up behind Zamora's car. Chavez remarked to Zamora that he looked like he'd just seen the devil, and Zamora replied that he just might have.

He motioned for Chavez to follow, and with Zamora recounting his tale, they walked towards the site where the strange craft had landed. What they found was a patch of scorched grass, with sagebrush burning in the center of the circular burnt patch. Equally spaced around the perimeter were four circular depressions about four inches wide and depressed three inches into the earth. Sgt. Chavez decided this needed to be looked into further. He radioed into the station and they got into touch with their captain. Soon he and a FBI agent, who happened to be in Socorro at the time, were on the site. After the site was inspected and the officers interrogated, the sighting, although never ridiculed by the staff of Blue Book or other governmental agents, was never solved and the craft and its occupants never identified.

Blue Book classified this case as unidentified, and J. Allen Hynek, the leading scientific advisor to Blue Book, and later well-known UFO author, researcher, and advocate was convinced that in this case, Officer Zamora indeed saw something land that did not fit the profiles of anything known to him or the United States Air Force at the time. Zamora felt somewhat vindicated, when two days later, Orlando Gallego and his family reported seeing an object shaped like an egg with four legs as it landed and took off near his home in La Madera, New Mexico.[12] When police officers arrived on the scene they found burnt marks and indentations that matched the physical traces left behind where Officer Zamora had his sighting a short distance away in Socorro.

This is but one of the cases that made a believer out of Dr. Hynek. Although he was a strong advocate of the Air Forces position on flying saucers when he was asked to be a scientific consultant by Blue Book, sightings like this one, where competent, stable, and highly trained individuals witnessed craft and beings that were truly otherworldly, helped change his analytical mind. He began to accept and advocate the position that UFOs were real.

New Mexico

A short distance away and a mere four days later, a pilot at Holloman Air Force Base/ White Sands Testing Range had an encounter with the same or similar UFO as reported in the sightings prior, that he would not soon forget. The pilot of an RB-57 bomber on a routine bombing run/training mission, flying just a few miles west of San Antonio, New Mexico,[13] but still on the grounds of the White Sands installation, radioed back to the tower that he was not alone in the sky. When they inquired what he was referring to, the pilot (whose name was withheld from the original report) informed mission control that there was a UFO tagging along with him as he carried out his mission to test some new ordinance.

The tower asked for a description, and the pilot radioed that it was white and egg-shaped, decorated with a prominent red insignia that he did not recognize. The pilot decided to take another pass over the hovering object. Once he had the plane turned around and was heading back to the area where the UFO was sighted, the pilot excitedly radio mission control that the object was on the ground. At this point, radio communication with the plane was lost. The plane subsequently resurfaced back at the base a short time later, with one very excited pilot.

A ham radio operator, who transmitted the report to APRO for investigation, monitored the entire training mission. When the heads of APRO, Jim and Coral Lorenzen, tried to investigate the matter, all their efforts were stonewalled by Major Quantanilla of Project Blue Book, who wanted to know the name of the ham radio operator in return for information about the bomber's encounter with the now-familiar egg-shaped UFO seen throughout the southwest on the ground and in the skies in April of 1964. Needless to say, the ham operator wanted no part of the Air Force thus the investigation was over before it could begin.

Santa Barbara County, California

On September 15th, 1964, the testing of an Atlas missile at Vandenberg Air Force Base took a weird turn for those involved when unknown to them, a UFO made an appearance near one of our ICBMs (intercontinental ballistic missile) in test flight.

At the time, Dr. Robert Jacobs was a 1st Lieutenant in the Air Force, assigned to film all the test firings and flights of rockets and ICBM the Air Force conducted at Vandenberg Air Base in California. On this day, using a motion picture camera attached to a telescope on a platform situated on a nearby hilltop, the team was tracking the flight of an Atlas missile. A radar set tracked the missile as it flew out over the Pacific, and then relayed the position of the rocket to the tripod on which the camera was mounted, which in turn kept the camera trained on the rocket at all times. The new procedure worked so well that due to their exuberant celebrations over their success, neither he nor any of the 120-man team he commanded saw the missile's encounter with the UFO sixty miles above the Pacific Ocean until a debriefing several days later.

Lieutenant Jacobs was ordered to proceed to his superior's office. Upon his arrival at the office of Major Florenz Mansmann, the Chief Science Officer of their unit at Vandenberg, Lieutenant Jacobs was introduced to two men from Washington. The major proceeded to roll the film of the missile test flight, and much to Jacob's surprise, during the part of the film when he and his team were celebrating, an Unidentified Flying Object zooms into the field of view. The round object was very distinct and clear,[14] as it paced the missile and then began to hover over the rocket as it soared through the sky. After a blinding flash of light, the UFO began to circle the Atlas missile, followed by two more bright flashes. The UFO then flew off as the missile tumbled out of control, and splashed into the Pacific several hundred miles from its intended target.

At that instant, the major switched the lights back on and Lieutenant Jacobs was asked to explain what it was they had just seen, as if he was responsible for the UFO's appearance just because he filmed the event. He simply said that it looked like a UFO. At that, the major informed him that the event did not happen, and he was to forget about it all together. It was eighteen years before Lieutenant Jacobs mentioned anything to anyone. When he did, in 1982, as an Assistant Professor of Radio, Film, and TV at the University of Wisconsin, he gave credence to the belief held by many, that the government knows that UFOs are real and have done what they can to cover up any trace that these objects are here and can and do whatever they want, wherever they want, whenever they want.

Author's Note:

Our last series of reports from 1964 are several lesser known cases where each sighting of a UFO involved the craft landing and leaving behind some physical trace as to its visit. They are not very high-profile cases, with even less glitz and glamour, yet they are significant to the premise behind this book. These sightings cannot be attributed to hallucinations by delusional people. And, like the reports of the egg-shaped UFO in the southwest earlier in 1964, these cases show that UFOs are real, tangible objects. Only objects that are made out of some material and actually weigh a great deal could leave depressions in the earth and only some type of tangible machine would leave burnt patches in lawns and fields. Illusions, hallucinations, swamp gas nor Venus could leave the type of traces found at these and other sites where UFOs have made contact with the earth.

Montreal, Canada

Mr. Nelson Lebel, of Montreal, Canada, had his television viewing interrupted on the night of November 8th, 1964, by a strange site. Glancing out his window, Mr. Lebel spotted a round, luminous craft hovering over a cluster of trees about half a mile from his home.[15]

After contacting his army buddy, who happened to be a retired Canadian Army Officer and the local newspaper, he, his friend, and a representative of the newspaper went to the woods to see what they could find. What they found was consistent to what you would expect if a glowing object touched down in a wooded area. On the floor of the forest, they found a circular indentation in the ground and scorched grass and weeds. Above this spot, the branches of the surrounding trees lay snapped and scorched, as if something emitting a flame or heat, of considerable weight, had set down. Which is exactly what Mr. Lebel claimed to have seen.

Terryville, Connecticut

On November 30th, a medical official (name withheld during original report at his request) from Terryville, Connecticut made a similar report as Mr. Lebel had some twenty-two days earlier. While driving home, he saw a brightly glowing light fly over his car and descend into a wooded area a short distance away. He decided to go into the woods to investigate. When he turned towards a clearing where the object had come to rest, the object rose off the ground and flew at a high rate a speed over the top of his car. When he got out of his car to look at the area where the UFO had settled down, he too found indentations and burnt grass.

Staunton, Virginia

About one month later, on December 21st, 1964, Horace Burns, a gun shop owner from Staunton, Virginia, witnessed a UFO as it landed and took off from a patch of ground not far from Route 250. He claimed the object was cone shaped, about 125 feet tall and 75 feet wide at its base. As it floated over the highway in front of his car, he claims that some "invisible force" stopped his car's forward progress. When two DuPont engineers checked the area where the UFO had touched down, the ground was found to be highly radioactive, while ground a short distance away registered normally.

It took the Air Force almost a month to come up with the startling claim that Mr. Burns had a seen mirage that night. They never commented on how his mirage could have lefts behind radioactivity in the vicinity where he had seen the object. (Are they not concerned with something so trivial as radiation?)

Author's Note:

There have been many things written about 1965 in the UFO community. The reason is that this was the first year that the government had to deal with a flap of sightings that knew no numeric or geographic bounds. The sightings were reported at an alarming rate. People everywhere started taking more notice of these objects that, due to the government's misinformation, they thought did not exist or that only crazy people sighted. It was now known that these sightings were reportedly seen by elected officials, high ranking corporate executives, doctors, lawyers, clergyman, police and military. It would take the government sometime to once more make the general populace believe that UFOs were not a serious problem.

Washington, D.C.

Let's start off this year with a sighting that happened in our nation's capital during the evening hours of January 11th, 1965. At about 4:20 PM, at the request of one of their colleagues, while looking out the windows of their offices in the Munitions Building, two Army Signal Corps engineers thought they had been had by their buddy. He had claimed to have seen some strange lights hovering in the sky, and all they could see was an airliner, which appeared to be on a routine approach to National Airport.

Paul Dickey and Ed Shad were ready to rib their colleague for his bad eyesight, when they suddenly looked in the direction he was now pointing and they too saw the strange disc-shaped objects as they hovered in the sky at what they estimated to be 12,000-15,000 feet.[16] It wasn't long before the disc made a zigzag pattern across the sky as they flew south towards the Capitol Building.

Roaring in with after-burners at full throttle, two delta winged jet fighters made their way east over the heart of downtown Washington, D.C. and gave chase to the discs. It was no contest, as the objects easily out-distanced the fighters. Many people in and around the capital sighted these same craft for the entire month of January. And they were not alone. The flap spread over the world, heightening the concern of citizens in most of the industrialized nations of the world.

Custer, Washington

The very next day, January 12th, 1965, a UFO was tracked by United Stated Air Force personnel at Blaine Air Force Base in Custer, Washington. The base began tracking the object which had come down very close to the ground and followed closely the car of a federal law enforcement officer as he drove down a lonely road not far from the base.[17] He reported that the object was a glowing disc about thirty feet in diameter. It made no sound and had neither wings nor any visible means of propulsion.

A short time later, officials were called to the ranch of a local farmer who claimed that a flying saucer had just landed in his pasture. When base officials arrived on the scene, they found no flying saucer, but a there was a thirty-five-foot oval area in his field where the snow cover had been melted right down to the ground! According to the farmer, who wished to remain anonymous, the Air Force told him in no uncertain terms that he would be better off if he just forgot the whole thing! Not a very easy thing to do, as how often does an alien craft make a landing in your backyard? (I know I wouldn't forget it anytime soon!)

Williamsburg, Marion, Fredricksburg, and Hampton, Virginia

Almost two weeks later, on the night of January 25th, 1965, the Virginia State Police were called to investigate a report of an encounter a Richmond businessman had with a UFO.

The businessman, a real estate developer by trade, was driving along a highway in Virginia, when his car stalled after being approached by what he described as a large aluminum-colored inverted top.[18] The object hovered just feet above the ground next to the highway just miles outside of Williamsburg, and remained there for about twenty-five seconds, then took off at rapid speed, making a very audible whoosh as it flew over the witness's stalled car. As soon as the object left, the car started on the first try and the motorist was on his way to the first telephone booth he could find to report the strange encounter he had to the proper authorities.

According to the Virginia State Police logbook for that evening, about one half-hour later another Richmond businessmen had an encounter with the strange object. And on that same evening in the opposite corner of the state, a group of residents, including Woody Darnell, a police officer, his family, and several other law enforcement officers saw a UFO near their homes in Marion, a small town in southwest Virginia. According to the report he filed, he, his family and colleagues all saw a glowing object as it hovered over them for several minutes, before hastily exiting in a shower of "sparks." The objects reminded them of a "Christmas sparkler."[19] The area where the UFO took off from was still on fire when the government boys showed up from Byrd Field.

Tactical Air Command officials at Byrd Field attributed the sighting to a plane with an arc light attached to it. When questioned about the fire, they reported a hunter shooting at a squirrel could have ignited the tree! (Hey, at least they were getting more original—it could have been Venus that started the fire!)

Less than thirty minutes later, the same object was seen some 275 miles away in Fredricksburg. Obviously, the flyer of that *plane* had nothing better to do that night than frighten people throughout the entire state! This ridiculous explanation was shot out of the water when, the following day, most of the residents of this small community saw the same object, who then called up anyone they felt needed to know about this unusual visitation, jamming switchboards at police and radio stations with frantic calls about the same "sparkling" UFO that had been seen the night before. According to local air fields no planes were aloft that could have accounted for this sighting.

The next day, January 27th, 1965, found two NASA engineers watching a strange craft as it hovered in the sky above Hampton, Virginia. The two men, one a former Air Force pilot,[20] watched the object, that they claimed had several flashing lights, as it slowly descended and landed on the ground a short distance away.

One witness, engineer A. C. Grimmins told NICAP (National Investigations Committee On Aerial Phenomena) investigators that the object made a sharp zigzag before landing and then climbed rapidly out of sight and into the annuals of UFO history.[21]

Manresa Beach, California

Our next report is of a man who claims to have been taken aboard a landed UFO, who reported the encounter to the Air Force. They, for their part, proceeded to interrogate him. The results of the interrogation were recorded and it is from an account of those tapes that this report is taken. Though Mr. Padrick is a competent observer, his claims border on the incredible. The case is included here, because the information provided by him by the Air Force, if true, has a significant impact on how we should view the world around us.

While outside of his house near Manresa Beach, California, at 2 AM on the morning of January 30th, 1965, Sid Padrick,[22] a forty-five year old radio/TV technician, spotted the outline of a large saucer -shaped craft hovering low in the air behind a cluster of trees. As he stood watching, the craft came closer to him. He stated that it looked like two saucers put together, was about seventy feet in diameter and thirty feet high.

As the ship drew closer, he became scared and started to run away. Just then he heard a voice say, "Do not be frightened, we are not hostile," but he continued to run, until they added, "We mean you no harm." The voice proceeded to invite him onboard the craft.

Intrigued, he stopped and turned, walking slowly towards the craft that had settled down on the ground behind him. As he approached, a doorway opened and he entered. Once inside, he found himself in a small room, another door opened, and behind that there was a man awaiting him. He noticed a total of eight men and one very attractive woman aboard the craft. All looked very much human. All looked to be in their mid-twenties by earthly standards, with a Mediterranean complexion and faces that seemed to end in a rather pointed chin. They all wore two-piece "flight suits" that had no buttons or zippers.

The original crewman he came in contact with professed that he was the only one who spoke English. Padrick asked him the nature of their visit, to which the crewman replied, "Observation only." When he asked where the crew and ship came from, he received a cryptic answer. The lead crewman waited twenty-five to thirty seconds before responding to Patrick's questions, as if they were being processed and analyzed for the best possible answer which did not tell their visitor too much, but enough to keep him interested and calm.

Each room he was shown had a crewman that concentrated on the control panels in front of them, though, each crewman would observe him for the briefest period before refocusing their concentration on their task at hand. During the tour, he was brought to a room, which Padrick claims was filled with such beautiful colors, that words could not describe how it actually looked. The being asked him if he would like to pay his respect to the Supreme Deity! Shocked, Padrick did not know how to respond. But he managed to say that we on Earth have one and we call him God, and he asked the being if they were talking about the same thing. The being said that there is only one! So he kneeled and said his usual prayer. He came away with the feeling that though they were technologically superior, their relationship with the Supreme Being was very important to them, as if science and religion had become one.

Padrick was returned to the place where he was picked up and as he exited the ship, he felt the exterior, and it was hard, but surprisingly not metallic. It was unlike anything he ever felt before! He returned to his house and the clock showed that he had been gone for over two hours.

He reported his encounter to the Air Force the next day and was promptly grilled by a team lead by Major D.B. Reeder of Hamilton Air Force Base. The entire session was recorded by the USAF on audiotape. They tried to intimidate him at first, telling him that these craft are usually hostile, and he had no business going near one, no less actually agreeing to go onboard! (Strange words from a representative of an organization that swears UFOs don't exist...) They did tell him that there had been instances where the UFOs had shot down American Aircraft, and mention Captain Mantell by name! (Mantell died while chasing after a UFO in 1948. See Chapter 4.)Also, they informed Padrick that there was more than one group of aliens visiting earth, some hostile, some not. In return for this information, the major wanted Padrick not to mention this encounter. For over twenty years he did not, until Timothy Good, a researcher and prolific author from the United Kingdom, got him to open up and convey his story to him.

Only one person knows if this really happened or not, and he still stands by his story. Could the Air Force officer been playing Mr. Padrick for a fool? By all means, this is a distinct possibility...

...But on the slightest chance he was not, then the information he divulged was among the most import information ever leaked to anyone anywhere. This information, if true, proves that the United States Government has known about the existence of aliens and their purposes for being here for at least 45 years.

PHILIPPINES

Members of the crew of a United States Navy ship on a tour of duty in the Philippines, saw through binoculars and on their radar sets several UFOs as they sped overhead. On May 5th, 1965, the ships lead signalman (who wished to remain anonymous) spotted what he believed to be an aircraft bearing 000, position angle 21.[23] When he looked at the "plane" through binoculars, it was in actuality, three separate lights flying in close quarters. He reported his finding to his Commanding Officer, adding that he could not determine its height but they were moving faster than anything he had ever seen.

A short time later, four objects were picked up on the ship's SPS-6C radar. As they passed overhead, they spread out into a circular pattern and came to a halt directly over the ship. Here they stayed for three minutes. The ship transmitted IFF (Identification Friend or Foe) signals that went unanswered; meaning the hardware in the transponder could not identify the objects. The objects then took off at what was clocked at over 3,000 knots. The entire episode was recorded on radar tapes, was witnessed by the signalman and the other crewman topside at the time, and the ships' CO, XO and all other officers and crew on the bridge.

MACKAY, AUSTRALIA

Our next encounter comes from three dignified gentlemen down under. On May 24th, 1965, the three men, J.W. Tilse, a veteran airline pilot for Trans-Australia Airlines, John Burgess, a retired Australian army veteran of World War II, and Eric Judin,[24] an engineer, were enjoying the night air on the veranda of the Retreat Hotel on the outskirts of Mackay, Australia.

The object was first spotted some 300 yards from where the men were sitting. It appeared to be a brilliantly lit orb, with a rim around the middle and two banks of

intense searchlights. As it flew just above the tree tops, its lights, some yellow, some orange, all very brilliant, were cast down earthward, as if scanning the surface for God knows what.

The object's appearance so upset Burgess, that he wanted to retrieve his rifle and fire on the intruder. Tilse quipped that the object may fire back, and from its impressive appearance, Burgess checked his ego at the door and shot only concerned glances at the object as the lights dimmed and the craft settled down atop a small ridge a short distance away. The glare of the spotlights was still intense enough to prevent the witnesses from seeing if it actually landed or just hovered close to the ground. The object remained in this position for half an hour. The men made no attempt to approach the object.

As the object passed overhead, they saw that it had a tripod-like landing gear. Each leg had a light on it, and all three went out of sight when it passed overhead at about 300 feet. The object picked up great speed and flew horizontally on a northwestern trajectory until it was out of sight. Tilse, who claimed to have scoffed at other pilots when they claimed to have seen one of these, from that day on, knew that UFOs were real!

Valensole, France

On July 1st, farmer Maurice Masse, 41, left his wife and children at home in Valensole, France at 5 AM to work his lavender fields about one mile away. At approximately 5:45 AM local time, Maurice was about to start his tractor when he was distracted by a loud whistling sound.[25] Assuming it was another French military helicopter, as they frequently landed in his field, Maurice decided to go and have a chat with the flyers as he had done each time a helicopter had set down on his land.

Looking around as he rounded a stone wall, he was shocked. Settling down onto his field about 300 feet in front of him, was a white egg-shaped object with several legs. The machine was about 10-12 feet high and 8 feet at its widest point. (Very similar to the object Officer Zamora report in New Mexico.) Bending over his bushes were two small children.

Thinking he had the culprits who had been vandalizing his fields, Maurice approached the duo. As he got closer, it became quite apparent to him that these were not kids, and hell, they weren't even human! As the duo faced him, he noticed they were two small beings about three feet tall, with pale white skin, and heads three times the size of a normal human's head. They had dark piercing, lidless eyes, which also were much larger than the average person's and just a small hole where their mouths should have been. They had large ears, high cheekbones, and were completely devoid of hair. Wearing one-piece gray-green suits, there were no apparent buttons or zippers.

The beings became aware of Maurice when he was about twenty-five feet away. They became alarmed, and one pulled a cylinder from his waist band, and with a quick point

in his direction, Maurice could not move any part of his body, including his feet which were now seemingly anchored to the spot where he stood. The duo looked at him awhile, exchanging some grunts among themselves. Maurice stated that he did not sense any hostility from them, and soon thereafter they packed up their samples and returned to their ship. They entered it through a sliding door, the whistling began, and the ship lifted off, hovered briefly, and moved away quickly, disappearing from his sight after it had traveled less than 100 feet.

Mr. Masse was immobilized for another fifteen minutes before whatever had hit him had completely worn off. When he was able to move, he went over to where the ship had landed and saw the depressions from the landing gears, and a one-foot hole caused by a central pylon on the ships belly. The earth was somewhat squishy around where the object had set down, but upon further examination later in the day, it had hardened to the consistency of cement. Nothing has grown on the ground on which the UFO sat to this day.

Antarctica

On July 6th, 1965, at approximately 7:40 PM local time,[26] a lens-shaped object was witnessed by base personnel as it flew over the Chilean, Argentinean and British bases on Deception Island, Antarctica. The object was reported to change color from yellow to blue to white to orange as it zigzagged over the bases. The object suddenly stopped mid-flight, and hovered motionless as a meteorologist and officers of the Chilean army watched in disbelief. The sighting lasted a total of twenty minutes, which was long enough for pictures to be taken of this odd object as it hovered in the clear blue Antarctic skies, before disappearing over the horizon at an elevation of forty-five degrees. The witnesses reported that the object moved in a zigzagging motion as it silently flew at great speed across the skies high above the bottom of the world. The same or a similar object was reported earlier in the day from a military installation on the South Orkney Islands.

Shawnee, Chichasha, Oklahoma City, and Wynnewood, Oklahoma

The overnight hours of July 31st to August 1st, 1965 were very busy for the law enforcement officials in Oklahoma. Three different officers in Shawnee, Oklahoma reported seeing a diamond-shaped formation of UFOs that took almost forty minutes to fade from sight.[27] The objects were spotted just after 9 PM CST, and were reported to have changed color from red to white to blue-green, as they flew, sometimes side to side, over the Oklahoma landscape. The objects proceeded on their way and were spotted flying over Chickasha, Oklahoma, by Patrolman C.V. Barnhill. According to police dispatcher Lieutenant Homer Briscoe in Oklahoma City, they received between thirty-five to forty calls from citizens concerned by these unknown objects flying over

their communities. Officer Louis Sikes of Wynnewood, Oklahoma had the objects in sight for a full forty-five minutes, while Tinker and Carswell Air Force Bases both tracked the objects on radar.

Lieutenant Briscoe summed up the feelings of all the law enforcement officers involved when he said, "The people are concerned, and they want to know what these objects are... only we can't tell them." Neither of the bases could offer any explanation, but the Air Force, being as resourceful as they are, informed all the people of Oklahoma, that they had witnessed stars that night.

Cheyenne, Wyoming

During the early morning hours of August 1st, 1965, Lieutenant Anspaugh was manning the phones at the headquarters of Project Blue Book. That night he recorded the following calls concerning sightings of UFOs.[28] At 1:30 AM, he received a call from Captain Snelling of the United States Air Force Command Post near Cheyenne, Wyoming, who reported receiving fifteen to twenty calls from area residents claiming that they had seen a large, circular object that changed colors but made no sound as it flew overhead. Two officers and one airman radar controller at the base also tracked these objects on radar.

At 2:20 AM, Lieutenant Anspaugh received a call from Colonel Johnson, the commander at Warren Air Force Base, near Cheyenne, Wyoming, reporting that he had received a call from the base commander at the Sioux Army Depot who claimed to have seen five objects at 1:45 AM as they flew over his location. A half-hour later, he called again to inform him that nine more UFOs were sighted. At 4 AM local time, Colonel Johnson called to inform Blue Book that they had confirmed nine more UFOs had been sighted in and around Cheyenne. And finally at 4:40 AM, Captain Holwell, Air Force Command Post called both Project Blue Book and the Defense Intelligence Agency to report that a strategic Air Command Team at site H-2(?) had reported that they sighted and tracked a UFO for almost an hour as it made its way through the Wyoming night.

Though it is nice to know that Blue Book and the Air Force were so busy that night, it would be equally nice to know exactly what they did about all of those UFOs flying unhindered over the state of Wyoming. My guess is that they did nothing, which is all they could do.

Michigan and Minnesota

Later that week, on the Lake Superior side of Michigan's upper peninsula, many qualified observers made contact with a squadron of UFOs. On Michigan's Keweenaw

Peninsula, the United States Air Force maintained a radar station just outside the town of Houghton. On September 6th, 1965, the personnel on duty reported that they had made "strong"[29] radar contact with a small fleet of UFOs as they made their way west over Lake Superior. What they saw on their radar screens was a squadron of ten UFOs flying in a large V-formation. The unknown objects were flying at 9,000 MPH while varying their altitude from about one mile to three miles high.

A short time later, several UFOs traveling at high speed were spotted in and around the skies above Duluth, Minnesota. The Air Force did not follow up on this radar-visual sighting.

Planes did not and still do not fly that fast. Although meteors and comets could travel that fast, they do not fly on a level trajectory, nor do they group together to fly in formation! Hallucinations and atmospheric phenomena such as ball lightning are not picked up on radar. So as usual, the question remains: What was it these men tracked on radar going 9,000 MPH: easy; ten Unidentified Flying Objects, which demonstrated acceleration technology light years ahead of our technology in 1965 and still a ways in the future even as you read these words today.

Portsmouth, New Hampshire

The early morning hours of September 3rd, 1965 produced two incredible sightings from the state of New Hampshire. Three members of the Air Force's 509th Security Police Squadron were on guard duty at the main gate of Pease Air Force Base in Portsmouth, New Hampshire. Sergeant Robert Mark was the highest ranking Non-Commissioned Officer at the gate,[30] and he recalled that at a few minutes past midnight, an airmen yelled, "Look at that thing!"

Turning around, he was just in time to see a strange object as it dropped out of a clear, star-filled sky. The object leveled off at about 350 feet and was headed right towards the guard shack and the base beyond. The object had two bright lights, making it look like an oncoming B-52. When the airmen heard no sound, they soon realized that this was no plane.

One of the guards ran to the shack and picked up the hot line to the security center at the base, and he began to shout into the phone, attempting to describe the object that was heading right towards him. Sergeant Mark shook the man to help him regain control and assured him that this object was not going to harm them. (How he knew that I am not sure!)

The object passed over them and headed towards the north end of the base. As the object passed overhead, all the lights in the area went out, and remained out for nearly a minute. Though he described the object as long, he could not say for sure its size or shape due to the blinding light it gave off and the pandemonium going on around him.

Exeter, New Hampshire

About thirty minutes later and approximately ten miles to the southwest in Exeter, New Hampshire, two veteran police officers responded to a call of a car off the road that was blocking traffic. The car was parked just outside the city limits, and inside, the officers found two women in a state of fright-induced shock.

When they could snap them out of their near trance, the women reported that they had been followed for several miles by a silent, large aerial object that brightly glowed an intense red. After calming the women down and convincing them that it was nowhere in sight, the officers got the women to continue on their way.

At 1 AM, Patrolman Eugene Bertrand came across a lone woman sitting in her car by an overpass. When he asked her why she was sitting there, she replied that she had been greatly frightened by a large red object that followed just feet above her car for about twelve miles. When she reached the overpass, the object, which had several pulsating red lights, just took off up into the star-filled sky and disappeared. Soon, he had her back on her way and he returned to his patrol, not knowing that the fun was just beginning.

A short time later, while walking to his home in Exeter, New Hampshire, from Amesbury, Massachusetts, along State Route 150, Norman Muscarello was probably thinking about how he would spend his last three weeks before joining the Navy, not about a UFO that he would soon be having a frightening encounter with that morning. By 2 AM EST, he was within a few miles of Exeter, when he came upon an open field near Kensington, New Hampshire. Just then, a large object with pulsating red lights swooped down at him from out of the sky.

He claimed the object was bigger than a house, about 85 feet in diameter was his best estimate. As it silently "wobbled"[31] towards him, he saw that the object had five pulsating red lights that blinked in order: 1-2-3-4-5-4-3-2-1. Feeling the object may hit him, he ducked behind a nearby stonewall and remained there until the object had moved far away from him. At which time he ran towards a nearby house.

When he reached the home of Clyde Russell, he began pounding frantically on the door. When no one answered, he took off running for Exeter and the police station he desperately sought to contact. Not long into his mad dash, an elderly couple gave the obviously scared young man a lift into the police station. He rushed into the station and recounted his story to Officer Toland, who was seated behind the front desk. Muscarello hysterically recounted his strange tale to the officer. Muscarello wanted an officer to go back out there with him to be sure that the area was secure. Toland called car #21 back to the station. Within five minutes, Officer Bertrand, with the strange women's story still fresh in his mind, walked in, heard the story, and decided to take Muscarello back out to the spot where he had seen the object. Officer Bertrand, an Air Force veteran of the Korean War, was sure these sightings had a logical explanation. When they returned to the scene, his mind was quickly changed!

Back on the scene, Bertrand called Toland to inform him that he did not see anything, but he and the "kid" were going to walk into the field, thus he would not be able to raise him on the radio for a short time. As they walked down the sloping field on the opposite side from where Muscarello had ducked behind the stonewall, Officer Bertrand scanned the nearby woods with his flashlight. When they had walked all the way to a corral where Carl Dining kept his horses and still had seen nothing, Bertrand tried to convince Muscarello that he must have seen a helicopter.

As they turned to head back in the direction they came, the horses in the corral began to snort and wildly kicked at the walls behind them, and nearby dogs began to howl. Suddenly, Muscarello yelled that he could see it. Bertrand spun around in his direction to witness a large craft with red lights, just as the "kid" had described, as it slowly rose from behind the tree line in back of the corral. The object lifted itself up over the tree and slowly made its way towards them, moving, Bertrand recalled, like a falling leave, bathing the entire area, including the Dining and Russell homes, in an eerie blood-red light.

Muscarello was frozen in mid stride. Bertrand moved to draw his service revolver, but then thought that might not be a good idea. Afraid of radiation, Bertrand grabbed Muscarello and headed for the cruiser. Once inside, he radioed Toland and told him what he was seeing. From within the safety of the cruiser, they watched the object move over head and silently hover about 100 feet above them, lights still blinking in a raising-descending order, for several minutes. Then the object began to dart off in the direction of Hampton, New Hampshire, with irregular, odd movements.

Just then, Officer David Hunt pulled up alongside of them. He reported having seen an object while on patrol, which must have been the same one Bertrand witnessed, as it was also a large object with red lights silently making its way across the field towards Hampton. The way the horses bolted and dogs howled made a lasting impression on Bertrand. Back at the station, Toland was taking a call from a telephone operator who stated that two men at a pay phone in Hampton were excitedly describing to her that they need some assistance as a giant red flying saucer was swooping down on them, and before they could finish, the line went dead. He notified Hampton Police, who in turn notified the local Air Force installation, Pease Air Force, who already were aware that a strange, truly alien object was making its way across the New Hampshire countryside that night, and there was nothing they could do to stop it!

Angleton, Texas

Also that night, on a lonely Texas highway in the early morning hours of September 3rd, two law enforcement officers had an encounter with a large Unidentified Flying Object. At close to 1 AM CST, while Chief Deputy B.E. McCoy and Patrol Deputy Robert Goode were on routine patrol out of their station house in Angleton,[32] the two men saw a huge flying object as they cruised the back roads in their patrol car.

In the clear moonlit sky, these two trained law enforcement officers reportedly saw a cigar-shaped object that was close to 200 feet long and approximately 45 feet at its thickest point. What had originally caught their attention were the lights on each end of the object. On the front end sat a brilliant purple light and on the rear a less bright blinking blue light.

The officers drove a little further down the road, then decided to pull off to the side, where they both took turns viewing the object through binoculars. As they watched the object, the lights began to change in intensity, and without any warning, the UFO performed a "nose-dive" directly at the officers' car. The object leveled off at about 100 feet above the highway, and as it approached from slightly above the road in the brightly moonlit sky, they could make out the shadow of the object on the highway. Patrol Deputy Goode put the car in gear and at speeds in excess of 110 MPH, the officers traveled the short distance to Damon, Texas, both in a highly agitated mental state.

Once they had recovered, they decided it was their duty to go back out to the area to ensure the safety of the citizens who lived in the area to the best of their ability, in the event this huge object decided not to remain passive. When they returned to the area, they soon saw the strange lights below the tree line and watched as the object began to slowly rise into the air. When the intensity of the lights began to change, just like they had before the object dove towards their cruiser, the officers tore out of there and heading back to Damon, from which they filed their report.

Pretoria, South Africa

Later that month, on the night of September 16th, two South African police officers had their own encounter with a UFO. Officer John Lockem and Koos de Klerk were on routine patrol on a lonely highway just outside of Pretoria.[33] They were driving on a section of the highway that cut through a densely wooded area. Rounding a bend, both were quite surprised by the reflection of their cars headlights off the shiny silver hull of a disc-shaped craft blocking the road ahead. Lockem hit the brakes and there they sat, observing the copper-colored object.

They estimated that it was thirty feet in diameter, looking like two inverted saucers, with the top one softly glowing. Ten seconds later, the object roared to life, and leapt into the air on two bursts of flame emanating from two tubes on the belly of the lower saucer. The blast from these "jets" was so great that the officers reported seeing pieces of the asphalt shooting skyward, and even after the object disappeared, the highway surface burned hot with flames three feet in the air.

When the South African military conducted their investigation, the officers' story was corroborated by what the experts found: The highway at that site, had been broken and cracked by an object of intense weight, then burnt by a source of intense heat. No practical jokers using gasoline and a tin pail could have pulled this off, as the military originally claimed. The military soon deemed this a case of utmost importance that should be kept under complete secrecy.

MARTINIQUE

While anchored off the island of Martinique, the crews of three French Naval vessels witnessed a UFO as it performed an aerial ballet overhead. The three French vessels, two submarines, the *Junon* and the *Daphne* and a support ship, the *Rhone*, were on their way back to France having just completed a joint exercise with American ships that were retrieving a Gemini space capsule from the waters near Bermuda.[34]

One night, Michel Figuet, the helmsman for the *Junon,* while standing on the deck of the sub, witnessed a large object as it flew eastward out of the western night sky. To him it looked like a large ball of light, or perhaps a large disc as viewed head on. When the object was perpendicular to the vessels, it changed directions and began to head south and suddenly it made two downward loop-to-loop movements and then disappeared rapidly, which Figuet compared to the way a light bulb looks when it was turned off.

It was 9:15 PM when the object disappeared. He remained vigilant; scanning the skies for thirty minutes, when suddenly the object returned in the exact spot it had disappeared. The object reappeared much like a light bulb being turned back on! It even retraced its steps! While traveling up into the sky, the UFO made two loop-to-loops and then disappeared into the western sky at approximately 9:50 PM. He could hardly believe his eyes! He was concerned that perhaps he was having hallucinations. Rest assured, he was not seeing things. This aerial ballet was witnessed by 300 other crewman from all three vessels, including four French Naval officers and observers from a nearby weather observatory.

Here is an interesting case, as we have witnesses who are all highly trained observers, who spend much of their time scanning the night sky for clouds, planes, and other aerial devices/phenomenon. If they could not identify what they were witnessing that night, it is simply because it was no man-made aircraft nor naturally occurring phenomenon. And contrary to what their American counterparts would have done, the French Naval Ministry did not issue a statement contradicting the sailor with lame reasoning. No, they analyzed this report and filed it away for comparative analysis should this object or one like be seen again in the future. (Once again our American officials could take a lesson from their foreign counterparts.)

Author's Note:

As we entered into the Space Age, even astronauts[35] were seeing UFOs! Many of our first astronauts, including Gordon Cooper, Donald Slayton, Robert White, Joseph Walker, Frank Borman, James Lovell, Edwin Aldrin and Neil Armstrong have reported seeing strange objects while in space. Their reports have not been included here not because I in any way doubt the veracity of their claims, as they would make for the best observers imaginable, but because of the nature of their sightings, unknown objects in an unknown place, is beyond my scope and any expertise that I may have. I know what is and isn't suppose to be in the skies and on the ground, but have no experience at what is or isn't suppose to be in space. Thus I feel much more comfortable commenting on what I know about. However, for a good review of their and other astronauts sightings please reference end note #35 for this chapter at the rear of this book for a website that will surely pique your interest.

CHAPTER 8

1966-69

THE GOLDEN AGE OF UFOS

"In the firm belief that the American public deserves a better explanation than that thus far given by the Air Force, I strongly recommend that there be a committee investigation of the UFO phenomena. I think we owe it to the people to establish credibility regarding UFOs..."

~President Gerald R. Ford
While in Congress, 1966

Having just finished the last chapter, you may be thinking that the early sixties was a very busy six years for those people who spotted, reported, and investigated UFOs. But as you will soon see, the last four years of the decade were even a busier time for these people, and for those now infamous debunkers in the United States Air Force.

In 1965, there were several thousand sightings reported, and probably the same number or more of unreported sightings, throughout the United States. If the Air Force thought for one second as 1965 turned into 1966 that they would have a lull in the latest flap of UFO sightings, they were sadly mistaken. In the first month of 1966, it became all too clear, that they would have to keep the gears turning in their machine of misinformation, as once again, Blue Book's staff was up to their ears in reports of strange craft flying in the skies above the United States.

But as we will see, the USAF was not alone. As the number of UFO sightings increased in the United States, the number of sightings reported around the world increased proportionally. Now, either Americans were spreading their paranoia around the globe as the debunkers would like you to believe, or there was indeed a marked increase in the activity of these craft in the skies all around our planet.

Right from the beginning of 1966, the Air Force had their hands full. By the 23rd of January they would be overwhelmed. The folks at Blue Book just did not know when to quit! Although sightings continued to come in every day from reliable sources, they maintained their mission of debunking all UFO reports, no matter how credible the witness, which led them to create ridiculous cover stories debunking those cases they could not readily prove false.

As we have seen in the last few chapters, reports were coming in from the military, law enforcement, and airline personnel, as well as upstanding members of the community from places around the world. And this trend would only continue adding a lot of pressure on Blue Book's ultimate objective: convincing Americans that UFOs were nothing they needed to worry about, because they did not exist.

Pompton Lake, New Jersey

An event on January 22nd would greatly contribute to bogging this arm of the misinformation machine down. It was also these events of January 22nd, 1966, that would begin to put doubts into the minds of many thinking people across the country. On this night, near Pompton Lake, New Jersey, a UFO made its third visit to a local reservoir. This night several hundred reliable, well-informed middle-class suburban residents reportedly watched as an egg-shaped UFO hovered, zigzagged, and shot red lights down towards the reservoir's frozen surface.

Local residents first spotted the object on January 11th and then again on the 12th. This time, however, it put on an aerial display that lasted long enough for the word to spread among local residents that the strange object had returned. All those residents who claimed to have seen something strange that night described the same object in their filed reports. The UFO was egg-shaped and was awash in an eerie red glow.[1] It would jump around from one spot on the reservoir to another at high speed, and then shine a red light down towards the ice each time it hovered over a given area.

When it had finally departed the area, several reservoir guards who ventured out onto the ice found that wherever the red light was projected down, the ice was melted straight down to the waters' surface. The object being witnessed impressed the several hundred people who saw it.

The fact that this happed just a little over twenty-five miles from downtown Manhattan, and was unheard of at the national level until the report was published in Frank Edwards outstanding book *Flying Saucers – Serious Business*, simply boggles the mind. Had it not been for the collected works of the late Mr. Edwards, numbering in excess of eight books, the Air Force's ministry of misinformation may have succeeded in covering up the truth behind this and many, if not all, other UFO sightings. But thanks to him and all other authors, reporters, and journalists who have kept the truth about UFO sightings and encounters flowing out for public consumption, we may one day learn all the secrets of the UFO phenomenon.

When this information was released, the USAF had a hard time quelling the uproar. This was one of the few examples of UFO reports where many, many people witnessed the same object leave physical evidence of its visit. Many of the falsehoods that the Air

Force and the debunkers had issued were now, for a brief time, being challenged. And although the legions of Americans who fought to have the truth released about UFOs did not win their battle, they provided enough doubt to the general population, for many to take a second look at the UFO phenomenon. All of which spelled more trouble and even more work for the members of the Project Blue Book staff.

Brazil

For our next sighting we head down to Brazil, where an experience pilot for Lockheed aircraft, a General Motors executive, ten Brazilian Air Force pilots and the controllers in the tower of the local airport all encountered a strange white light. On February 8th, 1966,[2] while flying in a brand new C-30 cargo plane, Ken Armstrong, a veteran pilot for Lockheed Aircraft Company, was on a training mission, that found him teaching ten Brazilian Air Force pilots how to fly the big cargo plane. Along for the trip was an executive from General Motors, checking out the operations of a new acquisition to their corporate family.

When they were on final approach to the airport in Rio de Janeiro, Armstrong radioed for clearance to land. The controllers immediately informed him that they had been tracking a white light that had followed the C-30 for over thirty miles. Curious, Armstrong asked for and received clearance from the tower to swing around 180 degrees so he could try to get a glimpse of the strange light that the tower claimed was following his plane. Armstrong began his steep turn and instantly saw the UFO that had come to rest in the air over a church steeple about a mile from the plane's position. He gave the engines some extra throttle to try to close in on the UFO, hoping this would afford him a better look at the object. The UFO, looking like a sphere of white light, had no problem maintaining its distance from the oncoming, yet, lumbering cargo plane.

After chasing the object for sixty miles, he gave up his futile attempt to close in on the UFO and turned the C-30 around to return to the airport and land. As he turned, the UFO once again fell back into cadence with the plane and followed it back towards the airport in Rio. The UFO once again stopped to hover over the church spire, and several minutes after the C-30 landed, the personnel in the tower watched as the object sped off and vanished in the distance in a blink of the eye.

Skowhegan, Maine

It was business as usual on Friday night, February 11th, 1966 for the people in the town of Skowhegan, Maine. It was quiet, but then again it usually was in this small town. Patrolman Robert Barnes and Special Officer Everett La Pointe were on patrol in that town's Parkman Hill section at 11:25 PM,[3] when they sighted an odd light near the ground just a short distance ahead of the police cruiser. As they drove closer, they were surprised to see a circular ship, about twenty feet long, with a flat bottom, emitting a bright orange glow. It was silently making its way through the neighborhood at about twenty feet above the ground.

The officers, not knowing what to make of the object, followed it at a safe distance until it was lost behind houses that were on a road parallel to the one they were driving on. When they could not relocate the object, they radioed into headquarters to report what they had just seen.

At 2:30 AM, having come up short on answers as to what they had witnessed, the Skowhegan Police Department made a call to nearby Dow Air Force Base to see if they had anything in the air at approximately 11:30 PM. Better yet, they were hoping they knew what it was the two officers had seen three hours earlier. They confirmed that they had no aircraft aloft, nor did they know what it was the officers had seen. They did advise the Skowhegan Police Department that they and the FAA in Bangor were tracking a slow-moving, low-flying object as it made its way across the Maine countryside, and as was procedure, these few results of the call to the USAF were entered into the police log.

The next morning, the Bangor papers got the tip as to what the officers had seen; they not only questioned the officers, but also put a call into the nice people at Dow Air Force Base. When the reporters from Bangor questioned them about the slow moving, bright orange object they had tracked the night before, the officer in charge, contrary to the information provided to the Skowhegan Police Department, told the journalist that no such object had been tracked.

As it turned out, the newsmen were one step ahead of the Air Force. Before contacting Dow, they called the FAA office in Bangor and received confirmation from them that theirs and Dow's radar had tracked an unknown object across Maine around midnight the previous night. When confronted with this tidbit of information, the Air Force soon thereafter released an official statement that classified the object as ground clutter!

What the officers saw might have been ground clutter, but from where did this intriguing bit of clutter come from? Why had the Air Force given the reporters false information? And as one astute reporter asked, why hadn't this ground clutter ever affected the radar returns at Dow and Bangor before? Good question, but don't wait for the USAF to answer that one, because they won't!

Rio de Janeiro, Brazil

On March 12th, 1966, a small detachment of soldiers stationed just outside of Rio de Janeiro, Brazil spotted a bright oval object as it hung in the air close to a nearby factory. When the officer in charge, Colonel Jorge Alberto Silveira Martins,[4] found out about it, he had a look at the object himself. He was quite amazed, and soon placed a call to the Brazilian Air Force Base nearby to see if they knew what he was looking at.

Much to his surprise, the Brazilian Air Force Base's radar tower operators didn't have the slightest clue what the object he saw was. Becoming somewhat apprehensive, Colonel Martins called the commander of his post in Rio and was sent a detachment of soldiers to bolster his confidence. Thirty minutes after it was first seen, and before the reinforcements, who were bringing anti-aircraft batteries with them, arrived, the oval object decreased in brightness and slowly vanished from sight. Several minutes later, the UFO reappeared about one-half mile away from its original location, only to disappear for good just minutes before the troops arrived from Rio. To be on the safe-side, the troops were ordered to stay near the factory.

The next night, the UFO appeared again causing great panic amongst the gathered troops. Although the troops were on orders to only fire if fired upon, several troopers had to be physically restrained to prevent them from firing upon an object that quite evidently caused them great concern. Every man gathered there, watched as the object increased its radiance to such an extent that it was uncomfortable for most of the soldiers to watch it for any length of time. Every so often, it would emit intense beams of light, scaring most of those gathered. This continued until it disappeared forever later that night.

When questioned by their superiors, the Air Force, and the media, each soldier felt sure that they had indeed witnessed a craft from some planet other than our own.

Dexter, Michigan

It was Sunday night, March 20th, 1966, and truck driver Frank Mannors was relaxing at his home in Dexter, Michigan. At 8PM he stepped outside into a very still and crystal clear winter's eve for a breath of fresh air. His eyes surveyed the farmland and rolling hills that surrounded his home. Looking up, he began to scan the heavens, and shortly, his eyes were drawn to a silent white light that was "falling" towards the ground. Watching what he felt was a shooting star, Mr. Mannors admired how swiftly and silently this bright light was descending towards the earth. Then suddenly, this strange light stopped and hovered in midair, just above the tree line off in the distance.

Frank soon realized that this was not a shooting star, but instead, some aerial device under intelligent control. Fascinated, he continued to watch the light with great interest. Upon closer examination, he saw that the object also had red and blue lights, and a white light that appeared to be rotating.[5] He called for his family to come out and see this intriguing object. In seconds, his wife, son, daughter, and his son-in-law, joined Mr.

Mannors. They all recounted that the object would settle down to the ground, emitting a bright white light, and then it would ascend to treetop level and change color from white to red or white to blue.

The family watched and tossed around ideas as to what the object could have been, but unable to come up with any plausible explanation, Mr. Mannors decided it might be a good idea to alert the authorities. He notified the Dexter police of the object and its location, and hurried back outside to join his family as they continued to watch the UFO. Once back outside, Frank and his son, Donald, decided that they were going to get a better look at whatever this thing was. So they excitedly set out over the landscape heading in the general direction of the object. While they were gone, since the Dexter police had not yet arrived and Mrs. Mannor was becoming more and more anxious, she called the Washtenaw County Sheriff's Department to alert them that a flying saucer had landed near her home. Shortly, six patrol cars were on their way to the Mannors' home.

While driving up McGuiness Avenue, towards the Mannor's home, Dexter Police Chief Robert Taylor and Officer N.G. Lee both saw the object on the ground in a nearby swamp. As they viewed it through binoculars all they could make out was an intense red glow. Two Sheriff's Deputies who also were on their way to the Mannor's home soon joined them. On the opposite side of the swamp, Deputy's Stanley McFadden and David Fitzpatrick were joined by the two Dexter police officers, as all four entered the woods to try to get a better view of the object. As they shined their flashlights in the object's general direction, its lights went off. Then, they all heard a high-pitched noise, and Chief Taylor saw a red object streaking towards the Mannor's home.

When they arrived back at their patrol cars, Dexter Police Officer Robert Hunawill informed all the officers that, as he approached their location, he too had seen the red object. It passed overhead at about 1,000 feet and was joined by three other similar objects, then all proceeded to disappear into the night sky.

Well, contrary to their first impression, this call had not been a waste of time! All the officers converged on the Mannors home to take a report as to what the family had seen and then they would be adding it to their own. Once at the Mannors house, Frank and Donald recounted that they had gotten to within about a quarter of a mile of the object. It was about the size of an automobile with a yellowish-gray quilted surface. The red and blue lights were on either end of the ship, which was shaped like an irregular pyramid. It hovered about eight feet above the ground and they both thought they could see something turning rapidly on the underside of the ship. The ship then turned bright red, like molten lava, and all the lights went off, presumably as the officers tried to make their way in from the opposite angle. Both lost sight of it until the loud noise was heard and the object was then visible to them as it climbed into the sky.

The members of the family who remained at the house heard the loud-pitched noise and watched the object as it flew directly over their home. The officers finished writing up their reports and returned to their respective station houses. Then, at 10:30 PM, Chief Taylor's son saw an object in the sky flashing red and white lights as it slowly moved eastward over the town. He watched it for a couple minutes, then the UFO instantaneous changed course and zoomed out of sight over the western horizon.

At 11:15 PM, another pair of Washtenaw Sheriff's deputies on their way back to Ann Arbor saw a bright object in the sky and proceeded to give chase until they lost it behind a row of trees.

This case caused uproar, but the Air Force had the situation well under control by that Friday evening. Their resident expert at the time, deduced that the lights they had seen obviously had been will of the wisp, or in a more common vernacular, swamp gas! The fact that the light left the swamp and joined three others, and was seen later that night in different parts of Washtenaw County was never addressed. Marsh gases may glow over a swamp, but they do not rendezvous with other swamp gases and lead law enforcement officers on high-speed chases! The objects seen that night truly were Unidentified Flying Objects.

Cannock, Straffordshire, England

A week later, on March 27th, 1966, the passengers and crew of a plane in flight sighted yet another UFO. On this morning, Mr. and Mrs. Thomas Oldfield of Helmshore, Lancashire, England, were passengers aboard a British United Airways flight flying from Manchester to Southampton. At 8:10 AM GMT,[6] as the plane was flying 9,000 feet over Cannock, Straffordshire, England, at approximately 270 MPH, Mrs. Oldfield noticed what she assumed was a another airliner overtaking the airliner she was flying in. As she watched, it soon became apparent that this jet plane had no wings!

With her 8mm Minolta motion picture camera she had brought along to capture the sights of Southampton in hand, Mrs. Oldfield pointed the camera out the window and exposed several feet of film. When the film was developed at a Kodak processing plant in Hempstead, it was plain to see that she had captured a wingless, cigar-shaped object with four fins on one end, as it flew alongside the plane. The object was visible as it came from behind the wing, paced the airliner and then took off at tremendous speed. The fins can be seen to retract just before the UFO sped off.

Several images copied from the film appeared in the British paper, *News of the World* and created quite a stir. This, of course, brought in the British Air Ministry, who, following the lead of their American counterparts, declared that the image on the film was nothing more than the reflection of the plane's tail on the curved windows of the airliner's passenger compartment.

Although this is a nice story, it doesn't make an ounce of sense! How could the tail, which presumably was moving in the same direction and at the same speed as the window this so-called reflection was filmed in, possibly increase speed and fly past the airliner in a sudden burst of speed? Likewise, the tail of the plane would have to be inside the plane to be reflected and filmed from inside the cabin! These points notwithstanding, CBS television broadcasted a UFO special across America later that year, in which they used this story as an example of how normal things can seem extraordinary when viewed from unfamiliar angles! The producers obviously had never flown in an airplane, as all the plane windows I have gazed out during a flight always seemed to reflect the lights from the inside of the cabin. Had she filmed a couple of glowing objects that continually paced the plane, then the explanation offered by the British Air Ministry may have made sense. But, since the object was dark gray and cigar-shaped, came up to, then paced then speed away from the airliner, I tend to discount the reflection of the tail story. I tend to believe that this is just another case where there was proof that UFOs are real and all the experts chose to ignore the truth, offering instead illogical explanations that supported their untrue assertions that UFO do not exist. This, however, would not be the last time this object was seen.

Clayton, Australia

On April 6th, a science class witnessed this object or one very similar to it as it performed in Australia. Andrew Greenwood was busy about the business of teaching his students scientific principles at the Westall School, just outside of Clayton, Australia.[7]

His attention was averted to the classroom windows, when he saw a strange object rise up from its resting-place, behind a row of pine trees some distance across the schoolyard. He moved towards the window, and saw upon closer examination that it was a large, gray cigar-shaped object, now clearly visible through the classroom window as it began moving toward downtown Clayton. Soon the class had joined their teacher at the window and all watched intently as the object hovered and flew around the sky in a somewhat erratic fashion. The class had watched the object for over twenty minutes, when it disappeared from sight at the conclusion of one of its strange maneuvers.

Australian officials did nothing in the way of investigating the object.

Iowa City, Iowa and Golden, Colorado

Back in the good old US of A, on April 10th, 1966, in Iowa City, Iowa, sheriff, deputies, and state and local police officers all witnessed a red spherical object as it was descending over their city at 11:15 PM. Local radar at the Cedar Rapids Airport tracked the object as it was performing its maneuvers over nearby Iowa City.

Later, several police agencies in Colorado reported the same or a similar craft as it slowly flew over the mountains just to the east of Golden, Colorado. Hundreds of local residents witnessed the object, and according to Sheriff Dave Courtney, the object was not a plane or a helicopter. He believed then and today that the object was definitely something unusual.

Ohio and Pennsylvania

Several days later, on April 16th, Sheriff Deputy Dale Spaur and Special Deputy Barney Neff[8] were making preparations to impound a car full of electronic equipment that was abandoned along State Route 224, near Atwater, Ohio. Spaur had gone around to the back of the car, to get the license plate number, when suddenly, both officers became aware of a buzzing sound that was increasing in intensity very quickly. Looking around, both men saw a disc-shaped craft as it was rising out of the nearby woods.

The UFO was about 50 feet wide and 15 feet thick at its center and had a low domed structure on top. The underside was enveloped in a brilliant purplish light. In a matter of seconds, the ship was slowly flying over their heads at about 150 feet. Both officers reported experiencing a pleasant warmth from the purplish lights radiating from the crafts' underbelly. As it began to move away from them, a large antenna-like protrusion rose from what they assumed was the rear-end of the top edge of the disc.

When Spaur radioed in to headquarters to inform them what they were watching, the night sergeant ordered them to give chase to the object. Since the UFO was moving away at about twenty MPH, Spaur did not anticipate a problem keeping the object in sight. Boy, was he wrong! As the cruiser rolled down the road, the object began to increase in speed, and within moments a chase was on! The chase began near Atwater, Ohio and would not end for fifty-five minutes. The object the officers chased was about 1,000 feet above the highway, and at times, their pursuit exceeded 100 MPH, and much to their surprise, when they began to fall too far behind, the UFO would come to a dead stop and hover there until the cruiser could catch up!

As the deputies drove towards the Pennsylvania line, officers from several other police agencies joined them in their futile pursuit of the object. Police Chief Gerald Buchert of Mantua, Ohio, hearing the officers involved in the chase on the radio, went outside with his camera and snapped a picture of the object. Spaur and Neff were forced to end their pursuit when the cruiser they were in ran out of gas near Freedom, Pennsylvania. Although the officers had chased the object for eighty-five miles, their story was scoffed at by the Air Force, who promptly informed these two highly trained law enforcement officers that what they had chased was a satellite and/or Venus. Naturally, the officers involved disputed the Air Force's claim. They reasoned that since the object rose up out of a patch of woods before the chase had started, it was neither a satellite nor the planet Venus! Likewise, the Air Force Reserve Base in Youngstown, Ohio did not believe the object they tracked on radar was a satellite, as fighters were scrambled to intercept, but had to abandoned the chase, because the UFO was flying below their stall speed.

Here we have yet another case where the Air Force's explanation was plain old-fashioned misinformation!

Virginia and Washington

C.N. Crowder, manager of the Mobile Chemical Company of South Hill, Virginia was working late the night of April 21st, 1966. It was 9 PM by the time he had completed his day's work. As he exited the gate in front of the company warehouse and started down the road, he was more than just a little happy that the long day was finally over and he was headed for home. A short distance down the road, while rounding a slow, winding bend, Mr. Crowder came upon an object that blocked the entire road.

The object was cylindrical, looking like a metal storage tank,[9] about twelve feet in diameter and seventeen feet high, resting on the two-lane highway on four pod-like yard-long legs. Mr. Crowder stated it reminded him of a propane tank just sitting in the middle of the road. It had no lights, no windows, nor any visible openings. As he closed in on the object he flashed his high beams, and the object, shooting a white flame from its underbelly, shot straight up into the air, setting the blacktop on fire as it departed. Crowder made his way to the nearest police station to report his sighting. The police followed him back to the spot where they found a three-foot wide scorched spot on the highway that was still warm to the touch.

Later that night, the same or a similar object was spotted and almost rammed by a driver outside of Kent, Washington. Upon a follow-up investigation the next day, police investigators found the scorched area and four holes, three-quarters of an inch deep and half an inch wide, sunk into the blacktop forming a sixteen-foot rectangle. The blacktop around the holes was broken from the immense weight of the craft being supported on the four narrow legs.

A few days later, state police investigators led Project Blue Book official William Powers, an assistant to J. Allen Hynek at the time, to the spot where Crowder had seen the UFO. They tried to duplicate the scorch marks on the road by burning several types of accelerants on the blacktop, but none left the same or even a similar burn mark that the UFO had left. Powers took samples of the scorched blacktop back to Wright-Patterson Air Force Base in Dayton, Ohio for analysis, with no results ever being released for public consumption. Mr. Powers, to his credit, issued a statement upon the conclusion of his investigation at the scene to the local newspaper, the *South Hill Enterprise* stating he believed that Mr. Crowder did in fact see what he claimed to have seen, as he had no reason to make up such a story. He, however, could provide no definitive answer to the question that Mr. Crowder and the people in South Hill most wanted answered: What was the object that blocked the highway, leaving traces behind for all to see that night in rural Virginia?

Author's Note:

As you well know, we have recounted in these pages, many reports made by qualified competent, and even expertly trained observers who all claimed to have seen an object that looked and acted unlike any other aircraft on or from this planet. If a UFO landed on the White House's front lawn, do you think everyone would suddenly believe that UFOs were real? You know as well as I, that there would be claims that the whole thing was staged by a Hollywood production crew or something similar offered up by the government and the debunkers.

Well, as you will see now, and again in several other accounts that await, high-ranking government officials have seen UFOs and made reports of what they had seen, yet, the government still maintains their conspiracy of silence regarding the existence of UFOs.

Oscala, Florida and Beyond

In this instance, the then governor of Florida, while on the campaign trail, witnessed a UFO while surrounded by newsman and officials on a flight from one campaign stop to another. On April 25th, 1966, then Florida governor Haydon Burns was flying from Orlando heading towards Tallahassee,[10] cruising at 6,000 feet. In the vicinity of Ocala, the governor, his executive assistant, Frank Stockton, Florida State Police Captain, Nathan Sharron, and several newsman were enjoying the flight in the double-engine Corvair aircraft when the governor was paged by the pilot and asked to come to the cockpit.

Once the Governor was in the cockpit, the copilot Herb Bates pointed out the object he had first noticed upon takeoff back in Orlando. All three men watched the two bright yellow globes as they flew apparently side-by-side pacing the aircraft for several minutes.

The governor decided he wanted a better look at the objects, so he ordered the pilots to turn into the lights that were pacing the plane off the starboard wing. The governor then returned to the cabin and informed all assembled that there was a UFO or UFOs pacing the plane, and he had just ordered the pilots to turn and give chase to the objects. As they turned, all got a better look at the UFO, which now looked more like two crescent-shaped objects connected by a central "bridge" of some sort. The objects, as if reacting to the plane's encroachment into "their" airspace, proceeded to shoot straight up an out of sight in the blink of an eye.

This in combination with their unusual shape was enough to thoroughly impress all the witnesses onboard the plane. On the plane that night were two newspaper bigwigs: Bill Mansfield, Central Bureau Chief for the *Miami Herald*, and Duane Bradford, capitol bureau chief for the *Tampa Tribune*. Both saw the object and both were left with a new respect for the UFO phenomenon. Mansfield was quoted as saying that there was indeed something up there that night, something everyone present saw, and something that is yet, to that point, unexplained, as it remains today.

Bradford added that after the sighting, he no longer thought the whole UFO phenomenon was a laughing matter! This is a sentiment that most wish the government held.

CHARLESTON, WEST VIRGINIA

Our next account is extrapolated from a letter written to J. Allen Hynek,[11] after he resigned from Blue Book and began researching the UFO phenomenon using scientific methodology. The incident happened on May 4, 1966, and involved the flight crew of a Braniff airliner and an experienced air traffic controller, (whose name was withheld at his request) from whom Dr. Hynek received the aforementioned letter. Although when the case was investigated by Blue Book, they reached the conclusion that this sighting was caused by misidentification of landing lights, I will allow you to make up your own mind as to what you believe was encountered by these highly trained observers that night in the skies above the Midwest.

According to the air traffic controller who submitted the letter, he was working at the airport at Charleston, West Virginia on the night the sighting took place. At the time, he was a ten-year veteran of controlling air traffic, having done it for three years in the Air Force and seven years with the FAA. That morning at 4:30 AM, he received a call via VHF from Braniff Airlines Flight 42, requesting information on traffic in his vector. Looking at the radarscope, the controller radioed to Braniff that although he had no known traffic, his radar was painting a return of unknown traffic five miles off his 11 o'clock position. The controller followed by commenting that the traffic must be well below him as it was not transmitting the signal that was mandatory for high-altitude flight. Braniff responded that the traffic was above his position, 33,000 feet, and descending! The controller was baffled as the only known traffic was the Braniff flight, and an American Airlines flight twenty miles behind Flight 42. Thinking the unknown may possibly have been a U-2 or some other secret plane, he radioed the Braniff flight and asked the captain if he could describe what he was seeing.

The captain reported that this object was no plane! It was a mass of light changing color from white to red to green. Shortly, the object made a 180-degree turn and sped back the way it had come in excess of one thousand miles per hour, baffling both the pilot and the air traffic controller. The controller, knowing that the pilots of the American Airlines plane must have seen the object as it retraced its path back to wherever it came from, radioed the airliner to inquire if he could see the object, and the American Airlines captain politely refused to comment. When he did comment, in a letter to Project Blue Book, the American Airlines pilot claimed that he was thoroughly unimpressed with the sighting, as it appeared to him that what the Braniff pilot had seen was nothing more than the landing lights of another plane.

If this had been another plane with its landing lights on, why had the American pilot not seen the object as it passed by his plane, all of which was captured on the radar in Charleston? If a plane had buzzed two airliners, passing one with its lights out, the USAF, FAA, and federal government would surely want to find out who had put the lives of so many people in the air and on the ground in jeopardy. Blue Book accepted the landing light theory and closed the book on this investigation, showing no concern for these two possible midair collisions. Had this really been a plane buzzing these two airliners, it would have had to land somewhere, and if it did it would have been tracked by radar from Charleston to its destination. The authorities could have gotten that information and been there awaiting the pilot when he deplaned, had they wished too.

Am I implying that these agencies don't care? Absolutely not, as they and their families fly in planes and live under the skies where these aluminum monsters fly. Had this object truly been a plane, there would have been repercussions, which can only lead me to draw one conclusion: Whatever buzzed those planes that night was not any earthly vehicle.

Grafton, Australia

Returning once more to Australia, on the night of June 7th, 1966, two police Constable's chased a UFO that was flying above the small community just outside of Sydney, known as Grafton. This sighting actually made it into the local paper, the *Australian Dominion,* due in part to the description of the object involved and the caliber of the people who witnessed it. Constables E. Mercer and P. Woodman were sitting in the Grafton Police Station at about 8 PM local time[12] when a call came in from a citizen reporting that an odd-looking object was hanging over his part of town, and that the officers may want to have a look at it.

The officers went outside, and right where the man reported it to be, sat a strange light in the night sky. The officers retrieved a pair of binoculars from the station and through them they could make out that the object was a "ring" of light, alternating in color from red to white. Looking around, they could see hundreds of excited residents who also spied the odd object that looked to be hovering around 1,500 feet above the town.

The object began to leisurely move across Grafton, at which time, the Constables hopped in a cruiser and began to follow the odd light on its journey. They kept tabs on it as it went here and there all the way across town, stopping on several occasions to study a given area a little longer, then moving on its way. The officers followed it through the outskirts of town, and once outside the town limits, the object suddenly accelerated and sped off and out of sight. All in all, several hundred people saw the object as it spent two hours slowly flying over and possibly surveying the buildings and residents of the entire town of Grafton.

Abington, England

Our next sighting was made by several scientists in Britain. In Abington, England, on the night of June 17th, P.D. Wroath, a member of the British Astronomical Association, and Dr. R.S. Gilmore saw an odd-looking light in the night sky at about 7:50 PM GMT.[13] These two scientists trained their six-inch reflector telescope on the object.

What had appeared to be just a light, soon took on the shape of a cone of light, with a central dome-like structure and three equally spaced bright "headlights," hovering high in the sky over the beautiful English countryside. The object was high enough in the early night sky to still be reflecting sunlight, and through the telescopes magnification, they could discern patterns of shadows and light as any solid object exposed to a light source would have. By using some fundamental scientific principles, they calculated the distance and height of the object and found it to be twenty-eight miles downrange and almost eight miles high. More quick computations indicated the object was at least sixty feet in diameter.

The scientists, wanting to share this most fascinating observation with others, allowed five other unnamed witnesses to view the object through the telescope. The object moved slowly through the sky, hovering in place for thirty minutes at a clip, and after ninety minutes of being in view, the object was obscured by a cloud bank. The sighting was reported locally by The Observer in a very detailed account, impressing many with the credentials of the observers and the oddness of the object the scientist had seen.

Coralles, and Albuquerque, New Mexico

In the early morning hours of June 23rd, 1966, Julian Sandoval, a project engineer with NASA's Apollo Program and former USAF pilot, spotted a UFO in the skies above New Mexico.

While driving down Interstate 85 near Coralles, New Mexico at approximately 3:42 AM, Mr. Sandoval spotted a UFO hovering 12,000 feet above a radio antenna near Sandia Crest, Albuquerque. He stopped his car, and got out with binoculars in hand and began a fifty-one minute observation of this strange object. Through the binoculars, the object looked like a tetrahedron, or more simply put a three-dimensional pyramid[14] shining with a luminosity similar to that of an ordinary electric light bulb. Using the antenna as a point of reference, he estimated the object to be 300 feet long, and flying slowly, at about 35 MPH, at a height of 12,000 feet. On one end of the object he saw four blue-green lights.

The object was clearly visible in the moonlit night sky, and what a sight it was! When interviewed by NICAP, Sandoval mentioned that the object would brighten whenever it moved, leading him to believe that the luminosity and propulsion systems worked in tandem. According to the report placed by NICAP, Sandoval was sure that it was unlike anything the United States currently had or was in the process of developing!

After forty minutes or so, the object began a slow descent, and leveled off at about 9,000 feet. It remained there stationary, and then suddenly shot off at what Sandoval estimates was Mach 6 or six times the speed of sound, which was over three times as fast as any aircraft the United States had in 1966! This report was not even investigated by Blue Book. Could it be possible that they wondered how they could ridicule a man with the credentials of Sandoval without raising many a suspicious eyebrows all across this land? Instead they did the next best thing; they ignored this sighting all together, probably figuring what people don't know can't hurt them.

Rochester, New York

June 24th, 1966,[15] Rochester, New York was visited by an object that sounds strangely similar to the object seen over Vermont, in July of 1907, as covered in Chapter 3. At 8:30 PM, Sheriff's Deputy Joseph Bobortella spotted a cylinder as it spun its way over Rochester. He watched it as it hovered over Aquinas Stadium at Mt. Read Boulevard and Ridgeway Avenue for a full fifteen minutes. Officer Paul Sterling viewed the object through high-power binoculars as it hovered over the E.I. DuPont de Nemours plant that, at the time, was located on Driving Park Avenue. When he viewed the object, it appeared to him that it was about 150 feet off the ground. To him, it resembled an illuminated pipe fifteen feet long and two foot in circumference. And like its predecessor in Vermont, when it had completed its survey of the area, it disappeared from sight!

Clear Lake, Indiana

David Roth, a well known and successful Fort Wayne, Indiana, Realtor in the 1960s,[16] had gone to the train station to pick up his son, who was returning from the Great Lakes Naval Training Center for some rest and relaxation at the family summer home in Clear

Lake, Indiana. That night, July 22, 1966, was a bright clear evening. It was 11:25 PM, and as the two men made their way to Clear Lake on a country road, David, who was driving, was listening to his son, John, describe his Naval medical training when he saw something fly over the car. Thinking he may have imagined it, he said nothing.

After the third pass over his automobile, he asked his son who had suddenly fell quiet, if he too had just seen something fly over the car. Nervously, he responded in the affirmative. With that, David stopped the car and he and his son got out. Once outside they could see that the object was round and kind of saucer shaped. It looked to be about twenty-five feet in diameter, and they could see portholes ringing the upper portion as the object hovered silently about thirty-five feet above the roadway, a distance they both felt was uncomfortably close to their automobile.

As they watched, the UFO began to swing back and forth like a pendulum and in a matter of seconds had flown straight up and out of sight. They hurried the rest of the way home. Finding everyone there asleep, they also went to bed. They got little sleep, as the frightening experience still weighed heavy on their minds. The next morning, the Roths found out that several other local residents at Clear Lake had also had up close and personal encounters with the same or a very similar UFO. Without thinking twice, Mr. Roth, braving ridicule, informed the local authorities of the object he had seen. Though there was no investigation, the Roth rested easier knowing they had alerted the authorities to the unwanted intruder in hopes that it would not return.

Augusta, Georgia

At 3 AM on the morning of July 27, 1966, a group of soldiers on their way back to their barracks at Fort Gordon, Georgia from a training class that did not end until after 2 AM,[17] witnessed three objects, each about five miles from the other, that crossed the night sky at about 20,000 feet.

The soldiers described the objects as looking like stars that moved across the sky. Except these "stars" were not stationary, they moved quickly across the sky, and every fifteen seconds or so, the objects would change from white to red to green simultaneously.

The objects were seen all across the base and throughout Augusta, Georgia. Unbeknownst to the soldiers, according to published reports at the time, these were the same or similar objects that had been tracked all across Georgia two nights previously. According to Robert A. Bennett, Watch Supervisor at the Augusta Airport, their radar had tracked these objects and witnesses had viewed them with the unaided eye. At 3:40 AM he and four witnesses watched two white objects as they changed colors and flew in different directions, and then suddenly turned simultaneously and proceeded to accelerate out of their view. Then, at 4:25 AM, while Bennett was observing a cloud bank to the northeast of the tower, the two lights returned, towing a cylindrical object behind them. This time, he was able to view them for fifteen minutes, both with the naked eye and through binoculars. The objects were visible to the tower in Augusta, and the Air Traffic Control Tower at Atlanta's Fulton County Airport. Reports of these strange lights poured into police stations from all four corners of Georgia.

Prince George's County, Maryland

Then, on the 1st of August 1966, UFOs, very similar to those just reported, once again showed themselves near our nations' Capital.

Around 11 PM, Dr. Vasil Uzunoglu, a physicist and engineer,[18] was driving down the Washington Beltway on his way through Prince George's County. As he drove along, he was startled to see a large UFO speeding across the sky at a speed the doctor estimated was in excess of 4,000 MPH! The object came to a complete standstill above one house in particular, and while it was there, the doctor got a better look at it. He stated that the object was larger than the house it hovered above, was made of a dark-metallic material that showed up in, but did not reflect the light from, its rows of red, green, and yellow lights. The object remained stationary for several minutes, and then instantaneously accelerated to its initial speed, flying towards the southern horizon was soon out of sight.

Sebring, Florida

The following month, veteran pilot James J. O'Connor was flying his plane quite leisurely 9,500 feet above the outskirts of Sebring, Florida at 10 AM on a very sunny morning. As he began to climb to 10,000 feet, he notice a strange round object high in the atmosphere. He soon realized that the object was descending down as it was steadily increasing in size. He became somewhat concerned when he realized the object was not only descending, it was also matching the planes forward speed! It remained in the exact location above the plane until it had descended down to take up a position just several hundred feet above the plane. By this time, the object was huge!

O'Connor estimated the saucer-shaped object was at least 300 feet in diameter, and cast a shadow that engulfed the plane entirely. The engine's noise and everything else was overshadowed by the high-pitched whine the thing emitted filling the plane's interior and shaking him from the inside out. With mounting concern, O'Connor decided to stall out the plane and then let it drop several thousand feet before restarting the engine and pulling the plane out of its nosedive.[19]

At 3,500 feet, he started the engine, pulled the plane out of the dive, and then looked up to see where the object was. This was when he became very scared. As he looked up, he was stunned to see that the object had remained exactly the same distance above his plane as it had been before he put the plane into the dive. He began to take evasive maneuvers, putting the plane into a steep turn, first to the right, then to the left, and repeating the process several times. Still the object was above his plane; he could not lose it! With fear mounting, O'Connor reached for his .38 caliber pistol, and as he did, he noticed the UFO had turned on to its side, showing a topside that looked very similar to the bottom, and shot directly up into the atmosphere and out of sight!

O'Connor was understandably, absolutely amazed by this huge craft's ability to reverse direction and zoom straight up into the upper atmosphere as if it was not constrained in anyway by gravity! Upon touchdown, O'Connor filed a report with the FAA, from which this account was taken.

Now I ask you, would any person risk not only his good name, but also risk of attracting the type of attention that may be a detriment to their reputation, both private and professional, by making up such a story and then broadcasting it to the world by filing a report with the FAA, if he indeed did not have so frightening encounter with a UFO? If you were him, would you risk you career by making up a story, that, chances are, no one would believe anyway?

Prince Edwards Island, Canada (near Maine)

The following day, members of the Royal Canadian Air Force where refueling at their base on Prince Edwards Island, which is a short distance east of the Maine coast. As they went about their business at 6:30 AM,[20] eight airmen noticed a circular object as it passed overhead. The shiny object, as if responding to their stares, halted all forward progress, and began descending, coming to a rest just several hundred feet above the ground, several thousand yards east of the base. They watched it as it remained totally still and absolutely quiet for twenty minutes. Then, just like the object seen by O'Connor in Florida the previous day, the object without any prior warning, shot straight up and out of sight into the upper atmosphere.

Author's Note:

From this very busy year of reported sightings, the last two reports of UFO we will see here come to us from the flight crews of two airlines companies.

Luanda, Angola

Our first case happened on the night of December 7th, 1966. Captain Henrique Maia was piloting a Brazilian Airways Boeing 707 to Luanda, Angola, when at approximately 10:30 PM local time, while the plane was still out over the Atlantic Ocean, about one half hour from landing at the airport in Luanda, he noticed the plane was being paced by two "shiny, disc-shaped objects."[21]

Concerned that these objects were so close to the plane, he and the copilot decided it might be wise to try to shake these two unwanted visitors. So after alerting the passengers to the object and their plans, the pilots began to bank the airliner from side to side. They radioed Luanda to see if they had any known traffic in their vicinity. It is not surprising that the airport responded that they only had his airliner on their scopes.

Shortly before they reached the Angolan shoreline, the two discs retreated back into the darkness of the vast night sky. Once on the ground, the Captain made a complete statement to the Angolan authorities that was supported by the independent testimony of many of the passengers onboard the airliner who also saw the two objects as they paced the aircraft.

Mexico

A similar occurrence was to happen to another airliner and its passengers and crew on the 30th of December. On this night, a Canadian Pacific Airlines DC-8 was outbound from Lima, Peru on course to Mexico City, Mexico. In the cockpit, Captain Robert Millbank, was conversing with the rest of his flight crew that night, consisting of: Second Officer John Dennis Dahl, Navigator Mike Mole, Purser Joseph Lugs and pilot trainee Wolfgang Poepperi.

The plane was cruising at 30,000 feet and making good headway, traveling at 600 MPH through the clear, cold night sky. While relaxing in his seat at approximately 3 AM,[22] Captain Millbank noticed two odd-looking lights on the horizon. He reported that the lights were originally close together, but as he watched them, they began to grow larger and further apart. Being an experienced pilot with sixteen years of flying experience under his belt, he knew that these objects did not appear like any other stars he was accustomed to seeing each and every night. Nor were they planes, as he saw no red or green lights. Whatever they were, they were getting closer, and at a rapid rate.

Just then, the rest of the crew in the cockpit, alerted by the Captain's silence and intense stare, all glanced in the general direction their captain was looking. All watched as this one large object "intercepted" their aircraft. As it got closer to them, the flight crew could easily distinguish rows of smaller lights between the two really big ones. All agreed that these smaller lights looked like the windows and as the object passed off their left wing tip and across the face of the moon, they could distinctly make out a saucer shaped superstructure between the two large lights that now appeared to be on either end of the craft. They estimated that the object, whatever it was, was about as big or a little bigger than the DC-8 they were in, and flying much faster! The object passed the plane and accelerated out of sight.

Once on the ground, the entire crew filed reports with the authorities in Mexico City. While doing so, they made it abundantly clear that there was no way that the object they had seen was a planet or star, nor was it any type of plane or other aerial device. So again, it can be asked, exactly what was the object that passed so close and so fast to their plane high in the night sky above Mexico?

Texas

The sightings by pilots, crews and passengers did not cease as time marched on and 1966 became 1967. American Airlines Flight # 162 was on the last leg of a multi-stop trip from San Francisco to Houston on the night of January 16th, 1967.[23] Having let the majority of the passengers off in El Paso, the plane was airborne and on its way to Houston by 10 PM CST. Left on board were fewer than ten passengers, two of which were Dr. Philip Welsh of the Computer Applications corporation, and Miss Teresa Trittipoe of the Manpower Development Institute, both psychologists by trade. Miss Trittipoe was the first to notice a bright point of light that was following the plane through the star-filled sky. She watched in silence for several minutes as the object changed course and speed several times. Believing she was watching a UFO, she turned around to face Dr. Welsh and pointed out the object to him.

As they watched, the light began to dart about the sky, growing closer, than distant to the airliner, and changing course and speed at will, even reversing its course instantly on one occasion. They watched in stunned silence as the UFO performed feats that they were sure no terrestrial craft could. They did not inform the other passengers as most were sleeping. They felt that the pilots were aware of the object, as they repeatedly switched on and off the landing lights long before they landed, and banked right and left, a move that would tell the pilots if the object they were viewing was stationary, allowing them to confirm or deny that what they were seeing was a reflection from lights in or on the plane.

Immediately after the plane had completed these maneuvers, the UFO copied them exactly! The light was with them until just before the plane touched down in Houston, when it made a huge arcing swing up into the atmosphere and shot out of sight. Had the two witnesses not made a full report, this sighting would have remained unheard, as the pilots, whom the witnesses were sure had seen the object, reported nothing out of the ordinary had occurred during the flight! But as you have seen, unlike international flight crews, American flight crews who report UFOs have to undergo thorough interrogation, risk professional and public ridicule and oftentimes risk termination from these high paying, prestigious positions by reporting UFOs. All really good reasons to keep quiet about having seen a UFO!

Author's Note:

Several days later, the entire metropolitan area of Houston was under siege by Unidentified Flying Objects. The mini flap began on January 22nd, 1967 and lasted until the first week of February.

Houston

That night, Houston police received at least eight[24] verified reports from across the city, of a large object flying at tremendous speed while performing incredible maneuvers.

Among the observers that night was Dr. Albert Kuntz, a psychologist from the University of Houston. According to the doctor, he and a neighbor observed a boomerang-shaped UFO for over thirty minutes. The object had several red lights on it, and moved quickly, yet silently, through the dark night sky. The object would move about the sky, then stop, and reverse direction, retracing every move it made, until it had returned to the point where its movement had initiated. The sighting lasted until the sky became overcast, and the high-flying UFO could no longer be seen by those who viewed it from the ground.

Wharton, Texas

The sightings remained constant throughout the last week of January across the Houston area, and culminated with the following headlines on the front page of the *Houston Tribune* on February 23rd: "Saucers Buzz Wharton Treetops."

Wharton, Texas is a small bedroom community in Houston's suburbs, and according to the article, a sixty-foot-wide object had been seen in the skies over the area since January 22nd. The witnesses who viewed the object from as close as sixty feet to as far away as the upper atmosphere, included psychologists, three bankers, a radio station owner, a newspaper editor, and a teacher who described the object as performing feats that broke all known laws of aerodynamics. So anyone claiming that UFOs are seen over desolate country highway, and never near highly populated areas are obviously dead wrong as we have seen here and in many previous sightings.

Lane City, Texas

Before the headlines above had hit the front pages of Houston area newspapers, a man in his wife, while driving through nearby Lane City, Texas, had a close encounter with a large UFO as they drove down a lonely rural highway. K.R. Miller, a 33-year-old department store manager and four-year Air Force veteran, and his wife were driving just outside of Lane City when they spotted an odd red light in the sky.

As they watched the object, it soon became apparent that it was growing closer to them and dropping in altitude. Pulling off the road to get a better look, the stunned couple, watched as the fifty to sixty-foot-wide object, that appeared to be a saucer with a dome on the upper portion, with rows of red, green, blue and amber lights, settled down several hundred feet in front of their car. The object was at treetop level and crossed right over the highway, and, as if that wasn't enough, they saw two other similar objects hovering in the distance. The couple jumped into the car and quickly drove into Lane City.[25]

Once there, he called the editor of the *Wharton Journal,* Frank Jones. When Frank Jones arrived on the scene, awaiting him there were the Millers, Lane City mayor Melvin Weaver, and Marlowe Preston, the publisher of the *Wharton Journal.* All were watching a UFO hovering over the local sulfur plant. The light, which was about five miles away in New Gulf, Texas, was hovering over the plant when several other UFOs joined it. Through binoculars, they could see the circular crafts with their multicolored lights as they hung over the plant, until suddenly, they all shot forward, then made a ninety-degree turn and shot straight up.

These lights, if not studied through binoculars could have been mistaken for planes or other air traffic. Had the assembled group in Lane City not witnessed their incredible maneuvers through binoculars, this is what they probably would have been assumed to be. What they saw could not be explained by local authorities, including those folks from MIT who operated a radar station several miles away that shot signals towards the sun and moon twenty-four hours a day!

Great Britain

The morning watch for Great Britain's Coast Guard is usually rather busy. The morning of April 28th, 1967, is a day that eight members of the guard would not soon forget.

At 11:30 AM GMT,[26] eight guards in Brixham, Devon witnessed an unusual object as it flew over the British coast. According to Coast Guardsmen Brian Jenkins the men got a really detailed look at the object, as they used 25x binoculars to view the odd craft. Through them, the cone-shaped object appeared to be spinning while hovering in the air at an elevation of approximately 15,000 feet. The object was white and reflected the sunlight. The narrow end of the cone was pointed up, and at the base there appeared to be a triangular door. They estimated the cone was 150 feet wide and 200 feet long. It slowly drifted against the prevalent breeze, alternating its altitude from 15,000 feet to 22,000 feet as it drifted in a northwestern direction.

Jenkins placed a call to the Royal Air Force Base at Mount Batten, Plymouth, England. They made notes and informed him that they would contact the Ministry of Defense in Liverpool. The guards continued to watch the object as it drifted to a position about eight miles away. At 12:40 PM, a plane came into view as it flew over the UFO, then dived down towards the UFO and finally disappeared. (It was not reported in the sources from which this report is taken if the plane just left the area, disappeared behind clouds, or merged with the UFO.) Shortly thereafter, the UFO disappeared into a cloud bank.

Later that day, the Ministry of Defense informed the Commander of the Coast Guard station in Brixham, that what his eight men had seen was a refraction of sunlight in the ice crystals of the upper atmosphere.

(As absurd as this explanation is, at least they didn't claim the object was a weather balloon!) The eight men who viewed the object knew that what they had seen was a real, solid object, not a refraction of light. Unbelievably, the base commander sided with his men. When questioned about the Ministry of Defenses explanation, he stated that he felt that it was silly to imply that eight highly skilled observers working in and for the defense of their country, could mistake a refraction of sunlight for a solid object. He thought that it was very strange though, that his superiors had ordered him and his men not to discuss this object or the sighting with anyone!

Indianapolis, Indiana

Our next sighting once again involves one of the most competent, trained professionals included herein as witnesses of UFOs, an airline pilot. Only this time, the pilot witnessed the object from a slightly smaller machine he was piloting: an automobile. An airline pilot, at whose request will remain anonymous,[27] was driving home to his upscale suburb just to the northwest of Indianapolis.

It was about 11:15 PM, May 15th, 1967. As he turned onto the road that led to his home, he saw an odd craft floating in the skies over the fields that bordered his property. He estimated that the object was at an elevation of 1,000 feet. It was cigar shaped with a single bright white light on the front, a rapidly blinking red light on the rear with deep red pulsating lights connecting the two. The pilot hurried into his home and called the airport tower to see if they had this thing on their scopes. They confirmed that they had been tracking it now for several minutes. He inquired if any Goodyear blimps were scheduled to be in the area, to which the controller answered a resounding no, adding that at that moment there wasn't any known air traffic aloft, nor any weather balloon scheduled for release that evening.

Once off the phone with the airport, the pilot called the Marion County Sheriff's Office. They dispatched two deputies who were close by, to go and check out the UFO. First on the scene was Deputy Kenneth Toler, who reported that they could clearly see the object; it was like a fat cigar with lights on it. It appeared to him to be about fifty feet long and moved very slowly. He claims that they watched the object for almost a half hour, and then without warning, the UFO went from a crawl to moving so fast the eye had a hard time keeping up with it, as it climbed up and out of sight.

So on this night more than four decades ago, we had an airline pilot, sheriff's deputy, and a radar controller all observing an unknown object as it made its way through America's heartland unhindered on its mission by any of the agencies we employ to protect us. (And the powers that be say sightings like this never happen!)

Spain

Another flight crew encountered a UFO over the Spanish countryside on September 10, 1967. This time, it was the crew of a DC-6 outbound from the resort on Majorca Island, ferrying almost 100 Britons back from holiday, when they encountered a fast-moving UFO at approximately 5 PM GMT.[28]

The plane was cruising at 16,000 feet, about eighty miles northwest of Madrid, when the flight crew, consisting of Captain Fred Underhill, First Officer Patrick Hope, and Flight Engineer Brian Dunlop, spotted an odd object some miles in front of the plane. At first, the object appeared as a silver ball moving perpendicular to the plane. Interesting, yes, but intriguing no. When the object came to a dead standstill and then sped towards the nose of the aircraft, this weird object soon caused the crew to cease being mildly interested and quickly became extremely concerned. The object was hurtling towards their DC-6, moving at a speed the captain estimated to be in excess of 3,500 MPH! As it neared their plane, it became obvious that the object was indeed to one side of the aircraft.

As it grew closer, the crew could now see that the UFO was a strange cone-shaped object about 100 feet long and 80 feet wide, looking very much like an ice cream cone turned the wrong-side up. Whatever it was, it was made out of a shiny silver metal that reflected the light of the setting sun. When the UFO had made its way so as to be right alongside the airplane, it dived beneath the plane and shot out of sight. Captain Underhill is quite certain that what he saw was unlike any plane on earth, then or now.

Portland, England

On the 26th of October 1967, J.B.W. Brooks, who worked as a flight administration officer for British Airways and was previously employed by the Royal Air Force as an intelligence officer,[29] was out walking his dogs one breezy day near Moigne Downs, which is but a short distance from his home near Ringstead Bay, Dorset, England.

As he sheltered himself from the strong winds, he noticed an odd object as it streaked earthwards and quickly slowed and hovered slightly above the ground. Where it came down and hovered, the object was in a central location in the immediate vicinity of the USAF Communications Unit in Ringstead Bay, the Winfreth Atomic Power Station and the Admiralty Underwater Weapons Establishment in Portland, England. The time Mr. Brooks noted was 11:47 AM GMT.

The object consisted of a circular central section about twenty-five feet in diameter and four fuselages or appendages protruding near the sides, each seventy-five feet long. As it hung there in silence and perfectly still in a Force 8 gale, the four fuselages began to move. The two on each side connected together, stacking one atop the other. Then, the pairs connected length-wise at the rear of the ship making the craft about 175 feet in length, and very suddenly, the UFO was accelerating up into the cloud-filled sky and out of sight.

Why the UFO rearranged itself, he was unsure. But, he was definitely sure that this device was not of earthy design, as in his years in service to the RAF and British Airways, he had never seen anything even remotely similar to this object. Although the object intrigued him, his one dog, a 12-year-old Alsatian was very unnerved by the object, so much so that the well-trained and obedient pet would not heal at her master's command; instead she "pawed" at him as if begging to be taken elsewhere.

As we see here and in several other cases, UFOs can and do have a profound effect on animals, especially those animals with keener senses of hearing than our own, leading many to believe that although UFOs appear silent to us, they may in fact be emitting sound too high for us to hear, but well within the range of domesticated animals.

Hampshire, England

Two weeks later, in the early morning hours of November 6th, 1967, Karl Farlow was driving his truck on the road locally known as the B3347,[30] which connects Avon and Sopley, in Hampshire, England.

Suddenly, all the lights on his truck went dead. Since the engine remained running, he figured there was a bad connection someplace and pulled over to have a look. As he pulled over, he noticed an egg-shaped UFO giving off the most exquisite green light he had ever seen. The UFO was nearly as wide as the road, and hovered just over the left shoulder.

Coming in the opposite direction was a car, and when it had gotten to within thirty yards of his truck, its lights also went out and its engine failed. Mr. Farlow was petrified as he watched the object as it floated to the right side of the road, then back to the left side, and then accelerated out of sight.

At that instant, the truck's lights switched back on and the car's lights and engine also began functioning normally. Once he had pulled himself together, Mr. Farlow drove up to the Jaguar whose occupants, a veterinarian and his female companion, were obviously unnerved by what they had just seen. Together, they went to a call box and rang for the police.

First on the scene was Constable Roy Nineham, and he attested to the frightened state of all involved, and according to the report, where the object traversed the highway, the blacktop had melted. Mr. Farlow and the veterinarian were taken to the Christchurch police station and interviewed until 4:30 AM. The women with the veterinarian was taken to the hospital and treated for shock. Though nothing came of the police investigation, as the British Ministry of Defense did not feel this sighting worthy of their time, Mr. Farlow not only had memories to remind him of that night, but a hefty bill to repair the damage done to the truck's electrical system.

The fact that the truck's engine did not die in this and many other cases where trucks have come into contact with a hovering UFO, is a result of the differences between internal combustion gas and diesel engines. For whatever the reason may be, normal gas engines, lights, and televisions, will quit due to the odd electromagnetic radiation given off by certain types of UFOs. Diesels, being mechanically different from gas engines, seem to be immune to this electromagnetic radiation. If you read other books about UFOs, you will see that a large percentage of long-haul truckers claim to have seen UFOs as they are out driving under the night skies, while the rest of the 9-5 workers sleep soundly in their beds. Many have experienced the same odd circumstances that Mr. Farlow describes as they drive their rigs the world over.

Ashland, Nebraska

Our last account from 1967 comes from America's heartland. As is often the case, the sighting happened in the wee hours of the morning on December 3rd, 1967.

Patrolman Herbert Schirmer, a 22-year-old naval veteran, was on patrol in his hometown of Ashland, Nebraska. As he drove around, he had a gut feeling that something was not right. Throughout the area, dogs howled and cattle bolted. Schirmer stopped at one corral where a bull was kicking violently at the gate as if wanting to escape from his confinement because of some unseen presence. Once he was sure the gate would hold, he searched the area with his spotlight and went about his business of patrolling the Ashland countryside.

At 2:30 AM, as he was approaching the intersection where Highway 6 intersects with Highway 63, he saw a large vehicle that he thought was a truck with a flat tire, blocking the road.[31] When he flicked his high beams, the large object with several rows of lights disappeared straight up into the darkness of that winter night, or so he thought.

When he arrived back at the station house at 3 AM, he wrote in the police log, "Saw a flying saucer at 6 and 63, believe it or not."

This should have been the end of this sighting, but it was not. As the days turned into weeks the headache that started that night became worse. He could not concentrate and was slacking off at his new position as Police Chief. Finally, at the suggestion of members of the Condon Committee, he underwent hypnosis to see what it was that night that continued to bother him half a year later.

While hypnotized, the officer remembered that the UFO did not instantly shoot straight up and out of sight. In his mind's eye, he saw the crew of the ship get out of the craft, come to his car, and take him aboard their craft. While on board, he was told that they were landed to draw power from the local supply and meant no one any harm. He was informed that they could speak all of the languages of the inhabitants of this planet with the help of a translating machine. They were here to observe, yet military planes had harassed them, even shooting them out of the sky on several occasions. When he asked how they operated their craft to move so quickly, he was told that it was run via a crystal and generators that worked against gravity. He was shown the interior of the craft and put back into his cruiser, and then the ship rose up and departed.

Now if this all really happened I can't say, only Officer Schirmer can. But the people on the Condon Committee must have felt that his story had some merit, as they wanted to know more about it and convinced him to undergo hypnotic regression to allow him to give a detailed account of his encounter. Likewise, though he ended up quitting due to the whole ordeal, the people of Ashland had enough faith in this man to make him their police chief, so I would venture to guess that what the officer said happened that evening did happen. If his account did not match up so closely with the reported encounter that we have seen in New Hampshire and California, it would not have been included here. (For a detailed in-depth review of this case please go read *Beyond Earth* by Ralph and Judy Blum—like the books mentioned earlier by Frank Edwards it is also an outstanding work in the field of UFOlogy.)

Author's Note:

When compared with the middle of the decade, the last two years of this decade were very quiet in terms of numbers of reported sighting. So we will include here just the cream of the crop, and only those that measure up to our already-stated standards.

Redlands, California

For five unforgettable minutes, more than 200 residents saw and heard a large UFO as it flew over Redlands, California. The UFO first appeared in the skies over Redlands at 7:20 PM, February 4th, 1968. The UFO descended down from the heavens and came down to an altitude of 300 feet and hovered near where Columbia Street and Colton Avenue intersect.[32] Slowly, it began to move forward in a northwesterly direction for almost one-mile. Then according to those who witnessed the craft, the UFO once again hovered for a moment and then shot straight up and out of sight at approximately 7:25 PM.

The witnesses, who saw the object for a good five minutes, from all across town, all agreed that the UFO was disc shaped with a dome on top. They estimated that it was about fifty feet in diameter. It had a row of orange lights on the bottom and a row of alternating red and green lights above those. Those who viewed it felt sure that the object was rotating as it flew slowly overhead. The entire town heard the object as it passed overhead producing a high-pitched whine, which was caught on audio-tape by a local pastor recording his sermon.

Field researchers from the now-defunct Aerial Phenomenon Research Organization, as well as four scientists from the University of California at Redlands, investigated the incident. From the facts at hand, they all concurred that from the object's description, it was not any known aerial device. Nor could it have been a mirage or hallucination, as neither of these would have shown up on the recording the minister had made of his sermon. This gathered group of experts felt that these people had an encounter with but one of the many craft that have been reported over the years that we all refer to as UFOs.

Chascomus, Argentina

On June 3rd, 1968, Dr. and Mrs. Vidal, residents of the city of Maipu, Argentina, accompanied their neighbors who were headed to a family reunion in Chascomus, Argentina.[33]

They arrived in the afternoon, and after partaking of the festivities, they all set off for home around dusk. They followed Argentine National Route 2 back to Maipu. The Vidal's neighbors arrived home first, and agreed to wait until their friends were home before retiring for the evening. They figured they would not have to wait long, although they had lost sight of the Vidals, they left the party at the same time, thus they should arrive any minute.

When minutes turned to hours, the neighbors feared the worst, and decided they should go back to Chascomus and see if they could find the Vidals. On the way, the thoughts of their friends being in an accident mingled with the less fearful thoughts of finding their friends parked on the roadside with a stalled car or flat tire. When they had reached Chascomus and had not come across any sign of their friends, they made the eighty-mile trip back home in a state of bewildered confusion. Had they missed them? Had they gone somewhere else and returned a different route? They would have to wait and see.

The following day, they informed the Maipu police of the disappearance of the doctor and his wife. They immediately began an investigation to locate either them or their car. But when the first day passed and nothing could be found, it seemed as if the Vidals had disappeared without a trace. When their phone rang the next day, however, they were relieved to hear the voices of their neighbors. That relief soon turned to shock when Dr. Vidal informed them they were calling from the Argentine Consulate in Mexico City, thousands of miles to the north! Dr. Vidal informed his neighbors that he could not provide details at the moment, but asked if they could meet them at the airport in Ezeiza. When the Vidals arrived, they found a crowd of relatives and friends who were glad they were safely returned after their mysterious disappearance.

Both wore the same clothes they had on at the party several days before. Dr. Vidal looked beleaguered, but his wife was in bad shape. Mrs. Vidal was taken directly from the airport to a private clinic where she was treated for a "violent nervous crisis."

Once things began to return to normal, the doctor, against the consulate request, began informing people of his odd encounter. They had left the reunion right after their neighbors. He tried to maintain a speed that would allow him to keep his friends taillights in view at all times. Just outside of Chascomus, the radio began to sputter as the car ran into a dense fog. The next thing they knew, they were sitting along the roadside in broad daylight. Getting out to walk around and clear his head, he noticed that all the paint from his car was gone, leaving the cars sheet metal body panels glistening in the sunlight.

Mrs. Vidal began to come out of her groggy state and soon was awash with tears, and fearfully wanted to know where she was. The doctor did not know. Dr. Vidal got back into his car and started the engine, intending to drive somewhere to find out where they were. When a car came into sight, he stopped and flagged it down, asking the driver where they were. The passing motorist's information told them that they were on the outskirts of Mexico City—which sent Mrs. Vidal into sheer panic.

Upon arrival in Mexico City, they found their way to the Argentine Consulate where they told them of their weird experience. They were given a medical examination and their car was impounded and sent to a lab in the United States for testing. The Consulate made arrangements for their return to Argentina, informing them that it would be in their best interest not to mention the strange ordeal to anyone. But how could they not? Their friends and family knew they were missing, and everyone knew that in a day and a half, even driving at breakneck speeds through the Andes, the Vidals could not have driven the 5,000 miles to Mexico City. And what about their new car? How could they explain that it was in America undergoing tests without raising many suspicious eyebrows?

Although this account is a bit of a deviation from all others contained herein, I choose to include it because I truly believe the events related by Dr. Vidal happened exactly as he claims. Am I a sucker for weird stories? Do I hear an unusual tale and instantly assume aliens are involved? I can answer both of these questions with a resounding NO! Ask yourself these questions, as I did when first reviewing this case.

1. Would a successful doctor in any country risk losing the status he has attained and the income from a thriving practice just to get a little media attention? Probably not, thus I do not think this angle is a likely scenario

2. Could they have gotten to Mexico City in their car, which was on record with the Argentine Consulate as having been sent to the USA from the location of the Party in Argentina? Driving over 5,000 miles would require 2 ½ days of driving 100 MPH for twenty hours a day, another unlikely scenario.

3. Is there any other way they could have gotten to Mexico City? Sure, via an airplane, but what of their car. Would anyone abandon a new car for a little publicity that would not benefit them?

Add this to the fact that Mrs. Vidal was admitted to a clinic for treatment for what the doctors there felt was a real ailment and the facts stand up in support of my claim that something very unusual *did* happen to them. And although there was not a sighting per say of a UFO before they blacked out, the whole ordeal is in line with the reports made by many abductees of events that happen before and after an abduction.

It is my belief, as well as others better trained in the abduction phenomenon than I, that the Vidal case points to their having encountered something outside the realm of normalcy. Chances are that they, like the Hills, had an interrupted journey. Due to his wife's slow recovery, we will never know. In the best interest of his wife, her condition, and their place in the local community, Dr. Vidal felt it was better to forget about the incident than try to find out what really happened that night as they returned home from a joyous celebration only to find themselves in the middle of yet another unsolved mystery connected to the UFO phenomenon. Had they under gone hypnotic regression, chances are, after the fog rolled in, an ordeal similar to the Hills and many others, would have played itself out before they were returned to the roadside 5,000 miles from their point of origin.

Author's Note:

Undoubtedly, Phillip Klass was the government's Chief Debunker. So in interest of fair play, and in an attempt to give you the chance to determine if this moniker I assigned to him holds true, I will go through the next case a little differently. Up till now, we have listed the particulars of the sightings and then reported the possible explanations and or the official explanation afterwards. This time I will give you the expert's opinion first, so you can be the judge in deciding if the judgment was sound, based on the facts at hand. So here we go!

Madrid, Spain

On September 5th, 1968, thousands of people, including jet fighter pilots of the Spanish Air Force, witnessed an Unidentified Flying Object over the city of Madrid, Spain.

Now, the explanation that Mr. Klass has given states that what the witness had watched was a weather balloon of French design as it made its way above the Spanish Capitol on that late summer evening. He goes so far as to say that he believes that the balloon was one designed in Toulouse for the French Center for National Space Studies, which could have reached the reported altitude and remained there for several days.

Now let's see if this makes any sense. Barry James[34] filed a report with the United Press International news service on September 6th describing the events of the day before. According to his report the people of Madrid poured out into the streets that night to observe a bright object high in the sky as it slowly made its way over their city. When the reports came into the Spanish Air Force of the UFO over the capitol, an American built F-104 fighter was dispatched and vectored to the object's location. When the jet had a visual on the bogey, which at that time was hovering at 50,000 feet, it sped to intercept the unknown object. When the supersonic jet began to close in, the object shot up to 90,000 feet and continued on its slow meander over the Spanish landscape.

Another fighter pilot radioed confirmation that the object was still up there and traveling very slowly across the city. With the thousands of Spaniards in the streets, traffic was backed up for miles. Pictures taken of the object through high-powered telescopes show a triangular object that gave off a tremendous amount of light.

Now I ask you, in all honesty, do the facts of the report support Mr. Klass' conclusion? Had the object just drifted over the city reflecting light from the sun, which had set many hours earlier, this may be a viable explanation. Since part of the report fits the explanation, the debunkers capitalize on this and explain away the sightings, with no mention of the rest of the story. What Mr. Klass did not explain, nor could he explain, is how this French designed balloon managed to climb from 50,000 feet to 90,000 feet at a speed that a supersonic F-104 could not match? A balloon could not do this since its speed is determined by the wind, and winds are not faster than the speed of sound.

This case is no different from the countless others where the quasi-experts have claimed that pilots chased a weather balloon. The fact that the weather balloon is never caught by the speedier jet is never addressed, and still an *expert* will explain it away with complete success, once again making those who take UFOs seriously look foolish to those people who are not as informed about the intricacies of this truly baffling phenomenon.

LEARY, GEORGIA

Our last account is taken directly from the NICAP UFO report filed by the person who witnessed it. One evening in October of 1969, ten to twelve men were standing out of doors in Leary, Georgia at approximately 7:15 PM awaiting the start of a meeting. Their idle banter was interrupted by light on the horizon which began to act in a very strange manner. The men noticed a bluish sphere of light at about thirty degrees of elevation on the western horizon. It appeared to be moving towards them at a steady speed. Though there were stars in the sky that evening, the men were sure this was no star, and as it drew nearer, they came to recognize it for what it really was: a UFO.

The object drew close to them and still the night air was silent. The object made no sound whatsoever. The UFO was as bright as a full moon, and changed from bluish to reddish and was distinctly outlined against the early evening sky. The object appeared to stop, then move away, come close once more, and then hovered once again. It initially was the size of a star or planet when on the horizon, and when it had traveled to its closest point to the men, about 300 yards, it appeared to be as big, if not bigger, than the full moon. The object remained in view for ten to twelve minutes, and then disappeared.

Although it took the witness four years to file the report, it was well worth the wait. The one man from the group who filed the report makes for one highly believable witness. He is a Navy veteran trained in nuclear physics for service aboard one of the atomic vessels in America's fleet. Despite the risk of public humiliation due to his high profile job, this event had so profound an influence on him that he made the report to NICAP and even allowed them to use his name: James Carter. At the time of the report, Carter was Governor of Georgia and as we all know would go on to become the 39th President of the United States.

It was just three months after this incident, on December 17th, 1969, that Project Blue Book decided that in their opinion, UFOs posed no threat to the security of this nation, thus the United States Air Force should cease investigating the sightings of UFOs. Whoever said ignorance is bliss had the brass in the Air Force in mind! When asked by the American people to investigate these objects that so freely roamed the skies above the United States, they purposefully discredited and down played sightings routinely. This created a public ignorant to the facts and blissful in their eased minds. The general public was left unaware of the fact that UFOs are real, they're here, and that we may never know what their purposes are.

CHAPTER 9

THE 1970s
THE UFO PHENOMENON AFTER PROJECT BLUE BOOK

"I don't laugh at people any more when they claim they've seen UFOs, because I've seen one myself."

~Jimmy Carter
President of the United States of America
From an interview appearing in the *Wichita Beacon*
September 1973

After the government's agents of disinformation at Project Blue Book called it quits, thusly informing the world that according to them and in turn the United States Government, UFOs were not worthy of investigating nor a matter of national security, it became more difficult for people who had sightings to bring themselves to report them. As you will see, although the quality of the sightings and witnesses remains the same herein, the number of reports made by qualified competent observers decreased considerably. This is a direct result of the Air Force declaring UFOs as no threat to national security. By declaring this, the Air Force successfully laid the groundwork for those debunkers in the media to stress to the world that if the Air Force doesn't consider them a threat, they must not be real.

So those people in the past, present, and future who see these make-believe objects are not *playing with a full deck,* and their reports should be dismissed. In their view, the only people who would report a UFO, knowing that the USAF wants nothing to do with them or their supposed sighting, would obviously have to be mentally or emotionally unstable. Before making a report, those who had a sighting would have to consider how the report would impact their lives. Would they be labeled a kook? Would this cause them to lose their jobs, businesses, or social standing? Would they be the butt of many jokes and the object of much ridicule? Was it really worth risking any of the above just to try to get answers that would not be forth coming?

As you can probably understand, this one declaration by the USAF in many ways got them off the hook. By relegating the task of investigating these sightings to local law enforcement and those groups founded solely to investigate these and other strange occurrences, the Air Force could continue researching the sightings, chasing UFOs with the planes and gas that our tax dollars buy, without having to offer any explanations as to what the UFOs were and why they are here. Since they had already publicly declared that they were no longer in the business of conducting investigations of UFOs, they could brush aside any question about the subject, while coyly making insinuations about the veracity of those who see these things that the USAF claimed do not exist.

It becomes easy to see why many sightings go unreported. Everyday life is hard enough, so why bring more headaches down upon yourself? Be that as it may, if these folks in the following reports did not see exactly what they claimed to have seen, why risk all the aforementioned problems for a few headlines or a few minutes of fame. If they were not trying to find out the truth behind what it was they saw, would they risk so much? I think not.

CHINA, HUBEI PROVINCE

Behind the Great Wall lives an ancient race, whose people and customs our very different from ours in the west. One thing we all have in common though, is that the people of both the United States and China have and continue to see UFOs.

The following sighting occurred during the last week of September 1971. The man who made the report, Chen Chu was a member of the Peoples Liberation Army stationed in China's Hubei Province.[1] He and his unit were on a training mission in a valley just to the north of Dingxian City in central China. At 7:30 PM local time, Chu and several others noticed a ball of light as it rose from behind the tree line to the rear of their encampment's northern perimeter.

The ball of light was as big as a full moon and gave off a large quantity of a misty gas from its well-defined edges. The object began to emit more "gas" from its bottom and started a slow rise into the night sky. As it climbed, it would stop to hover for a few moments and then once again repeat what it had just done.

As it silently rose up and out of sight, those assembled could easily discern that this was no aerial machine like any they had every laid eyes on. The object had no windows, wings, engines, nor any tail. It was quiet, ruling out the possibility that it was a helicopter. The only familiar sight was a bright light attached to it. The troops, many of whom were still on edge from the commotion surrounding the failed coup attempt against Mao Tse Tung by General Lin Biao and Biao's subsequent death in an "airplane accident," quickly reported what they were seeing to their superiors. They swiftly dispatched a motor vehicle and a small detachment of troops to chase after the object. Due to the roughness of the terrain, the vehicle was forced to give up their chase.

IN THE SKIES OVER THE MIDWEST

The year 1973 was another year in which the country and the world experienced a major flap of UFO sightings. In February of 1973, the flight crew of a DC-8, whose names and the name of their airline are withheld here as per their original request when filing their report with NICAP,[2] spotted a UFO as they flew through the cold winter night. Around 2:30 AM CST, the plane was descending from an altitude of 21,000 feet, traveling in excess of 500 MPH. As they descended, the copilot spotted a light just under and slightly in front of the plane's right wing. He originally assumed this light, which looked to be about a mile away, was nothing other than another aircraft. The light was pacing the plane, and after watching it for a brief period, the copilot alerted the pilot to the object's presence.

Concerned that an airliner would fly that close to his plane, the pilot, continuing to observe the light with the copilot, tried in vain to raise the strange object via the radio. They could not raise the object, and after their final attempt, both men watched stunned, as this light closed the mile distance almost instantaneously, and once again paced the plane just 300 yards off and slightly above the planes right wing. Once the object settled into pacing the plane, the bright light from that morning's full moon allowed the men to see what the light was attached to, and soon they realized why they were unable to raise the craft on their radio. The light was being emitted from an oblong wingless, tailless, silvery metallic object.

They estimated its size as about forty feet wide and about eighty feet long. The pilots switched on their weather radar and the object did paint a return on their set. As if in answer to this, the object flew up and over the plane, pacing the plane from the exact same spot over the left wing of the plane. After a short time, it dropped down and disappeared from radar, only to reappear flying in excess of 1,000 MPH as it flew under the plane and out in front of the aircraft. It then made several up and down motions and after a sudden right turn, the object disappeared in the direction from which it came.

The pilots would never again scoff at those who claimed they had seen those strange lights in the darkness of night, as now they too had become believers that there are strange objects flying through the skies, and those objects, as we know, truly are unidentifiable.

SAYLOR LAKE, PENNSYLVANIA

The people who are year-round residents of the Saylor Lake area in northeastern Pennsylvania were treated to an aerial show on the nights of March 1st and 13th, 1973. On the 1st of March, over a dozen local residents, including Pennsylvania State Trooper James Hontz, watched as UFOs flew over the lake for over three hours and twenty minutes.

The witnesses claimed that the objects were round and disc-like; most had white lights, while a few had red or blue lights. The objects made no noise nor left any vapor trail as a plane's super-hot exhaust would have left in the cold night air. According to those on hand, the objects came in fifteen-minute intervals starting at 7:25 PM and continued till almost 10:45 PM. The UFOs were flying over the lake at about 1,500 to 2,000 feet heading towards the New Jersey border. They would fly overhead in small squadrons, which, according to Trooper Hontz, gave them the appearance of large flying Christmas trees.[3] In all the witnesses saw thirty-nine UFOs as they slowly made their way over the lake and then sped off with tremendous bursts of speed, making their way east and on to God knows where.

The control tower of nearby Allentown-Bethlehem-Easton Airport claimed they had not tracked any strange objects, but when queried, they and New York Air Traffic Control Center both stated that their radar would not track objects in that vicinity if they were below the 2,000-foot ceiling. When investigators asked the Air Force if any maneuvers had been scheduled for the 1st, one Major Larry Brown informed them that there were none that night in northeastern Pennsylvania nor Northwestern New Jersey.

Then, almost two weeks later, on the evening of March 13th, residents of Saylor Lake were treated once more to a show by the same or similar UFOs as they once again flew over this resort community. This time, however, there were twelve disc-shaped UFOs that flew altogether in one squadron. They flew low, slow, and were so bright that locals claimed that in the area around the lake, night became day for the entire time the UFOs flew overhead. When Major Brown was asked what these objects could be, he reminded the investigators that the Air Force was out of the "UFO business" and if they wanted help in solving their mystery, they should seek out help in the scientific community. He added that they would find that their mystery had a reasonable, logical answer, because as the major stated, "They always do." What the objects were that flew over Saylor Lake those nights in March of 1973 remain unidentified.

Author's Note:

We now come to October of 1973, a month that saw a massive influx of UFO reports and sightings made to police agencies, newspaper, radio and television stations and various national and regional investigative organizations. This flap caused much concern and fear, because the people who had the best tools to investigate and/or intercept and deal with these craft no longer cared what happened in the skies over America.

TUPELO, MISSISSIPPI

At approximately 8:30 PM on the night of October 3rd, 1973, Mr. and Mrs. G.F. Brown[4] were driving in their family car near Tupelo, Mississippi. As they made their way down the road, they spotted some strange lights in the sky. Mr. Brown pulled to the side of the road and they sat there watching in wondrous awe as a UFO with flashing red, yellow, and green lights slowly flew overhead. When it had disappeared, the couple remained parked by the road in hopes that it would return so they could get a second look at so magnificent a sight. Driving down the same road was National Park Ranger Thomas Westmoreland and three other rangers stationed at nearby Natchez Trace Park, as well as a deputy sheriff who was on routine patrol. They all stopped to investigate why the couple were parked alongside so desolate a section of highway, and while speaking with the Browns, who related their sighting to these law enforcement officers, just as the couple had hoped it would, the UFO returned.

Ranger Westmoreland described the object as being as big as a house, saucer-shaped, with round rotating lights. He estimated the object was passing overhead at 1,000 feet, making for quite a memorable sight. When the object disappeared this time, it did not return, leaving those who witnessed it in a state of awe from the wondrous sight, but also a bit puzzled as they could not figure out what this object could possibly have been.

EL CENTRO, CALIFORNIA

A similar event occurred two days later in El Centro, California. A retired schoolteacher and her adult daughter, (whose names were withheld at their request) were driving home on the night of October 5th, 1973. As they drove down the highway they came upon a crowd of vehicles consisting of several cars and a Greyhound bus all pulled off the road creating a mini-makeshift parking area. They decided that they wanted to see what all the excitement was, so they pulled over and joined the large group of people on the grassy slope next to the shoulder of the road.

Expecting to see an accident or a plane crash, this mother-daughter duo was quite surprised when they looked up at the object at which scores of others around them were staring. Off in the clearing was a large saucer-shaped object, engulfed in a glistening vapor.[5] The object was hovering in absolute silence above the roadside as the crowd stared in fascination at this object that was quite easily the most spectacular thing anyone of them had ever seen.

The retiree, her daughter, and the crowd around them, watched as the large disc began to rise ever so slowly, stopping only when it was about a quarter of a mile off the ground. It hovered there for a brief moment and then vanished right before their startled eyes. The shocked crowd dispersed, taking with them the memories of having seen a craft that was certainly alien to them. Just what it was, none of those assembled has ever found out.

NEW ORLEANS, LOUISIANA

The residents in St. Tammany Parish, near New Orleans, Louisiana, know where they were the night of October 10th, 1973. That night Lieutenant Robert Lonardo and Captain Huey Farrell were out patrolling the parish when the switchboard at their station house began receiving calls from people across the parish concerned with very bad television, radio, and CB reception.

At about 11 PM, Jimmy Fisher arrived at his home in the Avery Estates housing development to find a crowd of people standing outside and watching a large white glowing object as it silently hung over his house. As the UFO hovered over Mr. Fisher's house, the local dogs were howling themselves into a fit, and could be heard over the phone as he reported the object to the police.

Lonardo and Farrell arrived on the scene at just about the same time as Captain Noel Hampton. As they exited their cruisers all were shocked to see what Lonardo described as a "giant silver hamburger"[6] as it hung four to five hundred feet over Fisher's home. The object then began to move away, making a loud high-pitched whine that some present described as a cross between the sound that tires make as they travel at high speed down a road and a freight train. Others felt the noise sounded like the noise one might hear if they were in the middle of a tornado. Whichever way, the noise was recorded by Lieutenant Lonardo who had a tape recorder in his unit, and when played back for researchers, they could hear the background noise of people on the CB describing the object, followed by a loud whirling sound and then silence. And although they liked to make it abundantly clear they were out of the UFO business, when officials at nearby Keesler Air Force Base found out about the sighting, they were interested enough to request a full report by the officers on the scene. Unfortunately, submitting this report to the USAF did not provide answers to those who witnessed it hover over Avery Estates that October night in 1973.

DOVER, DELAWARE

Whatever it was they had seen in Louisiana, may have been seen several days later in Delaware.

On Sunday night, October 14th, 1973, a trio of women spent the better part of an hour observing a very similar craft as had been seen in Louisiana four days previous. These women, who were in Dover, Delaware,[7] watched the large, shiny object as it hung in the air over their neighborhood. After nearly forty-five minutes, one of the women telephoned the police.

When they arrived, they called their station and requested that the police helicopter stationed at the Dover Air Force Base, who by the way was observing the object and tracking it on radar, yet did not scramble any planes, be sent to investigate the object.

As the helicopter drew closer, the large silvery object, as is often the case, accelerated out of the area, ending any hopes that the police helicopter may be able to tell the police and the witnesses below what it was they were seeing.

ANN ARBOR, MICHIGAN

That same week, a man and his wife were driving through Ann Arbor, Michigan when they were startled by the appearance of a large, amber light in the cloud-filled night sky. The light descended down from above the clouds and flew on a parallel course with the car in which Mr. and Mrs. John Gilligan were driving. The object was in sight for more than a half-hour. When the cloud-cover had broken, the UFO was lost amongst the stars as it made its way up into the heavens. Though both John and his wife, Katie, could not identify what they object was, they were sure that it wasn't an airplane!

The reason this is included here is that, at the time of the sighting, John Gilligan was governor of Ohio[8] and certainly not prone to making wild accusations, nor creating fanciful stories about encounters with UFOs. This object must have made a lasting impression on the governor for him to risk so much bad publicity by reporting what he had seen, knowing it would be carried on the news agencies and wires throughout the country. That includes Ohio were he would have to face re-election. This type of news, could certainly generate bad publicity of the type that would be useful only to his opponent. So the chances of such a high-level government official reporting an encounter with a UFO would only be made if that person was sure that the object they were viewing was truly unidentifiable.

CHATTANOOGA, TENNESSEE

Later that week, on the evening of October 17th, 1973, Sergeant Lester Shell, 47, a traffic division supervisor with twenty years on the job, and Patrolman Harry Jarrett, 35, a nine-year veteran of the police force, were on routine patrol near Chattanooga, Tennessee. The night was pretty quiet until they were radioed to investigate a strange object that was sighted by twelve residents of a nearby neighborhood.

When they arrived on the scene, they found a cigar-shaped craft just twenty feet off the ground and emitting an intense bluish-white light as it silently hovered. They estimated that the craft was thirty to forty feet long and ten feet wide. They slowed their cruiser down and tried to approach the object. When they had gotten to within 100 yards, it slowly and silently rose straight up and out of sight.

Sergeant Shell, an experienced pilot, was quite sure that what they had seen that night was not a plane, star, nor a reflection of the moon. He was sure that they had witnessed was a tangible craft built by an unknown intelligence, and the object, whatever it was, surely was under some intelligent control. That was the same thing Officer Bill Kuykendall, 29, stated after he spotted the same or a similar UFO some five miles away at approximately 8:30 PM that same night.[9]

MANSFIELD, OHIO

On the night of October 18th, 1973, a Bell Huey helicopter belonging to the United States Army and stationed at the 316th Medivac Unit, which was based out of Cleveland's Hopkins International Airport, had a frightening encounter with a UFO. The crew consisted of the Commander of the 316th, Captain Lawrence Coyne, his copilot Lieutenant Arrigo Jezzi, Staff Sergeant John Healey and Crew Chief Staff Sergeant Robert Yanacsek. The crew was on their way back to Cleveland from Columbus, Ohio where they had gone to undergo routine physicals.[10]

In a report filed with the Federal Aviation Administration. Captain Coyne describes his and the crew's horrific encounter with a UFO. According to Coyne, their helicopter was flying level at 2,500 feet and was just outside of Mansfield, Ohio, when at 11:05 PM , SSG Yanacsek observed a red light out on the eastern horizon, on a ninety-degree angle to the helicopter's heading. Captain Coyne felt the light must be a radio tower's beacon light and paid little attention to it. Thirty or so seconds later, SSG Yanacsek informed the captain that the light was on an intersect course with them and closing at what he estimated was over 600 MPH. Fearing that the object was in reality a jet that they may soon collide with, Captain Coyne took the controls from Lieutenant Jezzi and immediately initiated evasive maneuvers by putting the helicopter into a power dive and leveling off once more at 1,700 feet.

Coyne tried to raise Mansfield Tower on both UHF and VHF, but was unable to do so. The crew feared a collision was eminent, but according to Coyne, when the object drew close, it slowed down instantly to 100 MPH to match the helicopter's speed. It remained over them for a brief time as they continued to fly home towards Cleveland. The object was cigar shaped and they estimated it to be about sixty feet long, and had no wings, engines, or windows. As it flew over the helicopter, a green light from the rear of the UFO shown down and engulfed the aircraft and its crew. The object then began a slow, moderate climb with the helicopter in tow. Before the object sped off on an westerly course, turning forty-five degrees and disappearing, Coyne, according to the report, noticed that his aircraft was in the process of being lifted up from 1,700 feet to 3,500 feet at a climbing rate of 100 feet per second. None of the crew reportedly felt the usual pull of gravity one experiences when making a sudden climb in a helicopter.

When the object had gone, Captain Coyne returned the helicopter to 100 MPH airspeed, and descended back to 2,500 feet and continued back on course to Cleveland. Ten minutes after the green light had ceased to shine into the Huey's cabin, the radio returned to normal and they radioed their base to report what had just transpired. When the FAA questioned them, all four men gave the same story detailing their fearful encounter with a UFO. The authorities could not hush this up, as there were witnesses on the ground in Mansfield who claimed they saw a UFO fly across the sky and hover over a moving helicopter, then both rose up and the UFO departed. Those on the ground were amazed by the intensity of the green light, as the witnesses reported it not only illuminated the helicopter, but the trees, ground and people below the helicopter with an eerily bright green glow.

The FAA, much like the Air Force, could not explain what it was the crew had encountered, but one thing is for sure, none of those four men will forget their encounter with that UFO, nor will they probably ever care to have another. In light of their harrowing experience in the skies above Ohio, I can't say that I blame them!

MALMOE, SWEDEN

UFO reports did not let up with the arrival of 1974. In January of 1974, UFO reports were once again coming in from around the globe.

In the early morning hours of January 26th, three airline crews witnessed a squadron of UFOs as they flew across Europe. At 2:49 AM local time, Captain Lars Berglund was at the helm of a Boeing 727 high above Malmoe, Sweden[11] when he spotted a curious light as it approached his plane. As the light grew closer, Captain Berglund soon realized that this was not one, but ten to fifteen saucer-shaped, luminous objects flying in a tight formation. The objects were flying above his plane at approximately 31,000 feet. They were orange in color and traveled faster than his jet was cruising. He called the attention of his copilot and mechanic to the area in the sky and they too watched as the squadron flew by. They were not alone up there that night, as two other flight crews, one English and one Norwegian, also witnessed the flyby of the exact same formation as it flew over Sweden that dark, cold winter night.

BAKERSFIELD, CALIFORNIA

Our next sighting comes from yet another high-ranking politician. This witness was also a governor at the time of his sighting, yet a mere seven years later, he would also hold the title of President of the United States.

On a flight made during the Spring of 1974, the then governor of California, and future 40th President of the United States, Ronald Wilson Reagan, his pilot Bill Paynter, and several security agents were flying over California in a Cessna Citation.[12] Between

9 PM and 10 PM that night, while flying near Bakersfield, California, Governor Reagan spotted an odd light trailing the plane at a distance of several hundred yards. The governor called Paynter's attention to the light, and together they watched as the round light became somewhat elongated as it accelerated past the plane at an astounding rate of speed. As it passed, Governor Reagan ordered Paynter to pursue the object, which he did for several minutes, until the object instantaneously changed course and shot straight up into the heavens.

Governor Reagan confided in Norman Miller, the then Washington Bureau chief of the *Wall Street Journal,* and according to him, the governor told him all about the sighting and that once the plane was on the ground, Governor Reagan told his wife, Nancy, the whole story and they subsequently went out and did a great deal of research on the subject of UFOs. When asked directly if he believed in UFOs thereafter, Ronald Reagan would respond that on the subject of UFOs, he was an agnostic! The perfect answer for a man on the campaign trail trying to become the most powerful man in the world!

Albany County, New York

On the evening of August 20th, 1974, the radar operator in the control tower of Albany (NY) County Airport was painting a return on his screen of an Unidentified Flying Object. Not wanting to get a second opinion from a superior, he decided to wait and see if the Air National Guard pilots aloft in a T-29 trainer would also see the object and get a verification on its ID that way. Within seconds, the Army personnel in the plane radioed the control tower to report that they had spotted a red light flying through the sky at tremendous speed. The tower confirmed that the object was also on their radar screen, but they had no other known traffic other than the T-29. They gave clearance for the T-29 to change course and pursue the object. When the Army plane had altered its course, the UFO streaked across the sky at a speed the radar operator calculated to be in excess of a mile per second, or 3,600 MPH![13]

The object, or one like it, came back to the Capital District several hours later. A New York State Trooper out on patrol from his Loudonville, New York barracks spotted a red object hovering low in the sky. Shortly after he radioed the Albany County Airport to see what traffic this could be, a brother trooper, Trooper Thomas Cole out of the Malta, New York Barracks reported that a red disc-shaped object had hovered several hundred feet over his car while he was on patrol in the area of the Knolls Laboratory, a subdivision of General Electric and the Atomic Energy Commission's Atomic Research Center. The object silently hung over his car for a brief time and then disappeared out of sight. He, like the authorities at the Albany County Airport, answered question about the sightings freely. And although a UFO was witnessed through the eyes of two state troopers, the crew of an army plane, and displayed on the scopes at the local radar tracking station, the official explanations was that all had seen a weather anomaly, one which remains unexplained to this day.

SEOUL, SOUTH KOREA

It was a crisp cool autumn evening on the night of November 21st, 1974, when Captain Joseph E. Sturdman and Lieutenant Victor. E. King were scrambled in their F-4 fighter to investigate an unknown blip appearing on the radar screens in the control tower of Osan Air Force Base, near Seoul, South Korea.[14] The object painting the return at their base was flying in an area north of Seoul, so it was assumed that the object was a North Korean plane either accidentally or purposefully testing the South and its ally's response time.

Captain Sturdman used the Ground Control Intercept Operator to vector him to the area of the object. GCI informed them to level off at 20,000 feet and proceed on a course heading of 355. After a while, GCI broke in on the radio and informed Sturdman that he should change heading to 340, his target was at 25,000 feet and zigzagging through the sky. Captain Sturdman felt that he might be on a wild goose chase, as planes do not and cannot zigzag through the sky. He climbed to 25,000 feet and once there, he asked his copilot and radar man Lieutenant King if he showed the object on his screen. He scanned the area and was about to answer in the negative, when the object jumped onto his screen. He informed Sturdman that, yes, it was there, and it was moving from side to side, just like the GCI had told them, but now they were headed right for it!

Suddenly, Sturdman could see the object. Dead ahead was a white-hot ball of light, which shot to the left of the plane, then straight up and finally went back to its right once again. Sturdman armed his 20mm cannon and tensely began to close in by turning to the right to intercept the object, which was still about a mile away. As they closed to within 1,000 yards of the craft, the UFO shot straight up 1,000 feet and ceased all forward motion, coming to a standstill as the F-4 raced towards it.

Sturdman knew this was no North Korean aircraft they were dealing with. He still felt it was making hostile moves, so he banked his craft so as to come across the object on a strafing run. As he closed in for the kill, the UFO sat there just waiting, and without any warning, it vanished from both eyesight and radar, and the plane flew through the airspace that had been occupied a split second before by an Unidentified Flying Object.

Unbeknownst to the crew, the object they had been chasing was spotted by members of the Tactical Operations Center of the US Eighth Army in Seoul, and reports had been coming in from guard posts and troops in the field near the De-Militarized Zone

(DMZ) since before they were aloft. More than eighty people had flooded the police switchboard in the city of Uijongbu with reports of the strange light.

When the F-4 touched down thirty minutes later, Captain Sturdman and Lieutenant King were met by a mob of airman wanting to know what had happened up there and what they had seen. Shortly thereafter, a full-bird colonel from the Air Force's Office of Special Investigations was debriefing them as they removed their flight suits, finishing up with a suggestion that they not discuss the sighting with anyone. Although the Air Force investigated this sighting in an attempt to find out what this unknown object was, if they were successful in doing so, neither Sturdman nor King were ever informed of what it was they sparred with in the skies over South Korea.

Spain

The following year, 1975, was only hours old when our first sighting occurred. On the night of January 2nd, 1975, six members of the Spanish military were working their way through that morning's shift at the Las Bardenas Reales bombing and gunnery range, located just a short ways away from the Zaragoza Air Base.[15]

At approximately 11 PM local time, the six men (whose names were deleted from the report used to gather this information) spotted two UFOs as they slowly made their way overhead. The main witness in the report used binoculars to get a better look at these odd craft. Through them he saw a craft shaped like an upside down coffee cup, with white lights on the upper and lower halves and alternating white and amber lights on the sides. He estimated the size as about ten to fifteen feet long, or being about the size of a small truck. One of the UFOs descended and either came to rest on the ground or hovered very close to it. When it took off up into the night sky and went out of sight, a bright, white light illuminated the entire area below it. The objects were in sight by the six viewers until 11:25 PM.

The men reported what they had encountered to their superiors, and the authorities of the Third Air Region of Spain appointed a judge to conduct an investigation to determine what these men had seen. He, mirroring American investigative conclusions, declared that all six men had a shared optical illusion, even though when interrogated, they all describe the incident in the exact same manner! Needless to say, the six witnesses wholeheartedly disagreed with the judge and the fruits of his *investigation*.

North Hudson Park, New Jersey

George O'Barski was the proud owner of a small liquor store in New York City's Chelsea section.[16] In 1975, even at the age of 72 years, each night, Mr. O'Barski would normally close up the shop around midnight and head back to his home in New Jersey.

On January 12th, he decided to check the inventory before heading home for the night. At 2 AM, he finally locked the place down, and braving the wicked cold, got into his car for the drive back home. Listening to the radio, he crossed the Hudson on that crisp and clear winter morning, and made his way through a section of New Jersey known as North Hudson Park.

Strangely and quite uncharacteristically, his radio began crackling with an intense static. Spinning the dial, O'Barski found that no stations would come in, so he switched the radio off. Just then, he heard a low, but intense, droning noise that seemed to fill his car. Looking out the window, he saw a strange-looking craft with long windows from which bright light poured, flying parallel to his speeding car. The craft reached a small hill near the Stonehenge Apartments and settled down onto the ground.

George stopped his car some sixty feet away from where the craft had come to rest. He described the object as being disc shaped with a domed topped. Long vertical windows ringed the entire craft. He estimated the craft as being thirty feet wide and about ten feet high. Amid mixed emotions, he sat and watched the craft. Slight fear was overtaken by curiosity, and his steadfastness was rewarded. While he watched, a door opened up on the side of the craft, and steps unfolded until they reached the ground. Much to his surprise, nearly twelve "midgets" in matching white uniforms and helmets marched down the ladder and scattered, each armed with a spoon-like device and a small bag. With diligence, the little "men" had filled their bags and went back inside their craft in less than five minutes. With a loud whirring noise, the object took off and it and its crew exited George O'Barskis' life as suddenly as they had entered.

He continued home, still trying to rationalize the weird spectacle that he had just witnessed. The next day, he still was not sure if he had witnessed these little men or was suffering from a lack of sleep that had induced a hallucination. When he pulled into the North Hudson Park where he had stopped the night before, sure enough, in the same area where he had seen the little men digging were twelve six-inch-deep holes!

The next time he saw one of his regular customers, Budd Hopkins, knowing he was interested in UFOs, Mr. O'Barski told Budd Hopkins of his sighting. He and several other investigators, including Ted Bloecher, New York's director for the Mutual UFO Network, investigated the sighting and found that several other people in the area had witnessed the UFO as it landed and took off from the park. One man, Bill Pawlowski, the doorman at the Stonehenge Apartments, saw the UFO land, and went to call the police. As he talked with them, he heard a high-pitched whine. So loud was the whine that it shattered the plate glass window in the lobby through which he had seen the UFO land and depart. His and other witnesses' testimony proved that Mr. O'Barski was not hallucinating that night, and what or who it was he saw that evening, he has never found out.

ALAMOGORDO, NEW MEXICO

When you think of reports of humans being abducted by spacecraft, you usually would not associate this phenomenon with any Air Force personnel. Our next case is just that, an alleged abduction of an Air Force airman by those who operate the craft we call UFOs.[17] (This report exists despite his employer steadfastly maintaining that UFOs do not exist.)

United States Air Force Staff Sergeant Charles Moody was a crew chief who was working the swing shift at Holloman Air Force Base on the night of August 12th, 1975. Once back in his home in Alamogordo, New Mexico, he found himself unable to sleep. So grabbing his smokes, he got into his car to drive to the edge of town and sit under the star-filled sky to relax and watch for meteors. As he watched the sky, he was amazed to see a disc-shaped craft as it descended to an altitude of 50 feet at a distance of 100 yards. Once the object had leveled off, it began to slowly move towards his car.

Frightened, SSG Moody jumped off his car's hood and hopped into the car to try to get out of there fast. He found the car's engine would not turn over, and as he watched the approaching craft, he felt a strange numbness engulf his body. Feeling the strange sensation leaving, he looked up to see the craft ascending into the night sky. He tried to turn the car over once more, and it started right up and he sped home. When he got home, he was surprised to find that there was an hour and a half that he could not account for.

The next day he told his wife he had a sore back and she found small puncture holes over his spine that were red and inflamed. Within the next few days, he developed a rash that covered his body. When he reported for sick call, he was taken to nearby Beaumont Army Hospital, where he was treated for a case of radiation poisoning! When he had recovered, he was returned to duty at Holloman.

Within the next few months, he began to recover the memory of what transpired during the missing time he experienced on the night of August 12th. What he remembered brought no comfort. He began to remember being taken aboard the UFO by its occupants. The beings he described were less than five foot tall with large hairless heads and large penetrating black eyes, and a small slit for a mouth, that communicated to him without speaking with their mouths. Disturbed and wanting to find out the rest of the story, SSG Moody notified APRO (Aerial Phenomena Research Organization) of his encounter and abduction. After he passed the Stress Evaluation Test APRO administered to try to discern if the subject was telling the truth, the APRO investigators began their investigation. And no sooner had they, then the military put up the stonewall. Although the doctors and nurses remembered treating the airman for radiation poisoning, his records could not be found. Moody himself was transferred from New Mexico to an airbase in Europe, thus effectively putting an end to APRO's investigation of a member of the United States Air Force who witnessed and was taken aboard a craft that surely was not of this world.

HONSHU, JAPAN

October of 1975 was a busy month for UFO witnesses and researchers.

On the 17th, more than fifty travelers witnessed a UFO descend and hover over Akita Airport in Honshu, Japan. The witnesses on the ground, as well as airline pilot Captain Masarus Saito of Tao Airlines[18] who flew past the object on his final approach, described the object as gold in color with two white lights, one on each end. The object looked like two pie plates placed on top of one another, in the classical UFO manner. The control tower warned all incoming and outgoing planes to beware the hovering craft. After several minutes, the object flew west and then out over the sea.

MAINE

Members of the 42nd Security Police Squadron stationed at Loring Air force Base, Maine, were very busy on the night of October 27th, 1975.[19] Staff Sergeant Danny Lewis was on duty that evening, guarding the perimeter of the highly restricted munitions' storage area. In the storage area, inside igloo-like huts behind a twelve-foot-barbwire-tipped chain-link fence that is guarded day and night by both human and canine members of the 42nd S.P.S., lay nuclear weapons.

At approximately 7:45 PM, manning the radar in the control tower of the base, Staff Sergeant James Sampley of the 2192nd Communications Squadron, spotted an unknown blip on his screen closing in on the base's northern perimeter. Simultaneously, SSG Lewis also saw the light, which he assumed to be a low-flying aircraft slowly approaching the base. Back in the control tower, SSG Sampley was not immediately alarmed, as the craft on his screen was still over ten miles from the base. So, as procedure dictates, he tried again and again to contact this "plane" to advise them that they were entering highly restricted airspace. Although he used every wavelength, both civilian and military, to raise the "plane," the base received no response.

Shortly thereafter, SSG Lewis was on the horn to the Command Post of the 42nd Bomb Wing, to inform them that an unknown craft had penetrated the base's perimeter and was hovering within 1,000 feet of the nuclear storage area. The alert was sounded and the threat this unknown craft posed was taken very seriously. Within minutes, security forces were pouring into the area of the munitions' storage area, and through the base command post, a request was sent out to NORAD bases at Hancock Field in upstate New York and North Bay in Ontario, Canada, for fighter support to chase off the object that was now circling ten miles to the north-northeast of the base's perimeter.

When the fighter support was denied, the Wing Commander increased his security posture at the base, requested the Maine State Police and local flight controls help to determine whom, what they now assumed was a helicopter, belonged too. The State Police had no helicopter in the air and local flight control was of no more help. The base remained on high alert so as to be prepared in the event the object decided to once more fly over the munitions' area. A short time later, the object disappeared from the radarscope at approximately 8:45 PM, but the alert lasted until well after sunrise on the 28th.

The next night, SSG Lewis was once again on patrol at slightly after 7:15 PM when he, SSG William Long and SSG Clifton Blakeslee all spotted what they assumed to be the running lights of an aircraft approaching the base from the north. The object was flying at 3,000 feet and this time, it stopped 3 miles short of the base's perimeter. The wing commander was notified by Lewis, and once again, within minutes, he and the Staff Sergeants were standing near the munitions' storage area observing an amber light with a white flashing light either near or attached to it. Once again the object was thought to be a helicopter, and once again the base's radar tracked it as it hovered some three miles away. They watched the object to the north of the base until 8:20 PM when the lights went out and it disappeared from both sight and radar.

It then reappeared over the end of the runway, where it was spotted by Sergeant Steven Eichner and his crew. They were working on a launch truck when they saw an orange-colored object appear at the end of the runway. They all agreed that the craft was no plane or helicopter, but instead was silent and looked like an elongated football. The object disappeared from their view and reappeared over the north end of the runway, near the munitions' compound. The crew jumped in the truck they were working on and sped down Oklahoma Avenue towards the munitions' area of the base. Turning left towards the munitions area, the truckload of men were surprised to see the object hovering just 5 feet off the ground and about 300 feet in front of them, well within the base's perimeter and dangerously close to the nuclear weapons. Eichner described the object as silent, without any doors or windows nor propeller blades or jets to keep it aloft.

Suddenly, all hell broke loose at Loring Air Force Base. Sirens were blaring and lights flashing as the security forces of SSG Lewis and company sped towards the scene. Eichner and his crew thought it may be best to retreat from this restricted area and decided to drive back out on the runway near their original position to watch this drama unfold. As the security forces closed in, the lighted object just simply disappeared. The object reappeared on radar and was tracked as it sped away, being lost to the base's radar when it reached Grand Falls, New Brunswick, Canada.

Although the 42nd Security police turned the munitions' area upside down, not a trace of the object could be found. With mounting concern, the Wing Commander sent messages out to the National Military Command Center in Washington, D.C., Chief of Staff of the USAF, SAC Headquarters and many others, alerting them to the events of the past two nights. Over the next two days, Loring activated the Security Police Battle Staff and requested and received a helicopter and crew from Plattsburgh Air Force Base in Plattsburgh, New York. Since the landing of the UFO near the munitions' storage area on the 28th, the object, although it appeared every night through Halloween, always kept several miles between it and the base.

This report was squashed by the military, and had it not been for the investigative efforts of Lawrence Fawcett and Barry Greenwood, this incredible encounter may have never come to light. Now here we have a case where a UFO was spotted in and around a highly sensitive military installation, where the details we have read were supplied by the people who were at the base when the object made its repeated visits. If this can happen and the American people not know about it, how many other times has an event of this magnitude occurred at the thousands of military installations around the world. Of course there will be those who might say these events did not occur, but it is a matter of record that the base requested the fighter support and the helicopter gunship for protection against the unknown intruder, an intruder that neither they nor we know the origin of some thirty-five years later. More disturbing than that is the fact that the military could not catch the craft, nor prevent it from entering a restricted area where nuclear weapons were stored.

Lewiston, Montana

The following month brought yet another intrusion by a UFO into the restricted area of a base where nuclear weapons were stored. The place, United States Air Force Launch Control Facility, which housed minuteman missiles awaiting launch, in Lewiston, Montana.[20]

The date was November 7th, 1975. (Names were withheld from original report at witnesses' request.) Two officers in the underground bunker were alerted when a sensor sounded the alarm that an unknown intruder violated their facility's security perimeter. The two officers in the bunker notified the Sabotage Alert Team (SAT), who loaded into a security vehicle and headed towards the area of the breach.

About a mile from their barracks, they could make out an orange light hovering near the Minuteman Silo labeled K-7. Driving there as fast as safety permitted, they closed in, and radioed back to the officers in the bunker that the object that had breached the site's security was a huge disc, that they estimated to be 300 feet in diameter, glowing so brightly, that its orange luminosity illuminated the entire launch site.

Not wanting to get too close to this very intimidating object, the men informed the officers that they would go no further. The huge disc slowly began to rise, and once it had reached an altitude of 1,000 feet, it appeared on NORAD's radar at Malmstrom Air Force Base, and two F-106 jet interceptors were launched in a fruitless effort to give chase to the object that moments before had been hovering over a highly restricted Minuteman Missile Silo. The jets never had a chance to make contact, as the UFO continued to rise until it was out of the radar's range (200,000 feet).

Though it did not return that night, the personnel at Malmstrom Air Force Base had sightings, both visual and radar, of the same or similar craft on November 7th, 8th and 9th. Once again, if the debunkers would like to verify this encounter, all reports of intrusion by unknowns at missile silos should surely be a matter of record at the Pentagon, the CIA, and/or the NSA, so go check, and you will find that the events that night transpired just as they are reported here, which unfortunately, doesn't help me sleep any better! Let us all be thankful that these visitors settle for observing these weapons in storage, instead of wanting to see the results of their detonation!

Canary Islands

Had the following encounter not been reported by a man held in such high esteem by his local community, it probably would not have been included here. But he was and it is!

The night of June 22nd, 1976, was clear and starry, the type of night that Doctor Padron Leon, a resident of the Canary Islands, would rather be enjoying on his veranda with his family, instead of performing a house call for a sick patient.[21] The doctor was in a taxi with Santiago del Pino, the patients' son, on their way back to his mother's home. As the car rounded a bend, the taxi's radio quit and all were engulfed by a strangely cold gust of air. Up ahead of the taxi, a large transparent craft, about the size of a two-family home, hovered over the roadway. Within the transparent walls could be seen two beings busily operating the control panels that the men assumed operated the crystal-like flying machine.

Dr. Leon was quite impressed by the two beings. He described them as having short legs and torso and a disproportionately large head. The driver of the cab flashed his high-beam's in an effort to get a better look at the craft and its occupants. When hit by the beam of the car's headlights, the object began to rise with a loud whistling noise. Scared, the men pulled off the road and sought shelter in a nearby house.

Once inside, the home owners, who were puzzled as to the cause of their poor television reception, soon found its cause. All four watched as the transparent UFO and its crew ascended and sped off at high speed. The doctor remains convinced that on this night he saw a machine and beings from another world!

TEHRAN, IRAN

Just after midnight during the early morning hours of September 19th, 1976, the Imperial Iranian Air Force Command Post in the Shemiran[22] section of Tehran, Iran, received several calls from local residents reporting unknown lights in the sky. Those at the command post called Brigadier General Yousefi, who at first told them the citizens were seeing stars, but after checking out the skies and seeing the strange lights, he ordered that a fighter be scrambled to investigate.

At 1:30 AM local time, an American-made F-4 fighter was scrambled and vectored to an area some forty miles north of Tehran where the object had settled into a silent hover. The UFO shone so brightly that it was visible from seventy miles outside of Tehran. It grew larger the closer the F-4 came, and when the fighter was within twenty-five nautical miles of the craft, it lost all communications and the instrument panels went dead. In a bit of a panic, the pilot turned away and began to head back in the general direction from which he had come. As soon as he had changed his heading, his communication and instrumentation all came back online and functioned normally. Once he reported this back to base, a second F-4 was scrambled, and when this fighter flew close enough to get a radar lock, the UFO departed the area at a speed that was just fast enough to keep twenty-five miles between it and the oncoming fighter. The pilot reported that he followed the object, not able to discern any details due to its intensely bright illumination, as it made its way south of Tehran.

Suddenly, as the pilot remained in pursuit of the UFO, a smaller object came out of the larger UFO and sped towards the F-4 at blistering speed. Fearful of his plane and his life, the pilot armed an AIM missile and aimed it at the small object. Instantly, his instruments and communications once again went dead! With no defensive arsenal, the F-4 pilot, using the skills he learned from his American trainers, took his plane into a full throttle nosedive to try to get away from the smaller object streaking towards his plane. The object trailed for a short distance, and when the plane did not turn back towards the larger UFO, the smaller one, instantaneously changed course and returned to its "mother ship" and disappeared within its brilliant glow. Just then, the F-4's communication and instrumentation came back online. As they leveled off from their free fall, they watched as another smaller object was shot out of the large UFO, descended until it came to rest on or just above a dry lake bed, giving off enough light to illuminate an area of several acres!

Low on fuel, the F-4 returned to its base in Mehrabad. Within minutes, the objects vanished. The next day, the area where the pilots felt the smaller UFO had come to rest was searched, but there was no trace of anything unusual. Had it not been for the recorded radar tapes showing two F-4 fighters pursuing and being pursued by objects that certainly were not of this Earth and the recorded audio transmissions, this case may have never found its way into the mainstream of UFOlogy.

GRENOBLE, MONTRAND, AND VOREPPE, FRANCE

On the night of November 5th, 1976, several witnesses reported a UFO from their varying positions in and around Grenoble, France.[23]

At 8:08 PM, a father and daughter witnessed a bright spinning UFO as it flew over their home. The UFO came out of the northwest sky and disappeared to the southwest of their position when it traveled behind the mountains near Montrand, France.

At the same instance, several miles away, a French physicist (called Dr. Serge in the material this account was taken from) was driving near Voreppe, France, when he saw a large illuminated disc in the sky above the French countryside. He pulled off to the side of the road and got out of the car in order to watch this spectacle very closely. This scientist described the disc's size in minutes of arc (angular measurements), which for our purpose, we will suffice to say it was quite big. It was white towards the center and bluish-white towards the edges. The whole object was surrounded by a greenish glow.

He watched the disc as it went from the zenith of the sky to the horizon in eight seconds. As it neared the distant horizon, it came to a complete stop, hovered for several seconds, and then took off in a different direction at a much greater speed. It disappeared behind some mountains some twenty-two miles distant. According to the physicist, the sighting was made during clear weather (local weather service indicated clear skies, a slight breeze and forty degrees), for just less than a minute, without any indication of noise being emitted as this large disc flew overhead and through the mountains of central France. "Dr. Serge" was convinced that the object viewed was not a plane nor any conventional device, but what it was he had and has no idea.

AUTHOR'S NOTE:

With the reported sighting that follows, we kick of the first of what will be numerous sightings of a large triangle or boomerang-shaped UFO. Although it has been reported as far back as 1951 and all across the United States since, as you will see, these UFOs will become the focal point of many people, researchers, and media types, as they were the exclusive shape of UFOs sighted in New York's Hudson River Valley throughout the next two decades. These objects have been sighted by thousands of people over a twenty-year period as they made what seemed like regular flights over New York's southern Hudson Valley Region. The majority of sightings were centralized over a stretch of the Taconic Parkway, a scenic, yet desolate, unlit highway connecting the Albany/Schenectady/Troy area to New York City, though you will note the other locations, as well. As you will see, the wide array of sightings and witnesses made these encounters a special favorite of the television series *Unsolved Mysteries* and *Sightings*.

MEMPHIS, TENNESSEE

This time, the triangular UFO made an appearance near Memphis, Tennessee.

One night in May of 1977, five officers of the Memphis Police Department made independent sightings of a triangular-shaped UFO.[24] Two officers came upon the object as they were responding to reports of odd lights hovering over a golf course. When they arrived on the scene, they saw the huge triangular UFO as it silently hovered some 500 feet above the course. They estimated it was at least as wide as a football field, and made absolutely no noise! One of the officers, wanting a better look at the object, took a hunting rifle out of the trunk of his car to get a close-up of the object through his high-powered scope. The minute the rifle was pointed at the object, it shot off across the horizon, from a standstill mind you, in less than two heartbeats! I don't have to tell you, but I will, that we did not and still do not have any craft, especially something of that size, that could accelerate from 0 to 36,000 MPH instantly!

PORTUGAL

On the 17th of June 1977, a Portuguese Air Force pilot had a harrowing encounter with a Flying Saucer. On this day, Sergeant Jose Rodrigues, who was a 23 year-old pilot in the 31st Squadron of the Portuguese Air Force, was flying in bad weather over the Castelo de Bode dam.[25]

At approximately 12 noon, his eyes were drawn to a dark object emerging from the white clouds to the right of his airplane. Without warning, the object sped towards his plane, coming alongside his craft, taking up a position just several meters off his 11 o'clock position as they both continued their flights through the thick clouds. He described the object as being disc shaped and dark in color with a smooth top section and a paneled lower section. He estimated that the disc was about forty feet in diameter. The object then flew off at tremendous speed. As it did, his aircraft began to vibrate vigorously. Also, the plane's magnetic compass fluctuated wildly, and Sergeant Rodrigues had to call on his training to remain focused on the problem at hand, forgetting for the moment his strange encounter with the UFO, and trying to right his plane which by now had slipped into a nosedive.

As the ground rushed up towards him, he managed to regain control of the vibrating plane just feet above the treetops and landed the plane in one piece at his intended destination a few miles away. When he landed, he was in such a state of stress-induced shock that he had to be helped to the infirmary, where the base doctor examined him.

The men on duty who saw Sergeant Rodrigues when he landed felt sure that engine trouble, even such that could cause the plane to nearly crash, would not have put the normally calm and cool military man into such a state of dishevel.

Aviano, Italy

On July 1st, 1977, Signor Benito Manfre, a night watchmen of Aviano, Italy, on his day off, was awaken from a sound sleep at approximately 3 AM local time by the non-stop barking of his dogs.[26] When he went outside to see what the cause of all the ruckus was, instead of seeing a cat like he had expected, Benito watched in awe as a large glowing disc silently hovered over the nearby Aviano Air Base.

At the base, USAF Airmen James Blake watched as the object, which to him looked like a slowly spinning 150-foot-wide top, which was silently hovering some 300 feet above a restricted area of the base. Seconds later, the entire NATO installation was thrown into complete darkness. Five or so minutes later, Benito Manfre's dogs ceased to bark once the UFO had silently rose up into the air and made its way out of sight in back of the mountains that lie just outside Aviano.

A short time later, the base's lights came back on and there was a slew of activity in and around the NATO installation. When questioned about the incident and asked to identify what Manfre had seen, the NATO base commander replied that he must have seen a reflection of the moon on some low clouds! As a side note, there were no clouds that night, that happened to be a couple hundred feet above this sensitive NATO base. (Nor is it likely that this *reflection* made dogs howl and plunged a strategic base into darkness and subsequent turmoil.) For this sighting, the moon filled in nicely for Venus, which as we have seen, according to the experts, has been mistaken as a UFO on countless occasions.

China

Six days later and approximately 6,000 miles away, people witnessed the over flight of two orange UFOs. At approximately 8:30 PM local time, on the 7th of July, 1977, a group of 3,000 Chinese citizens had gathered in an outdoor theater to watch a movie made by their communist brethren in Romania called *Alert on the Danube Delta*.[27] As they watched this movie, it was so engrossing that many found themselves staring up at the stars. Suddenly, a group within the crowd began to point into the air and shout to alert the rest of the people to two orange oval objects that were descending straight towards the assembled crowd. The objects passed very low overhead, and as they did so, they illuminated the area with their orange-colored glow. Many reported that they felt a kind of heat as the UFOs flew by. As panic ensued, the objects swiftly ascended and were out of sight in short order.

According to Chen Caife of the Zhangpo County Public Security Bureau and local doctor Lin Bing-Xian, in the commotion, people threw themselves to the ground to avoid the objects and many even stampeded away from the open-air theater, leaving two children dead and hundreds injured! I feel safe in saying that the moon, stars, Venus, planes, weather balloons, meteorological anomalies nor mass hallucinations could scare so many people so badly as to cause a stampede where two children died and hundreds more were injured. Those people at that gathering saw something that invoked great fear, something not of this Earth!

CHINA

Another sighting took place in China just several days later. Zhang Zhousheng was an astronomer with the Yunnan Observatory working out of the northern suburb of Chengdu City in China's Sichuan Province.[28]

On July 26th, 1977, at approximately 10:12 PM local time, he witnessed an object that he described in his own words as a "very astonishing and unexplainable phenomenon." In the skies above, he saw a spiral-shaped object that emitted green and blue light. Immediately, he wanted to share this experience with others, so he sought out his coworkers. When he reached their location outside, the object was still slowly making its way across the sky, and from all the commotion and staring at the sky, he quickly realized that his coworkers had already spotted the odd craft.

The spiral object moved from north to south and was seen for a full five minutes. The object was sighted by thousands of people in an area stretching over 100-square miles. What this spiral object was is not known. The fact that many people witnessed it, like the two orange UFOs in the previous account, makes these sightings hard to dismiss. These two sightings were nothing short of amazing multiple-witness sightings of Unidentified Flying Objects, made over the highly populated countryside of one of the largest countries on this planet!

AUTHOR'S NOTE:

As we close out the year that was 1977, we return to the good old USA to recount two sightings of the already, and soon to be frequently, mentioned boomerang-shaped crafts as they made their way over communities across this great land.

PLYMOUTH TOWNSHIP, NEW YORK

On November 23rd, 1977, at least six people witnessed one of these UFOs as it flew over the small community of Plymouth Township,[29] which is forty miles southwest of Utica, in Central New York. A farmer and his wife claimed that they saw a large boomerang-shaped object as it passed over their house. The object was emitting so loud a buzzing noise that their entire farmhouse shook.

CARROLL COUNTY, ARKANSAS

Then on December 15th, 1977,[30] many residents along a twenty-five mile stretch of Carroll County, Arkansas, including several police officers, public officials, teachers, researchers, and dozens of ordinary citizens witnessed a large UFO as it made its way over head. According to the witnesses' reports, the UFO was very big and shaped like a diamond. It was absolutely silent as it flew very low and very slow over northwest Arkansas.

This, or another object very similar to it, would be the center of an incident that occurred several years later in Texas, that has since become known as the Cash-Landrum Incident, where two women and a child came into contact with a diamond shaped UFO and grew very sick from their encounter.

AUTHOR'S NOTE:

Although the prior were not the best-documented sightings covered herein, one would think that our government and our military forces would be interested enough to investigate the reports of strange objects flying low and slow over locations throughout the nation. Unfortunately, there was no investigation done or any interest shown by any department of our government. It has grown all to evident that the government has either no interest in stopping or simply cannot stop these craft from roaming the skies, and if help was needed due to some situation in which one of these objects were involved, to whom could the ordinary citizen turn too? No organization, except the Armed Forces of the United States could even begin to handle a situation in which a UFO was involved. If they are not there to help, then we are on our own!

YORKSHIRE, ENGLAND

Sergeant Tony Dodd and Constable Alan Dale were on their normal patrol one night in the middle of January 1978 near Skipton, Yorkshire, England, when without any warning, their patrol became anything but routine. When interviewed about their sighting, both men were very eager to relate the events that transpired on that lonely country lane, not only because they would like to know what it was they saw, but also because of the profound effect seeing this UFO had on them then and now.

As they were driving down this dark, lonely lane in rural Great Britain, the men were both taken aback by the sudden illumination of the roadway ahead of them. As there were no streetlights, the first thing they thought was: *Where could the light be coming from?*

They soon had their answer! Pulling to one side of the lonely country lane, the police officers got out of the car just in time to watch a highly illuminated UFO pass directly overhead. They described the object as traveling at approximately 40 MPH at about 100 feet off the ground. It was circular with three round ball bearing-like protrusions on the bottom. The whole object glowed incandescent white, as if the metal that it was made from was white-hot or molten![31] There were lights "dancing" around the bottom that gave it the illusion that it was rotating around on a central axis.

The object silently passed over them and continued on its ways until it stopped over a dense patch of forest to the officers' left. The white disc hovered very close the ground, silent and still. Wanting to get another look at the UFO, the officers jumped back into their car and headed in the general direction of where the object had settled down. Although they could see the light in the trees upon reaching the small village of Conoley, the officers never came as close to it again as they had when they'd watched it earlier and with great awe.

When questioned, both officers felt sure that whatever the object was, it was no known aircraft. The silent, fluid motion of this oddly designed craft convinced them that as creative as those damn Yank's were, this object wasn't one of their newly designed airplanes! How right they were! Thus, the only thing we can categorize it as is a UFO!

Mt. Etna, Sicily

During the evening hours of July 4th, 1978, four friends were spending their leisure time conversing and enjoying the scenery near Mt. Etna, Sicily. It was about 10:30 PM when the group of friends, consisting of Antonina di Pietro, Italian Naval Officer Maurizio Esposito, and Italian Air Force Sergeants Franco Padellero and Attilio di Salvatore,[32] noticed a triangle formation of three red lights in the night sky. As they watched, one of the lights broke formation and flew down towards the group. Now watching with great interest, the men were in awe as this light flew over their position and disappeared down behind the slope of the mountainside.

They all climbed into di Salvatore's car and drove in the direction in which the object had disappeared. Rounding a bend on the twisty mountain road, from a large depression on the side of the road the quartet saw a "dazzling" light illuminating the dark countryside. They stopped the car, got out, and went over to the edge of the road. From this vantage point, the four friends watched an amazing scene! Resting on the ground a short distance down the hillside was a saucer-shaped object emitting a bright dazzling reddish light, with smaller red and blue lights ringing the underbelly.

The object was about forty feet wide with an illuminated yellow dome on the its topside. Next to the craft, they saw five or six very tall, thin beings. They were dressed in black coveralls and all were described as having blonde hair and very attractive human features. Two of the craft's occupants began to climb the slope towards the group.

Some unseen force instantly immobilized the four friends. The two beings came to within fifteen feet of the quartet and remained there as if studying them for several minutes. One motioned towards the saucer and they both returned. All climbed back into their craft and the lights all around it began to intensify.

When a car started down the road towards were di Salvatore's car was parked, all the lights on the UFO went out and the area was plunged into darkness, save the passing cars headlights. Once the car had gone, the UFOs lights all came back on, illuminating the area once again in a kaleidoscope of colors. The four friends all regained mobility and went back to the car and quickly drove down the mountain and back to the false safety of civilization.

Now sure, these people could have made up this whole story, and what a story it was! But, let us remember that three of the four were active military personnel, and for them to create a story for which they would undoubtedly be hassled over by their peers and more importantly by their superiors, would not be worth the problems it would create. Thus, it is my strongly held opinion that these military men reported an encounter that so greatly troubled them, that out of love or loyalty to their country and countrymen, they had sworn to protect, risked ridicule to inform someone in authority of what had happened to them, on the outside chance that this encounter represented something greater than a brief visitation alongside a lonely mountain road.

MICHIGAN AND WISCONSIN

Just after midnight in the early morning hours of July 28th, 1978, Mr. and Mrs. Gruss of Benton Harbor, Michigan, were outside their homes enjoying the cool night air of the Lake Michigan coastline. At about 12:20 AM local time, the couple saw a large, silvery colored cylindrically shaped object hovering about a mile above Michigan's Rocky Gap area.

The object remained stationary in this spot for thirty minutes. At 12:50 AM, it started to move in a southwesterly direction towards Gary, Indiana.[33] After much discussion about who to contact about the sighting, at 3:59 AM, the Gruss' called to report what they had seen to the St. Joseph Coast Guard Station several miles south down the Lake Michigan coast.

At 4:01 AM, those on duty at the Ludington Coast Guard Station spotted the same object heading west out over Lake Michigan. Further up Lake Michigan on the Wisconsin Coast, at 4:04 AM, the Coast Guard Station at Two Rivers, Wisconsin, spotted the object as it flew north. Ten 35mm pictures were taken of the object as it passed low enough over Two Rivers for the personnel there to distinguish several steady red lights and many white lights pulsing in random order. Further along up the coast and within minutes, the personnel at Sturgeon Bay Coast Guard Station spotted the object to the south of their position, high in the night sky, traveling in a northwesterly direction. At 4:25 AM, the strange silvery cylinder was spotted over the Green Bay Lighthouse. Those on duty that night watched as the object overflew their position and continued on its course to God knows where! The last sighting that morning by military personnel came at 6:36 AM, when a Coast Guard Cutter near Apostle Island in Lake Superior had the object in sight for five to six minutes.

These sightings by highly trained members of our military did *not* show up on national television's evening news. The debunkers claimed that the sightings were the reentry of space debris. One even claimed that the silvery cylinder was most likely a booster rocket. They did not find it necessary to explain how a falling rocket booster could possibly stay airborne for over six hours as it fell to earth nor how space debris falling to earth could be sighted changing course as it made its way over three states and two Great Lakes.

Near King Island, Tasmania

On the 21st of October 1978, 20-year-old flying instructor Frederick Valentich was flying his Cessna 182 from Moorabin, Victoria to King Island, Tasmania. He anticipated a routine flight, as he had made this trip many times before and the only weather conditions he had to watch out for was a scattering of clouds at 7,000 feet. He was flying that night not only to pick up a load of crawfish for the officers of the Air Training Corps, of which he was an instructor, but also to rack up some night flying hours to his credit.[34]

Upon his return to Melbourne, he was to attend a family reunion. At 6:19 PM, while flying over the Bass Straight, Valentich spotted a UFO. He radioed the control tower in Melbourne, using his designated call sign, Delta Sierra Juliet, asking if they had any known traffic in his vicinity, more specifically at the 5,000-foot level. They responded that there wasn't any known traffic in the vicinity he had inquired about. He radioed back to Melbourne that he had an unknown craft with four very bright "landing lights" flying a little too close for comfort.

Suddenly, the craft flew over the top of his plane at about 1,000 feet and at an incredibly high speed. He reported this development to the control tower and asked if they had any military planes in the area. Again they responded in the negative. Valentich was talking to Melbourne as the object once again approached his plane from the east. He then called to tell the tower that the craft was playing games with him that it would repeatedly pass over his plane at a speed he could not even make a guess at. Melbourne asked him what his position was, and he told them his coordinates, air speed, and elevation.

They then asked him if he could identify the craft, and after several seconds of dead air, Valentich responded (with a few seconds breaks in between each description), that it looked like an elongated object with a metallic looking surface covered with green lights. Then suddenly it disappeared. Melbourne asked him to confirm that the object just vanished. After several seconds of dead air, he responded that it was now approaching from the southwest, and Valentich asked Melbourne if they had any idea what type of aircraft this was that was playing a dangerous game of cat and mouse with him and his aircraft. Before Melbourne could offer any guesses, Valentich told the tower that the plane's engine was sputtering and no matter what setting for fuel mixture he tried the engine's performance would not improve. Melbourne asked him what he intended to do. Valentich radioed back that he was going to try to make King Island. Several seconds of silence was followed by Valentich's strained voice reporting to the controller that the object was coming once again, and now it was over his plane.

At 7:12 PM local time, Valentich informed the controller that whatever the object was, it was not a plane! The airwaves went dead and the plane disappeared off radar. Melbourne tried several times to raise Valentich, but no contact was made. His communication with Melbourne at 7:12 PM was the last anyone has ever heard from Richard Valentich.

Melbourne notified Search and Rescue to go on alert. When the plane did not reach King Island by 7:33 PM, an air/sea search was initiated. An intense search was conducted until October 25th, but no trace of the plane or the pilot, or even the radio survival beacon signal, could be found. The investigation into the disappearance of this man and his plane turned up little.

Flight controller Steve Robey, with whom Valentich spoke with on the night of his disappearance, informed the investigators that he believed Valentich's claim that a UFO was playing games with him and his plane. The rushed responses given to questions and tenseness in his voice alerted Robey that whatever was in the sky with the Cessna that night caused its pilot to be very concerned for his personal safety.

CHINA

Two days later, the same or a similar UFO was visible to many as it visited the skies above Lintiao Air Base in Gansu Province of China on the evening of October 23rd, 1978.

According to one of the eye witnesses, Chinese Air Force pilot Zhou Qingtong, it was at 8:04 PM local time, when he and the other pilots in his brigade, as well as several hundred citizens who lived near the base, were watching a movie in an open-air theater. As the movie played, just like in our previous Chinese encounter, commotion swept over the crowd as hands and eyes were pointing towards the cloudless star-filled sky, where a huge elongated object with two bright lights shooting bright beams of green light out in front of it made its way across the sky, moving in an east to west direction.[35] A sort of bright mist engulfed the object and formed a trail in the sky that remained for several seconds after the object crossed overhead. The object was rather low to the ground and flying at not too great a speed. Whatever it was, the object was very, very large, and created quite a stir among the people and the fighter pilots who all agreed that they had never seen anything like this object anywhere.

SAGINAW BAY, MICHIGAN

On November 1st, 1978, while returning from a refueling mission, the pilot of a KC-135 tanker was making his first approach to land, when somewhere between 10:30 PM and 11 PM they were ordered to check out the report of a UFO over Wurtsmith Weapons Storage Area.[36] Turning, he could see a white light, not unlike that of a strobe light flashing, in the skies above Like Huron. The UFO then headed south towards the Saginaw Bay area of Michigan.

Captain Higginbotham asked for and received permission to change course and follow the object. He headed south, trailing the UFO by about a mile, soon realizing that there were two craft, and the bright light was being flashed back and forth between the two. Whenever the tanker tried to close the gap, the UFOs would move forward just enough to keep the same distance between the tanker and themselves. They lost the UFOs when they began to cross Saginaw Bay, and being low on fuel, informed the control tower that they were returning to base.

On their way back, they once again spotted the UFO as it hovered once more above the Wurtsmith Weapons Storage Area. Captain Higginbotham landed the tanker and was soon thereafter interrogated by USAF's Office of Special Investigations, who requested that Higginbotham not discuss this incident any further. Thank goodness he decided not to comply with their wishes, as we would not have this sighting to include here to further prove that competent, technically trained observers do see UFOs, and still nothing is officially done to solve the riddle that is the UFO phenomenon for the public.

SPAIN

The year 1979 was not a very good year. Yankee great Thurman Munson died in a freak plane crash, NASA's first Space Station, Skylab, crashed back to earth, the Iranian Hostage Crisis ensued, and very few quality sightings of UFO were reported. The one that was, appears next.

A few minutes before 11 PM on the night of November 11th, 1979, Captain Francisco Lerdo de Tejada was piloting a big Super Caravelle passenger jet loaded with 109 mostly German and Austrian tourists from Salzburg, Austria to Tenerife, Spain when he spotted two large very powerful red lights.[37]

The lights were approaching the airliner from the 9 o'clock position and about ten miles away. In the blink of an eye they were right on top of the aircraft, stopping their approach at a one half-mile distance. The captain estimated the size of the object the lights were attached to as being relatively the same as a jumbo jet. The object would zigzag around, over and under the aircraft, passing too close for comfort at tremendous speed, flying every which way and back again as it played a dangerous game of cat and mouse with the infinitely less maneuverable airliner. The passengers were unwilling participants in this game as they were tossed around by the evasive maneuvers made by the captain to ensure his airliner did not collide with the rather large, yet agile UFO.

The situation worsened with the UFO passing ever closer, making flying the plane that much more difficult. In response to this development, Captain Tejada requested permission to make an emergency landing. Permission was granted and the plane touched down a short time later at the airport in Valencia, hundreds of miles from its destination.

Once on the ground, the UFO could still be seen hovering above the airport by the deplaning passengers. The passengers and crew, the airport director, air traffic controller, and several of the ground crew all witnessed the UFO hovering and then departing from the skies above the airport. While it hovered, the UFO was picked up by radar at the Los Llanos Air Base near Albacete, Spain. Two Mirage fighters were scrambled to the area to investigate the unknown object. The pilots closed in on the object and established a radar lock on it, only to have it play the same weird game with them as it had with the Super Caravelle airliner only minutes before! When it tired of this game, the UFO accelerated out of the pilot's sight and radar range. In what appears to be the normal course of events worldwide, an official investigation was conducted where witnesses were interrogated, stories retold, but no official explanation or conclusion was ever offered.

CHAPTER 10

THE 1980s

INVASION OF THE GIANT TRIANGLES

"In our obsession with antagonisms of the moment, we often forget how much unites all the members of humanity. Perhaps we need some outside, universal threat to make us recognize this common bond. I occasionally think how quickly our differences worldwide would vanish if we were facing an alien threat from outside of this world. And yet I ask – is not an alien force already among us?"

~President Ronald Reagan
Speaking Before the UN General Assembly September 21st, 1987

As the 1970s gave way to the 1980s President Carter's promise to uncover the truth about the UFO phenomenon and disseminate the information to the American people had all but been forgotten. Although he made an effort to make this promise a reality, the secrets were and are so safely guarded that even the president could not, or would not, get the information out to the American people. It may be the case that as Commander-in-Chief, Jimmy Carter was informed of what the government, military, and intelligence communities knew about the UFO phenomenon, and like those men who served before him, he decided the truth was too much for the public at large to accept and decided to allow the facts to remain secret. Or he could not gain access to the secrets and gave up to try to run the country, which at the time, turned out to be more difficult than cracking the safe in which the secrets behind UFOs were kept.

Ronald Reagan, like Jimmy Carter, had also had witnessed an Unidentified Flying Object when he was governor. Wisely, he made no mention of his experience nor promised any forth-coming revelations concerning the UFO phenomenon while campaigning for the presidency. His running mate, George Bush, was once the head of the CIA, and as such, probably had the answers to the questions that Reagan and all of us who have seen something unidentified wanted about UFOs and the UFO phenomenon. Some say that this inside information lead Reagan to state on several occasions and in front of millions of people, how he believes that the nations of the world would be forced to come together and fight as one cohesive unit, should we all become unwilling targets of a threat from outer space. (Please see the last Internet link in Appendix B.)

BISBEE, ARIZONA

Who says lightning doesn't strike twice? In the UFO phenomenon it often does, and this can be attributed to the fact that the beings that operate the UFOs are truly on some type of information gathering mission. Repeated observation of the flora, fauna, and indigenous population in a certain area would be a sensible and necessary part of their ongoing mission. This is exactly what occurred at the Phelps-Dodge copper smelting plant near Bisbee, Arizona.

On the night of October 23rd, 1980,[1] workers at the Phelps-Dodge plant watched as a large, round object hovered momentarily over one of the plant's two 600-foot smoke stacks. The object wobbled as it hovered silently above the stack. It projected a beam of light down the smokestack before departing the area.

As you will remember, in June of 1947, the same or a similar object was also witnessed by many of the workers on the job that day at the very same facility.

MORENCI, ARIZONA

Another incident occurred on the 23rd of October 1980, several miles away at the Morenci High School, in Morenci, Arizona. As parents and teachers were watching 110 members of the high school band practice their music and marches on the school's football field, the loosely organized practice turned into near chaos when a large, glowing object slowly drifted overhead. The object hovered over the field, as if observing the scared people below, before continuing on its original course and disappearing behind nearby hills. The witnesses described the same or a similar object as was seen by the employees of the Phelps-Dodge plant.

SPAIN

On November 11th, 1980, five flight crews from passenger airlines saw a UFO as it hovered near the main runway and buzzed planes in the airspace above and around Spain's Barcelona Airport. The five airliners that had encounters that night were Iberia Airlines Flights 350, 810, 1800, 1831, and Trans-Europa Flight 1474.[2] All had encounters, but only two filed reports.

Trans-Europa Flight 1474 Captain Ramos reported that, at 6:40 PM, he was flying his jetliner at 30,000 feet in the vicinity of Maella, Spain, about 108 miles out of Barcelona. As he and the copilot busied themselves flying their 727, they both happened to notice a green light in the sky slightly to one side of their airliner. The light began to grow as the object flew on a near collision course with the near fully loaded jetliner. As it flew closer, both pilots soon realized that they were not witnessing a plane racing towards their craft, but one of those things that they hoped only someone else witnessed: a UFO!

The pilots described what they saw as appearing very much like a spherical soap bubble flying at a tremendous speed towards the vicinity of their aircraft. As the bubble closed in on the aircraft, the copilot switched off the autopilot and the captain put the plane into a mini dive of 400 or so feet. The object crossed in front of the plane and disappeared to the south of their craft, but not before both men saw a second, but much smaller sphere tagging along behind the bright green sphere. The entire sighting lasted just about one minute.

Flight 1831 was taxiing on the runway at Barcelona Airport when the cockpit crew saw the green sphere fly towards the airport and hover over the end of the runway. Being restricted from take off by the presence of this craft, the captain of this 727 tried to signal the object as it silently hovered over the end of the runway by flashing his bright landing lights. No sooner had he ceased flashing the lights, the green sphere just disappeared into thin air. The crew of Flight 1831 and many witnesses around the airport watched to see if the object would reappear, but it didn't. After confirming with the tower that there was no longer any traffic at the end of the runway, Flight 1831 was airborne and on its way within minutes. Please note the date of this encounter. It is exactly one year to the day after Captain Tejada, flying the Super Caravelle from Austria to Spain, witnessed a UFO in the skies above Barcelona, Spain, as reported in the last chapter. This sighting is very much like the sighting at the Phelps-Dodge plant, as it may represent yet another return visit by some intelligence to a given area, as part of a continuing process of observation.

MISSOURI

The boomerang-shaped UFO that we talked about in the last chapter made its first reported appearance in the 1980s on the night of November 18th, 1980. This would be but one of the hundreds of sightings of this craft that would occur throughout the decade. This night it was sighted over north central Missouri by scores of witnesses.[3] Hundreds of people, including twelve police officers, witnessed a triangular UFO as it blazed an erratic trail across northern Missouri.

The UFO was seen for a total of four hours as it slowly zigzagged its way across the Show Me State. Witnesses near Kirksville, Missouri, first sighted the object. The object meandered its way over this small city of just over 17,000, and as it made its way west, a controller on duty at the FAA facility outside of Kirksville spotted the object on his radar screen as it passed by at a whopping 45 MPH! By the time he got someone to cover for him so he could go outside to see what this was, the triangular object was just visible as it slowly disappeared behind some of the local terrain. The object went west out of Kirksville and was witnessed by many more people as it made its way over the smaller communities of Novinger, Green City, Milan, Reger, Humphreys, Osgood, Galt and Laredo, before making its last appearance of the night over Trenton, Missouri. This type of behavior by this specific type of UFO would be repeated many times in the skies above the communities of New York's lower Hudson Valley in the years to come.

Rendlesham Forest, England

Thursday, December 25th, 1980, Christmas Day, would be the starting point for one of the most amazing encounters with UFOs ever recorded. At about 11 PM that Christmas night, an English farmer, whose home lies not too far from the Woodbridge NATO Air Base, was enjoying the holiday programming on television, when he was angered by lights he took to be from a USAF aircraft playing what he called "silly beggars" in the night sky above his fields.

When he investigated, he could tell they were not planes, but what they were he could not ascertain. A couple hours later, in the early morning hours of Friday, December 26th a strange blip was tracked on radar at Heathrow International Airport as it made its way across the English countryside. It was tracked on radar until it vanished from the screen near Woodbridge and Bentwaters Air Bases. On duty that night near the east gate to Woodbridge Air Base were USAF Airman Joe Borman and Sergeant Jerry Stevens, both attached to the 81st Squadron's Security Police.[4]

At close to 2 AM GMT, the two men were leaning on the hood of their jeep discussing what they would do when their respective tours of duty were over. Both men were startled by the appearance of an unknown light in the night sky that appeared above the dense woods that bordered the base. After watching it for a moment, Airman Borman turned to his sergeant and asked him what that light over the forest was. Sergeant Stevens, uttering the first thing came into his mind, said that it was probably just the lighthouse at Orford Ness. Looking slightly to one side made him suddenly realize that the light was not the lighthouse, as it could be seen as a distinctly different light several degrees to the south of the unknown object in question. Stevens noted that he was unaware that any traffic that would be coming in that night, unless it was an airplane making an emergency landing. Airman Borman informed Stevens that he did not think the light was a plane as it was hovering in one spot. Stevens replied that a plane coming head on could give the illusion that it was hovering, when in reality they are moving in a straight line and growing closer. The object appeared to be a round light glowing like a magnesium flare that had been dropped out of an aircraft, only there were no other craft in the area at any altitude that could have dropped a flare.

Borman interrupted the sergeant's speech, by commenting that if the object was a plane it was crashing! As both watched, the light moved slightly to the south and then made a beeline into the dense woods. Borman thought out loud, "Jesus, what was that thing!"

Sergeant Stevens quickly radioed the base to inquire if they had any known traffic inbound on runway 27. Base wanted to know if they had a problem, and the wise sergeant informed them that they *might* have a problem over runway 27. The tower informed the security officers that they would check for traffic, and when the voice returned on the radio, the security officers knew before the controller told him, that there was no known traffic in the area.

Back at the base, the officer in charge wanted to know what was the nature of the problem. Stevens informed them that they had seen a light first hovering over and then crashing into the woods near their present location. Night Command informed them to stay at their current position, as back up was on its way to their location. They asked Stevens if anyone was out there with him and he told him that he was accompanied by Airman Borman. Night Command then inquired if they could estimate the area in which the light was seen to come to rest at, and they both answered that they could. At 2:30 AM two security officers, Airman Jim Archer and Airman John Cadbury arrived at the east gate to join Borman and Stevens.

INTO THE WOODS

Before setting out into the woods, Borman and Stevens were ordered to remain at their post and Archer and Cadbury were ordered into the woods. Much to their dismay, they were ordered to leave their M-16s behind, just in case the need should arise for them to leave the base property. They got the approximate coordinates from Stevens, jumped back into their jeep and drove through the gate and out onto a concrete pathway that ran parallel to the perimeter fence in the general direction of the English Forestry Commission offices and the Tangham Wood farm. When the concrete ended, they drove down a dirt path used primarily by forestry officers, and when that ended, they had to get out and walk. Heading into the utter darkness of the dense forest, the airman remembered their standing orders: Find the crash site and look for wreckage to determine whose aircraft it was and apprehend any survivors and return them to base to inform the authorities there as to what their mission had been.

Archer and Cadbury slowly made their way through the dense woods, continually commenting on how this little exercise was going to turn out to be an exercise of futility. Suddenly, through the trees ahead, both could see lights, a mixture of red and blue, pulsating a short distance off the ground. Archer grabbed his walkie-talkie to report back to base what they had encountered in the woods, but it was not working. They tentatively continued through the woods in the general direction of the lights making sure they kept a constant fix on the lights ahead of them.

When they got closer, they could not believe what they were seeing! In front of their unbelieving eyes was a craft about ten feet wide and eight feet high. The object was triangular in shape and was made out of some material that glowed with an eerily bright white light. The light was bright enough to illuminate the ground below it as well as the trees surrounding it. A band of red and bluish-white lights could be seen across the object, giving it the appearance of a brightly lit Christmas tree. Out of the base of this pyramidal craft, three tube-like landing gear legs could be seen. Archer asked Cadbury if he was seeing the same thing. When he did not answer, Archer took his eyes off the object and looked in the direction where his partner had been standing. Archer was shocked to see that Cadbury was inching his way towards the object!

Archer tried to scream to his partner, but just stood there in stunned silence as his partner came to within feet of the unknown object. As if alerted to Cadbury's presence, the object withdrew the landing gear and began to float silently, yet gracefully upwards. When it had reached the level of Archers' head, the object began to move away from the two men. Gracefully, and quite slowly, the object made its way through the forest dodging the trees effortlessly as it headed towards a fence and the grassy clearing beyond. The object raised itself over the fence and bobbed like a cork in water, as if enticing the men to follow it and follow it they did!

Once over the fence and in the field, the airmen watched as the glowing object hovered and then shot straight up into the night sky, filling the woods with a bright light and whipping the barnyard animals into a frenzy of bellows and stampedes. The bright light from the departing craft gave way to the darkness that enveloped them, and with it came a loss of their senses, which caused them to lose track of their assigned duties and just kind of mull about in the woods.

At the base, mayhem was erupting. It was 3:30 AM and the two airmen sent into the woods had not made contact in over half an hour. From the tower came the report that a bright object was seen rapidly ascending from the general area into which the men had been sent. The officer on duty decided something needed to be done and quick. Several squads were assembled and given the order to go out into the woods and not to return until Cadbury and Archer were found.

At 3:45 AM, one of the search parties came across the two men as they stumbled in bewilderment through the dense thickets. They were returned to base and debriefed.

At 4 AM, Colonel Ted Conrad decided that since the men had left the base and made contact with this object on English soil, the local constabulary needed to be brought into the loop.

At 4:11 AM, they called the local police and about twenty minutes later they met with two Bobbies at the edge of the forest near where the object was encountered. The two officers, showing little or no enthusiasm, took the details of the colonel's report and returned to their station. Both had taken more than enough reports from locals of UFOs; they did not need the Americans giving them more of the same!

UFO Traces

Later in the day after the sun broke nights gloomy hold over the English countryside, a Master Sergeant from the 81st Security Squadron was sent out to where the airmen had made contact with this UFO to check for any physical traces. Sure enough, in the dense woods right where the airmen told the officers the object appeared to have set down, there were three depressions forming an equilateral triangle with twelve-foot sides. Still later in the day, a specially equipped A-10 Warthog anti-tank airplane made several passes over the woods to see if there was any lingering radiation. The plane's sensitive equipment picked up some lingering radiation, prompting another call to the local police, who once again responded with the same lack of enthusiasm.

At 8:30 PM that Friday night, December 26th, a four-man detachment was on routine patrol near the east gate of Woodbridge, where the object had been first sighted some twenty hours earlier. As they went about their patrol, the men spotted some strange lights twinkling in the night sky. After several minutes, the lights disappeared. Not long thereafter, one man in the patrol spotted a glowing light in the woods near the spot where Cadbury and Archer had their encounter the night before. They wasted no time in reporting what they were seeing. They radioed in to Sergeant Alan Benson who was on duty at neighboring Bentwaters Air Base[5] and reported the lights in the sky and the glow emanating from the woods. He radioed Lieutenant Englund, the shift commander, to inform him of what was going on. Englund, in turn, called deputy base commander Lieutenant Colonel Charles Halt to request permission from him for he and Sergeant Benson to head out and join the four-man patrol near the east gate of Woodbridge. Englund and Benson made the five-minute drive to where the four-man detail obediently waited near the eastern most gate of Woodbridge. With midnight approaching, the lieutenant, sergeant and the four-man patrol, piled into jeeps, took at least one fully loaded M-16 and headed down the same path into Rendlesham Forest that Archer and Cadbury had taken almost a day before.

Back Into the Woods

When they had come to the end of drivable roads, they also disembarked their vehicles and set out on foot. As they picked their way carefully through the thick woods, an eerily strange curtain of light could be seen with what appeared to be a rolling fog beneath it. The object within the fog looked to have a red light on top and a band of blue lights ringing its midsection. As the men approached this odd object, it, like the craft seen the night before, began to back away at a speed that allowed it to keep a constant distance between itself and the oncoming soldiers.

The airman closest to the object reported that the air was filled with static electricity, enough to make his hair stand on. Lieutenant Englund was convinced that the prudent course of action was to get the hell out of there! So he and the other five men retreated from their position, back toward the safety of their vehicles. As he left, Sergeant Benson noticed that the humans were not the only scared creatures in the woods that night. Much like the retreating soldiers, deer, squirrels, rabbits, and other wild game were making their way away from the location of the strange fog-enshrouded craft.

When they had reached their vehicles, they radioed back to Lieutenant Colonel Halt to report and see how he wanted them to proceed. Like the night before, this detachment was told to hold their position, Lieutenant Colonel Halt was on his way with enough back up to flush whatever it was out of Rendlesham Forest!

CONVOY

Lt. Colonel Charles Halt arrived with a convoy of vehicles and nearly thirty additional military personnel shortly after midnight on December 27th. The personnel were distributed and ordered to scout the area for any traces the intruder may have left behind.

The mission was unfolding with mixed results when, suddenly, the peculiar fog, which glowed an odd yellowish-green, appeared once again just ahead of a small group of soldiers, including Sergeant Benson and Airman Cadbury.[6] All the animals on the neighboring farm began to bolt and whine. Benson looked around to see if there was something else at large that could be causing the uproar.

Through the trees, a small red light could be seen navigating around the many obstacles in the dense forest. Benson ordered the airman with the radio to get a message through to Lieutenant Colonel Halt. Unlike the previous night, the radio worked just fine and when Halt was informed of their location, all eyes turned to that location where Benson and his men stood. They could also see the light weaving a strange path through Rendlesham Forest.

Halt wanted to get a better view of the object, so he and several men tried to move to a point on the edge of the clearing, which afforded an unobstructed view of the object. This also allowed them to get a look at it through one of the "Starlight Scopes" the military uses to turn night into day. Halt was recording the events as they unfolded on a handheld tape recorder. On the tape, he describes the object as being yellowish and close to the ground. As he watched it, the object appeared to be moving slowly towards him, when suddenly smaller lights began to shoot off of the yellowish object.

Benson and Cadbury were witnessing these events from a closer vantage point. They watched as the red object floated silently towards their position in the clearing and when it became engulfed within the yellowish mist it imploded with an enormous flash of light. When their eyes had recovered from the bright flash, resting on the ground in front in the center of the clearing was a strange-looking craft. The object had a pyramid-shaped dome on top, yet the middle widened into a curving base so as to hide any landing gear the craft may have had.

A Look Through the Startlight Scope

The men were ordered to contain the situation until backup could arrive. Just like the previous night, the object slowly lifted itself off the ground and began to move backwards towards the tree line on the far side of the clearing. They got permission to go forward and they pursued the retreating craft. Lieutenant Colonel Halt and his men moved forward also, crossing the open field and stopping at the edge of the tree line to get a look at the object through the Starlight scope. The airman with the scope looked through its viewfinder at the object, which was about 250 yards away. Through the scope, he could see the object was still moving from side to side. In the middle was a dark spot that oscillated, appearing to him to look very much like an eye opening and closing. The flashes of light that emanated from the craft were so bright that he felt as if they would burn his inner eye. According to Halt's tape, the time was 2:44 AM; they had been chasing these lights in the forest for over an hour.

At 3:05 AM, the object began to shoot bright strobe like lights into the air. Suddenly, two half-moon-shaped objects with multi-colored lights flashing about their "hulls" appeared in the sky to their north and about five miles away. As Halt recorded their appearance on his tape recorder, the objects in the sky changed from half-moons to full circles. With their full attention on the objects in the skies, they did not notice that the object on the ground had moved very close to them and was now in back of their current position.

The airman with the scope refocused on the craft and informed Halt that it was moving towards them and a lot faster than before and shooting beams of light in all directions. Halt recorded on the tape that what he was witnessing was unreal. The light coming off the object was penetrating the trees as if they were not there. The craft sped faster and faster, dodging trees and shooting off bright penetrating beams of light. All involved knew that this was no man-made object, nor was it a star, swamp gas, or Venus! As it flew nearer to them, the craft made an instantaneous right angle turn, and in an instant, was lost amongst the stars in the upper atmosphere.

A fraction of a second later, they were hit by an icy blast of air, which had a concussion so strong that all were knocked unconscious for several minutes. One airman did not fully recover until hours after they had returned to base! As the men recovered and began to make their way back to their vehicles, Halt made two final entries onto his tape recorder. One at 3:30 AM stated that the object on the ground was gone, but the two in the sky remained. The last at 4 AM recorded the fact that one object remained airborne flying erratically and shooting beams of light down towards different areas of Rendlesham Forest.

INVESTIGATIONS

Unlike many of the other instances where objects buzzed or entered the perimeter of military bases, there was a lengthy investigation of this incident. The resulting investigation lead to investigations by US Senators and Prime Minister Thatcher, debate in the English Parliament, and for a short time, a strain on the special friendship we enjoy with the United Kingdom. (For a more in-depth telling of this incredible encounter please consult the book *From Out of the Blue* by Jenny Randles.)

The explanation offered by many experts was that the highly trained Air Force personnel varying in rank from Airman to Lieutenant Colonel actually were frightened out of their minds by the broad sweeping light of the Orford Ness Lighthouse. They offered this explanation even thought the object was seen by many people over a two-day period, left landing marks, was sighted through sensitive military hardware, illuminated the woods and ground below and around it, moved around trees, and several were seen in the sky.

IMPACT

Now, as many of you probably already know, from this reported incident has sprung claims of alien abductions, meetings between government people and aliens in the forest, military cover-up of same, and so on and so forth. These claims have succeeded in doing only one thing: lessening the impact that this sighting had on the entire UFO phenomenon. For the first time, there was an encounter between many military personnel in close proximity to two major air bases and several unknown objects, one that was actually on the ground and within shooting distance of a large detachment of Air Force Security officers. They saw craft that could perform maneuvers and functions that violated all known laws of physics.

Oddly, the story did not leak out for several years, and when it did, the media did their usual skewed and inaccurate reporting of this fantastic encounter. CNN was noted as playing segments of the Halt recording and then ending their short report with the conclusion that the experts offered (light house light) as the unquestionable explanation as to what so many service men had witnessed. This was very successful in creating within the unindoctrinated mind of the masses that, yes, these men had seen something, but it was just light from a lighthouse, thus effectively cementing in those minds that nothing spectacular happened at all. Of course, in reality, the events that transpired should have signaled the world that UFOs are real and that they are here.

KENT, NEW YORK

After having dinner at her mother's home in Kent, New York, Monique O'Driscoll, a well-respected member of the community and an employee of the Brewster Mental Health Clinic, and her daughter, were driving back to their home in Brewster, New York. At about 8 PM, February 26th, 1983, the music they were listening to on the radio was replaced by a loud, furious hissing noise. The noise was so deafening that they shut the radio off and amused themselves by looking at the very picturesque sky, cloudless with a bright moon as it illuminated the hills of the surrounding countryside.

As they drove, Monique's daughter saw some bright lights on one of the hillsides and pointed them out to her mother. As she mentioned that it was probably a house, the lights began to move. Monique was impressed by the brightness of what appeared to be a craft with no fewer than fifty lights decorating it. As it moved, her daughter mentioned that the craft was probably flying over White Pond,[7] and with a hint of apprehension, she asked her mother, "You're not going to follow it are you?"

Monique found herself turning down the road that led to the pond. Up ahead, about a quarter of a mile away, they could see the craft off to their left. It then flew directly over the car, and as it did, both women watched out the windshield as it flew directly overhead and on its way out over the pond. As it passed overhead, neither heard any sound whatsoever. Monique was daunted by the size, estimating the V-shaped object was about 200 to 300 feet from tip to tip, and made out of a structure of tubes that appeared to her very much like an iron bridge.

They pulled the car over to the side of the narrow road. Monique got out of the car. Her daughter was scared by the object and elected to remain in the car. Through the birch trees alongside the road, she could see the boomerang-shaped craft as it hovered over the pond. For some unknown reason, Monique felt a great need to get closer for a better look. With her daughter screaming at her to get back into the car, she headed to a small open area where she could see the red and blue lights of the craft reflecting off of the ice, completely unafraid of the intimidating large craft that hovered nearby.

She noticed that there were also several amber lights scattered in and about the red and blue lights, with one large amber light in the center of the craft. Having watched the craft for three or four minutes, it slowly began to move away. Monique found herself asking aloud, "Please don't go; I would like to get a better look at you." Suddenly, the craft stopped, made a 180-degree turn and slowly started to drift towards her. Her daughter's screams pleading for her to get back in the car and leave so the craft would not take them, began to sink in and she turned and headed back towards the car, keeping an observant eye on the craft as she did so. As she walked towards the car, she began to feel a bit scared and the craft stopped and turned and flew up towards Farmers Mill Road. She jumped into the car and followed it once again. They followed the craft up Farmers Mill Road to the point where it crosses Gypsy Trail Road and stopped the car.

In a house a short distance away, Mr. and Mrs. Donald Nandi saw the object and called the police in Carmel and Kent, New York. The law enforcement officers at the other end of the phone informed them that many people had seen some odd lights in the sky that night.

Outside a short distance away, Monique once again got out of her car and was watching the craft as a car going by pulled alongside her. In it was her friend Rita Rivera. They talked about the object and the fact that no one would ever believe them if they told their story of what they were seeing. She too had seen it over White Pond but unlike Monique was afraid to drive near or past it for fear her headlights would attract the craft's attention. When the craft began to move away, they got into their respective cars and followed it until it was out of sight.

DANBURY, CONNECTICUT

Shortly after Monique and Rita lost sight of the craft, Herbert Proudfoot, a teacher in his hometown of Danbury, Connecticut and two friends, both air traffic controllers, saw the same or a similar craft as they drove in Proudfoots' car down I-84. Pulling off I-84 at one of the Danbury exits, one of the passengers pointed the odd formation of lights on the horizon out to the two other occupants in the car. Proudfoot pulled to the side of the exit and the three of them got out of the car and watched as the boomerang-shaped cluster of lights slowly made its way in their direction. They heard no noise as the craft passed overhead at about 1,000 feet. Nor could either of the air traffic controllers (who shall remain anonymous at their request) identify the lights as any known aircraft. The trio lost sight of the craft behind a stand of tree some miles away. All mentioned a phrase that would be heard frequently by researchers investigating the Hudson Valley UFO sightings: The experience, the size of the craft, and the silent passage was all like something out of *Close Encounters of the Third Kind!*

PUTNAM COUNTY, NEW YORK

Dennis Sant, at the time, the Deputy Clerk for Putnam County, New York, and his two children were on their way home from church on the night of March 17th, 1983.[8] As he pulled into the driveway at approximately 8:40 PM, he spotted a large triangle-shaped object hovering over his yard about fifty feet from his home. They all jumped out of their car and ran to the backyard, but the object was gone.

He took the kids inside and informed them to get ready for bed. As he was speaking to his children, he experienced an overwhelming need to go back outside. As soon as he was out the door, the object could be seen about 300 feet away as it hovered 50 feet over I-84. He went back inside, got his father and his two kids and they all went back outside for a look at the strange craft.

Back outside, they could once again see the craft as it hovered over a truck that had pulled to the side of the road on I-84. They could also see the many cars that had stopped and the occupants of them, who had gotten out of their cars to watch, as this incredible machine silently hovered over the normally busy interstate.

Watching it as if in a trance, Sant remembers thinking at the time that he wished he could get a better look at the craft. Just as with the previous sighting, no sooner had he thought this, than the object pivoted and began to slowly float towards his position. It stopped about forty feet away from Sant and his family, hovering about twenty feet above a telephone pole at the edge of his yard. He recalled the object was well over 300 feet wide with lights of red, green, and white covering its underside. He watched the object for at least three minutes, and all the while, its lights seemed to intensify.

As the object left, he jogged to keep up with it, not wanting to lose sight of it. He followed a bit longer, and then suddenly became frightened that it might land. As he stopped chasing it, he watched it in awe as the huge, silent machine slowly floated over his pond and then back over I-84 and out of sight, leaving in its wake, hundreds of dumb-founded witnesses.

Carmel, New York

Several days later, on March 24th, 1983, Dr. Lawrence Greenman, his wife, Joan, and their three daughters, were spending a quiet evening in their home near Carmel, New York, relaxing and watching the television.[9] It was slightly after 8 PM when Joan noticed a bright light through the living room window moving in the northwest sky. After watching it from the couch for several minutes, she and the entire family went outside to see what it could be.

Coming towards them from the west was a large bright light. Joan returned inside for a pair of binoculars. Once outside again, she looked at the hovering object through the binoculars. All she could discern was a row of lights that appeared to be in a zigzag pattern. As she looked closer, she could see that the lights were attached to a dark green metallic structure. The object began to turn and Joan could see that the object was boomerang shaped.

Suddenly, as they all watched, the object shot a bright beam of white light down towards the ground. In the beam, Joan, still using the binoculars, saw a small red light that was lowered down from the bigger object and then headed off away from it in a northerly direction at a very high speed. The large boomerang shut off the white beam of light that it had been projecting downward and slowly moved off towards the south, then turned and headed east in complete silence.

The amazed family went back inside their home to discuss what the odd craft could have been, wondering if they alone had witnessed this incredible sight. As they would see in the next morning's paper, they were one of the thousands of people who saw this object that evening.

YORKTOWN HEIGHTS, NEW YORK

Only minutes later, Ed Burns, a Program Manager, who would go on to become a Vice-President, for IBM was driving north on the Taconic Parkway towards his home in Yorktown Heights, New York, when the music on his car's radio began to fade away only to be replaced by intense static. While switching the channels, he happened to look up and ahead of his car on the right; there was a pattern of lights. He watched them as he continued driving, and as the lights came closer, he could make out a distinctive triangle shape. The lights passed over the top of his car as the ship slowly crossed the highway.

A short distance ahead, he pulled to the side of the road and joined twelve other vehicles that had only moments before been speeding up the Taconic, that now sat idle as drivers and passengers stood outside watching this huge triangle-shaped craft as it silently moved towards them.

As it passed overhead, Mr. Burns, very impressed with the object, mentioned to those around him that it appeared very much like a lighted city in the sky.[10] The huge object hovered directly over their position for a short time. Mr. Burns described the object as triangle shaped with many colored and white lights covering it. The colored lights flashed in a synchronized pattern, while the white lights remained constant. Absolutely no sound could be heard from the huge object at any time during the sighting. After a minute or two, Burns stated that the craft then began to move in a Z-pattern as it made its way up the Taconic. He stated that although the craft seemed to be moving very slowly at first, in a second or two, it seemed to have moved a great distance away.

Although this night the boomerang-shaped object had produced much excitement throughout the Hudson Valley, there were still many more sightings and much more excitement to be had by local residents.

Not long after Mr. Burn's sighting, the Yorktown Police Department began receiving so many calls reporting the strange object that their phone's switchboard became congested. Likewise, traffic on the Taconic Parkway and many streets in surrounding towns were becoming backed up due to drivers and passengers abandoning autos to view the extraordinary craft passing silently overhead.

One of the many people who were watching the object was William Hele, who at the time was the chief meteorologist for the National Weather Corporation. As he drove on the Taconic Parkway, in the area near the Westchester County Airport, he noticed slow moving, but intensely bright lights on the horizon. Though he watched the lights for only a short time, his interest was piqued. So Hele decided to do what many others around him had done, pull off to the side of the road. Even with all his experience and years of looking skyward as a meteorologist, as the object approached, Hele became dumbfounded as to what it was he was seeing. Though he could not identify it, he knew it was no conventional aircraft. The lights were beginning to form a V-shape, which he estimated to be about 2,000 feet off the ground. As it approached, it descended to approximately 1,000 feet and slowed to a crawl as it noiselessly passed overhead. The V-shaped object had a multitude of lights that changed colors as if each had a rotating prism inside.[11] As the object flew by, Hele was stunned when all the lights went out and he could see nothing in the sky, no craft, no formation of planes, nothing, except stars. Moments later, the entire craft was once again overhead pulsing with an assortment of colorful lights that changed rapidly as it silently continued on its trek.

Around this same time, Yorktown Police Officer Kevin Soravilla saw what he at first believed to be a jet in trouble. This initial observation was drastically altered when this V-shaped pattern of lights made a 180-degree turn, turning as if on a central axis, then slowly drifted away. Knowing no plane or planes could perform such a maneuver, his sighting that night left Officer Soravilla wondering exactly what it was he had seen.

A short distance away from Officer Soravilla was the police station in New Castle, New York. It also began to receive calls about strange lights in the sky. At about the same time, Officer Andy Sadoff, a five-year veteran of the force, who was out on patrol, spotted the lights in the sky as she sat parked in a driveway on Cross Ridge Road trying to catch speeders in a radar trap.[12] Over the top of a nearby hill, she spotted a group of intense lights as they slowly passed over the hill's crest. As she watched, the object kept coming and coming, and soon she sat staring at a huge silent machine as it slowly floated overhead, turned, and then flew out of sight. Sitting shaking her head, trying to figure out what the hell she'd just seen, Officer Sadoff was surprised several minutes later by the return of the huge boomerang-shaped craft.

The V-shaped object had green and white lights and moved with a gliding motion as it made its way over her cruiser. She estimated the UFO was at least 300 feet from tip to tip. Locking the doors, she stuck her head out the window, watching intently, as the object came to a dead stop over her car. As it hung overhead, she could see a huge, dark, metallic form that the lights were attached to. The object started to move away, and Officer Sadoff was still surprised that she could not hear any noise coming from this gigantic machine. The UFO flew back the way it had come and disappeared behind the hill over which it had first appeared. Her sighting lasted about eight minutes.

CROTON FALLS, NEW YORK

Seven months and several days later, on October 28th, 1983, Jim Cooke, a biomedical engineer, who at the time of his sighting was developing machines for the emerging field of medical laser surgery, was driving to his home in Mahopac, New York from nearby Croton Falls, New York, at about 2:15 AM.[13] As he drove up Croton Falls Road from Route 6, nothing in his engineering experiences could prepare him for the sighting he was about to have.

Rounding a bend in the road, Mr. Cooke spotted some lights in the early morning sky. Thinking it was just a plane; he paid little attention to them and continued driving. As he approached the Croton Falls Reservoir on his left, the lights sped towards his car and descended in the area near the reservoir much faster than an airplane or helicopter safely could do. He slowed down to take another look in the direction of the lights. Looking through the trees, he could see that the lights had been shut off, but a large dark object hovered over the reservoir at about the treetop level. The object appeared unlike anything he had ever seen before.

Cooke stopped his car, got out, and watched the object through the trees for several minutes. After working up the needed courage, he picked his way through the trees towards the shoreline. Once there, he saw that the object was triangle shaped and hovering just 15 feet above the surface of the reservoir, about 200 feet from his position. He estimated the object was 100 feet long at the base and 30 feet long at its apex, and most amazingly, the object made no sound whatsoever.

Suddenly, intensely red lights appeared on the ship's sides. Then a red shaft of light descended from the craft and appeared to be probing the water below and whatever lay beneath its tranquil surface. He noted that the material the ship's hull was made out of did not reflect the lights when they came on. The ship moved to four different locations above the reservoir, remaining at 15 feet above the water at all times. Each time the craft stopped, the red shaft of light descended from the object and probed the water below.

As the object made its way around the reservoir, as would be expected on a highly traveled road even at that time of night, several cars passed by on Croton Falls Road. Each time Mr. Cooke heard a car coming, all lights were extinguished on the object.

Once the car had passed, the lights would come on and the UFO would continue its probing of the water below. When the UFO had completed its survey of the reservoir, it silently rose up and flew away in the direction from which it had come. Cooke was very impressed with the craft that he had watched for nearly fifteen minutes. After the sighting he had no idea what it was he had seen or from where it could have come from.

Author's Note:

Although the boomerang-shaped UFO was not the only one sighted in 1983, these sighting best illustrate the point I am trying to get across: These sightings contradict everything skeptics and the government have led the American people to believe about UFOs. Here, contrary to the skeptics' claims, we have sightings by qualified observers (police officers, meteorologists and engineers), people who have nothing to gain by creating UFO stories (IBM Executives, County Clerks), and large groups simultaneously observing huge, well defined UFOs as they hovered over New York's Hudson Valley. Once the sightings started to make headlines, skeptics were quick to chime in with their two-cents worth, declaring in the way that only they could, that all these people having these sightings were mistaken in the reports they made. They did not see a huge UFO. What they were witnessing was several ultra-light aircraft as they flew in formation.

Although there was a squadron of rogue pilots making these dangerous flights, the objects reported prior were not planes. Witnesses took pictures and videos of both the above object and the squadron of ultra-lights. In each case where the planes flew overhead, the engines could be heard and the formation of lights was not as well defined. The objects reported above and below were one large object with many lights, not several small objects flying in formation. This is attested to by the fact that as it flew overhead, a structure could be seen between the lights. Had this been several small aircraft, some clouds, many stars, or even the moon, would be visible between the lights due to there being no structures connecting them. Likewise, even engines as small as those of ultra-light aircraft could be heard as they sputtered along through the night sky, and in each of the cases we have reviewed, the object sighted was completely silent.

The maneuvers performed by the UFOs reported here, like 180-degree turns, hovering above patrol cars and lakes, both frozen and thawed, would not be possible by any aircraft other than helicopters. Had the lights been a group of helicopters, they would not only be easily heard, but their downdraft would also be easily felt. In none of the cases reported are loud engines heard nor blasts of air felt.

DANBURY, CONNECTICUT

On July 12th, 1984 the boomerang-shaped UFO made an appearance in and around Danbury, Connecticut. Just before 11 PM that night, Edward Mulholland, who was an engineer at Perkin-Elmer Corporation in Norwalk (which made many components for the Hubble Space Telescope), spotted some odd lights hovering over a golf course near the Danbury Airport Exit off of I-84.

Exiting the interstate to stop and take a look at these lights, Mulholland parked his car near the local fairgrounds and left his auto. The lights soon took the shape of a large ship with many lights on it. Suddenly these multicolored lights went off and were replaced by intensely bright blue lights. The craft hovered about 500 feet above the course, and when it began to move off, it did so at a very slow speed. The object moved off towards the east, made two left-hand turns and then floated away.

Keith Reid was next to spot it. While driving down I-84, the object became visible to him and his passenger near one of the Danbury exits. They followed it for a short distance, and when it hovered in an open field, he stopped the car and they got out to take a closer look. The object's lights were changing color from white to red to orange to green to blue to white and then repeating the sequence. They described it as triangular in shape and very large.[14] The object left at high speed, and as it did so, its lights faded away until nothing could be seen except the blackness of the night sky.

CANDLEWOOD LAKE, CONNECTICUT

Dr. Richard Long, a law professor at St. John's Law School in New York City, was relaxing at his home on the east side of Candlewood Lake with his wife and nephew when they spotted a triangle formation of lights in the night sky. The craft moved to their left and then settled down into a hover a short distance away. As it began to move, all the lights went off and the craft vanished. Dr. Long thought it wise to report what he saw so he called the Danbury Police to report his sighting of the quickly becoming well-known Hudson Valley boomerang-shaped UFO.

PEEKSKILL, NEW YORK

On June 14th, 1984 a New York State Power Authority Police Officer, whom we shall call Steve (due to his wish to remain anonymous), was walking a routine patrol at the Indian Point Nuclear Power Plant near Peekskill, New York, when an odd grouping of lights in the distance caught his eye. Steve, a three year veteran of the Power Authority Police, who was a veteran of both the United States Army and the New York State Police, noted the time, 10:15 PM, and looking up at the lights, could tell that whatever he was seeing, it was definitely heading towards the facility. The lights appeared to be white with a yellowish hue, and arranged in the shape of a large boomerang.

After watching the lights for approximately ten minutes, he looked over towards the Consolidated Edison facility that boarders Indian Point, and saw no fewer than ten Con-Ed employees starring up at the approaching lights, which had now come to be within a quarter mile of Steve's position. Steve radioed the other workers on duty that night at Indian Point to alert them to the strange lights, so they, like he, could get a glimpse of this odd sight. Two other officers responded to his call. Together they watched the object for another twenty minutes. Of the twenty minutes it was in view, during the last fifteen minutes, the object was seen to hover silently over one of the power plant buildings.

The object had ten lights that formed the now familiar boomerang shape, and they were steady and quite intense. So bright were they, that they made the bright security flood lights on the building below come on! Steve estimated that the lights on the ship were ten times the brightness of the security floodlights, and the incredible ship, that they estimated to be larger than a football field, dwarfed the eighty-foot-tall building it was hovering over. The object then slowly drifted off towards Peekskill and out of sight. When asked if what he had seen could have been a formation of small planes flying in formation, Steve answered with a resounding *no*! Having flown helicopters in the military, he knew that a formation of planes or helicopters would produce enough noise that it would be easy enough to hear. The object they saw was silent. Also, with the twenty-five MPH wind that blew constantly that evening, no light plane or helicopter could have flown so tight a formation so perfectly. What convinced him most of all though, was the fact that, as the lights approached, a plane flying much higher than the object disappeared for a few seconds when it passed in between the lights, which is exactly what would happen if the plane passed behind a solid body that the lights were attached to. Likewise, when the object turned to fly away at the end of the sighting, it turned as if pivoting on some unseen central axis.[15] Ultra-light planes would have to make a wide banking turn. They would not be able to hover, nor turn like this!

Read on, as this would be the first of two extraordinary sightings of a huge UFO over the highly restricted airspace over this nuclear power plant.

Sighting Two

Five weeks later, on the night of July 25th, 1984, Steve was once again on duty at Indian Point, when another guard put out a broadcast that the UFO had come back. This time, all available personnel, including two supervisors, raced outside to see the object. Once outside, Steve noticed that the object was coming from the same direction as it had come from during the first sighting. This time, though, the lights that made up the boomerang formation were not steady and of only one color. That night, the lights were blinking and changing in color from white to yellow to blue as the craft approached the only reactor that was active that evening.

As it came closer, he could make out a blinking red light in back of the light that formed the point or front end of the boomerang. As the object was passing over their position at about 500 feet, the men could walk and keep pace with the object. One of the officers in the control center aimed the camera on top of a 95-foot-tall security tower in the direction of the object. It was so large that the officer had to pan the camera 180 degrees to view the object in its entirety.

All who watched the object as it headed towards the reactor, agreed that the lights were definitely attached to a central structure, as the multitude of stars visible that night could not be seen between the lights as the UFO passed overhead. As soon as the object had passed over the east gate entrance to Reactor Number 3, all security systems went offline, including the computer that controls the security devices and communications.

One of the supervisors began to get nervous because this huge object's presence was barely thirty feet away from a working nuclear reactor. He hurriedly called nearby New York National Guard Command at Camp Smith, to see if they could identify what was over Indian Point. They could not. All the Security Police could do was sit and hope that the object would leave like it had several weeks before. As if to put all the officers at ease, the UFO spun around 180 degrees and slowly began to drift back in the direction from which it had come.

The following day, all officers at the facility were informed that nothing had happened the night before, and that was the official story they were to stick to. The need to contain this incredible sighting was understandable. Indian Point was a controversial plant, and so shortly after the Three Mile Island disaster, the last thing the plant's operators wanted was for local people, who were already afraid of the reactors, to be thinking that they had flaky, UFO-sighting guards policing the nuclear power plant in their back yard.

Local radio personality Gerry Culliton had received information that the sighting was a hoax perpetrated by a group of pilots flying ultra-lights in formation and that the New York State Police arrested the pilots of the small planes. When researchers contacted the State Police, they knew nothing about any pilots being arrested for flying in tight formation over this highly restricted airspace. Nor was there any mention of where the incredible planes that silently hovered over the plant could be found for inspection! And as we all know, that is because pilots in planes were not responsible for the sightings the Power Authority Police had in June and July of 1984.

KISKI VALLEY, PENNSYLVANIA

On the night of August 20, 1984, in Pennsylvania's Kiski Valley,[16] Vandergrift, Pennsylvania, Police officer Joseph Caporali and local politician William Ziegmound witnessed strange craft as they flew through the northwestern portion of the night sky. What first was one large craft, they watched split into three smaller craft. Being mobile in the cruiser allowed them to view these strange objects from several different vantage points. Once the objects had separated, Ziegmound got a pair of binoculars, and through them he could see that the one object that was flying here and there, was shaped like a perfect square and had two red strobe lights on one end and two green strobe lights at the other. All three came together in a triangle formation and flew off. The lights appeared to be about 150 feet apart, very large and flying at approximately 15,000 feet.

The very next night, at approximately 11:20 PM, local resident Lori Powell saw the same or similar objects as they flew silently and quickly through the clear night sky. Ms. Powell's father, William, had witnessed a stationary green light in the sky several nights before. And on the night of August 22nd, three more Kiski Valley law enforcement officers witnessed a large craft with red, white, and green lights as it hovered over Leechburg, Pennsylvania, bringing to an end a localized flap of UFO sightings that occurred throughout the month of August in the southwestern corner of Pennsylvania.

LANZHOU, CHINA

Captain Wang Shuting was piloting a Boeing 747 belonging to the Chinese Civil Aviation Administration on the Peking to Paris run on the evening of June 11th, 1985, when at approximately 10:40 PM while over Lanzhou, China, his flight encountered a UFO that almost forced him to make an emergency landing.

Flight CA 933[17] was on schedule and running smoothly when the captain at 39 degrees 30 minutes north and 103 degrees 30 minutes east spotted a UFO. The object was coming fast, and from a quick calculation, the pilot came to the conclusion that it would cross the path of the 747 dangerously close. Ready for evasive maneuvers, Captain Shuting watched as the object continued to grow until it was unbelievable in size! As the object passed a safe distance in front of the plane, the pilot reported that he estimated the object was six miles in diameter (no that is not a typo!) and illuminating a twenty-five square mile area! It was elliptical in shape and had a very bright center with rows of bluish lights around its periphery.

SWITZERLAND BORDER

In August of 1985, pilots flying an Olympic Airlines flight from Zurich, Switzerland, to Athens, Greece, spotted a huge UFO near the border of Switzerland. A short time later, yet another huge UFO was spotted by the passengers, including forty-five journalists, and the crew of a 737 enroute to Buenos Aires.

ALASKA

Over a year later, on November 17th, 1986, another extraordinarily large object would be witnessed by yet another pilot. At 5:10 PM, pilot Kenju Terauchi was piloting a Japanese Airlines 747 cargo plane through the frigid skies above Alaska.

He, his first officer, and the flight engineer spotted two lights about the size of a 727s[18] fuselage about 1,000 feet in front of their airliner. He radioed Anchorage Control Center to see if they could identify the traffic. Although the transmission was garbled with static, Anchorage received enough information from Captain Terauchi to radio back that they could not identify the traffic that now appearing on the radar screens at Anchorage and onboard the aircraft. Anchorage then called the military, which bore no results. The two objects then flew off into the darkening sky.

Before the atmosphere could return to normal inside the 747 cockpit, another object appeared on the plane's radar. Whatever it was, it was huge and coming towards them quickly from the rear of the aircraft. Anchorage also was tracking this huge object. The incredibly large object flew over the plane, disappearing into the same region of sky that the two smaller lights had a short time earlier. Kenju Terauchi watched in awe as the pale white UFO, the size of two aircraft carriers (about 2,500 feet long!), was flying faster than his 747! Terauchi felt this huge craft must have been the "mother ship" that carried the two 727-sized UFOs that he had seen just minutes before. He and the crew were becoming frightened and he requested permission to land at Anchorage. Shortly after the transmission, at about 5:39 PM, the mammoth UFO streaked across the sky and out of sight. This pilot was not afraid to relay his sighting to the media and it was on the wire in no time.

GULF BREEZE, FLORIDA

The events of November 11th, 1987 would alter the lives of hundreds of people and be but the starting point of a flap of sightings that would last well into the next decade, creating controversy far and wide. The focal point of these sightings was the small town of Gulf Breeze, Florida. Gulf Breeze sits on a peninsula in Pensacola Bay. The town is surrounded by military installations including the Pensacola Naval Air Station and Eglin Air Force Base.

At 2:30 AM, Mrs. Zamitt, the wife of a retired navy captain, was roused from her slumber by her barking dog. When she went outside, she was shocked to see a UFO shining a bluish light down onto her boat-dock. The object sat silently for several minutes and then shot out of sight.

Later that morning, outside his home at about 8:15 AM, Jeff Thompson was observing a circular object about thirty feet in diameter and fifteen feet high. It had two rows of dark spots through its tan center, a small dome at the apex of its silver top and a small protrusion coming down out of its dull tan lower section. The UFO was about 400 feet off the ground and sat silently until two jet aircraft sped in its direction. The UFO first rose up about 200 feet and then, just before the planes screamed overhead at low altitude, the UFO shot straight up and out of sight, flooding the area in a white light as it made its departure. The jets veered off and returned to one of the nearby air bases.

A Close-Up Shot

Slightly after sunset, a local contractor and father of two teenagers with his long time wife, was sitting in the office he built in his home when he saw a strange light in the darkening sky. At about 5:05 PM Ed Walters[19] went outside to get a better look at the odd light. Once outside, he quickly realized that what he was seeing was a very unusual craft. Walters dashed back into his house to grab the Polaroid camera he frequently used in the course of building homes. Camera in hand, Ed stepped back onto his front porch stairs and took four pictures of this object, then went back inside for another pack of film. Once back outside he snapped another photo, and realizing the object had changed course and was now moving towards his home, he went out into the street to get a close-up shot of this UFO. Once there, he was hit by a blue beam of light coming down from the UFO. He suddenly found that he could not move and began having difficulty breathing. He tried to scream out for help, but could not. He struggled to move or break free, until a voice projecting reassuring thoughts began playing in his head. Ed was lifted three feet off the ground, and as this happened he claims the air was permeated by an ammonia smell that made him want to gag. Suddenly, Ed was set down and the UFO quickly departed as a plane passed overhead. Back in the house, Ed's wife noticed the concerned look on his face and then smelled the ammonia/cinnamon smell emanating from him. He told her what had happened and they sat down to decide how this should be handled.

Same Old Skeptics

They decided to give the photos to the editor of the *Gulf Breeze Sentinel,* Duane Cook. He decided to publish the photos showing a UFO very much like the one described by Jeff Thompson earlier. Duane Cook was very surprised when his mother, Doris Somerby, called him and informed him that she had seen the exact same object that was in the picture he printed just five minutes before Ed Walters had his encounter as she and her husband walked their family dog.

It took little time after the astounding photos were published for the experts to proclaim that the photos were faked. Since Mr. Walters, a successful businessman who had little or no reason to try to make money by faking picture and creating stories of amazing encounters with a UFO, had used a Polaroid camera, it was said that the images were obviously the result of double exposure. The experts claimed that he took a model of a UFO, snapped a picture of it, and then took a picture of the sky outside his home, right over the UFO picture already exposed on the film. Though this is possible, upon examination by photographic expert and Navy employee Dr. Bruce Maccabee, who painstakingly pointed out how and why the pictures could not have been faked as the experts claimed. He declared that in his professional opinion the photos were legitimate.

Ed's encounters would continue through 1987 and into 1988. On January 12th, he took the most astounding photo of the same UFO as it hovered over the highway in front of his pickup truck.[20] In the picture, the UFO can be seen to be slightly wider than the road and about as tall as the telephone poles on either side of the roadway. The light it was emitting through its underside illuminated the surface of the road and can be seen as it reflects off the painted hood of his truck. His ordeal would go on to allegedly include repeated abductions and many more photo opportunities.

Ed was not alone, though, as over the next decade, hundreds, if not thousands, of people would see strange lights in the sky above Florida's panhandle. These objects would be captured by both still photography and videotape, backing up the fact that Ed Walters did see and photograph something very unusual. Exactly what these objects were remains a mystery to this day.

Belgium

Our next report was also the beginning of another flap of sightings; only this time they took place in Belgium.

On November 29, 1989,[21] just outside of the town of Eupen, some seven short miles from the German border, two Belgian Gendarmerie's, which are Belgian State Law Enforcement Officers, who were on routine patrol, came across a field that was lit up like a football stadium. Curious as to what it was that could be lighting the field so brightly, Officer Heinrich Nicoll and his fellow law enforcement officer pulled off to the side of the road and got out of their car. Above the field hung a huge triangle-shaped UFO. It hung silently in the air as three incredibly bright, white lights on its underside illuminated the field. In the middle of its "belly," there was a small dome extending down towards the ground, on which a blinking red light could be seen. They reported what they were seeing to their dispatcher Albert Creutz, and asked him to contact the military to see if they were testing any new craft in the area.

The object then began to slowly move away from the officers. So they got back into car and followed the object as it crawled across the Belgian countryside. The object seemed to be scanning the ground, as if studying it and all things on it, with two red beams of light that, to the officers, looked very much like lasers. The object once again hovered over a field and Nicoll and his partner stopped and exited their vehicle. Contacting their dispatcher Creutz, they found out that he had contacted four local airports and no one showed any traffic. Whatever it was they were seeing was either not registering on radar or too low to be picked up.

Suddenly, from behind a nearby stand of trees, another triangle-shaped craft exactly like the first slowly rose into the night sky. The two ships then slowly flew off and out of sight of Nicoll and his partner.

If Creutz had any doubts about what the officers in the field were seeing, his doubts were soon erased when he watched in awe as one of the giant triangles flew overhead not more than 500 feet from his office window. Approximately six minutes later, and eight miles away in nearby Kelmis, Belgium, Gendarmerie Dieter Plumanns and his partner watched one of the triangles as it slowly floated overhead. The triangle proceeded to hover over the top of the town's cathedral, and as it did, Plumanns and his partner watched as the red blinking light detached itself from the underside of the ship and floated down towards the building, then circled around in back of it. Once the light had returned to the ship it shot straight up and out of sight.

These two officers gave a description of the object they had seen that matched exactly in every detail the description of a silent triangle that Nicoll, his partner, and Creutz had given of the object they saw just minutes before.

The following month, Belgian Colonel Andre Armant and his wife were driving down a Belgian highway when they spotted a huge triangle-shaped craft silently hovering alongside the roadway. As it moved closer to them, a white light engulfed the car, scaring the colonel's wife to near hysteria. They soon departed the area and the craft continued on a course for Brussels where it was videotaped at precisely 2:23 AM by local resident, Marcel Alterano.

Though this sighting wraps up our reports from the decade of the 1980s, as you will see, it was just the first of many sightings of the triangle-shaped UFO that would soon be as common a sight in the skies over Belgium as the boomerang-shaped UFO was over New York's Lower Hudson Valley.

CHAPTER 11

1990 – 1999

Dangerous Skies

"It reminds me of the days of Galileo when he was trying to get people to look at the sun spots. They would say that the sun is a symbol of God; God is perfect; therefore the sun is perfect; therefore spots cannot exist: therefore there is no point in investigating..."

~ J. Allen Hynek
Former science advisor, Project Blue Book
Newsweek November 21, 1977 (p.97)

By the 1990s, the UFO phenomenon came into its own. It seemed that everyone was being abducted by aliens and reporting their horrifying experience in many books, articles, and television appearances. Alien merchandise flooded the shelves of many stores throughout the United States. You could see key chains, tee-shirts, notepads, folders, and television commercials/programs all graced by the now familiar features of the bug-eyed "gray" aliens.

None of this, though, helped to bring to the forefront the fact that our government was not telling us the truth about the UFO phenomenon. As I write this, the official government stance on UFOs still is that they do not exist, thus they pose no threat to the people of the United States of America. Still, people, as they have since time immemorial, continued to see Unidentified Flying Objects flying through the skies above countries all around the world and will continue to do so until those who pilot them decide to stop coming.

Although the sightings made in the 1980s were dominated by reports of the triangle-shaped UFO, the sightings in the 1990s would be dominated by reports of an old favorite: the cigar-shaped UFO, that was buzzing airliners the world over!

Russia

On March 21st, 1990, citizens in Pereslavl, Russia spotted a huge disc-shaped UFO across the vast expanse of blue sky above their town. Those that witnessed this odd disc-shaped aerial craft reported that it was about 150 meters wide, had two blinking lights (one at the 3 o'clock position and one at the 9 o'clock position of the disc's rim) and moved at least three times as fast as a MIG fighter aircraft. Those who saw it claimed that the lights blinked quicker as the craft went faster. The craft flew through the sky in giant *S*-patterns. According to General Igor Maltsev,[1] then Chief of Air Defense for the former USSR's Air Forces, the military received more than 100 reports of the strange object from across the Soviet Union. The military knew what was happening, as the craft was also appearing on their radarscopes as it flew overhead.

According to Lieutenant Colonel A. A. Semenchenko, at 9:38 PM, he was scrambled in his jet interceptor to see exactly what it was popping up on radar screens at several military installations. Aloft for less than thirty minutes, at 10:05 PM, he made a visual sighting of the UFO, which was altering speed, course, and altitude as it flew through the night sky. The object did not respond to his IFF (Identify-Friend or Foe). Although it had shown its capabilities beforehand, the object did not speed off as the jet approached. The object actually overflew the jet and continued on its predetermined course. Lieutenant Colonel Semenchenko could make out that the object was disc shaped and he was quite positive that the object had no wings or tail, nor was there any visible means of propulsion. As he viewed the object with his eyes, it could also be seen as a distinct blip on the MIG's radar screen along with the passenger aircraft flying in the vicinity of Pereslavl. On orders from his superiors, Lieutenant Colonel Semenchenko returned to base.

The object was on radar screens across the region for at least another hour as it circled aircraft and hovered motionless on several occasions. Describing the object, General Maltsev noted that the object's movement was not accompanied by any sound whatsoever. He stated that its maneuverability was astounding, seemingly able to break all the known physical laws of motion and inertia as it defied earth's gravitational pull. Russian officials did not offer any explanation as to what was witnessed that night by hundreds of residents on the ground, several radar installations, and the pilot sent aloft to investigate the strange unidentified object.

BELGIUM

Returning once again to Belgium, the huge triangle-shaped UFOs made their first appearance of the new decade on the night of March 30th–31st, 1990.[2]

On this night, Gendarmerie Captain Jacques Pinson was called to a residence outside Brussels when several persons enjoying a night of leisurely entertainment spotted two triangular patterns of lights slowly making their way across the night sky. Upon arrival at the home, he too saw the objects. They were not alone, as several other police officers on patrol were also viewing the objects. Soon, several NATO installations, including Glons and Semmerzake Air Bases, had the objects on their radar. They estimated the object was aloft in the vicinity of where the people and the Gendarmeries were having their sighting.

It wasn't too long thereafter that two Belgian F-16 Falcons were sent up to investigate the two triangle-shaped UFOs that were flying very slowly across the Belgian countryside. With help from the Gendarmeries on the ground, the two F-16s were vectored into the area where the UFO were hovering and the triangle-shaped UFOs were soon spotted by the F-16 pilots, who quite easily got a lock on the targets. As the planes closed, the objects, which originally had been flying at 25 MPH at 7,500 feet, dove at speeds calculated to be in excess of 1,000 MPH to hover motionless below 750 feet. Three times this action-reaction occurred. Each time the object climbed back into radar range, the F-16s would lock on them, and the UFOs would once again dive down below the detection of the plane's onboard radar. When the UFOs tired of this cat and mouse game, they accelerated out of view in a blink of the eye.

This and many of the Belgian Triangle UFO sightings have been explained away by the American Military as sightings made of the now world-renowned Stealth Fighter/Bomber F-117 and the B-2 Stealth Bomber. Although each are V-shaped, neither are capable of performing the feats witnessed by the people who came into contact with the "Belgian Triangles." Neither of these planes can fly in excess of Mach 1 (760 MPH), thus they would not have been able to fly out of sight in a matter of seconds. Conversely, although these planes are slow, neither can fly at speeds approaching 25 MPH, which is but a fraction of the stall speed of any jet fixed-winged aircraft. Nor could either silently hover over fields and buildings as the triangles have been reported to do in many sighting throughout Belgium. And having had my doors and windows rattled by the roar of a B2 flying overhead to celebrate a graduation ceremony at Rensselaer Polytechnic Institute a short distance from my home, I can vouch for the fact that this plane is by no means silent!

Once again we are seeing the misinformation machine at work, trying to explain away sightings of objects, which the witnesses knew from their size, speed, and performance, could not have come from any country on this planet at this point in time.

Soviet Union

On October 8th, 1990, local radar installations of the Soviet Air Force in the Chechen capital of Grozny, watched in awe as two huge targets suddenly appeared on their radar screens.[3] The object's size and odd movements created a big enough stir to have a jet interceptor launched to investigate what many felt would turn out to be a malfunction of the radar detection system.

At approximately 11:30 AM local time, Major P. Riabishev took off in his MIG fighter to look for these intruders into Soviet airspace. According to radar, the objects were at approximately 15,000 feet, and as he soared ever upward into the clear sky, Major Riabishev saw nothing but a scattering of high-altitude clouds. Having gone further than he had cared to go on this wild-goose chase, the major radioed back to base that he found nothing and was heading for home.

Just then, way off in the distance over his right shoulder, a reflection of sunlight in his peripheral vision caught his attention. He turned towards the flash of light off to his right, and as he closed in on it, Riabishev became increasingly uneasy about what he was seeing. Ahead of him he saw two, huge, cigar-shaped craft reflecting the bright noontime sun. One was streaked with silver and approximately 1,200 feet long. The second object was also cigar-shaped, except this one's hull was dull and non-reflective, and amazingly, it appeared to be over a mile in length! The objects were flying "sideways" at great speed and as he bought his plane into pursuit of these two craft, they disappeared in less than a second! Stunned, the Soviet officer returned to base to inform his superiors of the incredible aerial devices he had witnessed.

Skibo, Minnesota

Two days later and a half a world away, the residents of the small town of Skibo, Minnesota,[4] watched as strange, lighted objects appeared over nearby Hoyt Lakes. As the calls came into the police dispatcher, at about 9 PM, she informed two officers that they might want to go out and look for these objects, if nothing else, to calm the residents of that area and end the influx of calls.

When they arrived in the Hoyt Lakes vicinity, they also saw the UFOs as they hovered and darted here and there in the night sky. About an hour later, Air Traffic Controllers in Duluth began to pick up returns of unknown objects as they hovered and flew around above Skibo at high speed. After about an hour of this, the objects formed a rough circular formation and remained stationary. This formation was picked up on local Air National Guard radar as the 11 o'clock hour approached.

Final confirmation that something odd was indeed in the skies above Minnesota that night came from a passing airliner's crew. The commercial airliner was flying at 11,000 feet and about 45 miles to the west of Hoyt Lakes when its crew radioed into Duluth to report that they were watching two large, glowing lights that appeared to be at about 1,000 feet below their craft. Both appeared round and glowed with an intense deep red, almost blood-like, light. The objects appeared to be hovering and spaced out a few miles apart. When they inquired with ground control if there was any other traffic in the area, Duluth informed the pilots that there was no know traffic in the area other than their airliner. The pilots, not wanting to report a UFO, continued on their way, and not long thereafter, the strange lights left the area, but not after causing a great stir in this usually quiet corner of the Land of a Thousand Lakes.

I realize that this sighting was not as spectacular as some of those that we have reviewed, but it is a sighting that points to the factual existence of UFOs. Here we had several UFOs witnessed by hundreds of witnesses below the objects near the Hoyt Lakes region, and an airline crew above them. It was picked up on radar. All proving that the object seen was a tangible object of unknown origin, not stars, planets or any other natural phenomenon that may have been misidentified by those who were witnessing it. Since no follow up was conducted on this sighting, we will probably never know more details.

Soviet Union

Returning to the old Soviet Union, on the night of December 13th, 1990, the radar station at Kuybyshev, Russia, had an intense encounter with Unidentified Flying Objects.

At seven minutes past midnight, the men on duty at the radar station near the town known as Samara, watched with interest as a strange blip suddenly appeared on their radar screens. Whatever the intruder was, it appeared to be about the size of a strategic bomber (comparable to our B-52), causing the men at the station much anxiety. The object was closing in, and once it was within sixty miles of the base, the Friend or Foe Warning System used to determine if the craft was or wasn't Soviet, failed. The men were left to decide whether they should sound the alarm and notify the nearest air base that an enemy bomber may have intruded deep into the interior of the USSR, or wait to see if the blip on the radar was due to a malfunction, or perhaps a Soviet plane that had strayed off course.

When the object was within twenty-five miles of their position, the one large object broke up and soon was many small objects heading towards the radar installation at Samara. The alarm was sounded at their small installation and a group of soldiers were ordered out into the compound to prepare for a possible attack. Once outside, the soldiers saw a triangular-shaped object approaching the compound. When they were out in the middle of the compound, the object shot 30 feet over their heads and came to a stop, hovering about 150 feet from the restricted area near Station 12, which was a mobile, short-range radar array.

Suddenly, there was a bright flash, and when the men looked up, they saw that the array's upper antenna were ablaze. The fire burned so intense and quick that, within moments, the array had collapsed to the ground. The officers and men present claim that the object was about 45 feet long and 10 feet thick.[5] None reported seeing any windows or openings, nor any visible means of propulsion. All were adamant that the object's hull looked very much like a burnt log. Not knowing what to do, the soldiers felt it would be best not to make any aggressive movements. The men watched the object as it hovered silently until approximately 1:40 AM local time. Then it rose up and disappeared into the night sky.

When Soviet officials analyzed it, they found that the metal had been melted from a sudden and very intense burst of heat. What could have caused the effect on the tower at this location, they could not say.

Author's Note:

The middle months of 1991 found the UFO community abuzz due to a sudden increase in the sightings of a particular type of UFO over both American and European airspace. Sighting were being reported by the crew and passengers of airliners on both sides of the Atlantic of a strange cigar-shaped object flying through the skies at high speed and in close proximity to many of the airlines' planes, passengers, and crews.[6]

England's English Channel

On April 21st, 1991, Captain Achille Zaghetti was piloting an Alitalia McDonnell-Douglas MD-80 on approach to London's Heathrow International Airport. As they flew over the English Channel and were within a few miles of the southeastern English coast, the pilots began their controlled descent from 22,000 feet. Cruising at 380 knots towards Heathrow, the plane descended at approximately 1,200 feet per minute.

At 8 PM, Captain Zaghetti spotted a long, brown, cigar-shaped object as it came across his plane's line of flight. He then pointed out the object, which was flying about 1,000 feet above the airliner, to his copilot. Immediately, he radioed Heathrow to see if they had any other traffic in the area. They informed him that they had him and an unknown object flying above his airliner on an east-southeast heading, and on the last sweep it appeared to be about ten miles behind the airplane. Since it was now just passing the plane, the UFO was moving at quite a clip! The object continued on its heading and disappeared out of sight.

England

Both pilots of a Britannia Airways Boeing 737 saw the same, or a very similar object, while the airliner was enroute from Dublin, Ireland, to London, England, on the afternoon of June 1st, 1991. Like our last airliner, this one was on final approach to London's Heathrow International Airport.

At approximately 2:38 PM, the fully loaded airliner was cruising at 8,000 feet in a holding pattern, when the pilots saw a cigar-shaped object fly at high speed past their airliner's port side and disappear in the vast expanse of the bright blue sky.

ESSEX, ENGLAND

A little more than two weeks later, on June 17th, 1991, four passengers onboard a Dan Air flight from London's Gatwick International Airport to Hamburg, Germany saw a wingless, cigar-shaped object pass below the airliner they were flying in.

At approximately 6:30 PM, as the plane was climbing into the evening sky over Essex, England, one of the passengers, German engineer Walter Liess, saw an object he described as appearing gray and being shaped in every proportional way to a cigar. He stated that the object was traveling on a course that was parallel to the plane but going in the opposite direction. The object could be seen to travel up and down, like a porpoise swimming in the ocean, as it flew by the airliner. Although none of the crew aboard the plane, nor radar on the ground caught sight of the object, the four passengers were sure of what they had seen in the skies over England.

LONDON, ENGLAND

The following month, there was yet another sighting of the mysterious cigar-shaped UFO near London, England.

At 5:45 PM, on the afternoon of July 15th, 1991, the pilots of a Britannia Airways 737 spotted a black cigar-shaped object as they were on the final leg of their flight from the Isle of Crete to London, England. The plane was at 15,000 feet and was descending towards London's Gatwick International Airport when both pilots spotted the object that was but 1,600 feet above and ahead of their airliner. Within seconds, the object was passing within 300 feet of the 737, and a mere 30 feet above it! Air Traffic Control in London saw this near miss and was heard to warn another aircraft that the object had veered towards it, but the pilots of that airliner claimed not to have seen anything.

CALIFORNIA

On August 5th, 1991, the crew of a United Airlines Boeing 747, flying 23,000 feet above and 50 miles to the northeast of George Air Force Base in California, had an encounter with the same, or a very similar, craft as had been seen over England.

The pilot spotted a wingless, cigar-shaped craft as it flew towards his plane at supersonic speed. Although the object was in sight for just a few seconds, the pilot was sure that it was no aircraft. As it flew by at supersonic speed, just 500 feet away, the pilot, though he is not sure what it was, could rightfully attest to the fact that the object, which traveled at speeds in excess of the speed of sound and did not make a sonic boom, surely was not like any plane he had ever seen!

Russia

I would assume the fear of flying knows no national boundaries. Thus, working for an airlines would surely help a person overcome this fear, since they would know the ins and outs and behind the scenes operations that go on daily at any major carrier that makes flying one of the safest modes of transportation. When an airlines' employee does fly with the airline they work for, they can usually expect a nice, calm, routine experience. This was just the opposite of what occurred when Igor Yadigin, an airline mechanic for Aeroflot, traveled from Voronezh to St. Petersburg, Russia during the early morning hours of August 20th, 1991.[7]

Aeroflot Flight 2523 took off from Voronezh, Russia at 1:35 AM local time. Thirty minutes into the flight, Igor was invited into the cockpit to join the crew. Once there, he could observe how the airliners he helps to keep running are operated. He also could soak in some of the breath-taking panoramic views visible only from the pilots' cabin.

While looking out one of the cockpit windows, the pilot noticed and pointed out to the others there, a huge milky-white sphere of light. Inside this sphere, was an emerald-colored sphere, and together they were flying some miles off in the distance in the same sector of the sky where the Great Bear constellation was easily visible to the assembled Aeroflot crew. The crew studied the object and in a report, they stated that the object was about the size of an airliner that would have been flying at 2,500 feet some thirty miles away. As they watched, a bright beam of colored light was emitted by the craft, just before what appeared to be another airliner quickly changed its heading to avoid a possible midair collision. The object traveled a little faster than the plane and was in view for an additional fifteen minutes before it sped off and out of sight.

Brookfield, Ohio

Just after midnight one cool autumn night, Ray Anne Rudolph was on duty taking calls for the Trumble County, Ohio 911 Emergency Dispatchers' office.[8] On that night in October of 1994, just after the clock had struck midnight, her switchboard began lighting up with calls. The callers, some out of concern and others out of sheer fright, were calling 911 to report that they had seen strange lights in the skies over Brookfield, Ohio.

After the number of calls began to mount with all the callers reporting the same thing, Ray Anne decided it may be wise to alert some of the police officers in the field of the developing situation. Liberty Township officers, Patrolman Stephan Remner and Sergeant Toby Melore were on a break when the call was broadcasted over the radio. Ray Anne alerted the officers to the fact that many people in the northern section of the township were seeing what she believed to be a plane, perhaps in trouble and looking to land, flying low over the homes of concerned citizens. Sergeant Melore informed Remner that he would go and check out what was causing all the commotion. Putting his lunch on hold, he returned to his cruiser from the local coffee shop, and proceeded to drive to the area.

While enroute, an elderly gentleman walking his dog on Samson Drive flagged Sergeant Melore down. The older gentleman claimed that a large bluish-purple object had just left the area after silently hovering over his home for several minutes. Not knowing what to make of the information he just received, Melore continued down Samson Drive to see if he could catch a glimpse of whatever it was that was responsible for creating such a fuss. After driving about a quarter mile further down Samson Drive, Sergeant Melore was baffled by the sudden and unexplainable events that unfolded.

As he was driving down the street, his radios went dead, and the car's engine and all of its lights inside and out shut off. As the cruiser rolled to a stop, he put the transmission into park to try to restart the engine. There was nothing when he turned the key. Suddenly, after several failed attempts to restart the cruiser, his entire vehicle inside and out was bathed in an intense white light. Startled, Sergeant Melore, got out of his car to see what was shining this incredible amount of light down onto his cruiser. When he got out all he could see was white light, even shading his eyes did not help cut through the bright light. After about thirty seconds, the light started moving away from the cruiser. As it did, he could then see that above the bright light was a saucer-shaped object that made absolutely no noise.

When the object had moved several hundred feet further down Samson Drive, the engine in the officer's car started up and all the lights, and both radios came back on as if they'd never ceased operating, all without any prompting from the officer! Sergeant Melore hopped back into his cruiser and threw the shifter into drive and the chase was on! Sergeant Melore's cruiser did not stand a chance of being able to keep up with the object, so as it began to out-distance his cruiser, Melore broadcasted a call to the dispatcher and all other units in the field describing what he was seeing.

Now, Roy Anne back at Trumble County 911 was beginning to get scared. Sergeant Melore was supposed to go out and spot a low flying plane and instead he was in pursuit of an Unidentified Flying Object! Three other units in the vicinity responded to Melore's broadcast and headed in the direction he had told them the UFO was traveling. Monitoring the officer's broadcast, Roy Anne Rudolph decided to call the Air Traffic Controllers in nearby Youngstown, Ohio, to see if they knew what it was flying over the Trumble County countryside. They informed her that not only didn't they know what the traffic could be; they did not have it on any of their radar screens! This heightened the anxiety she was already feeling, leaving her slightly sorry she called them at all.

Out in the field, the officers chased the object north towards I-82, and as they did, one of them stopped their cruiser and got out his binoculars to try to get a better look at this weird craft. Through the binoculars, the object appeared to be solid and shaped like a saucer with a small dome on top. The UFO was covered with lights of varying intensities, colored in many shades of red, blue, purple, and white.

A short distance away, having monitored the broadcast in his cruiser, Lieutenant James Baker of the Brookfield Township Police Department decided he was going to go to the highest point in Trumble County to see what this UFO, that he had heard about but not seen, looked like. He quickly drove to the old NORAD radar tower that was no longer in use. Once there, he raced up the stairs to the top platform and marveled at what he was seeing. From his vantage point, he saw not one but three of these saucer-shaped craft that appeared exactly as the other eleven officers who witnessed them described. He watched as the loose triangle formation of ships changed color in sequence from blue to red to purple to white. The objects continued north, and Lieutenant Baker watched until they were no longer in sight.

When asked, the officers readily described to those willing to listen to their stories what it was they had seen that night. When the information went public on a NBC broadcast (*Confirmation – The Hard Evidence of Aliens Among Us?*), an astronomer named James McGahee informed the viewing public that the officers had not seen any UFOs at all! He claims that twelve highly trained law enforcement officers were scared out of their wits by and chased a natural phenomenon miles down the back roads of Ohio. According to McGahee, the bright light that shone on Sergeant Melore's car was the result of a bright fireball. Although he did not mention how a fireball could hover in place, he did mention that the car stalling was just a coincidence. The rest of the officers who saw the strange object(s) in the sky that were changing colors, obviously were duped by the scintillation of distant stars.

Police officers regularly recognize stars and can distinguish them from moving objects. Not only do stars not participate in police chases, they also do not hover and then continue on along the highway when they choose. Stars, too, would not have a solid structure shaped like a saucer with a dome on top, above it. A fireball may radiate some light, but enough to light up an entire street and be so bright as to cause a person to shield their eyes is highly unlikely. These officers did not see stars, planets, or fireballs. What they saw was one of the many varieties of craft that we have come to call UFOs.

Author's Note:

As we have seen in the past, when individuals who work in the aviation industry within the United States encounter something unusual in the air or on the screens of their radar sets, we the American public, do not always hear of their experiences. To avoid unwanted publicity from the media or their employers and coworkers, those employed in the aviation industry try to either sweep these incidents under the carpet or purposefully forgot what they saw and when they saw it. Let's face it, we all know how hard it is to land a high paying job, let alone one where you could work your entire career! Thus, it is easy to understand why pilots, stewards, or stewardesses, air traffic controllers, or others employed in the airline industry might not want to report an encounter with an UFO.

The sighting listed herein previously, and the one that follows, reported by those in the field of aviation deserve to be touted as the most reliable proof that there have been, are, and will continue to be Unidentified Flying Objects roaming the skies. So without further adieu, lets launch right into our next sighting where, once again, a cigar-shaped UFO is spotted visually by an airline flight crew, and in addition, on the radar screens of air traffic controllers in both the private sector and the United States military.

TUCUMCARI, NEW MEXICO

Our adventure begins at 10 PM on the night of May 26th, 1995. (Since the information contained in this report was ascertained by the Freedom of Information Act, names of the controllers and flight crew were deleted by the Feds before the information was turned over to the original source from which this report was taken.)

America West Airlines Flight 564 was cruising over New Mexico, slightly off course because they were skirting a thunderstorm to avoid the associated turbulence. Flying at approximately 39,000 feet, the pilot caught a glance of a strange object in the skies over what was estimated as Tucumcari, New Mexico, a small southwestern town of 6,800 people, located about 200 miles east of Albuquerque and 80 miles northwest of Cannon Air Force Base.

The pilots studied the object for a while and decided that a call to Albuquerque Air Route Traffic Control Center would be the best way to find out what they were watching. Using their designated call sign of Cactus 564,[9] they called into the air traffic controller to report what they were seeing and inquire if they knew what it was. The controller asked them to describe what they were seeing. Not sure they wanted to broadcast to the world what the object looked like, the pilots hesitated for several seconds and then transmitted the following to the controller on the ground. The pilots of America West 564 informed the controller that they were watching an object off their right wing and almost 10,000 feet below their 757. The object, which was illuminated against the black clouds of the passing thunderstorm by frequent lightning strikes, appeared to have a blinding strobe light turning counter-clockwise; it was shaped like a cigar and in the range of 300 to 400 feet long! Air Route Traffic Control informed the America West pilots that they did not show an object on their radar, nor did they have a clue what could be flying there at that time of night. If they were willing to hold on, he would check to see if another controller or perhaps another center had the object in sight or knew what it was.

The controller asked some of his colleagues if they knew if the military had anything in the air that time of night and all responded that they did not. He then called Fort Worth Center and they neither saw the object on radar nor knew who or what was flying in the area. He then radioed Cannon Air Force Base to see if they had anything up that night. They stated they did not and inquired why he was asking. Albuquerque responded nervously, that a pilot was seeing a 400-foot-long cigar-shaped object as he flew in the vicinity of Tucumcari, then added the comment that, "This is not good!" Cannon AFB replies, "What does that mean?" and Albuquerque responds, "It's a UFO or something; it's that Roswell stuff again!" (Please keep in mind that this transcript is taken from one that is available to all by submitting an FOIA request to the government.) Cannon AFB responds that they haven't seen anything like this, nor do they know what it could be. Striking out on all attempts, Albuquerque radioed America West and informed them that Cannon Air Force base had no planes, weather balloons, aerostats (which are 100-foot-long balloons with platforms that carry specialized radar to a height of 15,000 feet over restricted air space), nor any type of craft up that night and no one in the area had any idea of what they were seeing.

The object was now out of sight of the America West pilots (presumably obscured by the storm clouds they were skirting), who stated that in their combined several decades of flying, had never seen anything that remotely resembled it, and were quite shocked to find out that no one could identify the huge cigar-shaped object.

Though the sighting was over for the pilots, the controller in Albuquerque was still a bit disconcerted by the object sighted by the two experienced pilots. He proceeded to radio the nearby NORAD installation. Once they responded, he informed them that two America West pilots had seen a 400-foot-long cigar-shaped object with a strobe light on it flying at 30,000 feet, quipping that the object was straight out of the *X-Files*. He asked if they knew what the object was, and after a bit more chatting, NORAD informed him that they knew of no object out there, but would monitor the area in greater detail. Though Cannon Air Force Base, NORAD, and later Holloman Air Base, were interested in this sighting, no known follow up was conducted, leaving the controller and pilots at a loss, still pondering what the huge object was flying over the desert that night.

New York City

Captain Phil Bobet, an experienced pilot with over 15,000 hours of flight time, was piloting Swiss Air Flight 127 from Philadelphia, Pennsylvania, to Boston, Massachusetts on August 9th, 1997. He, his flight crew, and passengers set off from Philadelphia's International Airport in a big Boeing 747[10] for the routine 57-minute flight at 4:50 PM. They headed north, accelerated to 390 MPH and climbed to 23,000 feet. The weather was clear as a bell with only a scattering of clouds over New Jersey. After a little more than a quarter-hour in the air, the plane was passing just to the south of New York City. After turning the plane to the northeast towards Boston, Captain Bobet handed over the controls to his copilot and began to address the passengers in the cabin.

He was glancing out the left cockpit window as he pointed out the World Trade Center, Ellis Island, the Statue of Liberty and other landmarks to the passengers on the left side of the plane. As he turned to look forward once again, both he and the copilot spotted a glowing white object headed right at the cockpit. The object was dead ahead and closing fast. Before any evasive action could be taken, the cylindrical or cigar-shaped object was passing a couple hundred feet above the plane at an incredible speed. The object passed so closely that the copilot actually ducked down in a reflex reaction to the object passing just over the top of the cabin.

It was 5:07 PM when Flight 127 radioed Danbury Control Sector of the Boston Air Route Traffic Control Center. Captain Bobet requested any information on high-speed traffic in the area, stating that his airplane had just experienced a near miss with a cigar-shaped object, which passed very closely overhead at extremely high speed. Air Traffic Control in Danbury asked Captain Bobet if he could identify the traffic that just passed him. He responded no, but was sure it wasn't a plane as it traveled too fast! Captain Bobet described the object the best he could, as cigar-shaped with no wings. He could give no better description, as the object was moving so fast that any other details of the craft could not be seen.

The plane proceeded on its way and landed at Logan International Airport in Boston at approximately 5:50 PM. The next day the flight crew was interviewed by representatives of the National Transportation Safety Board, the Federal Bureau of Investigation, and the FAA's Civil Aviation Security Office. After an extensive interview and an actual investigation, the finding that was released was that the plane had a near collision with a weather balloon. (How a weather balloon could fly that fast and appear as a white glowing cigar is unknown and unmentioned by the experts.) And although weather balloons are released from Upton, New York, some 45 miles northeast of the planes encounter, each day at 3 AM and 7 PM, they are tan, brown, red, or black, are not self-illuminating, and take less than half an hour to rise to 23,000 feet, make their readings, after which they slowly return to earth.

Captain Bobet, interviewed after the fact, feels that these agencies were delinquent in their finding that claim he almost hit a weather balloon. He and his flight crew are sure that whatever it was they saw that afternoon was not of this world! It is important to note that within this exact same airspace, just one year before this encounter, TWA Flight 800 exploded, after, according to some witnesses, being struck or colliding with a high-speed cigar-shaped object. The *coincidence* of the similarity of the unknown craft in both reports and their interaction with airplanes in this very busy air corridor is quite unsettling to say the least. Subsequently after the above mentioned encounter and after John F. Kennedy Jr.'s plane was lost in the same area and Egypt Air Flight 990's odd crash, there began to appear much talk in certain circles of a new Devil's Triangle forming off of the northeastern coast of the United States.

Hot Lava Springs, Idaho

Sitting on the front porch of their cabin in Hot Lava Springs, Idaho, Janice Price and her son were enjoying the coolness of the night air. At around 11:15 PM, June 20th, 1999,[11] they both became perplexed by the sudden appearance of a beam of bright white light being projected down into the woods near their cabin.

The light moved through the woods and out onto the driveway where it suddenly stopped, as if who or whatever was shining it down towards the earth, was startled to see the driveway in this densely wooded area. There was no engine noise, thus they ruled out a search and rescue plane or helicopter as being responsible for this beam of light, which was eerily illuminating their driveway. Nor could it have been an incredibly bright fireball, bolide or meteor, as none of these natural phenomenon can hover over a given area.

Suddenly, the light switched off and the entire forest went silent. Unnerved by this, Mrs. Price remained still for several moments and then went into the cabin to discuss what had just happened with her brother-in-law. As soon as she turned to look back outside, an intensely bright white light lit up the house and all the woods surrounding it like it was all of a sudden daytime once more. According to Janice Price, the light was very much like the light produced by an arc welder. As she watched, the light began to move and the shadows cast by the trees danced around in unison as it moved away from the cabin. Mrs. Price claimed that the effect created on the surrounding forest by the moving light was so intense as it made the trees appear to move and that it nearly made her dizzy. Her son, who had remained on the front porch the entire time, agreed that the light from the object made the trees appear to move and this was unworldly to say the least.

A short distance away, recently retired Air Force pilot Owen Mitchell had just gone to bed. Having just closed his eyes, he bolted upright, startled by an intensely bright light illuminating the entire area around his home. Sitting straight up in bed and looking out the window, he saw a white orb glowing with a fierce intensity as it was passing through the star-filled night sky. Although he saw it for only a few seconds, he was sure that it was heading west, was shaped like a ball, and though it was white in the center, its edges appeared bluish in color. He, like Mrs. Price, likened the light it gave off to the light given off by an arc welder. And although it hurt his eyes to look at it directly, the object so fascinated him that he could not stop watching it the entire time it was in view. Having spent twenty-six years on active duty in the Air Force, Mitchell was quite sure that this was not any aircraft in existence!

London, England

Rounding out the last year of the 1990s, we have two cases from the fall of this year. On October 26th, 1999, a report appeared in the *London Daily Mail*[12] of an airliner's near miss with another bright object, not unlike the one reported by the flight crew of Swiss Air flight 127 in 1997 off the east coast of the United States.

The MD-81 airliner took off from London's Heathrow International Airport. As it was climbing into the skies above the English countryside, the crew spotted a bright light headed towards them as they passed the 3,500-foot mark. The object rushed towards the craft, and just like in the Swiss Air case, the object was on top of the aircraft and passed it before any evasive action could be taken. This Unidentified Flying Object passed within 20 feet of the MD-81's fuselage, thoroughly shaking up the entire cockpit crew. Due to the fast movement of the craft, this flight crew, like Swiss Air's, could not describe the object in any detail, except it was a bright, not any airplane they had ever seen, and flew at an incredibly fast speed.

Washington State

The following month, one of the Geosynchronous Orbiting Environmental Satellites that the National Oceanic and Atmospheric Administration has in orbit to monitor the Earth's weather patterns snapped a picture of a huge UFO.[13] The satellite was taking pictures at 2:45 PM GMT above the coast of the state of Washington. One of the photos shows a huge UFO, that many like to refer to as a "Mother ship," as it made its way through the satellite field of view, flying about 100 miles above the earth's surface.

The UFO only appears in a certain number of the photos as it, unlike the satellite, was moving. In the photos, the UFO, which is not a smudge, lens flare, or computer glitch, can be clearly seen to have structures, including numerous windows. When the camera on the satellite took a close up of the UFO, steam could be seen coming off its hot hull as it passed through the water vapors in the upper atmosphere. The object in the photo has yet to be identified by any government agency, but can be seen in the archives of the University of Colorado.

CHAPTER 12

2000 TO THE PRESENT
NEW MILLENNIUM, SAME OLD STORY

"I believe that these Extraterrestrial vehicles and their crews are visiting this planet from other planets which obviously are a little more... advanced then we are..."

~Colonel Gordon Copper
Mercury 7 Astronaut
In a letter to the United Nations 1978

I would like to start off this chapter by mentioning that the fact that there are fewer sightings in this and the previous chapter are not indicative of a decrease in sightings of strange aerial craft. The fewer numbers are due to what many call the "Ridicule Factor." Most witnesses during this time frame have not been willing to give their names and occupations; instead they request to remain anonymous so they are not laughed at by friends, neighbors and co-workers, and in some cases lose their jobs and/or standing in their communities. Though not included here for the above reason, it is worth mentioning that there were major flaps of UFO sightings in both Pennsylvania and Texas in the closing years of this decade where hundreds of witnesses in each state all reported seeing strange objects in the sky, and as usual, no follow up was conducted by anyone other than the UFO investigative organizations like MUFON (Mutual UFO Network). Now let us get to the sightings!

ILLINOIS

In the early morning hours of January 5th, 2000,[1] truck driver Melvern Noll noticed a strange light to the northeast of his position. As the object flew closer to him, it began to resemble a two-story house. This "house" had red lights on its underside, and as the object slowly and silently flew past his position, Mr. Noll noticed that there were two rows of horizontal lights on the side emanating a dull white light. He watched in awe as the craft flew off in a southwesterly direction, approximately 500 feet off the ground, making its way very slowly and utterly silent.

Mr. Noll was privileged to see the object for another few minutes before it disappeared from his view. When the slight shock of seeing such a fantastic sight had worn off, Mr.

Noll thought it best to report what he had seen to the local police in Highland, Illinois. He relayed his sighting to the Highland dispatcher and suggested that she contact her counterpart in Lebanon, Illinois, the town nearest to where the UFO disappeared from Mr. Noll's line of sight. Thinking that this "UFO" might really be an aircraft experiencing difficulties, she relayed the information to the Lebanon dispatcher and suggested they send an officer to investigate.

At about 4:10 AM local time, the Lebanon dispatcher radioed Officer Ed Barton and informed him to proceed to Homer Park, where he was to watch for a large illuminated object slowly flying low overhead. Officer Barton asked dispatch if this was some kind of joke, and when dispatch assured him this was not a joke, he headed over to Homer Park. Once at the park, he noticed nothing unusual in the skies, so he continued past, driving towards Illinois State Route 4. As he neared Route 4, much to his surprise, Officer Barton noticed two large "brilliant" white lights off in the northeastern sky. Once at Route 4, he headed south back towards Lebanon watching the lights out of his driver's side window.

Thinking what he was watching was a plane in trouble, Barton plotted and intercept course, in case the trouble became worse and the craft came down. Once back in Lebanon, he turned off of Route 4 and onto Route 50, heading towards a bridge that would offer him a wide panoramic view of the sky and the lights as they approached his position. After crossing the bridge, Barton pulled his cruiser off to the side of the road and watched as the lights came to a stop and hovered over the northeast end of nearby Summerfield, Illinois.

He noticed the lights looked to him to be attached to some type of solid object that was somewhat shaped like an elongated triangle. When the object, that he was certain was no aircraft, began to move in his direction, Officer Barton turned the lights, engine, and radio off to enhance his ability to observe this peculiar object. Watching the elongated triangle pass overhead slowly and in complete silence, Barton estimated it to be about 75 feet long and 45 feet at its widest point. He saw a large, bright white light in each of the triangles' three corners and in the middle towards the rear, was a small red light. He noticed that as the lights moved through the sky, the stars between the three lights disappeared, indicating to him that this was a solid object. The object passed by him no more than 1,000 feet above and 100 feet away and Officer Barton watched in amazement as the triangle pivoted on its axis and picked up speed instantaneously heading off and out of sight in a southwesterly direction. After clearing his mind, Officer Barton radioed dispatch to inform him of all he had just witnessed.

As Officer Barton was finishing his report of the sighting, Officer Paul Martin of the nearby Shiloh, Illinois Police Department, radioed to state that his encounter was just beginning. As he drove in his cruiser on the south side of Shiloh, Officer Martin watched, as the lights in the sky grew closer to him. Once close enough for a good view, he noticed that the object was triangle shaped with three bright lights, matching the description of all those who had seen it previously that morning. He estimated that the object was about 1,000 feet in elevation and about a quarter mile from his position, and he watched it as it flew west until he could no longer see this intriguing object.

Over in Millstadt, Illinois, Officer Craig Stevens listened intently to the radio traffic as his fellow law enforcement officers described the strange object flying silently and purposefully over southwestern Illinois that morning. He thought for a moment to figure out where he could get an unobstructed view of the sky, and was soon headed off to Liederkranz Park in the north end of town. It was at 4:29 AM, not long after he had parked his patrol car in the park, that Officer Stevens was on the radio to dispatch, letting them know that he could now see the object as it flew towards his position. As it passed, he too described it as triangular in shape with three bright white lights, flying low, slow and silently through the clear night sky. The object disappeared off to the northwest, but was also reported by an officer of the Dupo, Illinois Police Department that preferred to remain anonymous. Whether the object was simply sightseeing in nearby St. Louis, Missouri or taking a quick look at nearby Scott Air Force Base, we will never know, but one thing is for sure, that January night will not soon be forgotten by any of those that witnessed this incredible Unidentified Flying Object.

Turkey

A year and a half later and half a world away, another strange object was spotted by two well-trained observers. At about 12:30 PM local time on August 7th, 2001,[2] 1st Lieutenant Ilker Dincer, an instructor for the Turkish Air Force's Squadron 122, flying his T-37 Trainer with student pilot Lieutenant Arda Gunyel, took off from his home base in Izmer, Turkey and headed out into the Gulf of Candarli for a practice flight.

Once at 15,000 feet, they began to practice engine stoppage and other emergency maneuvers. As they proceeded with their practice, from out of nowhere, an object appeared slightly ahead of their T-37. They both described it as being pyramid shaped with one large protruding leg, and glowed with an eerie extremely bright light. Upon Lieutenant Dincer recovering of his senses, he radioed flight control describing the object that he was seeing. He informed them that he was going to move in to take a closer look. Much to the two pilots surprise, the control tower responded that the only object on their radar was the T-37. As he banked his training jet to move in for a closer look, to his horror, before they could intercept the UFO, it had intercepted them!

Though, they could not see anything on their radar screens, any doubt that the control towers staff may have had as to the events unfolding in the skies above were dashed by the frantic radio message from Lieutenant Dincer that he and the UFO were in a literal "dogfight" over the Mediterranean Sea! Over the radio came frantic reports from Lieutenant Dincer of how the UFO went from being ahead of the T-37 to just off its wing, then to its rear and finally settling in over the cockpit, scaring the two pilots to a point of near hysteria.

Much to the two men's relief, as suddenly as the UFO had appeared, it flew away at a fantastic speed. As fast as the T-37 could manage, the two pilots returned to base. Upon their arrival, and seeing they were visibly shaken, their superiors debriefed the two pilots. The encounter managed to make its way to Turkish news, and when the military was faced with widespread questions from the Turkish public wanting more information on the two pilots whose plane was buzzed by a UFO, the Defense Ministry pulled out a page from the old Project Blue Book manual! Their official explanation was that some strange aerial device did not buzz their two pilots and jet aircraft. They had simply had a close encounter with a weather balloon. How the Turkish people could feel safe with pilots who went to pieces when encountering a weather balloon was not touched upon.

Millbrook, New York

Friends of Bruce Cornet, PhD, had been telling him about their regular sightings of UFOs near their home for many weeks when he decided to go and see if there was anything to these sightings other than over active imaginations. On the night of August 20th, 2003, at approximately 9:37 PM, he found out that his friends imaginations had nothing to do with what they were seeing.

Standing outside his friend's house in Millbrook, New York,[3] he and his friend both noticed two bright lights approaching their location at a speed estimated to be about 10 MPH. The lights became a structured craft with black surface and a multitude of colored lights as they came to within a few hundred feet of the pair at an altitude of no more than 500 feet. The two objects stopped, hovered, made a sharp right turn and headed off for parts unknown. During the brief encounter, Cornet noticed the oddly shaped craft's lights did not illuminate its surface as you would expect so many light to do, making its overall appearance that much more mysterious.

Mexico

On March 5th, 2004, the crew of a Mexican Air Force Recon/Patrol plane had an historic encounter with an Unidentified Flying Object. It was groundbreaking in the study of UFO encounters because it was the first time that UFOs, eleven to be exact,[4] were tracked on radar and a Forward Looking Infra Red (FLIR) camera, but not seen by the naked eye of the observers.

On that historic afternoon, the eight-member crew of a Mexican Air Force Merlin C-26A were busy about their work looking for drug runners in the airspace above the Ciudad del Carmen region of Campeche, Mexico. The twin-engine aging plane was loaded with all the latest detection equipment, including AN/PS Bravo Victor 3 radar and Zapphir II Forward Looking Infra Red (FLIR) cameras. Piloting the Merlin that afternoon was Major Magdeleno Munoz; his radar man was Lieutenant German Ramirez and the FLIR operator was Lieutenant Mario Vazquez—all members of Mexico's 501st Aerial Squadron.

At approximately 5 PM local time, while using the FLIR cameras, Lieutenant Tellez spotted an unknown object at 10,500 feet about 38 miles away from the C-26A. Lieutenant Tellez notified the pilot, Major Munoz of the bogey. Thinking the object may have been a drug smuggling plane, he turned the C26 towards the bogey, and alerted their home base of their actions and the location of the bogey, in case the base needed to launch interceptors to intercept this probable smuggler. The C-26A closed on the object, and although it came to within two miles of the object's location, none of the crew could see it with the naked eye. However, the radar and FLIR operators had a lock on their invisible foe.

Suddenly, the radar and FLIR operators watched their screens in disbelief as the object flew away at an incredible rate of speed. They notified a bewildered Major Munoz in the cockpit and he swung the lumbering aircraft around 180 degrees and headed back towards their original course. As quick as it had disappeared, the object reappeared on the radar and FLIR screens directly behind the aircraft, again two miles out. As Major Munoz was reporting back to base of the disappearance and reappearance of the object, another object appeared on both radar and FLIR screen two miles out, directly in front of the aircraft. Much to the crews terror, more objects appeared on the scopes until eleven UFOs in all, that could not be seen by the naked eye, had surrounded their aircraft keeping two miles between the plane and themselves at all times.

The crew responded by adhering to their training and conducted themselves as if they were under attack, reporting every step of the way back to their base, while trying to come to a rational explanation as to what was out there surrounding their aircraft. No such explanation was forthcoming. After twenty-four excruciating minutes, the objects simultaneously flew off at high speed, disappearing from both the radar and FLIR screens. Since they never actually saw the objects, none of the crew could give an estimate on size, nor report on their color or makeup.

The radar and FLIR tapes told another story. Once examined, they confirmed the presence of one, then two, and finally eleven objects flying aloft that encircled the C-26A, yet never closing to within more than two miles, then disappearing altogether, while performing unthinkable acceleration and instantaneous course changes, unlike any achievable by even the best interceptors available today.

Upon their return to base, the crew was debriefed and the report filtered its way up the chain of command, making it all the way to the Mexican Minister of Defense, General Ricardo Garcia, before being reported to the people via a television program entitled, *Great Mysteries of the Third Millennium* broadcasted on Mexican Television on May 9th, 2004.

Author's Note:

The following set of sightings are a bit lacking in the necessities I have aforementioned as warranted for inclusion herein, but because of the quality and expertise of the witnesses involved, who all wished to remain anonymous, I have included it here as further proof of the ongoing phenomenon.

Chicago, Illinois

At approximately 4:40 PM on the afternoon of November 7th, 2006, Chicago's O'Hara International Airport was abuzz with activity.[5] Passengers coming and going. Planes arriving and departing. A member of United Airlines ground crew was busy performing his daily task when an odd feeling gripped him. Without knowing why, he felt a strange and all-encompassing urge to look up; so he did. What he saw riveted him to the spot where he stood.

Much to his surprise, hanging low in the sky above Gate C17 was a dark disc-shaped object. After staring in awe for a short time, he snapped back to reality and his first thought was for the safety of passengers about to take off. Should this object move in the wrong direction at the wrong time, a mid-air collision could result. So he radioed the pilots of Flight 446, that was moving away from the gate to proceed to the runway for takeoff on its flight from Chicago to Charlotte, North Carolina.

Much to the pilot's surprise, in the air where the crewmen had said to look, was what they described as a disc-shaped object that appeared to be rotating as it hovered low in the sky. Listening in his office to the crosstalk on the radio, a United Airlines manager decided to go outside to see if he could see the same thing the other UAL employees were seeing. Sure enough, once outside he could see a disc hovering above the gate below the heavy cloud cover which had settled in at about 1,900 feet that day. He immediately returned to his office to confirm the sighting with his Operations Center and then called the FAA.

Meanwhile, another UAL pilot who was employed to shuttle planes from one place to another on the ground at the airport had just settled into his twenty-five-minute trip moving a big Boeing 777 from the International hanger to the United Airlines hanger. At some point in his trip, he too saw this disc-shaped object hovering over Gate C17. He also described it as a gray, disc-shaped object that was producing a sort of turbulence beneath it that look to him like a heat mirage you would see when driving on a black top road on a hot summer's day. He kept tabs on it till he had to park the 777 in the hanger and lost sight of it for a few minutes. When he had returned outside, the disc was gone, but where it had been hovering, there was a big hole in the thick cloud cover, so large and vertically deep that clear blue skies could be seen through it.

And though the Chicago newspapers and many media outlets, like CNN covered the story of no fewer than five highly trained, qualified observers having seen a strange object hovering over one of the busiest airports in the world, no follow up investigation was done by any federal agency. Now in the post 9/11 world of airport security, had an unauthorized helicopter or balloonist been hovering so close to a major airport, the person responsible would be in for some serious repercussions, but not one thing was done in this instance, because there was nothing that could be done, as the perpetrators of this airspace violation were not of this world!

Channel Islands of Alderney

At approximately 2 PM GMT, April 23rd, 2007, Captain Ray Bowyer[6] was ferrying his passengers at 4,000 feet from Southampton, England and was on landing approach to Aldeney Airport on the Channel Islands of Alderney. That day he was at the controls of a Trislander, a small propeller-driven aircraft, when he was caught by surprise by an odd sight. What he first assumed to be light reflecting off windows or glass on the ground in Guernsey, another Channel Island to the west of Aldney, took on a whole other characteristic when he viewed the lights thru binoculars.

As he looked through the binoculars, he realized what he was seeing were not ground reflections, but appeared to be lights attached to a long cigar-shaped object suspended on the horizon, gleaming with a sparkling yellow color. The strange object he saw looked to him to be roughly the size of a 737 or possibly even a bit larger. Bowyer noted that the craft had well defined edges with a gray patch on the left side of the "fuselage."

As the approach to landing continued, Captain Bowyer saw another object matching the first in color, but this one was off in the distance. However, not only Captain Bowyer saw these objects! Several of his passengers saw them, Captain Patrick Patterson flying a Jetstream aircraft from the Isle of Man enroute to Jersey saw something matching Captain Bowyers description, and on the ground in the airport control tower, air traffic controller Paul Kelley saw a contact where Captain Bowyer's "unidentified" was hovering.

Upon landing, he reported his sighting to the Civil Aviation Authority. The story spread like wildfire across the news medias of the world. Though this sighting consisted of a report of a UFO confirmed by multiple independent highly trained witnesses that appeared on local radar set, unfortunately, like so many others before it, this sighting was not investigated by the British Ministry of Defense, in this instance because it occurred in French Airspace!

CHAPTER 13

OUTSIDE THE PARAMETERS
MORE REPORTS OF THE ONGOING PHENOMENON

"I've been convinced for a long time that the flying saucers are interplanetary. We are being watched by beings from outer space."

~Albert M. Chop
Deputy Public Relations Director, NASA
True Magazine, January 1965

As you have probably noticed, since the turn of the twenty-first century, there weren't many UFO encounters reported that I could include in this book for reasons I've stated (including the "Ridicule Factor.") Again and in addition to those prior reasons, it is not because the sighting have tapered off as if some UFO fad was fading; instead it was because the sightings reported did not measure up to the qualifications for inclusion that I set forth at the beginning of this book. As you may remember, I promised to include only UFO reports that were of craft that could not be mistaken for anything other than sophisticated, highly advanced machines. Also, I promised to only include those sightings that contained the name and occupation of observer to prove they were competent witnesses, and the day, date, time, and location of the sighting.

But, so as not to leave you with the impression that sightings have all but fallen by the way side, I wanted to take this opportunity to show you some sighting that were important to me and the on-going phenomenon, even though they fell shy of the bar I set for inclusion. As you will see, sightings did not taper off in the first decade of the 3rd Millennium; in fact, they are on the rise. According to the National UFO Reporting Center (NUFORC), from January 1, 2000 to December 31, 2010, 46,824[1] people reported having had encounters with objects they could not identify. Reports have been coming in fast and furious with no signs of any let up.

The vast majority of these sightings are probably misidentifications or natural phenomenon. The findings in Project Blue Book records and the British Ministry of Defense which has just released many files, concur that roughly five percent of the sightings they investigated ended up being classified by them as unidentified. If we apply that percentage to the reports made to the NUFORC, we find that 2,314 reports may have been of actual Unidentified Flying Objects. If we apply that percentage to the reports made to the NUFORC, we find that 2,314 reports may have been of actual Unidentified Flying Objects. But let us not forget that those 46,824 sightings are tallied from but one UFO investigative organization. Image how large the number would be from all reports filed with UFO investigative groups around the world. Even those numbers would be dwarfed by the number of sightings that occurred and were never reported.

For this chapter, I have chosen to share with you two older incidents, one I am personally familiar with, one that had a profound effect on the UFO community, and many cases from the last decade, some of which have not been fully investigated but are amazing none the less. So let's dive right in to the sightings!

Thomaston, Connecticut

In the past, I have made many trips to Thomaston, Connecticut to visit relatives. Being an avid walker, the picture postcard like, quintessential New England small town was just the place to explore. One sunny Saturday afternoon as I made my way southwest down Main Street from St. Thomas' church, passing the Soldiers Monument complete with cannons, flags, and a monument to those who have served, I found myself in front of a very beautiful brick Victorian edifice known as the Thomaston Opera House. As it turns out, it is a multi-use building which functions as a theater for live plays, the police station, the town hall, and all the associated departments that make up the town government. Being a real fan of Victorian architecture, I was determined to get pictures of this magnificent structure from every angle possible.

Having taking several pictures of the front and sides, I went around back into the parking lot. As I continued taking pictures, a sign caught my eye. On the yellow metal triangle was a picture of Steven Spielberg's *ET* pointing up in the air, placed near the curb of the cross walk on that section of Clay Street, as if saying: *Watch for passing space ships!*

Well, needless to say, that was enough to pique my interest, but as it was Saturday, I could not go inside the town hall to ask about this sign, so instead, I went into many of the local *mom and pop* stores, wandered around a bit, and casually struck up conversations with some of the workers. When I asked about the sign, I made sure they knew I was not apt to make fun, as I knew that the people in this region take UFOs very seriously. Thomaston is located not far from the Hudson River Valley where thousands of sightings took place in the 1980s, and the area has also had substantial sightings in its own right. As the folks opened up to me, I discovered one story of a mass UFO sightings that struck me as incredible due to the odd physical effect associated with it, and with a little research an incredible story emerged.

Low and Slow

At 9 PM on the evening of January 9th, 1986, twenty miles northeast of Thomaston, the greater Hartford area police departments were deluged with callers reporting a large object with lights flying low and slow over north-central Connecticut. Though they dismissed the first calls as nonsense, since the phones still were ringing off the hook at 9:15 PM, the police became concerned that the people were actually seeing something way out of the ordinary.

Cruisers were sent to investigate the area the reports were coming from and they found a traffic jam on I-84 from many cars stopped to view the UFO. The object slowly and silently headed west and was seen in nearby Torrington at 9:30 PM, having taken thirty minutes to travel roughly twenty miles. The object turned southwest and at 9:45 PM; it was seen by many residents of Thomaston, including the ones I was speaking with that Saturday in the stores.

They described the object as a large solid triangle, made of a dark grayish material that did not reflect the red and white lights on the craft. The object flew slowly overhead, stopping briefly at the southwest edge of town and moved on as silently and mysteriously as it had arrived.

The story does not end there.

A UFO on the Clock

Four days later on Monday, January 13th, the same, or a very similar, object was seen slowly drifting over Thomaston from 10 to 10:30 PM. This time, before it departed, it hovered over the football field for a time. The physical effects left behind by this alien visitor were discovered the next day. When the entire town awoke to start a new day, the school, public, and commercial buildings ,as well as private residences all found that *every* electric clock in town was ten minutes *fast*!

The folks speaking with me who all requested to remain anonymous, alluded to the fact that the aliens must have known the history of the town, as Thomaston was once home to the clock factory of the famous Seth Thomas, from whom the town took its name. How appropriate they felt it was that whoever piloted the machine that floated over their town those two cold nights in January of 1986 chose to use clocks, the one thing their town was famous for, to leave behind a reminder of their visit.

Arizona and Nevada

The next series of sightings took the world by storm in March of 1997. In and around Phoenix, Arizona,[2] many thousands of people witnessed a huge boomerang craft with lights along its bottom.

The first reported sightings of the boomerang shaped craft came in from a witness in Henderson, Nevada at 6:55 PM PST. The V-shaped object had six lights on its belly and was heading from the northwest to the southeast. He stated that the UFO was about the size of a Boeing747 and made a sound like the rushing wind as it passed by his location.

The next witness was a former police officer from Paulden, Arizona. As he left his home, he saw the lights about twenty minutes after the first sighting. The witness claims he got into his car and was driving northbound, when at 8:15 PM MST, he saw a group of orange lights in the sky. The witness immediately returned home, found his binoculars and watched the object until it disappeared into the southern horizon.

At 8:17 PM, reports started pouring in from the Prescott, Arizona area. One such report was made by John Kaiser, who while standing outside with his wife and sons in Prescott Valley, Arizona, spotted a group of lights to the northwest of their position. Through his binoculars, Mr. Kaiser watched the object for about three minutes. He described it as triangular shaped with many lights, which were all red except the light on the "nose" which was clearly white. The object was fairly low to the ground and passed over their heads and disappeared into the night to the southeast of their home in Prescott Valley.

Another unnamed witnessed reported that while taking pictures of the stars, she spotted a large cluster of yellow-white lights in a V-formation. The point of the "V" pointed the way the object moved as it was observed crossing the sky from the northwest, disappearing into the northeast horizon.

A short time later, while driving north on Highway 69 about ten miles east of Prescott near Dewey, Arizona, six people saw a similar cluster of lights in the sky. Near Phoenix, Tim Ley, his wife Bobbi, son Hal, and Tim and Bobbi's grandson, Damien Turnidge could see the lights when they were still over the Prescott area. They watched as the lights moved in their direction. As they did so, they changed their first opinion that the lights were separate craft, and became convinced that the lights were all attached to one huge UFO. As the object drew nearer, the Leys described it as looking like a very large carpenter's square with five lights attached to it. Concern was soon felt by the witnesses, as the object continued to move towards their position, and in fact, its flight path made it head right up their street towards their home. The object was only about 150 feet above them when it silently passed overhead, and then made its way between two peaks in the Squaw Peaks Mountain Range and out of sight, headed in the general direction of the Phoenix Sky Harbor International Airport sometime between 8:30 and 8:45 PM.

Once on the other side of the mountains, witnesses in Glendale spotted the lights. Bill Greiner, a cement truck driver guiding his loaded mixer down the mountain roads just north of Phoenix and a confirmed skeptic before his sighting, became a diehard believer after. He witnessed the lights as they came to a stop and hovered near Phoenix for in excess of two hours.

Later that night, a young man driving to Los Angles, California, spotted the object outside of Kingman, Arizona. Just after the sightings, there was minimal press coverage in the Phoenix area—that is until a front page story in the June 18th, 1997 edition of *USA Today* brought the sightings to the attention of the country and the world. Soon after the *ABC* and *NBC* television networks picked up the story and reported on it extensively. As a result of all the media coverage, both the *Discovery* and *History* channels produced documentaries about the sightings in and around Phoenix.

Interestingly, the Governor of Arizona at the time, Fife Symington III, made light of the whole situation by calling a press conference to state that the culprits responsible for the *Phoenix Lights* had been caught, and one of his aides was escorted to the podium dressed as an alien. Later, he would change his tune, stating that he also had seen the lights and as a pilot and ex-Air Force Officer, he can attest to the fact that whatever it was he saw, it was not planes, flares or any of the other explanations handed up by the local pseudo-experts. In fact, to him it looked quite otherworldly, resembling nothing of man-made design he had ever seen before or since.

Lights returned to the skies above Phoenix in both 2007 and 2008, but never would the excitement match that caused by the 1997 sightings that encompassed people in two states.

DOUGLAS, GEORGIA

A multiple-witness sighting took place on the evening of April 28th, 2000, near Douglas, Georgia. Mr. and Mrs. Williams were driving near Highway 84 at 8:45 PM[3,] when she and her husband both noticed a bright orange light hovering just over the tree tops. Knowing that most aerial devices have white, red, or green lights, the Williams knew this was something out of the ordinary. The object appeared to be moving slowly, so they decided to take a closer look. They turned off the main road and headed in the general direction of the orange light.

As the Williams sped up to close in on the object, the one light became two lights, separated by a row of six very bright lights. The whole object still emitted an incredibly brilliant orange light. As they watched, two red balls of light appeared on the left and right side of the orange object. As they closed in on all these weird lights, a group of trees blocked their view of the lights for a short time and when they had passed the trees, the Williams' saw the four red lights, but the larger bright orange object was gone.

The red lights flew around in a confused pattern, and shortly after the Williams had pulled off into a field, the red lights disappeared likewise.

The next day, Mrs. Williams returned to where they had seen the lights the night before, to search for some physical evidence of what they had seen, but could find none. Little did she know that at the same time of their sighting the previous night, another couple driving near Nicholls, Georgia also saw the red lights near the tree line from a completely different point of view. A week later, another couple witnessed the same, or a similar, bright orange light hovering near the Green Acres community outside of Douglas. Whatever they were, the lights found something very interesting in and around Douglas, Georgia, requiring a second and possibly more visits to this community.

Marysville, Pennsylvania

A witness traveling through the area near Marysville, Pennsylvania had an encounter with an incredibly large UFO during the early morning hours of September 19th, 2000.[4]

While traveling down the road the witness drives everyday to get to work, the witness, as so often was the case, was admiring the serene beauty of the mountains and fields that surrounded the valley in which the roadway was built. Sometime between 4:30 and 4:45 AM, the witness noticed what looked like stadium lights over a field, approximately a mile away. Now, he knew there was no stadium in the field he drove by every day, yet the bright lights were definitely there, seeming to hang motionless quite low over that field.

As he closed the distances between himself and the odd bright light, he was shocked to see that the lights were indeed hanging in the sky at a very low altitude, were white in color, round in shape and very large. As he neared, he rolled down his window to listen for any sound that may be coming from the lights but there was none. Now very close, what he thought was one object, clearly became two distinct lights, both still and low and about the size of football fields. He was struck by the fact that the light they produced lit up the entire sky. As they hung motionless, he soon passed the lights, and as he drove further down the road closer to work, the gravity of the situation and the awe of what he had just seen made him turn his car around and head back to get another look. Though he was gone no more than a few minutes the two huge lights were gone, practically having vanished into thin air.

Ohio

A report of a UFO was received by the Waynesville, Ohio Police Department on the evening of April 25th, 2001[5] from some excited local residents who quite by chance had looked out their window and spotted a UFO. They called the Warren County

Communications Center, which in turn dispatched an officer to the 4600 block of Wilkerson Road to investigate the alleged UFO.

Upon arrival, he called into headquarters to inform them that there was an object he could not identify in the sky. As near as could be figured, the object was hovering over the Girl Scout Camp near the Stoneybrook Nature Reserve. The object was described as being oval shaped with blue and red lights circling it. Hoping for an easy solution to this ever deepening aerial mystery, the Warren County Communications officer placed a call to nearby Wright Patterson Air Force Base in Dayton, Ohio to see if they had something, or knew what was, aloft that evening above Waynesville. The air traffic control tower operator informed the dispatcher that Wright had nothing in the air that night and he had no idea what it was the officer was viewing. Wanting to see the object for herself, the dispatcher verified with the patrolmen that the UFOs were still there, and he confirmed that he was looking to the south from his position in Waynesville and the objects were right where they had been since his arrival. So the dispatcher went outside and from the communication center located in Lebanon, Ohio, she looked to the south towards Waynesville and she also saw the UFO.

Soon, an Ohio State Policemen stationed at Caesars Creek, located to the east of Waynesville, confirmed that he too saw the object. The UFO was witnessed for close to an hour that night before it slowly moved off and out of sight. All persons involved that night could plainly tell that what they were seeing was neither plane nor stars, and all shared an anger and frustration that they could not give definitive answers, be it to the citizens or fellow officers, of what it was they had witnessed.

The next night at approximately 9:48 PM, another UFO was reported by citizens of the Wilkerson Road area and by an officer near the Waynesville Airport. The final event of this mini-flap occurred around 5 AM the following morning. A female motorist reported to Ohio State Patrol that as she traveled down Route 122 near Genntown, Ohio, which is a mere five miles from Waynesville, a large triangular-shaped object with super bright lights pursued her car sending her into quite a panic, as I'm sure we all would have felt had we been in a car pursued by a UFO!

WAYNE, NEW JERSEY AND LONG ISLAND, NEW YORK

On the afternoon of June 2nd, 2001,[6] a man and his daughter were driving near their home in Wayne, New Jersey, when his daughter saw a black boomerang-shaped craft hovering in the sky above their car. It had no lights and hung silently at an elevation her father estimated was 1,000 feet in the sky. They watched it for approximately eight minutes, when very slowly it pivoted away from them as if turning on an axis, made one complete revolution, rose up so the apex pointed skyward, and disappeared very quickly into the cloud cover. The witnesses stated that the craft moved quite easily through the sky and seemed to have no problem defying gravity.

A little more than an hour later, a very similar craft was seen over Long Island, New York by eight people who were passenger in a private jet. A couple, their two children, and four friends had taken off from the Teterboro New Jersey Airport into a thick cloud cover, at 6:45 PM. They quickly broke through the clouds and about fifteen minutes later, one of the passengers brought everyone's attention to an object off the right wing of the aircraft. Behind and about 2,000 feet above the plane was a large boomerang-shaped object standing out against a bright blue sky. They watched the object for as long as they could before they lost sight of it, observing that it was about as big as a 747, had neither windows nor lights and was unlike anything any of them had ever seen before.

NEW JERSEY

Six weeks later, New Jersey was the site of yet another series of encounters with UFOs. Early Sunday morning, 12:30 AM to be exact, on July 15th, 2001, a large flying triangle was sighted near Newark International Airport.[7] Shortly thereafter, witnesses traveling on the New Jersey Turnpike reported that, as they were southbound, they noticed upwards of 100 cars pulled over to the side of the highway with their occupants standing alongside watching a large V-formation of lights. Some even claimed that they saw airliners on normal approach to Newark International, being diverted around the large collection of unknown lights.

While this was happening, the nearby police station in Carterert, New Jersey, was being swamped with calls by alarmed citizens reporting strange lights in the night sky. One such concerned citizen was a funeral director out on a death call who phoned his father, a Right Reverend of the Ukrainian Orthodox Church, at 12:40 AM, telling him to get outside quickly and see the collection of lights hovering over the Carterert Shop Rite Plaza. Once outside, the Reverend saw several sets of lights, all in triangular patterns, looking like a small fleet of UFOs moving east in a tight military-like formation, heading towards Staten Island, New York. He estimated the craft to be about 3,000 to 4,000 feet high and moving in unity.

These sightings were so widespread that they were carried by *The Newark Star Ledger*, New Jersey 101.5FM, and television stations WABC, WNBC, and CNN affiliate WNY, all broadcasting out of New York City.

On July 25th, 2001,[8] a request was submitted by the National Institute for Discovery Science via the Freedom of Information Act, to get radar information from the FAA for the relevant July 14-15th time frame. The tapes revealed that there was a high number of returns that had no transponders as all aircraft are required to have; they moved both faster and slower than planes would normally fly in that airspace, confirming that what those hundreds of witnesses saw were actually some unknown aerial devices, flying unhindered, through some of the most crowded airspace in the world.

Author's Note:

In 2002, we see a lot of UFO activity and encounters occurring across the pond in Europe.[9] Here are but a few.

Russia

On May 11th, 2002, two squadron of unknowns were picked up on Russian radar as they converged from different directions, on a base near the Ural Mountains. Needless to say, the base was put on full alert, and witnesses on the ground swear to the fact that at approximately 2:05 AM, the sky was lit up by an aerial battle waged between these two squadrons of UFOs. Witnesses described laser-like weapons being used by both sides in a sight none would ever forget. Of course, the Russian government denies any such knowledge of the aerial combat above their base, so perhaps they should have gotten in touch with their soldiers on the ground, so that they could get an idea of what transpired that night!

Seville, Spain

At 9:45 PM, on the evening of July 23rd, 2002, a witness identified as L.L.R., was driving down a road on property belonging to the Boliden-Apirsa Mine near Seville, Spain.

Suddenly, he saw a small light heading towards his vehicle from the opposite direction. Since the object showed no signs of slowing down, he turned on his high-beams to alert a possibly distracted driver to his on-coming car. To his great dismay, his actions did not change the lights' direction of travel. There was no doubt in L.L.R.'s mind, a collision was imminent, so he turned away to shield his face and neck in anticipation of a severe impact.

There indeed was a collision. Whatever it was he hit, simply burst into an explosion of many colored lights. Thus there was no accident, no crushing of metal, no breaking of glass, nothing. Rather disconcerted by this event, he jumped out of his stopped car to search for wreckage near or under his car and any casualties that there may have been. Much to his surprise he found nothing, except a mark on his hood where contact was made. On the hood he found some sort of thick watery-like substance that vanished when he touched it. Wanting nothing more than to put some distance between him and the site of this weird incident, he hopped back into the car, and to his shock and dismay, he had trouble starting it, as the battery refused to work.

DEVON, CORNWALL, ENGLAND

The next month, on August 3rd, 2002, a flurry of calls were received by BBC *Radio Cornwall*, in Devon, Cornwall, England, of a strange light seen landing in a field and then disappearing. So many calls were received that the sighting was also reported in the following morning edition of *The Western Morning*.

PORTSMOUTH, ENGLAND

Almost a year later, at 9:37 PM, the evening of May 15th, 2003,[10] witnesses traveling along a twisty back country road near Portsmouth, England noticed a very brilliant egg-shaped object in the sky above the flowing English countryside. The witnesses stated that the object was definitely not any known type of aircraft, and they were convinced of this fact by the speed, rapid direction changes and side-to-side maneuvers the craft made.

Intrigued, they pulled over to the side of the road and parked so they could watch this incredible device without crashing their automobile. After watching the object for just a few minutes, it began to move towards the car. When it was practically over the car, the witnesses had to shield their eyes as the car was engulfed in a blinding white light. Through shielded eyes, they noticed the dashboard clock hands were spinning around quite fast. As fear gripped them, the object suddenly vanished, leaving them feeling quite bewildered as to what had just happened to them. The clock on the dashboard ceased working right then and there.

MANSFIELD, NOTTINGHAMSHIRE, ENGLAND

Less than two hours later, another witness in Mansfield, Nottinghamshire, England, witnessed a UFO from the relative safety of his backyard. This time it was a group of three spheres in a tight grouping that moved over a small portion of the sky for over fifteen minutes, leaving the witness with the impression that they were searching for something or somebody.

DUNOON, ARGYLLSHIRE, SCOTLAND

Eight days later on the 23rd of May, 2003, a couple was out for a Sunday stroll walking near the West Bay area of Dunoon, Argyllshire, Scotland, and as they strolled along, they were surprised to see a very large and silent greenish-yellow oblong-shaped object fly very quickly overhead from north to south, disappearing right before their eyes.

The couple noted that they see Royal Air Force fighters fly training missions regularly, and this object was no plane!

Durango, Colorado

Tim Butler, a Durango, Colorado, sound engineer reported to the *UFO Roundup* that near the end of September, 2003, he saw a sixty-foot-wide boomerang-shaped object, as it swooped down and over Fort Lewis College, fly around Smelter Mountain, cross the Animas River, and finally disappeared behind Paradise Ridge, headed in the general direction of the airport. The entire event lasted only about three minutes, but it is three minutes he will never forget! Mr. Butler described the object as silver in color, had no visible military or civilian markings, and lacked a cockpit, any stabilizing equipment, or a visible means of propulsion. Nor did it have a single window. There was not one rivet visible anywhere on the craft. What impressed him the most was the total silence and the lack of any heat distortion trailing the object as it passed by and flew off out of sight. Having attended many air shows since he was a child, Mr. Butler feels sure that had this been some type of plane of any design or style, he would surely have recognized it for what it was. He could not because as we know what he saw that day was in every sense of the word, an honest to goodness UFO!

Rochester, Indiana

At 10 PM, April 8th, 2004, Bev Carpenter[12] was at home in Rochester, Indiana, when much to her surprise she sighted what she called a *humongous* UFO. According to her report, the object was disc-shaped with three lights on the left and right sides, was at least 100 feet wide and about 400 yards from her home. While the UFO was in the vicinity her house, the lights flickered and her computer malfunctioned.

Her 13- year-old granddaughter saw the UFO her grandmother witnessed, too. Robbie Crull, who lives near Ms. Carpenter, also saw a UFO that she claims was the same as the one her neighbor witnessed, so close to her home that she felt it may have been in her yard. Another witness, Gene Winters, saw the UFO in his backyard as it hovered merely fifty feet over his pond.

MUFON Indiana Assistant State Director Roger Sugden and State Section Director Stewart Hill went to investigate these sightings. They found a circle of downed tree limbs in the yard behind Ms. Carpenter's house where the object was reported to have hovered for a while. They also found high magnetic readings at the Winters' pond and at another site. The sightings had gained some interest by the local television station WSBT, who sent news reporter Ray Roth to the Carpenter home to meet with and interview Roger Sugden. Out back in the area where the UFO hovering had left high magnetic readings, was the site Roth chose for the interview. As they walked from the yard to the site filming a questions and answer segment, the camera, which was working perfectly, began to have audio problems, producing only a buzzing noise in Roth's ear and on the filmed footage. Sugden tried his tape recorder with the same result. Upon playing the tape back, an overwhelming buzzing could be heard in the background of the two men conversing. When they walked out of that area, the camera's audio and the tape recorder worked just fine, just as they had a short time earlier.

Willoughby Hills, Ohio

On Wednesday, June 16th, 2004 a veteran Ohio deputy sheriff and his wife saw the same UFO from two different locations in Ohio.[13] The Deputy's wife was driving along State Route 91 near where it intersects with Route 306, in the vicinity of Willoughby Hills, Ohio, when she was surprised to see a large odd-looking object in the sky. Upon closer inspection, she found that she was looking at a large boomerang-shaped object to the right of her car and about 100 feet in the air. It just sat there silent and motionless for the entire time she had it in view, which was about two minutes. She lost sight of the object due to driving conditions and traffic on the road.

She could not wait to tell her husband what she had seen. As it turned out, he saw the same thing from slightly further away. The deputy was out on patrol when he saw the object. It was self luminous, did not reflect the afternoon sun, and as he watched it, the boomerang-shaped object slowed down and appeared to get bigger. He last saw the object heading east towards the Perry Nuclear Power Plant, when it just vanished. It did not accelerate off, the deputy insisted, it just vanished right before his eyes.

Bracknell News, England

On July, 19th, 2005,[14] Maurice Jones and his daughter, Alaina, were outside their home in the Crown Wood's section of Bracknell News, England, bird watching with binoculars when they spotted an odd craft.

Mr. Jones states that his daughter was the first to see the object. They described it as brown, cigar shaped and apparently metallic, as the sun reflected off of its surface. They yelled for neighbors to come out and see, and all observed it, as the spinning object slowly floated over their homes, hovered for approximately twenty minutes, and then much to the shock of all gathered, the object just disappeared into thin air.

Exeter, New Hampshire

The next day the same, or a similar, object was spotted in Exeter, New Hampshire, by a retired US Navy veteran. The witness, was not only in the Navy for twenty-two years working as an Instructor Flight Engineer, but also worked for the Boeing Aircraft Company in Everett, Washington, as a quality assurance manager on the production line that produced the Boeing 777. At approximately 3:15 PM on the afternoon of July 20th, 2005, framed in a partly cloudy, blue sky, the witness saw a huge cigar-shaped craft hovering almost completely still. He was in shock from the size of the UFO, as it appeared to him to be about twice the size of a Nimitz Class Aircraft Carrier (roughly 2,000 feet wide), and hovered at what he estimated to be 2,500 to 3,500 feet. A strange cloud that resembled an orange/red flame began to billow out of the bottom of the craft, as it approached him at less than 100 knots (115 mph). The billowing cloud reminded him of how exploding Napalm billows out away from the blast site. At that moment, it seemed to him as if the air was igniting underneath this huge craft. As fear gripped him and he was about to run indoors, he saw something that defies all logic. The object swelled to twice its original size, roughly 4,000 feet long, and much to his surprise and relief, this incredible machine just disappeared right before his eyes, much as the cigar-shaped object had done the day before in Bracknell News, England.

Author's Note:

The spring of 2005[15] was the beginning of a mini-flap of UFO sightings in the Keystone State, which lasted into the winter of 2006. What follows are but a few of the reports received.

Fayette County, Pennsylvania

In Fayette County, Pennsylvania, in either late March or early April, a man was walking alone near the town of Smithfield, when he was accosted by two strange lights about the size of footballs. He stated that they glowed very brightly, and appeared to be under intelligent control as they flew past him a little too close for comfort and made their way further down the road, passing under a railroad bridge before disappearing out of sight.

Vandergrift, Pennsylvania

On August 24th, 2005, in Vandergrift, Pennsylvania, a man was busily packing his automobile for an upcoming trip, when he noticed movement in the sky out of the corner of his eye. At about 5:20 AM, he saw a bright silver UFO that looked like a large flat football flying in the early morning sky. It made no noise and he watched it as it passed overhead coming from the northeast horizon and then headed off towards the eastern horizon.

Suddenly, from the direction of Pittsburgh, a second UFO appeared on the scene, racing to catch up with the first one. This one was triangular shaped and had several lights on it. It slowed down to match the speed of the football-shaped object. Then both shot off with the triangle UFO, seemingly chasing the football-shaped UFO until both were lost from sight.

SCHWENKSVILLE, PENNSYLVANIA

At 9:35 PM on the night of January 14th, 2006, a man returning a book to the Perkiom Valley Library near Schwenksville, Pennsylvania, saw a huge light moving across the sky.[16] The object was about thirty yards distant and the witness claims it was cylinder-shaped (cigar shaped?) and several football fields wide (perhaps the same object the retired Navy Chief saw in Exeter, New Hampshire the year before?), with three rows of lights. The middle row was brilliant, with almost blinding intense red lights, while the top and bottom lights were yellow in color.

The witness quickly returned home for a camera as he wanted desperately to capture this sight, but when he had returned outside, the object had flown behind some trees and was soon lost to sight.

SOUTH SHORE, KENTUCKY

Once again, on April 28th, 2006, a large cigar-shaped object would be sighted, this time in South Shore, Kentucky.[17] The witness states that while he was attending a family reunion, at about 6 PM, his brother started screaming for everyone to look up into the air. When they did look up into the blue, sun-filled evening sky, they all saw a huge cigar-shaped object coming towards them from the northwest. As it neared the family reunion, it slowed down nearly to a crawl, an eerie turn of events which made all present feel as if it was observing them. So terrifying was the scene, the witness's aunt passed out from shock.

The cigar-shaped UFO then instantly picked up speed as two jet interceptors were heard to approach and the entire family, except the unconscious aunt, watched as the fighter chased the object off into the distance and out of sight towards Grayson, Kentucky.

The sighting was reported to the South Shore Police Department, the NUFORC, and was covered by the *Daily Times*.

SPRINGFIELD, MISSOURI

A witness reports that on the night of July 14th, 2006,[18] a women and her husband in Springfield, Missouri, were letting their dogs out, when they noticed a very large light in the sky that appeared to be exceptionally low to the ground. In fact, upon closer observation, the incredibly bright light was lower in the sky then the top of a cell phone tower that stood between the couple and the UFO. The light was so bright, that they could not make out any shape or form, but noted that the light was about the size of a softball held at arm's length and so bright that though the object was some distance from them, the light hurt their eyes. The light went straight up and came straight back down, several times, then settled into a hovering posture.

Some type of helicopter soon entered the scene, and the couple watched as it made three very wide arcing circular passes around the obviously much bigger object. Then, as if on a suicide mission, the helicopter headed straight for the object! The couple watched as the UFO began to slowly make its way up towards the heavens, but the couple feared that the fast-approaching helicopter might actually crash into the object. Luckily, it passed below the object, which was so big that it made the helicopter look very small in comparison. The enormous ball of light increased its speed and as it did so, the light changed to a multitude of flashing lights and a giant strobe spun on its bottom as it accelerated out of sight into the northwestern sky.

WARSAW, POLAND

On the morning of January 20th, 2007, approximately seventeen triangular-shaped UFOs appeared in the skies above the Sluzec district of Warsaw, Poland.[19]

The witness reports that she awoke at 1:15 AM, needed a cigarette, and went outside onto her balcony for a smoke. Once outside on the balcony of her home near the Okecie Airport, she saw seventeen isosceles triangles scattered throughout the sky. All had one apex pointed east. Each had three red lights in the corners and the red lights were connected by a thin row of blue lights. She noticed that one of the triangles was three times the size of the other triangles. She was soon joined by her dog, and once he was outside, he began barking at the objects and immediately returned to the safety of indoors. The witness continued to watch the objects for over an hour until they all simultaneously slowly rose up into the heavens and disappeared.

KEIGHLEY, ENGLAND

Keighley, England was the site of a multiple witness UFO encounter, where many people saw many UFOs.[20]

The reporting witness went out for a stroll at 8 PM the evening of September 22nd, 2007. Once outside, he noticed a flickering ball of red light up in the sky, and as he walked he kept an eye on this oddity. A short time into his stroll, he passed a group of people sitting in their garden watching another section of sky. As he was passing, he could hear them speaking amongst themselves, and then a shout rang out, stating, "Here comes some more, they look quite spaced out!"

With this, he looked in the direction they were watching, and sure enough, he saw two UFOs silently passing by and flicker with orange/red light. Excited at this peculiar turn of events, the witness wanted others he knew to also see it, so he phoned a friend telling him about what was happening. When he went outside, he too saw the UFOs.

As they all watched, the UFOs would pass overhead, and once gone, two more would appear on the horizon where the last two had come from and follow the same flight path over the people and on their way to God knows where. The pattern repeated itself for an hour, and the witnessed was astounded at the number of UFOs he had watched pass overhead.

The people in Keighley were not the only ones having strange encounters that night! Roughly thirty-five miles southwest of Keighley, guests at a wedding reception in Manchester reported that, at 10 PM, they could also see the squadrons of UFOs moving across the heavens quite high up and all at the same speed.

AUTHOR'S NOTE:

Three years after the last one, 2008 brought another wave of sightings across Pennsylvania.[21]

HATBORO, PENNSYLVANIA

At 10:20 PM, on March 28th, 2008, Rich Ferello was out taking his dog for their evening constitutional near his home in Hatboro, Pennsylvania. While looking into the sky to the east of his position, he noticed a plane flying at very high altitude.

Suddenly, four objects appeared flying low and in utter silence. Each object had blinking and non-blinking white lights on their sides and front, with at least one red white light on top. The objects came from the west headed east and abruptly turned north, obviously not following any of the FAA mandated flight paths as they flew around the sky, appearing as if they were searching for something.

Mr. Ferello returned inside his home and alerted his wife and son to the presence of the four UFOs. They also saw them and concurred that they were quite out of the ordinary. After fifteen minutes of observation, the UFOs simply accelerated off into the northwest sky and out of the Ferello's field of vision.

LEVITTOWN, PENNSYLVANIA

On April 20th, 2008, Denise Murter was awakened at 3 AM in her Levittown, Pennsylvania, home by what sounded like a screen being ripped apart. Much to her dismay, her dog was in an agitated state, growling at whatever or whoever was ripping the screen. Having made a quick survey of her home and finding nothing, she looked into the back yard and saw something she wasn't expecting.

In the sky behind her house was a UFO hovering in absolute silence. It had lights on its surface and emitted a cone-shaped light from its bottom down towards the earth. After watching mesmerized for thirty minutes, she finally broke the spell and went to get her husband, Dan, and together they watched this strange object for almost another half an hour before it left as mysteriously as it had arrived.

This was not to be their only encounter. Over the next few months, they had three more sightings, each of thirty minutes duration, one on May 20th, one on June 12th and another on July 8th.

Doylestown, Pennsylvania

Then on June 3rd, 2008, in Doylestown, Pennsylvania, Cliff Vandegrift was awakened from a sound sleep at 4:20 AM, and without knowing why, looked out the window. As he peered into the early morning darkness, he noticed a small cloud that was moving towards his home at a very slow speed. Except the closer it got, the less it looked like a cloud. The notion that what he was watching was a cloud was soon dispelled as the object took on the form of a dark gray, kind of a stretched-out hexagon. As it got closer, the hexagon UFO appeared quite large.

Mr. Vandegrift got out of bed and went to his open window for a better look. He estimated that the object was about 100 feet across, flying at approximately 600 feet and was completely silent. He went outside and watched as the object circled his property twice and then proceed to go back the way it came, gained altitude, and disappeared out of sight.

Levittown, Pennsylvania

Back in Levittown, Pennsylvania, at 1 AM the morning of June 25th, 2008, Anthony Gurka heard a strange noise as he was relaxing on his front porch. Looking around, he found that up in the sky was a boomerang-shaped UFO floating slowly past at about 1,000 feet elevation.

Philadelphia, Pennsylvania

On July 26th, 2008, Sunnie DeAngelis-Gardner was returning from work to her home in Philadelphia, Pennsylvania, at approximately 11:45 PM. Bringing her car to a halt for a stop sign just a few blocks from her house, she noticed an object in the sky over the woods near her home. She described it as being shaped like an "H," reminding her of an Imperial Tie Fighter from the movie *Star Wars*. It had red and white lights covering its body.

As she slowly drove the remaining blocks to her home, she lost sight of the object behind the tree line.

Philadelphia, Pennsylvania

Eight days later, also in the City of Brotherly Love, at approximately 10:10 PM on August 3rd, 2008, Tony Fusco was watching the sky from the comfort of his balcony when he heard an electronic type sound in his right ear. Not thinking too much of it he continued sky watching, until the sound was heard again just a few minutes later. Turning to his right, he noticed a ball of white light approaching his position. As he watched it, it did not shimmer, blink, nor flutter. It was just a ball of light, and as it got nearer, it vanished in a red flash of light.

Author's Note:

Our next sightings garnered much attention, as a series of widespread reports were received from Texas between August of 2007 and February 2009,[22, 23] centered on the Stephenville-Dublin areas.

Stephenville, Texas

On August 15th, 2007,[22] at 7:15 PM, a woman was photographing the sunset. Later that night, when she was reviewing her photos, she noticed a strange craft in nineteen of the photos. This was the start of something incredible.

On December 10th, 2007, Cecile and Misti Ford were driving north on Highway 108 at 7:30 PM, when they saw an oval-shaped UFO. The craft was moving along slowly as it made its way northwest from the northeast horizon.

Suddenly, the craft accelerated to an incredible speed and disappeared into the northwestern sky in a blink of an eye.

The very next day in Stephenville, Texas, at approximately 9:30 PM, Brian McCabe's dog alerted him to the presence of a very large black triangular-shaped UFO as it made its way low and slow over his neighborhood in total silence.

Old Boston, Texas

Then, on December 21st, 2007 a witness in Old Boston, Texas reported that, at 8:13 PM, he watched as a light on the horizon quickly advance on his position, and then fly overhead and out of sight at what he approximated was 5,000 mph. The object was flying at what the witness estimated was 10,000 feet. It was covered with approximately 20 orange-gold lights on its perimeter, forming a rectangular shape that he estimated to be one mile long by half a mile wide. He knew this was one solid object due to the fact that as the lights passed overhead, the area between the perimeter lights blocked out all the stars in the night sky.

Sometime during the afternoon of January 8th, 2008, Steve Allen, a pilot and local businessman, reported sighting the same, or a similar, object as was seen in Old Boston. Mr. Allen described the object as one mile long by half a mile wide, moving very fast. Very soon after he spotted it, the object began to be chased by two F-16s running at full speed with after burners engaged and sonic booms echoing throughout the area.

Three unidentified law enforcement officers in three different locations also reported witnessing the object. All agreed on the size and speed of the object, but as one was inside his cruiser, only two could confirm the silence of this gigantic UFO.

FORT WORTH, TEXAS

Later that same day, at about 6 PM, there were sightings of two different UFOs near Fort Worth, Texas.

Witnesses describe one of the UFOs as a large, stationary object with bright lights hanging silently in the sky just to the southwest of Fort Worth.

In the same general area, other witnesses reported seeing a large cigar-shaped object that moved from the southwest to the west and out of sight.

Yet another witness saw an object with eight stubby wings make its way across the skies of the Fort Worth suburb of Burleson.

A short time later, at 6:10 PM, a witness was driving on Highway 67, just west of Chalk Mountain, when something out of the corner of his eye caught his attention. In the western sky, he saw two objects as bright as wielding torches dancing in the sky. Suddenly the two lights flew off in different directions with tremendous bursts of speed.

LAKE PROCTOR, TEXAS

Ten minutes later, a witness reported that they were at their home in Lake Proctor, Texas, and were alarmed by their dogs who were barking their heads off out in the yard. The witness grabbed a flashlight and a gun and headed outside, expecting some sort of animal to be the cause of the ruckus. Instead, what they found was the dogs barking in the general direction of Dublin, Texas, Headed towards them in the sky from that direction was a number of lights, which the witness took to be a squadron of military planes flying in formation. But as they grew closer, the witness was shocked at the absence of the roar of all those jet turbines that should have accompanied a squadron of planes. All that was heard was the dogs barking.

Intrigued, the witness's eyes were transfixed on the strange lights until they had passed out of sight. The witness looked down to see if the dogs were alright as they had stopped their barking, but they were nowhere to be found in the yard. They were later found hiding under a piece of furniture in what quite obviously was a very frightened state.

STEPHENVILLE, TEXAS

At 6:30 PM that night, while walking the dog on the Legends Golf Course in Stephenville, Texas, a witness reported seeing two lights in the sky as bright as arc welders' flames. The objects made no noise as they flew in the general direction of Dublin, Texas. It has been found out by investigators (thanks to a Freedom of Information Act request), that as all these sightings were unfolding, local Doppler radar was painting unexplainable returns. One such return had no transponder and was tracked moving at 700 MPH towards the east.

BROWNWOOD, TEXAS

On January 8th, 2008, a mother, her 15-year-old daughter, and young son were driving home through Brownwood, Texas. At 7:10 PM, as they crested a hill, they were surprised to see huge blinking bright yellow lights scattered across the landscape very near the ground. They stopped the car and got out to watch the lights, and after a few minutes all the lights lined up and simply blinked out.

GRANBURY, TEXAS

Later that night, near Granbury, Texas, a 45-year-old witness was traveling on Highway 4 at about 8:50 PM. They saw an object in the sky about the size of a blimp that had red lights at the front and rear. The witness stressed that it was flying too low and slow to be any conventional aircraft.

RISING STAR, TEXAS

The next night, January 9th, 2008, a 44-year-old witness was headed south towards Rising Star, Texas, when a little ways outside of Cisco, on Highway 183, at approximately 10 PM, he spotted an object with five strobe lights flying at about 1,000 feet. The lights would come on in sequence from first to fifth and repeat the pattern. It was only in view for twenty to thirty seconds.

DUBLIN, TEXAS

On the 10th, at 6:30 PM, a 51-year-old witness was in her pickup truck at their spread in Dublin, Texas awaiting her husband who was out plowing. As she sat sky watching, she saw six lights in the sky as bright as headlights coming towards her location from the right. When they were directly in front of her, the lights simple extinguished themselves right before her startled eyes.

STEPHENVILLE, TEXAS

Later that night, at 8:45 PM over in Stephenville, Texas, a 53-year-old witness reports they were driving home when they saw a group of lights in a giant V-formation. Though the object was close, due to the brightness of the lights he could not see a body they may have been attached to. Upon arrival home, he took a quick look at the lights and raced inside to get a camera. Seconds later, upon his return outside, the huge formation was gone from sight.

PILOT POINT, TEXAS

At 6:50 AM on the morning of the 11th in Pilot Point, Texas, James Beatty was entering onto State Route 455 from Running Bear Road when he saw a bright white object cresting the hill on the other side of the local dam. The object hugged the ground and approached to within fifty yards of the witness's vehicle. The witness described the object as being metallic, gray or black in color, had three white lights on its paneled bottom, a canopy of some sort that ran nearly the length of the fuselage, and a rectangular rear end with three large round openings. What struck him most, as was the case with many of the witnesses, was the fact that the object made no sound whatsoever.

TEXAS

On January 22nd, 2008, while flying at 30,000 feet from Nashville to Dallas/Fort Worth, a witness reported that she watched out the plane window as a cigar-shaped object moved towards the plane and then shot back down into the clouds.

STEPHENVILLE, TEXAS

On October 28th, 2008[23] a witness in Stephenville, Texas, shot cell phone video of bright star-like lights hovering, making circles in the sky, and sudden sharp right angle turns, before being chased off by six fighter planes of unknown type.

A few days later, while driving the lonely roads between Proctor and Stephenville, Texas, on the night of October 23rd, 2008, at 7:50 PM, Jessica Clark and Hanna Fair spotted a UFO flying off to the right of their car. They said that the UFO consisted of a row of three orange-yellow lights that were very bright. These lights would be in one place for about ten seconds, then disappear and reappear in another place almost instantaneously. The pattern would repeat itself four times, and after the fourth time, the lights disappeared and did not reappear.

DUBLIN, TEXAS

Forty minutes later, at 8:30 PM, Ashleigh Cole and three others were horseback riding on the Dublin, Texas, ranch that she manages. When they came around a barn on the property, they all saw three big orange lights hovering about 100 feet off the ground. They all agreed that the balls were about as big as basketballs held at arm's length and were about 450 feet away. The lights, which appeared elliptical, would blink on and off in a random sequence and were attached to some sort of craft that was estimated to be about forty-five feet long. Silently, the object began moving from west to north, and after about five minutes into their observation, the lights just disappeared.

Also at 8:30 PM that night, Kirk Horn and his family, save one son, were watching television at his ranch that lies five miles from both Stephenville and Dublin, Texas. Suddenly, his oldest son Nick crashed through the door yelling for his family to come outside and see the UFO hovering on the other side of the house. Once outside, they looked where Nick had told them to, but the object was gone.

A few moments later, the UFO, a bright orange round light, reappeared hovering in a field a little less than two miles away. As they watched the object hovering in the field, they heard the sound of jets, and looking up, they saw seven jets converging on their spot, three from the west and four from the south. A moment later the orange UFO simply disappeared into thin air as the family watched in disbelief.

HAMILTON, TEXAS

A third sighting, from 8:30 PM that evening, comes to us from Max and Carole Derden, who live just outside of Hamilton, Texas, which is about thirty miles south of the locations of the two previous sightings.

From his back patio, Mr. Derden saw two different sized objects moving along quite slowly at what he estimated to be 20 MPH at an altitude of 3,000 feet. He noted that the smaller object had three large round orange lights, while the larger object had nine lights on it, which he was sure was reflected off of some type of metal hull the larger object was made of. To this mix arrived twenty to thirty iridescent green cones of light that moved around kind of erratically. As in previous sightings, the orange lights on both objects blinked on and off. The Derden's watched this light show for about twenty minutes, before all the lights vanished from sight.

EVANT, TEXAS

Later that night of the 23rd, Greg Plyant of Evant, Texas, spotted three round orange lights in the sky that blinked on and off, and formed sort of a curved arrangement as if the object they were attached to was also of round design. The UFO was suddenly joined by five or six military jets and soon exited the airspace. He would again see the same lights in the sky on the nights of 28th and 30th of October, 2008.

HICO, TEXAS

The last reported sighting from October 23rd, 2008 came from Mrs. D'Ann Wheeler. At about 9:15 PM, she and the friend she was visiting near Hico, Texas, were outside that perfect autumn evening, and as they were admiring the stars, they noticed two objects in the sky. Each had three vertical orange lights. The objects were hovering about 60 degrees above the horizon at a distance that was estimated to be 1.5 miles. The witness claimed the object hovered quite still, with the lights not blinking but rotating back and forth 10 to 15 degrees, and were about the size of baseballs held at arm's length. These lights would intrigue many more witnesses than just Mrs. Wheeler and her friend. As reported in the Hico newspaper, the entire crowd assembled for the Hico High School Junior Varsity football game, including spectators, players, and coaches were mesmerized by the lights so much, that the game came to a halt until the lights disappeared!

AUTHOR'S NOTE:

These are but a small percentage of the sightings reported in what has become known as the Stephenville Encounters, which have been covered in many newspapers and on many radio and television stations, as well as having a full episode of the *UFO Hunters* on the History Channel devoted to it. Mind you, local investigators, primarily the dedicate volunteers from MUFON Texas, are still investigating these sightings and will continue to do so until the whole story is known.

Though the government quickly tried to explain these sightings away as a misidentification of a squadrons of F-16s, they, as usual, failed to explain how an F-16 could fly low and slow, in total silence, and blot out a 1 mile by 1.5 mile swath of stars in the sky, or better yet, hover for long periods of time. But these facts do not sway everyone as to the governments' deceit. Not long after these sightings, I had the chance to speak with some relatives who work at Fort Hood, Texas. Having not seen them since the early 1990s, I was interested in what they thought about these incredible sightings happening all around them. They looked at me as if I had two heads and explained to me that the mystery had been solved by the government and proceeded to tell me the official F-16 story with great earnest. This goes to show that anyone can be drawn in by the stories haphazardly thrown together by governments with something to hide. It's easy to accept the experts at face value if one does not have all the facts at hand. This is definitely sad, but all too true and widespread throughout the populace.

POYNETTE, WISCONSIN

On June 18th, 2009, a retired deputy sheriff reported a UFO she spotted near her house in Poynette, Wisconsin.[24] The witness, a well-respected woman in her early fifties, with over a decade of experience in law enforcement, was just falling off to sleep with her two dogs in her bedroom at a little past midnight. As she was drifting into unconsciousness, she was riveted awake by a low, intense humming noise that seemed to be coming through the drapes that covered the big window in her master bedroom. Whatever the noise was, she knew she wasn't imagining things, as her dogs had jumped off the bed and were standing near the window.

So she walked over to the window; and seeing through the drapes that the motion activated lights in the driveway were on, she decided to go into her bathroom, which afforded her a better view of the driveway. As she walked to the bathroom, the noise seemed to grow in intensity. Looking out the bathroom window she saw nothing in the driveway. So she glanced up and found the source of the noise was nothing that she was expecting to see!

Hovering over nearly the entire length of her 400-foot driveway was a gray object with three very bright white lights in a line that stretched from the furthest tip of the object to just about its rear. Alone and slightly to the left of the other lights, at the rear of the craft, was a red and white flashing light. The object must have been less than thirty feet up as the motion detectors proximity switch was set to thirty feet and only motion within that distance would activate it. She watched as the object moved slowly south towards a meadow, eventually disappearing behind a nearby hill.

Leasburg, North Carolina

What started out as an overnight camping adventure in the backyard, turned into a nightmare for a Leasburg, North Carolina man on September 11th and 12th, 2009.[25]

The main witness is a family man who owns an auto body shop next to his home. His son and a friend headed into the backyard to begin their first-ever camp out at 9PM on the 11th. At 11 PM, his two chained-up dogs began barking, and fearing for the safety of his son, the witness ran out into the backyard to see what the commotion was. He looked around and found nothing unusual, so he walked back to his house.

At approximately 11:45 PM, he decided things were alright and his son was not in danger, and as he was going to head back inside, he turned around for one last look and spotted a large black triangle hovering 150 feet above his yard. The triangle was as wide as his yard, 125 feet, and one tip of the triangle was pointed directly at the witness. The object sat motionless, silently hovering above his yard. It had an orange light in each of the three corners. Behind the triangle, the witness could see four more objects, one star-like object, one round object and two egg-shaped objects ranging in color from yellow to orange and in size from eight to ten feet in width. The smaller objects took turns descending into the woods in back of his property remaining on the ground for two to three seconds then ascending back up to the big triangle. This went on for about four minutes. Then the witness went into his house to get his handheld DVD recorder. Though he had used it with no problems earlier in the day, when he tried to film the craft, the device would not work. (It did, however, work fine the next day with no recharging or adjustment.) So he returned inside to grab his handheld, one million candlepower spotlight to shine on the object allowing him a better view of this once-in-a-lifetime sight. When he shone the spotlight on the object, the surface of the triangle did not reflect the light, but absorbed it.

Then suddenly, as if in retaliation, the triangle shot an intense beam of bluish-white light down at the witness, who curled up as best he could to protect his face and head from the beam. Though it lasted only a few seconds, the beam left a lasting impression on the witness, who claimed it produced an intense heat and burning sensation wherever it hit him. When the beam was shut off, the witness ran into his house and watched as the triangle and the four smaller craft slowly drifted off towards the south.

A short distance away, two of the smaller lights accelerated straight up at incredible speed and disappeared. The triangle rotated up pointing the end that had been facing him when the beam hit him towards the heavens. Then it and the two remaining smaller objects shot up and out of sight at an astounding speed.

On Saturday the 12th, the witness felt extremely sick and nauseous all day. His neck and shoulders were tender to the touch, and developed a redness not unlike a severe sunburn. For the entire day he had a metallic taste in his mouth that reminded him of copper pennies.

NEAR LITTLE ROCK, ARKANSAS

A flight attendant reports that, on a routine commercial flight, she and a pilot witnessed a UFO on January, 5th, 2010.[26] The flight attendant stated that she was in the cockpit talking with one of the pilots as the airliner cruised along about 100 miles southwest of Little Rock, Arkansas. As they conversed, they both noticed a bright oval-shaped object hovering in the sky. As they took a closer look at it, the object proceeded to shoot a beam of light down to the ground. Visually following the beam down to the ground, they saw that the beam was illuminating a round object far below them.

When the object "noticed" the airliner, it shut off the beam and began to pace the plane just 500 feet away for nearly 30 minutes. As is often the case, the pilot and flight attendant decided not to report the object to the FAA for fear of ridicule. So afraid of some type of ridicule or harassment were they, that when they reported the UFO to the MUFON Case Management System via the MUFON website, they even declined to use their names for follow-up by trained investigator.

NEAR RUSTBURG AND RICHMOND, VIRGINIA

In the early morning hours of April 30th, 2010, at roughly 6:47 AM, a huge cigar-shaped UFO was spotted near Rustburg, Virginia.[27] Another witness, 111 miles to the northeast, while out for a walk along the James River in Richmond, Virginia, encountered that same immense UFO, around 6:30 PM that evening. While walking, the witness spotted a low hovering cigar-shaped UFO, about 2,000 feet up and a half mile inland from the river.

The object was described as being about 300 feet long, with a metallic body made up of alternating dark and light sections. The witness could see no wings, tail, engines nor markings of any type. No sound of any type could be heard. As the witness watched this huge aerial device just sit there, without any warning, an incredibly bright and intense clear white strobe light began flashing from the belly of this aerial beast. The flashing lasted a short while and then stopped, only to be followed by a similar intensely bright red strobe light. The red light went out and no more lights were observed. The craft pivoted in midair, turning forty-five degrees before becoming motionless once again.

Continuing on the walk caused the witness to lose sight of this huge UFO, but nothing will ever erase the image of that incredible sight in the memory of this witness. With a little bit of investigation, this witness learned that the scientist and government employees of both the Surry and North Anna Nuclear Power Plants in central Virginia also had sightings of cigar-shaped objects seemingly interested in their places of employment.

NEW YORK CITY

Our next sighting happened in broad daylight, within the busiest air corridor on the planet, over the largest city in America, and was filmed and witnessed by hundreds, if not thousands of observers.

The afternoon of October 13, 2010, was as beautiful an autumn day as a person could ask for. Sunshine, blue skies, and mild temperatures were the order of the day for the residents of New York City. Around 1:30 PM, the FAA and NYPD began receiving calls from hundreds of people in the Chelsea District of Manhattan, concerning bright objects hovering in the blue skies above lower midtown.[28] Onlookers and videographers were blocking streets looking at and filming these odd, stationary, bright circular objects. According to some of the witnesses, one object was seen "falling" out of the sky, and it split into three which formed a triangular-shaped pattern as they hovered. The three lights were soon joined by others.

To review what the witnesses saw, log on to YouTube and search UFO NYC Oct 2010, and you can see many videos taken that day for yourself, and see if you believe the explanation that was offered up in print and over the airwaves by our now infamous pseudo-experts.

The very next day, without batting an eye, all these sightings were explained away as balloons that escaped from guests at a teacher's engagement party. In my opinion, they may as well have said the lights were swamp gas, as both explanations hold about the same amount of credibility. Balloons surely do not fit the bill of what observers reported seeing, one light that split into three, than were joined by more objects, and all while hovering over Chelsea. Although silver balloons reflecting the bright sun that day could look like what was seen and filmed that day, any balloon that size would be blown all over the skies by the updrafts from the skyscrapers and the nearly incessant breeze that blows in from New York Harbor. Even if they were not blown away, surely they would have risen up and out of sight, not remain at a constant height. I feel that there is no way party balloons could remain in one spot so long.

If you were to check the time stamps on those YouTube videos I mentioned, I think you would come to the same conclusion, as they show the UFOs were in sight for at least ninety minutes. Per FAA Spokesmen Jim Peters, anyone releasing a weather balloon over Greater New York needs to notify someone of the release, and notification was not received by them or the NYPD, thus also effectively eliminating weather balloons as a possible explanation.

El Paso, Texas

Coincidently, a similar incident where three lights appeared and formed a triangular formation only to be joined by additional lights happened again four days later in El Paso, Texas, where they were explained away as stunt planes flying night drills! (If nothing else, the pseudo-experts in El Paso are at the very least more creative than those in the New York City media!)

Manitoba, Canada

Many travelers aboard a train in Manitoba, Canada had their itineraries disrupted when they and the train they rode upon encountered UFOs about two hours north of Fox Lake.[29] The encounter began on December 10th, 2010, as the train made its way across the wilds of Canada, when engineers, conductors, and passengers on the train spotted blue and green lights hovering near the tracks. As it approached, one of the hovering lights shone an incredibly bright light at the train. The light was so bright that it lit up the entire area. The bright light ceased and engineers reported seeing red lights join the blue and green ones, before they all shot straight up and out of sight. Whatever the light was that the UFO had illuminated the train and its surroundings with, it totally disabled the train's reception of satellite signals. Thus, until the signals could be reacquired and processed, the train, its crew, and passengers were effectively stranded for a couple hours in the vast Canadian wilderness.

CALGARY, ALBERTA, CANADA

Twenty-eight days later, on January 7th, 2011, a witness in Calgary, Alberta, Canada reported spotting lights similar to the ones that stalled the train in Manitoba. At about 10:30 PM, he was standing outdoors taking in the beauty of the Canadian Rockies. As his eyes wandered, his attention was drawn to a large green light that had smaller red lights "orbiting" it. The witness watched the lights move quickly to the west and out of sight in the abundant clouds out that night. The witness could not make out any structure the lights may have been attached to, and though unsure of what it was he saw, he definitely knew this object was no plane!

JERUSALEM, ISRAEL

As you will see, 2011 is shaping up to be a very busy year for UFO sightings and reports, so let's get right to them. At about 1AM the morning of January 28th, 2011, a UFO was reportedly spotted hovering over the city of Jerusalem, Israel.[30, 31] What appears as a white orb of light can be seen hovering high above the city for a short time, only to descend quickly, hover over The Dome of the Rock, an Islamic holy site. After a few moments, a burst of light precedes the UFOs acceleration straight up and out of view.

Now, there are already stories of how this is proof that aliens are here, and counter theories of this being a very well orchestrated hoax, but I believe that all videos (and there are at least four of them on YouTube) need to be thoroughly analyzed by experts—and no, not YouTube or blogging experts, actual photographic experts like the well-respected expert Dr. Bruce Maccabee—before it can be determined if this event was real or hoaxed. I have watched all four videos on YouTube and elsewhere and though the video that shows a close-up of the Dome of the Rock and the UFO coming down to hover near the Dome before taking off looks like a forgery, the other three, which are videos taken by three independent witnesses from different places around Jerusalem (one of the videos was definitely filmed by two witnesses at the Armon Hanatziv panoramic lookout near Mount Zion), may very well stand up to rigorous investigation. Nick Pope, who ran the UFO program for the United Kingdom's Ministry of Defense, proclaimed rightly that if these videos are real, they are some of the most incredible videos ever shot; if they are not, they are a very well-planned and coordinated hoax. View them for yourself by going to YouTube and searching Jerusalem UFO 2011 and decide what you think.

Even if one of the posted videos is a hoax, could it have been hoaxed on purpose by someone who wanted to, or was paid to, discredit the other three videos that are not so easy to explain? Stranger things than that have been done to purposely mislead the public into believing that UFOs do not exist!

ALLENTOWN, PENNSYLVANIA

On February 27th, 2011, a witness from Allentown, Pennsylvania,[32] reported that while on Roth Street, approximately one block from where Roth Street intersects with Fairmont Street, a huge football-shaped UFO was observed above a cluster of trees but lower than the flight path of normal air traffic.

The witness described the object as being self illuminated, red at the tail end, but the rest of the craft was a soft, but intense, white. The object looked as if it was self illuminated and appeared much as frosted glass would look when light was shining through it. The UFO was much larger than the two commercial airliners spotted flying higher above. In fact, much to the dismay of the witness, the size of the UFO was estimated to be roughly equivalent to that of a cruise ship. And that cruise ship-sized UFO was simply hanging silently above the trees. The witness was certain of two things. This was no meteor or any other natural phenomenon nor conventional aircraft. And, having watched it move out of sight diagonally, the witness knew this object was under intelligent control; by whom or what has yet to be answered.

CALIFORNIA

From March 6th, 2011 comes our next report filed by a person driving down the main road that leads on and off Camp Pendelton, California.[33] As the witness drove down the main street of the base, their eye was caught by a shiny object hovering in the sky in the general direction of the base's runway and air base. The object was round, flat and long, almost perfectly cigar shaped. It appeared to be made of metal which was reflecting the bright afternoon sun quite intensely. Suddenly, as if "spooked" by something, the object darted off to another part of the sky, leaving a line of light as it went from its original location to the new one. This happened a few times before the object disappeared into the clouds at an incredible speed, with no evident engines, nor any noticeable noise.

The witness claims that in all the years spent in the military observing every conceivable type of conventional aircraft, this was nothing like anything he had ever seen before.

CULPEPPER, VIRGINIA

At about 9PM the evening of March 7th, 2011,[34] a group of witnesses in Culpepper, Virginia, watched as several triangle-shaped UFOs flew slowly and erratically over their heads. It appeared to the witnesses as if they were looking for something or someone or making a type of survey of the area.

The objects were described as having one red light in front and two blinking white lights at the rear. One witnessed saw a spot light shine down towards the ground for just a moment. The lights would slowly and silently sweep from one side of the sky to the other, covering what the witnesses estimated to be several hundred square miles every pass. At one point, one of the objects flew just several hundred feet above the assembled witnesses, and the most that could be heard was a low humming noise. Every so often, the red and white lights would be replaced by intense white lights for several seconds, and then revert back to the less intense one red and two white configuration.

Pennsylvania

On the evening of the 26th of March 2011, three friends saw a triangle shaped UFO while driving home in Pennsylvania.[35] The witness reported that while driving, bright headlight-like lights were seen on what was thought to be a helicopter hovering in the sky not far down the roadway they were traveling on. When they had driven closer to the object, which was now hovering not far above the car, they soon realized that this was no helicopter!

The first clue was the lack of the roaring sound made by a helicopter. The next was the way the object appeared when viewed from their frighteningly close vantage point. The object took on the shaped of an obtuse scalene triangle, with its edges covered in oddly placed red, green, and white lights. Much to the dismay of the witnesses, as the car passed beneath the UFO on their way to home and safety, the object began to pace their car, except now the oddly placed red, green, and white lights had been replaced by one red and two white lights, one in each corner. Much to their relief, a short way down the road, the triangle-shaped UFO sped away in an instant, only to take up a position hovering in the sky, still visible, but quite a distance from the car. Then right before all three of their startled eyes, the craft simply vanished into thin air.

Pembroke Pines, Florida

At 12:05 AM, March 27th, 2011, a witness, while riding his motorcycle, saw two UFOs in the night sky. The witness was just passing the guard gate at the entrance of Century Village in Pembroke Pines, Florida[36] where his mother resides, when he saw two dark red, almost burgundy-colored UFOs. Higher up in the sky to the left of these lights, the witness saw two commercial airliners, thus confirming in his mind that what he was viewing was something else altogether.

The lights appeared much larger than the planes and the witness felt that they were two distinct craft of some unknown design, which was verified when they began to fly in different directions. Intrigued, the witnessed stopped his motorcycle, climbed off, and watched the nearer of the two dark red lights. As it passed through, and then under, some clouds, the red light went out and the UFO appeared to be a charcoal gray-colored disc shaped object about one mile directly overhead. The disc had a smaller circle in the middle with straight lines radiating out toward the edge, giving it the appearance of a full *Trivial Pursuit* game piece. The object then headed off in a westerly direction, at what the witness estimated to be five times the speed of the commercial aircraft he saw passing, or probably at close to 2,500 MPH!

After the initial shock of seeing such an otherworldly sight, the witness regained his senses, and wanting to get some pictures or video with his phone, he hopped back onto his motorcycle and began chasing the object. Racing down the highway at a high rate of speed, the witness began to lose sight of it near the intersection of State Route 27 and Okeechobee Road. The witness sped onto I-75 and headed west in pursuit of the object, but it was totally out of sight.

Abandoning the chase, the witness turned around to head for home in Coral Springs, Florida. Once there, he began to search the web to see if anyone else had ever encountered a similar object and much to his surprise (but not ours!), he found that many pilots and law enforcement officers and others had reported seeing objects much like the ones he had seen that morning.

Missouri

In the early morning hours of April 5th, 2011, a retired police officer in Missouri was awakened by his German Shepherd at approximately 3:15 AM.[37] Leaving his sleeping wife in bed, he followed his barking dog, which was leading him towards the rear of his home. Assuming she heard something he did not hear in the backyard, he headed towards the back door, with the dog barking ceaselessly. As he passed through the kitchen, he noticed a bright bluish-white light flooding in through the kitchen windows and the window in his back door. Perhaps it was his thirty years as a police officer that made him think that the light must be coming from a helicopter looking for a suspect.

All of a sudden a great, uneasy feeling overcame this veteran police officer, as he realized he heard no noise whatsoever. So great was his unease that he decided his next best course of action was to return to his bedroom to retrieve a loaded gun. He went to the back door once more, and opened it, at which time the light blinked off. Looking around the yard, he saw nothing. He then looked up and saw the source of the light.

Floating silently in the sky above was a dull black triangle-shaped object that was the width of his backyard, making it about fifty feet wide. Oddly, his faithful German

Shepherd would not come near the now open back door. Hearing a noise near the fence, but unable to see through the darkness, the retired officer retrieved a flashlight from a drawer in the kitchen. As he got it, he heard an animal-like clicking noise behind him but he saw nothing. Returning to the back porch, he shone the light towards the fence where he had heard the noise, not believing what was illuminated in his beam. Near the fence, stood a four-foot gray humanoid being with big eyes, just staring at him.

Within a second, the being simply vanished before the witness's startled eyes. The witness stressed that the entity did not leave, nor run-off; it simply vanished. Looking up, he saw nothing, as the ship vanished as fast as the being had. His thirty years of policing and all the training and experiences that go along with it could not prevent him from being frozen to the spot in great fear. When he gained his senses, his first instinct was to phone 911, but remembered how he and other officers felt about the people who made UFO reports—he thought twice and did not phone anyone. Instead, he went around the house locking everything that locked and returned to bed only to be shocked once more. Feeling as if ten to fifteen minutes had elapsed since he left his sleeping wife, he was shocked to see that a full ninety-one minutes had passed and the fear he felt before returned once more.

The following morning, he noticed that he had what looked like a nasty sunburn on his face, neck, and arms. When his wife noticed the burn, he told her of the light the night before but not of the humanoid, nor the missing time.

Cedar Rapids, Iowa

At 10:33 PM, the evening of April 8th, 2011, three friends were driving east on Highway 30, approximately 10 miles west of Cedar Rapids, Iowa.[38] Per the witnesses, there were a lot of clouds that night with the ceiling being a mere 300-500 feet high. The witness who was driving the car was the first to spot the strange light in the sky. The passenger in the back seat stated that, as they drove along, a bright ball of light that looked to be flashing like a strobe light appeared after coming down from above the cloud cover and remained hovering off to the left of the car. The witness estimated that the light was 30 to 40 feet wide and flashing in an irregular manner, but with a distinct rhythm. Its light was bright and appeared to be bluish-white in color, and it was not a mass of light but an object circular in shape. The flashes of light were all contained within the circular perimeter of the object, with the light forming the distinct circular shape when the flashes or pulses occurred.

Due to the object remaining stationary, as the vehicle drove down the road, the passengers lost sight of the strange object. Wanting another look at this incredible sight, when the first opportunity on that divided highway presented itself, the driver turned around and headed westbound back towards the place where the light had been, only to be disappointed to find the object had either increased its elevation taking it out of their sight or had vanished altogether.

Arizona

The morning of April 29th, 2011 was clear and sunny. A family of four, driving on route 17N from Scottsdale to Sedona, Arizona, was enjoying their trip, with the wife behind the wheel, the husband in the passenger seat, and their two children in the backseat.[39]

The wife recounts that as they neared the exit for Camp Verde, a small cigar-shaped, silver object came into her field of view, moving from west to east over the highway, a short distance down the highway from their car. She described it as silver in color, cigar- or disc-shaped, with no wings, tail, nor contrail following it. Since her husband was engrossed in his cell phone, she alerted him to the presence of the object by exclaiming, "Look at the UFO!"

He immediately looked up from what he was doing just in time to watch as it changed course, turning north, flying parallel to the highway, and almost instantly disappeared into the distance.

After the object disappeared, the couple tried to rationalize what they had seen but could not. Every plane, helicopter, bird, and cloud seen on the rest on the trip was compared to the object, but none came close to resembling that mysterious interloper that had intruded upon their pleasant journey.

Texas

On the afternoon of May 5th, 2011,[40] five Texas neighbors' witnessed a UFO as it overflew their normally tranquil neighborhood. Two neighbors, who had spent the afternoon together, went outside to say hello to another of their neighbors. As it was a beautiful day, the trio decided to sit in the grassy island in the middle of their cul-de-sac. As they sat enjoying the afternoon, two of the small group noticed a solid red point of light in the afternoon sky, as it moved east to west. Its brightness struck the friends as odd, as it was brighter than the silver fuselages of planes that would normally be seen in the sky, and in the bright sunny sky of that day, they would not expect to see a red light that intense, yet there it was!

As the friends discussed the possibility of it being a balloon or a red plane, the object came to a dead stop, began to pulse intensely, and slowly flew off in the opposite direction.

The trio saw yet another neighbor, and called her over to look at the strange object that they were seeing. As the four friends watched, from out of thin air, another red light appeared near the first one. They began to alternately pulse brightly and then vanish. A fifth neighbor brought out a pair of binoculars and observed the object very closely for several minutes. Even through the binoculars, the witness states that no apparent form could be seen, other than an intense red light. Soon thereafter the lights disappeared. Though the five neighbors watched the sky for more than an hour after the disappearance of the lights, nothing more out of the ordinary was seen.

Bayfield, Colorado

Four friends were camping in the Pine Creek campsites near Bayfield, Colorado, on the night of May 8th, 2011.[41] As they sat sky watching, an odd light was spotted between two peaks to the north of their position. What caught their attention was the fact that the light was excessively bright, even brighter than landing lights of a commercial jet.

As it drew closer, the single light became three separate distinct lights, all in a line with a red light above them. The craft these lights were attached to was a mere 500 feet off the ground and appeared to be descending. The object passed silently, low overhead, and as it did, they saw that the craft was diamond shaped and had an additional four or five lights on its underside. There was one red light in each corner and one in the center. The craft banked slightly and then disappeared into the south. About ninety minutes later, either another low-flying object that matched the first identically, or the same object, flew overhead from the same heading and also disappeared to the south.

CHAPTER 14

EPILOGUE

"We're sending them out. Why shouldn't someone be sending them here? Just think when Pioneer 10 finally leaves our solar system, it becomes our first UFO to all the other star systems!"

~Dr. Margaret Mead
American Cultural Anthropologist

Well, are you convinced yet that the government knows more and is much more interested in the UFO phenomenon than they have let on? Do you feel that the government and their so called experts are telling us less than the truth about what UFOs are and where they may come from? I hope so, as that was my goal in writing this book—to educate people to the truth concerning the UFO phenomenon, that UFOs exist and the government has known about them for quite some time. They've set up many organizations to investigate UFOs that promised to answer our questions concerning them, like Project Blue Book, the Condon Committee, and Projects Grudge and Sign; all had a job to do, and they did it well. They acted as a public relations conduit that disseminated what the government wanted known to the media and in turn to we, the people. The combined result of their work, the skeptic's cynicism, and the media's below-par covering of sightings has lead to what I like to call the Ridicule Factor. This factor has kept people from reporting what they see out of fear of ridicule and retribution, which has helped the secrets the government keeps remain safely hidden.

This can and will change if people begin to report what they see in mass numbers. Fads fade, but an ongoing phenomenon/problem never goes away until answers are found, and that is where you come in!

Every person can have a hand in forcing the government towards full and final disclosure. If you have a sighting, report it to one of the organizations listed in Appendix A and B. Organizations such as MUFON, CUFOS, NICAP, and NUFORC all have places on their websites to report a UFO, and it can be done in complete confidence, if you so wish. If you are really adamant about disclosure, write one of the officials who represent you at the federal level to voice your complaints and concerns with the secrecy surrounding the UFO phenomenon. An easy way to find their address is to Google "find my US Senator" or "find my member of the House of Representatives." I say to write your representatives instead of the president, as all things must go through proper channels and the aforementioned people represent us directly and make the laws, so they are the people who need to see the light first and foremost!

Do not be afraid to voice your concerns and opinions as every elected official works for us, not the other way around! Remember all the men and women before you who you have read about in this book (including presidents, governors, pilots, etc.) had the courage it took to bury their fears and concerns and report to the world what they saw. Add to that list famous celebrities and entertainers, like Will Smith, John Lennon, David Bowie, Mohammed Ali, Jackie Gleason, Olivia Newton-John, Jamie Farr, and Dick Gregory, amongst others, who have had encounters with UFOs and shared them with the world. Your voice speaks louder than you know when we all speak together as one body, looking for answers.

So remember, knowledge is power! And so as to be well versed in the subject matter before writing any official or discussing the matter openly in public with family and friends, read more books about the UFO phenomenon. Any of those listed in the bibliography would be well worth the read as they are all treasure troves of information by exceptional authors.

Do not wait for someone else to do this for you, as they won't. Nor should you think that the UFO phenomenon is going to just go away one day, as it will not. It has been here since the dawn of man, maybe even before! And quite possibly it will be here even after we are gone or until we no longer interest the beings in those fantastic machines that defy time, space and our understanding of the universe.

Appendix A
UFO Organizations from Around the World

MUTUAL UNIDENTIFIED FLYING OBJECT NETWORK (MUFON)

2619 11th Street Road, Greeley, Colorado 80634

Phone: (888) 817-2220 or (970) 352-5319

Fax: (970) 352-5365

Website: www.mufon.com

MUFON is the largest UFO organization in the world today. Founded in 1969, the Mutual UFO Network, Inc. is an international scientific organization composed of people seriously interested in studying and researching the phenomenon known as Unidentified Flying Objects (UFOs) by combining their mutual talents, areas of expertise and investigative efforts.

THE J. ALLEN HYNEK CENTER FOR UFO STUDIES (CUFOs)

P.O. Box 31335, Chicago, Illinois 60631

Phone: 1-773-271-3611

Website: www.cufos.org/

The Center for UFO Studies (CUFOs) is an international group of scientists, academics, investigators, and volunteers dedicated to the continuing examination and analysis of the UFO phenomenon. Their purpose is to promote serious scientific interest in UFOs and to serve as an archive for reports, documents, and publications about the UFO phenomenon.

CITIZENS AGAINST UFO SECRECY (CAUS)

Peter Gersten

8624 E. San Bruno Drive, Scottsdale Arizona 85258

Phone: (480) 609-9120

Website: www.v-j-enterprises.com/caus.html

Citizens Against UFO Secrecy (CAUS) is an Arizona based, public interest organization which is formed upon four principles:

1. CAUS believes that this planet, and the people on it, are interacting and in contact with a non-human form of intelligence;

2. CAUS is against any and all secrecy surrounding, involving and relating to this contact;

3. CAUS believes that the people have an absolute and unconditional right to know about this contact;

4. CAUS believes that it is through the judicial process that the truth will be set free and secrecy ended.

THE FUND FOR UFO RESEARCH (FUFOR)

P.O. Box 7501, Alexandria, VA 22307
Website: /www.ufoscience.org/

The Fund for UFO Research, was established as a nonprofit corporation in the District of Columbia on August 1, 1979. FUFOR is not a membership organization per se. Instead, it raises and disperses research funds for proposals approved by a national board. Each year, the Fund also awards a cash prize, the Donald E. Keyhoe Journalism Award, to both the print and electronic media journalist whose work about UFOs is judged the best among those submitted. FUFOR also issues a number of reports and monographs each year, the sales of which support future UFO research projects

THE BRITISH UFO RESEARCH ASSOCIATION (BUFORA)

Clarendon House, 117 George Lane, South Woodford, London E18 1AN
Phone: 08445 674 694
Email: enquiries@bufora.org.uk
Website: www.bufora.org.uk/content/

BUFORA is a nationwide (UK) network of around four hundred people who have a dedicated, non-cultist interest in understanding the UFO mystery. Within that membership are many active investigators and researchers working with the direct claims of witnesses to collate the data necessary to bring that understanding nearer. A loose federation of UK regional UFO groups called the British UFO Association was formed in 1962. In 1964, many of these groups decided to amalgamate all their activities under the BUFOA banner and the organization was renamed the British UFO Research Association.

THE INTRUDERS FOUNDATION

Budd Hopkins, Director

PO Box 30233, New York, New York 10011

Phone and fax: 1-212-645-5278

Website: www.intrudersfoundation.org/

Specializes in cases of reported abductions by extraterrestrial beings. Organization formed by abduction researcher Budd Hopkins to provide support and a forum for abductees to discuss their experiences.

VICTORIAN UFO RESEARCH SOCIETY (VUFORS)

P.O. Box 1043, Moorabbin, Victoria 3189

Australia

Phone: (03) 9506 7080

Website: www.ozemail.com.au/~vufors

Provides information regarding the UFO subject to both VUFORS members and to any person on the Internet with an interest and has been made possible by the members of VUFORS throughout the world.

Appendix B
UFOs on the World Wide Web

Here is but a sampling of the thousands of websites devoted to UFOs, aliens and other related phenomenon.

Those that follow represent the best the web has to offer:

dspace.dial.pipex.com/town/square/el82/cufog.htm

www.bufora.org.uk

www.coasttocoastam.com/

www.cufos.org

www.fufor.com/

www.mufon.com

www.nationalufocenter.com/

www.nuforc.org/

www.ozemail.com.au/~vufors/

www.sightings.com

www.ufoinfo.com/newsclip.shtml

www.ufologie.net/htm/quotes.htm

www.v-j-enterprises.com/caus.htm

Endnotes

Introduction

1. Tomilson, 7
2. U.S. Department of Health and Human Services
3. Institute for Energy and Environmental Research
4. Freedom of Information

Chapter 2

1. Michel, 1969
2. Blum, 39-41
3. Vallee, 1965, 19
4. Blum, 42
5. Blum, 42
6. Vallee, 1965, 23
7. Flammonde, 51
8. Vallee, 1965, 23
9. Lore & Deneault, 41
10. Vallee, 1965, 24-25
11. Friedrich, 44-48
12. Vallee, 1965, 26

13. Lore & Deneault, 60-61

14. Lore & Deneault, 65-66

15. Edwards, 1992, 290-291

16. Flammonde, 23

17. Dennett, 8

18. Flammonde, 69

19. Vallee, 1965, 31

Chapter 3

1. Lore & Deneault, 91-93

2. Lore & Deneault, 97

3. Blum, 60-61

4. Vallee, 1965, 48

5. Lore & Deneault, 106

6. Vallee, 1990, 133

7. Flammonde, 132

8. Lore & Deneault, 141

9. Good, 1988, 15-17

10. Blum, 68

11. Lore & Deneault, 126-127

12. Hall, 23

Chapter 4

1. Flammonde, 156

2. Lorenzen, 18

3. Ruppelt, 31

4. Flammonde, 167-169

5. Blum, 75

6. Vallee, 1965, 91

7. Flammonde, 170-171

8. Flammonde, 218-240

9. Flammonde, 167 and Lorenzen, 18

10. Flammonde, 258-260

11. McDonald, 69-70

12. Ruppelt, 93-94

13. Randle, 32-33

14. Edwards, 1966, 23

15. Ruppelt, 97-98

Chapter 5

1. Ruppelt, 106

2. Vallee, 1965, 98

3. Ruppelt, 106

4. Edwards, 1966, 22

5. Edwards 1992, 294-295

6. Vallee, 1965, 98

7. Lorenzen, 27-28

8. Edwards, 1966, 91-93

9. Lorenzen, 30-32

10. Flammonde, 313

11. Ruppelt, 110-111

12. Randle, 37

13. Ruppelt, 110-111

14. Lorenzen, 38-39

15. Flammonde, 317

16. Wilson, 15

17. Good, 1988 and Flammonde, 319-321

18. Ruppelt, 19-20

19. Story, 255

20. Michel, 1956, 95-97

21. Steiger, 62-65

22. David, 41-44

23. Good, 1988, 271

24. Edwards, 1966, 36-37

25. Flammonde, 327-328

26. Edwards, 1991, 191

Chapter 6

1. Edwards, 1966, 37-38

2. Edwards, 1966, 37

3. Edwards, 1967, 48-49

4. Edwards, 1991, 190

5. Good, 1988, 189-190

6. Vallee, 1965, 98

7. Good, 1988, 141-143

8. Good, 1988, 224-25

9. Edwards, 1967, 20-21

10. Good, 1988, 226

11. Good, 1988, 130

12. Hall, 41

13. Edwards, 1966, 28-29

14. Story, 200-201'

15. Blum, 102

16. Edwards, 1966, 38

17. Edwards, 1966, 103-104

18. Story, 297-298

19. Lorenzen, 153-157

20. Good, 1988, 147-148

21. Lorenzen, 92-93

22. Edwards, 1966, 31-33

23. Randle, 107

24. Hynek, 87-90

25. Edwards, 1966, 62

26. Blum, 102

27. Edwards, 1966, 63-65

28. Davis, 227-230

Chapter 7

1. Lorenzen, 180-181

2. Story, 298-299

3. Vallee, 1965 210-211

4. Good, 1988, 228-229

5. Lorenzen, 186-187

6. Edwards, 1966, 1

7. Edwards, 1964, 92

8. Edwards, 1964, 45

9. Wilson, 6

10. Edwards, 1966, 175-176

11. Lorenzen, 219-221

12. Brookesmith, 81

13. Lorenzen, 224-225

14. Good, 1988, 292-293

15. Fuller Incident at Exeter, 31-33

16. Steiger, 137-138

17. Fuller Incident at Exeter, 31

18. Edwards, 1966, 54

19. Steiger, 140-141

20. Edwards, 1966, 54

21. Fuller Incident at Exeter, 31-32

22. Good, 1988, 293-298

23. Hynek, 93

24. Edwards, 1966, 52-53

25. Brookesmith, 83

26. Lorenzen, 234-236

27. Fuller Incident at Exeter, 35-37

28. Hynek, 1972, 209-210

29. Edwards, 1966, 167

30. Fawcett & Greenwood, 58-59

31. Fuller Incident at Exeter, 9-12

32. Edwards, 1966, 170

33. Edwards, 1966, 56-57

34. Vallee, 1990, 23-24

35. Website www.syti.net/UFOSightings.html

Chapter 8

1. Edwards, 1966, 1

2. Edwards, 1967, 35-36

3. Edwards, 1967, 25-26

4. Lorenzen, 271-273

5. Edwards, 1967, 7-10

6. Edwards, 1967 36-37

7. Lorenzen, 273

8. Edwards, 1967, 28-29

9. Edwards, 1967 146-147

10. Edwards, 1967 31-32

11. Hynek, 83-86

12. Edwards, 1967, 60

13. Edwards, 1967, 61

14. Edwards, 1967, 105-106

15. Lorenzen, 274

16. Edwards, 1967, 64-65

17. Edwards, 1967, 62-64

18. Lore & Deneault, 185

19. Edwards, 1967, 67

20. Edwards, 1967, 68

21. Edwards, 1967, 126-127

22. Steiger &Whritenour, 1976, 45-46

23. Edwards, 1967, 127-128

24. Edwards, 1967, 142-143

25. Edwards, 1967, 143-144

26. Good, 1988, 61-61

27. Edwards, 1967, 152-153

28. Steiger &Whritenour, 1976, 46-47

29. Good, 1988, 63

30. Good, 1988, 64-65

31. Blum, 101-121

32. Story, 299-300

33. Steiger &Whritenour, 1969, 46-47

34. Good, 1988, 149-151

Chapter 9

1. Good, 1988, 210

2. Cornett, 35, 60-61

3. Spencer, 1977, 16-17

4. Spencer, 1974, 18-19

5. Randle, 141

6. Blum, 128-129

7. Flammonde, 18

8. Blum, 177

9. Spencer, 1974, 23-24

10. Blum, 193-194 and Good, 1988, 302-303

11. Fawcett, 1975, 51

12. Good, 1991, 80-81

13. APRO Bulletin, 1974, 1,3

14. La Porte, 15-16

15. Good, 1988, 151

16. Clark, 67 and True Magazine Staff, 6-9

17. Story, 233-234

18. Brookesmith, 109-110

19. Fawcett and Greenwood, 16-22

20. Fawcett and Greenwood, 27-30

21. Good, 1988, 153-154

22. Good, 1988, 319-321

23. Vallee, 1990, 27-28

24. Hynek and Imbrogno, 187

25. Good, 1988, 154-155

26. Good, 1988, 144-145

27. Good, 1988, 211

28. Good, 1988, 212

29. Hynek, 187-188

30. Hynek, 188

31. Good, 1988, 116-117

32. Good, 1988, 146-147

33. Fawcett and Greenwood, 75-76

34. Good, 1988, 175-181

35. Good, 1988, 213-214

36. Fawcett and Greenwood, 42-43

37. Good, 1988, 156-157

Chapter 10

1. Hynek and Imbrogno, 188

2. Good, 1988, 157-158

3. Hynek and Imbrogno, 157-158

4. Randles, 10-25

5. Randles, 26-28

6. Randles, 37-46

7. Hynek and Imbrogno, 9-13

8. Hynek and Imbrogno, 19-21

9. Hynek and Imbrogno, 27

10. Hynek and Imbrogno, 29 and NBC's Unsolved Mysteries

11. Hynek and Imbrogno, 30-31

12. Hynek and Imbrogno, 39-41 and NBC's Unsolved Mysteries

13. Hynek and Imbrogno, 1-3

14. Hynek and Imbrogno, 93-95

15. Hynek and Imbrogno, 140-149

16. Graziano, 7-8

17. Good, 1988, 218-219

18. Clark, 57

19. Good, 1989, 200-210

20. Walters, 107-111

21. NBC's Unsolved Mysteries

Chapter 11

1. Good, 1991, 28-30

2. Good, 1991, 31-32 and NBC's Unsolved Mysteries

3. Good, 1991, 30-31

4. Brookesmith, 142

5. Brookesmith, 143

6. Brookesmith, 146

7. Brookesmith, 144

8. NBC Special Confirmation – The Hard Evidence of Aliens Among Us

9. Michaels, 165-176

10. Durant, 19

11. Filer, August 1999, 13,23

12. Filer, December 1999, 16

13. Filer, 199 week 42, 2

Chapter 12

1. Marler, 3-8

2. Sekerkarar, 3

3. Dennett, 223-224

4. Connelly, 3-4

5. Maranto, 3-5

6. Clarke, 146-147

Chapter 13

1. Website www.nuforc.org/webreports/ndxevent.html

2. Website http://en.wikipedia.org/wiki/Phoenix_Lights

3. Filer, July 2000, 18

4. Filer, November 2000, 8

5. Young, July 2001, 3-6

6. Filer, August 2001, 10

7. Filer, September 2001, 14-15

8. Filer, October 2001, 12-13

9. Filer, October 2002, 13

10. Filer, July 2003, 11, 13

11. Trainer, December 2003, 21

12. Sugden, May 2004, 11

13. Young, October 2004, 10

14. Filer, November 2005, 16-17

15. Gordon, April 2006, 18

16. Filer, April 2006, 14

17. Filer, July 2006, 17

18. Filer, September 2006, 16

19. Filer, March 2007, 16

20. Filer, November 2007, 20

21. Ventre, September 2008, 3-6

22. Hudgeons, May 2008, 3-12

23. Webb, February 2009, 3-6

24. Lang, August 2009, 8-9

25. Lang, October/November 2009, 5-6

26. Filer, May 2010, 13

27. Filer, July 2010, 18

28. Filer, November 2010, 17

29. Filer, February 2011, 14

30. Website www.youtube.com/watch?v=z0JFul9ffs8&feature=related

31. Website www.youtube.com/watch?v=Fu4ri2GozIY&feature=related

32. Website www.ufocasebook.com/2011/allentownpa.html

33. Website www.ufocasebook.com/2011/camppendletonca030611.html

34. Website www.ufocasebook.com/2011/triva030711.html

35. Website www.ufocasebook.com/2011/pennsylvaniatri032611.html

36. Website www.ufocasebook.com/2011/floridadiscs032811.html

37. Website www.ufocasebook.com/2011/montanapoliceman.html

38. Website www.ufocasebook.com/2011/iowaflashes040811.html

39. Website www.ufocasebook.com/2011/az041911.html

40. Website www.ufocasebook.com/2011/texasdaylight050511.html

41. Website www.ufocasebook.com/2011/colorado050811.html

BIBLIOGRAPHY

Books

Blum, Ralph & Judy. *Beyond Earth : Mans Contact With UFO's*. New York, New York: Bantam Books, 1974

Brookesmith, Peter. *UFO : The Complete Sightings*. New York, New York: Barnes and Noble Books, 1995

Clark, Jerome. *UFO Encounters: Sightings, Visitations and Investigations*. Lincolnwood, Illinois: Publication International, Ltd., 1992

David, Jay. *The Flying Saucer Reader*. New York, New York: Signet Books, 1967

Dennett, Preston. *UFO's Over New York A True History of Extraterrestrial Encounters Over the Empire State*. Atglen, Pennsylvania: Schiffer Publishing Company Ltd., 2008

Edwards, Frank. *Flying Saucers – Here and Now!* New York, New York: Bantam Books, 1967

Edwards, Frank. *Flying Saucers – Serious Business!* New York, New York: Bantam Books, 1966

Edwards, Frank. *Strange World.* New York, New York: Bantam Books, 1964

Edwards, Frank. *Stranger Than Science.* New York, New York: Bantam Books, 1959

Edwards, Frank. *Strangest of All.* New York, New York: Bantam Books, 1956

Fawcett, Lawrence and Barry Greenwood. *Clear Intent-The Government Cover-up of the UFO Experience.* Santa Rosa, California: Spectrum Books, 1984

Flammonde, Paris. *UFO Exist!* Toronto, Canada: Ballantine Books, 1976

Fuller, John G. *Incident at Exeter.* New York, New York: Berkley Medallion Books, 1966

Fuller, John G. *The Interrupted Journey.* New York, New York: Berkley Medallion Books, 1966

Good, Timothy. *Above Top Secret – The Worldwide UFO Cover-up.* New York, New York: Sidgwick & Jackson Ltd, 1988

Good, Timothy. *Alien Contact – Top Secret UFO Files Revealed.* New York, New York: William Morrow, 1991

Good, Timothy. *The UFO Report*. New York, New York: Avon Books, 1989

Hall, Richard. *UFO Evidence*. New York, New York: Barnes & Noble Books, 1997

Hynek, Dr J. Allen. *Night Siege – The Hudson Valley UFO Sightings*. New York, New York: Ballantine, Books, 1987

Hynek, Dr J. Allen. *The UFO Experience*. New York, New York: Ballantine Books, 1972

Lore, Gordan and Harold Deneault. *Mysteries of the Skies*. Upper Saddle River, New Jersey: Prentice Hall, Inc, 1968

Lorenzen, Coral. *The Great Flying Saucer Hoax*. New York, New York: Signet Books, 1962

Michaels, Susan. *Sightings: UFO's*. New York, New York: Fireside Books, 1997

Michel, Aime. *The Truth About Flying Saucers*. New York, New York: Pyramid Books, 1956

Randle, Captain Kevin, USAF Ret. *The UFO Casebook*. New York, New York: Warner Books, 1989

Randles, Jenny. *From Out of the Blue*. New York, New York: Berkley Books, 1991

Ruppelt, Edward J. *The Report on Unidentified Flying Objects*. New York, New York: Ace Books, 1956

Spencer, John. *No Earthly Explanation*. New York, New York: Bantam Books, 1974

Steiger, Brad. *Project Blue Book*. New York, New York: Ballantine Books, 1976

Steiger, Brad and Joan Whritenour. *Flying Saucer Invasion Target Earth*. New York, New York: Award Books, 1969

Story, Ronald. *The Encyclopedia of UFO's*. Garden City, New York: Dolphin Books, 1980

Vallee, Jacques. *Anatomy of a Phenomenon*. New York, New York: Ace Books, 1965

Vallee, Jacques. *Confrontations*. New York, New York: Ballantine Books, 1990

Vallee, Jacques. *Dimensions*. New York, New York: Ballantine Books, 1988

Vallee, Jacques. *Revelations*. New York, New York: Ballantine Books, 1991

Walters, Ed and Frances. *The Gulf Breeze Sightings.* New York, New York: Avon
Books, 1990

Wilson, Dr. Clifford, Ph.D. *The Alien Agenda.* New York, New York: Signet
Books, 1974

Periodicals/Journals

APRO Staff. "New York Police See UFO." *APRO Bulletin* July-August 1974

Clarke, David. "The UFO Files – The Inside Story of Real Life Sightings" *The
National Archives.* United Kingdom 2009

Clark, Jerome and Lucius Farish. "Unsolved Mysteries from the UFO Archive"
UFO Report All Issues of 1975

Connelly, Dwight "Unique Mexican Encounter" *MUFON UFO Journal* June
2004

Cornett, Robert Charles. "Stapleton This is Flight 239: We're Being Followed!"
Official UFO Magazine April 1976

Durant, R.J. "Swiss Air Jet Has "Near Miss with UFO" *MUFON UFO Journal*
September 1999

Fawcett, George D. "The Unreported UFO Wave of 1974" *The UFO Report
Magazine* Spring 1975

Filer, George. "British Passenger Jet Has A Near Miss" *MUFON UFO Journal* December 1999

Filer, George. "Filers Files" *MUFON UFO Journal* August 1999

Filer, George. "NOAA Satellite Picks Up Giant UFO In Earth Orbit" *Filers Files* 1999 Week 49

Filer, George. "Filers Files" *MUFON UFO Journal* July 2000

Filer, George. "Filers Files" *MUFON UFO Journal* September 2000

Filer, George. "Filers Files" *MUFON UFO Journal* August 2001

Filer, George. "Filers Files" *MUFON UFO Journal* September 2001

Filer, George. "Filers Files" *MUFON UFO Journal* October 2001

Filer, George. "Filers Files" *MUFON UFO Journal* October 2002

Filer, George. "Filers Files" *MUFON UFO Journal* July 2003

Filer, George. "Filers Files" *MUFON UFO Journal* November 2005

Filer, George. "Filers Files" *MUFON UFO Journal* April 2006

Filer, George. "Filers Files" *MUFON UFO Journal* July 2006

Filer, George. "Filers Files" *MUFON UFO Journal* September 2006

Filer, George. "Filers Files" *MUFON UFO Journal* March 2007

Filer, George. "Filers Files" *MUFON UFO Journal* November 2007

Filer, George. "Filers Files" *MUFON UFO Journal* May 2010

Filer, George. "Filers Files" *MUFON UFO Journal* July 2010

Filer, George. "Filers Files" *MUFON UFO Journal* February 2011

Filer, George. "Filers Files – What's the Buzz?" *MUFON UFO Journal* November 2010

Friedrich, George. "UFO's: Heavenly Crosses?" *Argosy UFO Magazine* March 1977

Gordon, Stan. "Stan Gordon Reports Wide Range of Pennsylvania Sightings." *MUFON UFO Journal* April 2006

Graziano, Doris and Joe. "Press Reports" *APRO Bulletin* November 1972

Hudgeons, Steve. "Cluster of UFO Sightings in Erath County, Texas. November 2007 to February 2008." *MUFON UFO Journal* May 2008

Lang, Richard. "Retired Deputy Sheriff Sees, Hears Large UFO" *MUFON UFO Journal* August 2009

Lang, Richard. "The SIP Project Star Team Report September 2009" *MUFON UFO Journal* October/November 2009

La Porte, Richard. "Exposed: The Air Force Cover-up on UFO's!" *Argosy's UFO Annual* 1975

Maranto, Sam. "Incident at O'Hare" *MUFON UFO Journal.* February 2007

Marler, David B. "Illinois Police Track UFO Near Scott AFB." *MUFON UFO Journal* March 2000

McDonald, James E. "Symposium on Unidentified Flying Objects." Prepared for the United States House of Representative Committee on Science and Astronautics 1969

Michel, Aime. "Paleolithic UFO Shapes." *Flying Saucer Review.* November-December 1969

Sekerkarar, Esen. "Turkish Military Pilots Encounter UFO." *MUFON UFO Journal* September 2002

Spencer, John. "The Turbulent Year of 1973." *Argosy UFO Magazine* March 1977

Steiger, Brad and Joan Whritenour. "Pilots and UFO Encounters." *Argosy UFO Magazine* July 1976

Sugden, Roger. "Indiana Witness Reports Humongous Disc-shaped UFO with Two Sets of Lights." *MUFON UFO Journal* May 2004

Tomilson, John. "Citizens of Nice, France Saw UFO's in 1608." *MUFON UFO Journal* February 2009

Trainer, Joseph. "Colorado Boomerang Shaped Object Lacks Characteristics of Aircraft." *MUFON UFO Journal* December 2003

True Magazine Staff. "The Sighting at Stonehenge Apartments." *Flying Saucer Quarterly* Summer 1976

Ventre, John. "Signs Over Bucks County, Pennsylvania – Over 100 UFO Sightings Reported Over the Summer." *MUFON UFO Journal* September 2008

Webb, Richard. "Citizens The Second Wave of UFO Sightings Near Stephenville, Texas, Fall 2008." *MUFON UFO Journal* February 2009

Young, Kenny. "Ohio Sighting – Object seen by Civilians and Police Officers." *MUFON UFO Journal* July 2001

Young, Kenny. "Ohio Sighting Deputy & Wife Apparently See Same UFO From Different Locations." *MUFON UFO Journal* October 2004

TELEVISION PROGRAMS

NBC's *Unsolved Mysteries*

NBC Special, *Confirmation – The Hard Evidence of Aliens Among Us*

WEBSITES

Freedom of Information. http://www.foia.af.mil/shared/media/document/AFD-070703-004.pdf

Institute for Energy and Environmental Research. http://www.ieer.org/comments/fallout/nasltr0904.html

National UFO Reporting Center. http://www.nuforc.org/webreports/ndxevent.html

Phoenix Lights. http://en.wikipedia.org/wiki/Phoenix_Lights

U.S. Department of Health and Human Services. http://www.hhs.gov/1946inoculationstudy/findings.html

UFO Casebook. http://www.ufocasebook.com

Location Index